I0121436

THUNDER GOD, WONDER GOD

EXPLORING THE EMBLEMATIC VISION OF

JONATHAN EDWARDS

THUNDER GOD, WONDER GOD

EXPLORING THE EMBLEMATIC VISION OF

JONATHAN EDWARDS

Rob Boss

Foreword

Gerald McDermott

JESociety
Press

WWW.JESOCIETY.ORG

Paperback Edition May 11, 2023
ISBN 978-1-7379026-5-2
© 2023 Rob Boss

A publication of JESociety Press
Visit www.jesociety.org

ImagesofDivineThings.com

All rights reserved. No part of this publication may be reproduced, distributed, or transmitted in any form or by any means, including photocopying, recording, or other electronic or mechanical methods, without the prior written permission of the author/publisher, except in the case of brief quotations embodied in critical reviews and certain other noncommercial uses permitted by copyright law.

For permission requests and inquiries,
Email: rob@jesociety.org
Web: www.jesociety.org

Cover art: *View from Mount Holyoke, Northampton, Massachusetts, after a Thunderstorm—The Oxbow* (Thomas Cole, 1836).

PRAISE FOR THIS VOLUME

"Although scholars have long known about Jonathan Edwards' fascination with signs, symbols, types, and emblems, Robert Boss's study goes well beyond what others have done before. His wide-ranging comparison of Edwards with other figures of the period, but especially his exhaustive catalog of images ("emblems") in nature from which Edwards drew deep spiritual meaning, adds significantly to understanding Edwards. The book also suggests how Edwards' use of emblems could aid contemporary believers in finding more riches in Scripture as well as seeing more of Providence in the natural world."

Mark A. Noll, author of *The Rise of Evangelicalism:*
The Age of Edwards, Whitefield, and the Wesleys

"Rob Boss has done it again. This is a marvelous introduction to Edwards' typological vision. Enchanting indeed."

Douglas A. Sweeney, Beeson Divinity School
Samford University

"This is a deeply fascinating book which demonstrates how out of touch we moderns are with Edwards's God-centered vision of the world. Boss takes us deep into Edwards's typological and emblematic interpretation of nature, giving us both a rich scholarly study as well as a 'how to' manual packed with visuals designed to stir our theological imagination in Edwardsean ways. Many thanks to Rob Boss for pointing us back to Edwards's God-infused vision of interpreting the natural world!"

Robert W. Caldwell III, Professor of Church History
Southwestern Baptist Theological Seminary

"Rob Boss's clear and concise writing, combined with his deep knowledge of the subject matter, makes this book a must-read for anyone seriously interested in understanding the thought of one of America's most important religious thinkers. He masterfully unfolds an intelligible understanding of Jonathan Edwards' emblematic vision. Any pastor, theologian, or Christian serious about reaching this generation must take the time to digest and understand this brilliant work. This writing ignites hope in a world that feigns hopelessness."

Marty Martin, Lead Pastor
Northstar Church, Panama City, FL

FOREWORD

RABBI ARI LAMM IS AN ORTHODOX RABBI in New York City whose Twitter threads on reading the Hebrew Bible are read by Jews, Christians, and "nones" all over the world.[1] In a day when Orthodox Jews and orthodox Christians are lamenting the decline of traditional faith, Rabbi Lamm is optimistic. Don't be fooled, he advises us, by statistics in the mainstream media. Beneath the radar are millions of young people who are searching for God but not in traditional ways.

This book by Rob Boss shows that Jonathan Edwards has the keys to the treasures millions are seeking. Let me explain by saying something that might surprise readers about God's seeking and the millions of those seeking him.

The Bible says God himself is seeking people to worship him in spirit and in truth (John 4:23). This is a very Jewish way of talking about God, different from some Christians who characterize God as somewhat indifferent to human fates.

The other thing about God that might surprise readers is that God's way of reaching people is through the particular, not the universal. This surprises many because it has been a mainstream Christian belief that Jesus came to universalize the particular—from the particular people the Jews and their particular land to all the peoples of the world and all the lands of the world. Jesus, in other words, is commonly thought to have come to perfect what was imperfect in Judaism, its focus on particularity.

This was neither Edwards's view, nor that of the New Testament. Jesus endorsed thoroughly the teachings of Torah (Matt 5:17–19), which are all about particularity, and Paul endorsed not only God's choosing his particular

---

[1]https://twitter.com/AriLamm/status/1560611614226882560?lang=en.

Jewish people (Rom 11:28–29) but also their particular land promise (Acts 13:16–19).

As this book demonstrates, Edwards's dominating vision was of a *communicating God*. His God, who I would suggest is the God of the Bible, is a God who is continuously communicating his truth, goodness, and beauty through the near-infinite particularities of the world. In other words, God is constantly speaking. As Boss puts it, we are swimming in an ocean of God-planted signs, symbols, and emblems. If people do not hear, it is because they have grown deaf. They do not see his beauty through these emblems because they are blind.

In the scene at the beginning of his Introduction, Boss depicts the difference in perception between those limited to universals and those enriched with the beauty of particulars. For those whose eyes and ears are closed, a rose is merely the genus of a shrub in the family *Rosaceae*. A particular that is understood only by the universal of shrub and family of shrub. But for those with eyes and ears for the beauty of particulars, the rose is a sign from God that the sweet in life is always mixed with the bitter, and that true happiness comes only from carrying Christ's cross.

Those with open eyes and ears see beauty because God's beauty is in the harmony among different particulars. The number of particulars is infinite because they are the creations of an infinite God. And because he is infinite, each particular points to every other. This, among other things, shows why this cosmos cannot be understood mechanistically. It is more akin to an organism in which each cell communicates with every other.

Boss uses his skill with computers to illustrate both this interconnectedness of every part of the creation and Edwards's attempts to communicate this interconnectedness. As Edwards put it, all the universe is full of the "language of God" which can be learned only by learning the biblical narrative. But the learning is mutually reinforcing. The narrative teaches about nature, and nature helps us see the beauty of the narrative. Links to different parts of the Internet that link to other links, seemingly without limit, are carnal types of the interlocking antitypes of God's communication through nature and Scripture.

The unity of God's communications comes only from embracing its infinite particularities. The beauty of the One can be seen only by seeing the Many. This means we must refuse the temptation of lumping. Once we allow the left hemisphere to classify particulars into categories, we lose the beauties of the particulars because those beauties are beyond our words and concepts. As the philosopher Jan Zwicky puts it, we lose the *thisness* of the particular, which is the distinct way that each *this* focuses the "resonant structure" of the world.[2]

The poet Gerard Manley Hopkins famously suggests *thisness* in his poem "As kingfishers catch fire,"

> Each mortal thing does one thing and the same:
> Deals out that being indoors each one dwells;
> Selves – goes itself; myself it speaks and spells,
> Crying *What I do is me; for that I came.*[3]

Our world is content to lump individuals into classes and groups, as if the generalization suffices and the particular is finally unimportant. But even God, as McGilchrist suggests, created by dividing. His works on the six days were primarily works of separating—light from darkness, land from water, female from male. Yet each division into particulars created new things. Life emerges afresh in similar ways: chromosome pairs divide and are drawn apart, then re-form in new pairs to make a new cell. The beauty of life comes from dividing into particulars.[4]

It is contra-intuitive these days, but the new excitement for equality ironically blinds us to the beauty of harmony among differences. None other than Nietzsche recognized this.

> The coarser organ [of perception] sees much apparent equality; the intellect *wants* equality, i.e., to subsume a sense impression into an existing series: in the same way as the body assimilates inorganic matter . . . the will to equality is the will to power – the belief that something is thus and thus (the essence of judgment) is the consequence of a will that as much as possible *shall* be equal.[5]

McGilchrist explains Nietzsche's point: "The lust for control lies behind the demand that all shall be equal to – reducible to – something else. The process is one . . . of triumph by reductionism."[6] He who puts different

---

[2] Zwicky is cited in Iain McGilchrist, *The Matter With Things* (London: Perspectiva, 2021), 853.

[3] https://www.poetryfoundation.org/poems/44389/as-kingfishers-catch-fire.

[4] McGilchrist, *The Matter With Things*, 857.

[5] Nietzsche, *The Will to Power*, no. 511; cited in McGilchrist, *The Matter With Things*, 851.

[6] McGilchrist, *The Matter With Things*, 851–52.

individuals into a general class reduces them, overriding and eventually eliminating their individual differences.

This is the opposite of love. One might think that regarding a person as a member of a preferred group, and treating her as equal to everyone else in that group, is a considerate thing to do. But "he that would love, must love individuals, not generalities. You can admire or be attracted to womanhood, or manhood, but you cannot *love* them."[7] Blake wrote, "He who would do good to another must do it in Minute Particulars; General Good is the plea of the scoundrel, hypocrite & flatterer."[8]

This is what is pernicious about lumping persons and everything else we experience into generalities. It replaces the beauty of the individual in all of her particularity to something else, a generalized construct of our imagination. Uniqueness is lost in categorizing, as McGilchrist puts it.

The same holds true for nations. It is *de rigeur* to denounce nationalism and promote a globalism that regards nations as merely large examples of selfishness. But as Solzhenitsyn said in his Harvard commencement address,

> Were nations to disappear, we would be impoverished in exactly the same way as if all people suddenly became alike, with the same character and the same face. Nations are part of the wealth of the human race. Although generalized, they are its individuals. The smallest of them has its own special colours and hides in itself some special facet of God's design.[9]

Intriguingly, the Church in the new heavens and new earth will be differentiated according to nation, language, tribe and people—but not race (Rev 7:9). God decided when and where each of us would live on this terrestrial globe (Acts 17:26), and these national—which means religious and cultural identities—will be retained in the eschaton. These are among the particularities celebrated by the biblical authors and by Edwards in their portrayal of the divine beauty that is a harmony among differences.

In the last century both theological and literary scholars pronounced that at the end of the day all reality is linguistic—made by words and understood through words. Thus diversity, and whatever beauty comes from it, is a matter of language. But is this true? If so, what does that say to those who

---

[7] Ibid., 850–51.

[8] Blake, *Jerusalem,* chap. 3; cited in McGilchrist, 852.

[9] Alexander Solzhenitsyn, "A World Split Apart," June 8, 1978. https://www.americanrhetoric.com/speeches/alexandersolzhenitsynharvard.htm.

have trouble with language? Grandma with Alzheimer's? Babies who have yet to grasp language? The profoundly retarded? It is worth mentioning that those who have declared this dogma are typically the most linguistically gifted. A bit like the man whose only tool is a hammer thinks everything is a nail.

Far truer to reality was the conviction that human words are neither controlling nor ultimate. Yes, the divine Word is ultimate. But his Word is a person, and his reality transcends all human words. That is part of why Edwards said the best way to represent the triune God, who is the God of Israel and Father of the Messiah, is by music. For music is its own language that fills the spaces opened by the fissures that human language reveals.

Edwards believed in the divinity of the words of Scripture. But just as they could be distorted without eyes of faith, so too their meaning went beyond merely human concepts. This is why he prized the multiple images of Scripture, and its parables, whose stories and pictures communicated more of God's beauty that any theological system could. Because they were stories and images rather than syllogisms or theorems, there is infinitely rich correspondence between them and the world of emblems in the universe. Only in tracing the patterns among these two realities can one see the divine beauty.

This is what awaits those seeking God. A divine beauty that is infinitely fascinating—while also frightening–because it is a harmony of infinite particularity. This is a divine diversity profoundly more interesting than any human diversity celebrated by political agendas.

Seeing the emblems and the harmonies among them is the key for millions searching for God. May this book help open their eyes and ears.

Gerald McDermott is Distinguished Professor of Theology at Jerusalem Seminary and Distinguished Professor of Anglican Theology at Reformed Episcopal Seminary in Philadelphia.

PREFACE

THIS TEN-YEAR PROJECT, initially published as *God-Haunted World* (2015), has grown significantly since its first iteration. The most visible development is the addition of Part Two, which places Edwards' "Images" among emblematic works from early modern writers. This provides the reader of Part One with a deeper understanding of Edwards' emblematic world and an opportunity to compare his emblematic thought to other emblem writers.

It is my belief that Edwards' emblematic and typological world view remains relevant today, and this is the reason for the update and expansion of this work. Academic interest in typology has waned in recent years. It does not receive the same amount of scholarly attention as it did in the 1970s. As per research on Jonathan Edwards' typology, his reading of the Old and New Testaments has been deemed orthodox. His application of the typological principle to the natural world can be interpreted as either a betrayal of his theological beliefs or as a deepening of the believer's understanding of divine communication and their role in the relationship with all creatures.[1] Notably, no independent chapter was designated for Edwards' typology in the recently published *Oxford Handbook of Jonathan Edwards*. This is not to say that the volume does not give treatment to Edwards' types and shadows—Paul Helm, Stephen R.C. Nichols, William Dyrness, Christi Wells, Kathryn Reklis, Avihu Zakai, and Robert Brown devote some sections or space to Edwards' typological world view in their respective chapters.[2] Yet, this "honorable mention" of the topic reinforces the perception of its academic wane. This

---

[1] Anna Svetlikova, "Jonathan Edwards' Typology as Language," *Theologica Wratislaviensia* 7 (2012): 159.

[2] Douglas A. Sweeney and Jan Stievermann, eds., *The Oxford Handbook of Jonathan Edwards* (Oxford: Oxford University Press, 2021), 116–17, 171–72, 176–78, 298–301, 309–10, 316–19, 327–35.

book explores a road less traveled and will introduce Edwards as an emblem writer, showing him to belong to the company of early modern emblem writers.

Douglas A. Sweeney notes that Edwards "boasted of an all-pervasive typological passion, one that gave his thought a unique, and rather striking, spiritual focus."[3] In an endorsement of Gerald McDermott's *Everyday Glory*, which echoes Edwards' typological passion, Sweeney opines,

> The natural world McDermott describes is the world I want to inhabit and sometimes do. Profound faith is required of those who want to live there constantly, far more faith than most moderns are able to muster every day. But for those with eyes to see and ears to hear its wondrous beauty, it is gleaming with an eternal weight of glory that exceeds our paltry efforts to reproduce, abstract, or counteract it. It enchants the bodily senses—and awakens the spiritual senses—with its still too elusive satisfactions.[4]

Charles Hambrick-Stowe's work on Puritan piety and devotional practice offers an angle of research on Edwards' typology that is rarely mentioned today. Hambrick-Stowe notes that the emblem book, a form of devotional literature that combines visual aids with contemplative verse and draws on medieval iconographic traditions, arose as a sub-genre in the early seventeenth century. Some of the most popular Protestant emblem books were written by George Wither and Francis Quarles, whose work was directly inspired by Jesuit sources.[5]

Shakespeare's use of language and imagery, as discussed by Tibor Fabiny, owes a debt to the emblem tradition, and Edwards uses the term "emblem" as a synonym for types, but students of Edwards' typology have yet to make the connection between the two.[6] Fabiny sees the ongoing relevance of Edwards' typology for faith and culture, especially in our technological age. Edwards can help thoughtful Christians use the Bible's concrete images to

[3]Douglas A. Sweeney, *Edwards the Exegete: Biblical Interpretation and Anglo- Protestant Culture on the Edge of the Enlightenment* (New York, New York: Oxford University Press, 2016), 73.

[4]Gerald R. McDermott, *Everyday Glory: The Revelation of God in All of Reality* (Grand Rapids, Michigan: Baker Academic, 2018), Back cover.

[5]Charles E. Hambrick-Stowe, *The Practice of Piety: Puritan Devotional Disciplines in Seventeenth-Century New England* (Chapel Hill: University of North Carolina Press, 1982), 29–30.

[6]Gerald R McDermott, *Understanding Jonathan Edwards: An Introduction to America's Theologian* (New York: Oxford University Press, 2008), 101.

make sense of the contemporary world—he encourages us to both preserve and renew our Christian imagination.[7] Gerald McDermott has carried this typological torch forward in a broad fashion with *Everyday Glory,* weaving a theological nexus from all spheres of life, along with a succinct summary of Edwards' natural typology.[8]

Fabiny's and Hambrick-Stowe's observations about emblems and emblem books call for further investigation into the back stories of Edwards and emblems. Mention of Francis Quarles (1592–1644), an English religious poet who was a populizer of the emblem book genre, occurs in Edwards' *Catalogues,* and one of Quarles' emblems is featured as a frontispiece in volume 11 of the Yale edition of Edwards' works.[9]

Francis Quarles stated in his emblem book *Hieroglyphics of the Life of Man* (1638) that, "Before the knowledge of letters, God was known by hieroglyphics; and, indeed, what are the heavens, the earth, nay, every creature but hieroglyphics and emblems of His glory?" For the early moderns, emblems were discovered in nature and everywhere else. The uneducated were made aware of emblems by the preacher in his sermons; they saw and heard emblems on the stage and in pageants and processions; they were surrounded by emblematic motifs in the visual arts: in church windows, coats-of-arms, paintings, and decorations.[10] The emblem informed and helped shape virtually every form of verbal and visual communication during the sixteenth and seventeenth centuries.[11] The emblem taught people how to live in the widest sense, and also how to die.[12]

Everyday life in the early modern period contained a plethora of mundane and trivial aspects, yet even these could offer valuable lessons to the mindful individual. The four elements, the heavens, four-footed beasts, birds, fish, plants, stones, and insects were all seen as emblematic, offering a means of instruction to those with an understanding eye. Physicians, preachers, and moralists became cosmographers, creating tangible links between the

---

[7] Gerald R McDermott, *Understanding Jonathan Edwards,* 105–6.

[8] Gerald R. McDermott, *Everyday Glory: The Revelation of God in All of Reality,* 49–58 See also Chapter 8 on Typology in Michael J. McClymond and Gerald R. McDermott, *The Theology of Jonathan Edwards* (New York: Oxford University Press, 2012).

[9] Jonathan Edwards, Peter J. Thuesen, ed., *Catalogues of Books,* vol. 26, *The Works of Jonathan Edwards* (Yale University Press, 2008), 105, 129, 232.

[10] Peter Daly, *Literature in the Light of the Emblem* (London: University of Toronto Press, 1998), 43.

[11] Daly, *Literature in the Light of the Emblem,* 44.

[12] Daly, *Literature in the Light of the Emblem,* 45.

physical world and the invisible world of moral, spiritual, political, and psychological entities. This map of the "Book of Nature" or the "Great Chain of Being" extends in a hierarchical order from the Throne of God to the smallest pebble on the face of the earth. The Renaissance mind was able to form intricate harmonies from the correspondences between the visible and the invisible.[13]

The emblem is a type of "combined art" in which a verbal phrase or slogan is coupled with a visual image, followed by a subscription. This intertwining depicts a cognitive process that documents the age-old idea of the world as a book, in which all observable occurrences are viewed as "readables" that comment on one another. The phenomenon's presentation is intended to be a documentation of the context—a communicative network or descriptive system of which the phenomenon is a component. This system is a microcosmic mirror, and many occurrences may be linked together to virtually document the world as a book. The emblem depicts Thing, Word, Picture, and Scripture as interacting and correlating components of the same created and creative process.[14]

A motto, a striking image, an epigram, and occasionally a few quotations make up an emblem. Often, emblems were created in a cut-and-paste manner, frequently taking inspiration from works of visual art, classical literature, and other emblems. Numerous subjects, including love, religion, morality, and politics, might be addressed by these emblems. They have thus been the focus of multidisciplinary research. The emblem mixes many mediums, a broad variety of themes, and numerous allusions to other works, making it crucial for understanding the early modern period. Additionally, it presents a fantastic opportunity for digital humanities study.[15]

The computer has the potential to serve as a new platform for emblematics in our contemporary day, in which symbols are rearranged and juxtaposed to discover or take on new significance.[16] Likewise, the emblematic mode of thought promotes integration and composition as well as the generation of

---

[13]John Manning, *The Emblem* (London: Reaktion Books, 2004), 30–31. An artist or writer who uses elaborate, often exaggerated metaphors, analogies, and other figurative language to make a point, eg., Donne, Shakespeare, and Milton.

[14]Agrell Beata, "Documentarism and Theory of Literature," in *Documentarism in Scandinavian Literature* (Rodopi, 1997), 47–48.

[15]Peter Boot, "Mesotext. Digitised Emblems, Modelled Annotations and Humanities Scholarship," Ph.D. diss. (University of Utrecht, 2009), 13–14.

[16]Charles Gere, "The Computer as an Irrational Cabinet," Ph.D. dissertation (London: Middlesex University, 1996), 84.

ideas as opposed to their mere interpretation. Electronic literature, video games, and even the design of websites all follow this pattern. This kind of thinking—to blend and compose—is consistent with emblematic epistemology and is also prevalent in most traditional poetry. This mashup of text, music, and image is common on memes and social media websites, which frequently reference modern myths and urban legends. Web pages usually link out to other sites beyond their own content.[17]

Peter Daly observes,

> The sheer quantity of emblems is enough to inundate both the individual and teams of scholars, so that as yet it is not possible to test methodically and accurately any single hypothesis against a large enough body of emblems. A task for the computer perhaps?[18]

A desire to take Edwards and the emblematic world view into the computational realm inspired me to create *Types Explorer,* part of the *Visual Edwards Project.* *Types Explorer* is a tool for exploring and visualizing emblem books and the emblems of the Early Modern period.[19] It is composed in the Python programming language and is used to create and analyze complex networks. *Types Explorer* can be used to create visualizations of emblem books and the emblems contained within them. It allows users to concatenate data and create custom networks, with the nodes representing the emblems in the books and the edges (connecting lines) representing the relationships between them. Users can annotate the visual representation of the graph, adding colored notecards and images to the nodes to provide additional information about the emblems. Interactive visualizations can be published to the web, are easily shareable, and can be embedded in other websites and blogs.

Types Explorer can be used to search and visualize the connections between different emblems within a single book or across many books, integrating networks of biblical imagery and other metaphors. Visually appealing network graphs help users explore the underlying themes, highlight nexus points in the networks, and gain a deeper understanding of the emblems

---

[17] Jonas Ingvarsson, *Towards a Digital Epistemology: Aesthetics and Modes of Thought in Early Modernity and the Present Age* (London: Palgrave Macmillan, 2021), 38.

[18] Daly, *Literature in the Light of the Emblem,* 7.

[19] Robert L. Boss, *Visual Edwards Project.* https:www.visualedwards.org.

and their messages. In Part Two, many of the sections conclude with a visualization created with the software.

The exploration of Edwards' emblematic/typological world view is quite exciting, especially since he described it as an almost limitless frontier. "The whole universe, heaven and earth, air and seas," and Scriptures are full of this language of God and there is not time enough in all the world to learn it all.[20] The possibility of weaving together the Book of Scripture with the Book of Nature, especially in our day of vast computing power and acceptance of augmented realities, in order to reinforce the truths of the Bible should be irresistible unless there is a failure of imagination and devotion.

> If we look on these shadows of divine things as the voice of God, purposely, by them, teaching us these and those spiritual and divine things, to show of what excellent advantage it will be, how agreeably and clearly it will tend to convey instruction to our minds, and to impress things on the mind, and to affect the mind. By that we may as it were hear God speaking to us. Wherever we are and whatever we are about, we may see divine things excellently represented and held forth, and it will abundantly tend to confirm the Scriptures, for there is an excellent agreement between these things and the Holy Scriptures.[21]

How to Read this Book

The reader of this book should feel free to read its chapters and various parts non-consecutively. Part One is comprised of denser material which introduces the reader to Jonathan Edwards and his place within the history of the emblematic world view. Chapter Two tells the story of the emblematic world view. Chapter Three outlines its reception by Protestant and early Evangelical theologians. Chapter Four frames Edwards as an emblem writer. Chapter Five provides a theological reconfiguration of his notebook "Images of Divine Things" and invites the reader to occasional meditation. Part Two is organized around the subjects contained in Edwards' "Images" notebook. Each subject section in Part Two contains a modernized paraphrase of an Edwards' notebook entry along with works by other emblem writers. Jump in wherever and enjoy!

[20]Edwards, Wallace E. Anderson, Mason I. Lowance Jr., and David H. Watters, *Typological Writings,* 152.

[21]"Images," no. 70.

Contents

PART ONE:
EDWARDS' EMBLEMATIC VISION

CHAPTER ONE: INTRODUCTION

IT WAS A WARM SUMMER EVENING in a small pub in the English countryside. E.O. Wilson, Iain McGilchrist, and Jonathan Edwards had gathered to discuss the nature and significance of creation. Wilson, the renowned biologist, spoke of the power of evolution, arguing that the natural world is a product of a long and unpredictable process of trial and error. McGilchrist, the psychiatrist and philosopher, spoke of the importance of the two hemispheres of the brain, and how they shape our understanding of the world. And Edwards, the theologian, spoke of the emblematic view of the universe and demonstrated with a rose how his emblematic world view compared with Wilson's scientific view and how it fit within McGilchrist's brain hemisphere theory.[1]

Left Hemisphere: *Rosa* (Rose) is a genus of shrub in the family *Rosaceae*. They are climbers. They are native to The Contiguous United States, Alaska, Canada, and Saint-Pierre Et Miquelon. They have achenes. Flowers are visited by Bumble Bees, Buff-tailed bumblebee, Bumble-bee-mimic *Anthophora*, and *Helophilus hybridus*. Individuals can grow to 3.7 m.[2]

Right Hemisphere: Roses grow upon briers, which is to signify that all temporal sweets are mixed with bitter. But what seems more especially to be meant by it, is that true happiness, the crown of glory, is to be come at in no other way than by bearing Christ's cross by a life of mortification, self-denial and labor, and bearing all things for Christ. The rose, the chief of all flowers, is the last thing that comes out. The briery prickly bush grows before, but the end and crown of all is the beautiful and fragrant rose.[3]

---

[1] Iain McGilchrist, *The Matter With Things: Our Brains, Our Delusions and the Unmaking of the World* (London: Perspectiva Press, 2021), 2, Kindle edition.

[2] Encyclopedia of Life, "Rose," Accessed February 4, 2023. https://eol.org/pages/29911.

[3] *Images of Divine Things* in *Typological Writings, vol. 11, The Works of Jonathan Edwards,* ed. Wallace E. Anderson (New Haven and London: Yale University Press, 1993), 52.

Edwards described the universe as a grand symphony, with each component of creation interconnected and each thing part of the greater whole. He spoke of how the entire universe was held together by an unseen web of divine love. He argued that God created the universe as a reflection of His own perfect attributes and that humanity's purpose was to recognize and glorify God. The discussion was robust. His remarks were strong, filling the crowd with amazement and wonder. Wilson and McGilchrist sat there intently listening, nodding in accord as Edwards spoke. His ideas had clearly struck a chord with them both.

The truth is out there. Something deep within us understands that there is more to this world than meets the eye, under a microscope, or via a telescope. Humanity detects something about the world that defies scientific discovery—realms beyond the visible spectrum that are inaccessible to reason alone. The world is a strange and wonderful place. Many people live in perpetual anticipation of coming into contact with a higher power or alien intelligence. We yearn to be moved by something bigger than ourselves.

Jonathan Edwards (1703–58) was a colonial clergyman and philosopher-theologian who went further than most theologians in investigating nature as a revelation from God. Edwards reveals a God-haunted world in his personal notebooks and throughout his preaching and writing, in which we are surrounded by signs, symbols, and emblems that serve as windows to spiritual reality. Edwards does not deny the radical nature of this perspective of creation, and therefore, in my opinion, it deserves serious examination. He admitted in his "Types" notebook that he was convinced that the universe, the sky, the air, the seas, and Scriptures all contain images of divine things, like a language has words.[4]

According to Edwards, creation demonstrates more than just intelligent design. That much was granted by deism (the common belief that God created the world but no longer interacts with it directly). Nature, according to Edwards, is neither a mechanism or natural selection working its way to an unknown end. Instead, the creation has an intelligible design that serves as a living message for those with ears to hear and eyes to see. This may seem strange, even alien, to the apparently informed and sophisticated ears of the twenty-first century. However, Jonathan Edwards is not a supporter of merely rational enlightenment. He is a strong believer in supernatural illumination, believing that humanity requires Divine and Supernatural Light to see the Truth. This light is only available through God's grace. Humanity

---

[4]"Types," *WJE*, 11:152.

is swimming in an ocean of signs, symbols, and emblems—communications from the Divine mind inviting man to return to the Creator.[5]

Though Edwards anticipated that his views would be seen as out of this world, his world view is not all that fantastical when compared to several currently prevalent guesses and beliefs, such as:

> A world of random multiverses and alternate realities, with dreams of interstellar and inter-dimensional travel,
> A world that brims with life because it was long ago seeded by aliens, and
> A world of beauty, art, technology, faith, feeling, and consciousness that arose from a practically infinite series of random events and interactions.

Now compare the above views with Edwards' biblically informed view of reality:

> A world that is spoken into existence and upheld by the Word of His power,
> A world whose origin is not muck, mire, and goo, but language and poetry,
> A world that is the result of Wisdom, not blind natural selection,
> A world of intelligible meaning in which every thing is a word,
> A world that is grammatical to its core,
> A world that exists in the mind of God in whom we all live, move, and have our being,
> A world that speaks of Christ, for whom even the rocks yearn to cry out,
> A world that groans for liberation,
> A world that was created out of the overflowing love of the Omnipotent, Omnipresent, and Omniscient God, and
> A world whose meaning is unlocked by the Bible,
> *This is the the God-haunted world of Jonathan Edwards.*

According to Edwards, God's revelation to humanity is divided into two books: the Book of Scripture and the Book of Nature. Protestants have appropriately emphasized the final authority of the Bible, *Sola Scriptura,* over the second book of revelation. Yet, "The rising age of science found

---

[5]*WJE,* 17:408–26

in Edwards an American interpreter who... had reformulated his fathers' faith and placed it in the context of a modern philosophy of nature."[6] In comparison to what Edwards promotes, the Protestant Reformation was a "negligible performance," according to Joseph Haroutunian.[7] Nature, according to Edwards, is giving much more than hollow praise to its Creator. He claimed that it is only "fit and proper" for God to construct the world in such a way that it reveals mysteries about Him and His reign. "The works of God are but a kind of voice or language of God, to instruct intelligent beings in things pertaining to himself," Edwards stated.[8] Let him who has ears hear.

A Former Baptist

As Edwards correctly predicted, the pushback to his world view would be significant. However, antagonism occasionally creates a chance for competing world views to flow together. *The Creation: An Appeal to Save Life on Earth* is one such providence. *The Creation*, written as a letter to a Southern Baptist pastor by noted Harvard sociobiologist E.O. Wilson (1929–2021), discusses the planet's ecological crisis and extends a hand to Baptists and Evangelicals in the hopes that they will join forces with the scientific community to save the Earth.

Wilson was raised as a Southern Baptist in Alabama but abandoned the church during his college years. He wished that science and religion might put aside their disagreements and work together for the greater benefit. At the end of his first chapter, Wilson made an intriguing statement: "I already know much of the religious argument for Creation, and would like to learn more."[9]

Wilson believes that early in human history, a false turn was made in an endeavor to "ascend from Nature rather than to Nature." The "ascent to Nature" is characterized as an acceptance of our natural heritage and submission to "the gravitational pull of the natural world on our spirit, and on our souls."[10]

---

[6]Sydney E. Ahlstrom, "The Romantic Religious Revolution and the Dilemmas of Religious History," *Church History* 46, no. 2 (June 1977): 77.

[7]Ahlstrom, "The Romantic Religious Revolution and the Dilemmas of Religious History," 77.

[8]"Images of Divine Things," *WJE*, 11:67

[9]E. O. Wilson, *The Creation: An Appeal to Save Life on Earth* (New York: W. W. Norton & Company, Inc., 2006), 8.

[10]Wilson, *The Creation*, 13.

In this regard, he believes that the teachings of Holy Scripture are insufficient. Humans have a sense of environmental stewardship, but no explanation has been provided due to the lack of education and an explosion of biological information. Wilson's response is that nature should be acknowledged as "opening up a broad pathway to the heart of science itself," and that humanity's fate is inextricably linked to the fate of the creation.[11] He envisions an "Encyclopedia of Life," which catalogs each species based on genetic coding, anatomy, behavior, life cycle, and environmental role.[12] Not just scientists, but also historians and poets, should commemorate each species' extremely convoluted evolutionary past. This is his "compelling moral argument" for preserving the creation.[13]

Edwards likewise sees creation as opening up a broad path, not to the heart of science, but to the heart of God. Edwards encourages us to return to creation via scriptural meditation. He instructs us to explore deeper into nature in order to discern the Mind that underpins all existence. Though the distance between the Edwardsean and materialist views could not be larger, Jonathan Edwards may be the type of believer Wilson is looking for, because Edwards understands that creation is priceless—it is a voice of God.

The mechanized world envisioned by the eighteenth century Enlightenment thinkers differs little from the flat world of materialism—flat because it lacks any transcendent spiritual dimension—of today's Neo-Darwinists. As an alternative to the materialist view, Jonathan Edwards continues to offer a spiritually-illuminating and rational return to a God-haunted world—a thoroughly Christian view of reality.[14] Edwards' view of nature may seem strange to many people who are unaccustomed to viewing the creation as

---

[11]Wilson, *The Creation*, 13–14.

[12]Wilson, *The Creation*, 19–23.

[13]Wilson, *The Creation*, 123.

[14]Edwards' sense of a communicative creation was mirrored half a world away in Germany by the radical pietist leader of the Counter-Enlightenment, Johann Georg Hamann (1730–1788). At first a disciple of the French Enlightenment, Hamann experienced a deep conversion in 1758—the same year that Edwards died. From that time forward Hamann was committed to challenging the faith in reason that characterized Enlightenment philosophy (James C. Livingstone, *The Enlightenment and the Nineteenth Century*, vol. 1, *Modern Christian Thought, Second Edition* (Minneapolis, MN: Fortress Press, 2006), 71). For Hamann, God is "the poet at the beginning of days." Hamann looked to Psalm 19 for his understanding of the nature and purpose of creation: "[T]he Creation, which is an utterance to created things through created things, for day speaketh unto day, and night proclaimeth unto night. Its word traverses every clime to the ends of the earth, and its voice can be heard in every dialect. To collect these together is the scholar's modest part; the philosopher's to interpret them; to imitate them, or—bolder still—to adapt them, the poet's" (J. G. Hamann, J. M. Bernstein, ed., "Aesthetica in Nuce: A Rhapsody in Cabbalistic Prose (1762)," in *Classic and Romantic German Aesthetics*

a communication from God. Even in his own day "[w]hat for him was an obvious reality written across the cosmos, was not so apparent to others walking through an eighteenth century New England meadow surrounded by maples in the fall."[15] These revelations remained opaque to those without the spiritual sense imparted to believers at conversion. But to the redeemed who have cultivated their spiritual sensibilities, an examination of the Book of Nature points to God's presence in every area of life. Just as one can "read" a person by paying attention to body language, in the same way, one can learn about the excellencies of the Son of God by viewing the beauty of the world. Belden Lane notes that "Edwards can go so far as to say that even though this is a less direct form of communication, in some respects it may be more reliable."[16] Edwards writes,

> So that when we are delighted with flowery meadows and gentle breezes of wind, we may consider that we only see the emanations of the sweet benevolence of Jesus Christ; when we behold the fragrant rose and lily, we see his love and purity. So the green trees and fields, and singing of birds, are the emanations of his infinite joy and benignity; the easiness and naturalness of trees and vines [are] shadows of his infinite beauty and loveliness; the crystal rivers and murmuring streams have the footsteps of his sweet grace and bounty. When we behold the light and brightness of the sun, the golden edges of an evening cloud, or the beauteous bow, we behold the adumbrations of his glory and

(New York: Cambridge University Press, 2003), 4). "Passion alone gives hands, feet and wings to abstractions as well as to hypotheses;—to images and signs gives spirit, life, and tongue—Where are swifter syllogisms? Where is the rolling thunder of eloquence begotten, and where its companion, the monosyllable of lightning?" (Hamann, 14). Graubner observes, "This address of God to man is made in a language of images: images, because man can only perceive with his senses; language, in order to make him understand something different from himself. In this way, every recognizable thing becomes a figurative speech in parables and metaphors. The language of God's Creation is poetry" (Hans Graubner, "Theological Empiricism: Aspects of Johann Georg Hamann's Reception of Hume," *Hume Studies XV*, no. 2 (November 1989): 382). Graubner notes that God is, as Hamann says, "'the poet at the beginning of the days' [...] his language is necessarily a language of images because of the link-up of human experience with the senses [...] the ontological status of the created world as an 'absolute,' that is, an indissoluble metaphor [...] God's condescension to man as a limited being who depends on his senses is shown in two ways: as God's language of Creation that can be perceived by the senses in nature, and as God's word that became flesh in human history" (Graubner, 382).

[15]Belden Lane, "Jonathan Edwards on Beauty, Desire, and the Sensory World," *Theological Studies* 65, no. 1 (March 2004): 52.

[16]Lane, "Jonathan Edwards on Beauty, Desire, and the Sensory World," 51.

goodness; and the blue skies, of his mildness and gentleness. There are also many things wherein we may behold his awful majesty: in the sun in his strength, in comets, in thunder, in the towering thunder clouds, in ragged rocks and the brows of mountains [...] this is a reason that Christ is compared so often to those things and called by their names; as, the sun of righteousness, the morning star, the rose of Sharon and lily of the valleys, the apple tree amongst the trees of the wood, a bundle of myrrh, a roe, or a young hart.[17]

Job 12:7–8 is echoed in Edwards' understanding of God's voice through the creatures of this world. Nature speaks to all of humanity in a voice that proclaims God's glory. Psalm 19 compares the scope of nature's broadcast to the sun, which circles the entire world providing heat and light. Because everyone on Earth absorbs heat from the sun, everyone has access to the language of the heavens.

Master and Emissary

Edwards' poetic view of the world resonates strongly with Iain McGilchrist's brain research. McGilchrist's books *The Master and His Emissary: The Divided Brain and the Making of the Western World* and *The Matter With Things: Our Brains, Our Delusions and the Unmaking of the World* are widely received breakthrough investigations of the human brain and how its two hemispheres interact to shape our view of the world.[18] McGilchrist contends that the right and left hemispheres of the brain have complementary yet distinct roles, and that this duality is necessary for proper functioning. The right hemisphere is the "Master," the creative and intuitive power underlying our thoughts and behaviors. It is the source of our capacity for metaphor, imagination, and insight. The left hemisphere, on the other hand, is the "Emissary," the analytical and logical force that processes and interprets the world. It is in charge of language, reasoning, and the organization of knowledge. The left hemisphere is used to manipulate the world, while the right hemisphere is used to comprehend it. We have been able to control the world to a degree that was unimaginable a few generations ago, but

[17]*WJE*, 13:278–80.

[18]*The Master and His Emissary: The Divided Brain and the Making of the Western World* (New Haven, CT: Yale University Press, 2019). *The Matter With Things: Our Brains, Our Delusions and the Unmaking of the World* (London: Perspectiva Press, 2021).

this has been done without a true understanding of it. McGilchrist offers an explanation of reality that is more accurate than what we have been accustomed to, and covers the fields of neurology, philosophy, and physics.[19]

McGilchrist contends that for us to be our best selves, the two hemispheres must work together. The "Master" must be permitted to lead, but the "Emissary" must be allowed to interpret and analyze. If either is allowed to dominate, the outcome is a distorted perspective of reality. McGilchrist argues that our current Western civilization has allowed the left hemisphere to dominate, resulting in an imbalance that has caused a variety of social and psychological difficulties. In contrast to the left, the religious disposition of the right hemisphere allows one to perceive the depths of creation. Such a view is opposite of the attitude of the left hemisphere towards creation, which sees itself as the ruler—distant, confident, controlling, wanting to have power over creation and either disregarding the mystery of existence or using it to its own benefit. This is the attitude that now governs our world, and unfortunately, not just in the West.[20]

> An increasingly mechanistic, fragmented, decontextualised world, marked by unwarranted optimism mixed with paranoia and a feeling of emptiness, has come about, reflecting, I believe, the unopposed action of a dysfunctional left hemisphere.[21]

One might summarize the two hemispheres' visions of reality as follows: the left hemisphere's view is of a world composed of isolated, fragmentary elements that are easily manipulated, decontextualized, abstracted, and mechanical. It is an inanimate universe that is useful for purposes of control, but does not provide a helpful guide to understanding the nature of what it encounters. The left hemisphere began to gain ascendency during the Industrial Revolution—a monumental effort by man to gain power over the natural world and create a world in the likeness of the left hemisphere. Goods were mechanically produced, identical and interchangeable, free from the 'imperfections' of being made by living hands. Natural processes that resulted in subtle variations of form were replaced by invariant forms, such as perfect circles, straight lines, and rectangles. Tools, mechanisms, and machines that make machines were created. These products were certain,

---

[19]McGilchrist, *The Matter With Things,* 10–11.

[20]McGilchrist, *The Matter With Things,* 1880–81.

[21]McGilchrist, *The Master and His Emissary,* 6.

iconic, identical, rectilinear, endlessly reproducible, mechanistic, fixed, and man-made.[22]

On the other hand, the right hemisphere's vision is of a world that is infinitely more complex, flowing, and interconnected. It is an animate universe that is truer to what is, but is more difficult to comprehend and express in language. This view of the world is essential for a broader or longer-term understanding, but is less useful for practical, shorter-term issues.[23] Shakespeare's plays are a vivid demonstration of the ascendance of the right hemisphere during the Renaissance. There is no regard for rules or labels, but rather a joyous appreciation for the diversity and complexity of humanity, instead of the standardization of personalities and behavior.[24] The world is alive with beauty and enchantment. Shakespeare's work has been compared to the hiddenness of God—the great poet, the creator is present and hidden everywhere.[25]

Today, the natural world, cultural tradition, the body, religion, and art, which were once sources of intuitive life, have been drained of their power and disenchanted. Many people now draw their reality from TV screens and computers instead of direct experience. The physical environment that was once the natural world, with its rhythms and cycles, has been replaced by an unyielding and inert environment of non-living surfaces, straight lines, and concrete masses. This has resulted in the left hemisphere's world becoming externalized, thus subverting the right hemisphere's tendency to check with the real world of experience. Logic now leads back to a solution within the system, instead of a need to break out of it.[26]

Reweaving the Rainbow

In contrast to Edwards' ideas, clever publications like Richard Dawkins' *Unweaving the Rainbow: Science, Delusion and the Appetite for Wonder* aim to refute a spiritual understanding of the universe and replace it with a reductionist view, purged of depth, in which we and the rest of nature are simply a bunch of random particles, futilely and haplessly, without thought, crashing into each other in predictable ways, existing only in a material form,

---

[22] McGilchrist, *The Master and His Emissary,* 386–87.

[23] McGilchrist, *The Matter With Things,* 52–53.

[24] McGilchrist, *The Master and His Emissary,* 303–4.

[25] McGilchrist, *The Matter With Things,* 1914.

[26] McGilchrist, *The Master and His Emissary,* Location 440–44.

and having no value other than utility.[27] His book title is a play on John Keats' lament that Isaac Newton's scientific discoveries were responsible for unweaving the rainbow. Despite the fact that Newton published his observations over three centuries ago, the debate over the nature of Nature has not been settled. Individuals like Dawkins continue to feel driven to purge the rainbow and the rest of Nature of authorial intent. The resulting "speechless universe" can only be given a voice by the poet-scientist.[28] Nature, according to Dawkins, should inspire us to write poetry. Edwards, on the other hand, *reweaves* the rainbow and reminds us that the rainbow, like the rest of creation, *is* poetry.

A Colonial Mininister and More

But who is Edwards and why is he important? Briefly, Jonathan Edwards was a Northampton, Massachusetts Congregational minister and theologian most famous for his role in the First Great Awakening. Though he is best known for sermons such as "Sinners in the Hands of an Angry God," Edwards wrote a variety of theological discourses, miscellanies, and treatises on issues such as religious experience, free will, redemptive history, ethics, and original sin. Along with his theological writings, Edwards was fully engaged with the Enlightenment and the challenges of deism. "Images of Divine Things," Edwards' notebook of types and emblems, is one of his more intriguing works from this engagement.[29]

Jonathan Edwards' World View

"Images of Divine Things" reveals that Edwards held an emblematic world view that he believed answered the question of God's relationship to the universe and the correlation between nature and Scripture. In general, an emblematic world view considers nature to be rich in moral and spiritual truths that are expressed symbolically or hieroglyphically.[30] On the basis

---

[27]McGilchrist, *The Matter With Things,* 13.

[28]Richard Dawkins, *Unweaving the Rainbow: Science, Delusion and the Appetite for Wonder* (Boston, New York: Houghton Mifflin Company, 1998), 16.

[29]Jonathan Edwards, Wallace E. Anderson, Mason I. Lowance Jr., and David H. Watters, eds, "Images of Divine Things," in *Typological Writings,* vol. 11 of *The Works of Jonathan Edwards* (New Haven and London: Yale University Press, 1993).

[30]Nancy Pearcey, *Saving Leonardo: A Call to Resist the Secular Assault on Mind, Morals, and Meaning* (Nashville: B&H, 2010), 177.

of empiricism and materialism, the Enlightenment's deism and mechanical philosophy rejected such ideas.

Recent Scholarship

Edwards, widely regarded as a pivotal figure in early American Evangelicalism,[31] has been dubbed "America's Theologian,"[32] "America's Augustine," "America's Aquinas," and "America's Kierkegaard."[33] Yet, Edwards remains an enigmatic figure who defies easy categorization. Edwards' intellect has been properly described as a wonderful mirror that provides an enthralling reflection of the beholder.[34] Whether the image reflected is one of deterministic Calvinism, philosophical idealism, or romantic mysticism, the image depicts a broad world view. Despite varying interpretations and reflections on Edwards, it is widely agreed that his world view is strongly emblematic.[35]

Edwards was not alone in his awareness of the Divine presence and voice emanating from creation. According to British historian Reginald Ward, early Evangelicals once possessed a coherent world view capable of placing the drama of redemption within a greater framework of thought.[36] However, in the aftermath of the eighteenth-century revivals, Evangelicalism

---

[31]Douglas A. Sweeney, *The American Evangelical Story: A History of the Movement* (Grand Rapids: Baker Academic, 2005), 23–25. Sweeney defines American Evangelicalism as a "a movement rooted in classical Christian orthodoxy, shaped by a largely Protestant understanding of the gospel, and distinguished from other such movements by an eighteenth-century twist." Sweeney is referring to the theology and practices that emerged during the First Great Awakening revivals, which highlighted the need of spreading the Gospel of Christ throughout the world. Though not a denomination, eighteenth-century Evangelicals share a shared understanding of the good news as justification by faith alone, as clearly stated in the Bible (Rom 3:28), and the significance of expending large resources to carry this message to the ends of the earth.

[32]Robert W. Jenson, *America's Theologian, A Recommendation of Jonathan Edwards* (New York: Oxford University Press, 1988).

[33]Joseph A. Conforti, *Jonathan Edwards, Religious Tradition & American Culture* (Chapel Hill: University of North Carolina Press, 1995), 1.

[34]Peter Thuesen, "Jonathan Edwards as Great Mirror," *Scottish Journal of Theology* 50 (1997): 42.

[35]This consensus will become evident by both the variety of sources cited and from the texts of Edwards himself.

[36]W. R. Ward, *Early Evangelicalism: A Global Intellectual History, 1670– 1789* (New York: Cambridge University Press, 2006), 132–33. In chapter 1, "The Thought-World of Early Evangelicalism" Ward describes a decidedly spiritual world view comprised of a milieu of Pietism, hermeticism, Paracelsus's vitalism and the alchemical tradition, anti-Aristotelianism and illuminism, radical mysticism and theosophy, Cabbala, and the far-reaching influence of Jakob Böhme (6–23).

shifted its emphasis to doctrines of redemption, leaving teachings of creation primarily to Unitarians and Deists. Salvation was easier to preach than creation themes.[37] The spiritual (or emblematic) vision of the universe was handed over to those without the Spirit. According to Mark Noll, the main focus on personal piety frequently leaves greater concerns of world view unaddressed.[38] Ward observes that, as a result of the increasing flood of Enlightenment materialism, which threatened to push God out of his own creation, literature supporting the spiritual world view vanished swiftly in the eighteenth century.[39] Rather than avoiding the Enlightenment challenge, Edwards embraced an emblematic world view that profoundly contradicted mechanistic notions of nature. In doing so, he constructed a complex typology that extended beyond the Old and New Testaments' link between types and antitypes and into the real world.[40] Edwards' typological expansion into nature rejected mechanical philosophy's unified world view in favor of the two books of medieval theology, the Bible and the emblematic Book of Nature.[41]

Recent studies have addressed Edwards' enchanted and emblematic view of nature, most recently Lisanne Winslow's *A Great and Remarkable Analogy* in which she applies her expertise in the biological sciences to the study of

---

[37]Ward, *Early Evangelicalism: A Global Intellectual History, 1670– 1789,* 133.

[38]Mark Noll, *America's God: From Jonathan Edwards to Abraham Lincoln* (New York: Oxford University Press, 2002), 37.

[39]Ward, *Early Evangelicalism,* 132–33.

[40]Knight notes that traditional exegetes would admit that God occasionally reveals spiritual truths through natural emblems, such as the rock that Moses struck as representing Christ. Yet, "ordinary rocks in nature hold no such honored place." Edwards contended that divine types cannot be confined to Scripture alone. "Edwards heard God's voice still sounding in nature, in human history, and in the flow of contemporary events." Janice Knight, "Typology," in The *Princeton Companion to Jonathan Edwards,* ed. Sang Hyun Lee (Princeton: Princeton University Press, 2005), 191.

[41]Avihu Zakai, *Jonathan Edwards's Philosophy of History: The Reenchantment of the World in the Age of Enlightenment* (Princeton: Princeton University Press, 2003), 113–16. In "Miscellanies" no. tt on "Devotion" Edwards illustrates the devotional, symbolically communicative nature of The Great Chain of Being by comparing it to the inner workings of a clock in which the "immediate communication between one degree of being and the next degree of being (every wheel immediately communicates with the next wheel), but man being the top; so that the next immediate step from him is to God." As the wheels of the clock, though inferior to the hands, drive the hands to point out the correct time, in the same way the lower orders of creation are designed to move man beyond himself to a devotion toward God. Edwards, *The Miscellanies, a–500, WJE,* 13:190.

Edwards' natural typology and discerns what she terms an *onto-typology*.[42] Gerald McDermott's *Everyday Glory: The Revelation of God in All of Reality* is a significant contribution to natural typology in the Edwardsean spirit. He presents the reader, in a manner both erudite and accessible, with a Christian vision of reality, exploring how God reveals himself in creation. Drawing on the insights of Edwards, Newman, and Barth, McDermott argues that meaning and divine signs can be found in nature, science, law, history, animals, sex, and sports. In doing so, he offers a robust theology of creation and a way to understand God's relation to the world.[43]

Earlier assessments of Edwards' natural typology include the writings of Janice Knight and Avihu Zakai. Knight claims in *The Princeton Companion to Jonathan Edwards* that Edwards' typological innovations were the interpretive key used to discover God's language in the established order, history, and Scripture, and that these communications would grow as the Millennium approached.[44] Zakai situates Edwards' philosophy of nature within the backdrop of the Enlightenment, surveying contemporary ideas as well as Edwards' reaction to the challenge of mechanistic philosophy. Zakai begins to emphasize the centrality of the emblematic world view to Edwards' approach in this way.[45] Zakai notes that many aspects of Edwards' thought, both in form and content, can be linked back to his conversion, the defining event in his religious identity. This experience led Edwards to reconstruct, among other things, the external world of nature and the realm of history, the "order of nature" and the "order of time," as well as the realm of ethics and morals, in accordance with the theological convictions he gained during his conversion. In all of these areas, he tried to re-enchant the universe in order to manifest God's unshaken absolute sovereignty in creation. To use Max Weber's thesis, Edwards' life of the mind is evidence of how fresh religious convictions lead to new ways of behavior.[46] Tibor

---

[42]Lisanne Winslow, *A Great and Remarkable Analogy: The Onto-Typology of Jonathan Edwards* (New Directions in Jonathan Edwards Studies) (London: Vandenhoeck & Ruprecht Gmb.., 2020).

[43]Gerald R. McDermott, *Everyday Glory: The Revelation of God in All of Reality* (Grand Rapids, Michigan: Baker Academic, 2018).

[44]Knight, "Typology," 190–209.

[45]Avihu Zakai, *Jonathan Edwards's Philosophy of Nature: The Re- Enchantment of the World in the Age of Scientific Reasoning* (New York: T&T Clark, 2010). See also, Avihu Zakai, "An Interview with Avihu Zakai." [on-line]; accessed 29 November 2022; available from https://www.jesociety.org/an-interview-with-avihu-zakai/; Internet.

[46]Zakai, "An Interview with Avihu Zakai."

Fabiny offers another current take on Edwards' emblematic vision of nature. Fabiny asks that Edwards' typology be evaluated in a broader perspective, among the typologies of Shakespeare, Luther, and metaphysical poets such as George Herbert. *Tropologia,* Benjamin Keach's unjustly forgotten work, is also included by Fabiny.[47]

Gaps in Current Scholarship

Some specific components of Edwards' emblematic world view have not been thoroughly explored in contemporary Edwardsean scholarship. In other words, Edwards' realization of nature's intertextual relationship with Scripture is an emblematic world view, and his "Images" and "Types" notebooks are emblematic examples of the emblem book genre. A comparison of Edwards' notebooks with the broader phenomenon of emblem writing, particularly the Evangelical works of John Bunyan and Benjamin Keach, reveals a significant relationship to the emblem book genre. Despite the recognition of "interpretive keys" and resonance with other writers and theologians in the larger emblem tradition, an in-depth analysis of his emblematic world view's precise doctrinal content is absent. This gap could be caused by a lack of interest in Scripture or a fear of doctrinal dispute. Nonetheless, Edwards, a Bible man, saw the world through the lens of Scripture. As such, a systematic scriptural study of "Images of Divine Things" and "Types" would strengthen current scholarship by bringing doctrinal precision to his world view, which was not only distinctly emblematic, but also substantially inspired by Scripture.[48]

Thesis

In light of these contexts, I will argue that Edwards' typological notebook "Images of Divine Things" is clearly a variant of the emblem book genre. The research will concentrate on the history, analysis, and hermeneutics of Edwards' "Images of Divine Things" and "Types" notebooks, which are

---

[47]Tibor Fabiny, "Edwards and Biblical Typology," in *Understanding Jonathan Edwards: An Introduction to America's Theologian,* ed. Gerald McDermott (New York: Oxford University Press, 2008), 98. Fabiny brings a new perspective to the study of Edwards (and of Keach) by pointing out that students of typology have not yet explored the connection between Edwards and the emblem tradition, "[nor] have the other parallels between Edwards and Shakespeare been noticed (101)." Fertile ground for research abounds in comparative studies of Edwards with Luther, Shakespeare, and the metaphysical poets.

[48]Belden C. Lane, *Ravished by Beauty: The Surprising Legacy of Reformed Spirituality* (New York: Oxford University Press, 2011), 170–200.

frequently disregarded by systematic and historical theologians.[49] This intertextual reading of nature and Scripture, which I shall refer to as Edwards' *reinscripturation* of the universe, will also be compared to other seventeenth and eighteenth-century readings of nature and Scripture.[50] I use the term "reinscripturation" to express Edwards' recovery and reassignment of Scriptural relevance to particulars of the natural world that had been *de-inscribed* during the Enlightenment. Edwards felt that the created order possessed an inherent linguistic element; just as the Bible is an inscripturated record of God's spoken revelation, so is the world that was spoken into being. While Edwards vigorously defended the Protestant theology of Scripture, he was not opposed to "hearing" God's voice in nature/creation, as other Protestants had done, including Baptist pastor Benjamin Keach, Anglican poet Francis Quarles, and many others. Edwards held that the "Book of Scripture is the interpreter of the book of nature," and that the Bible is the sole accurate and authoritative interpretation and application of creation's signs and types.[51]

> The book of Scripture is the interpreter of the book of nature two ways, viz., by declaring to us those spiritual mysteries that are indeed signified and typified in the constitution of the natural world; and secondly, in actually making application of the signs and types in the book of nature as representations of those spiritual mysteries in many instances.[52]

Outside of the interpretive authority of Scripture, the voice of nature is hazy at best. Apart from the specific revelation of the Scriptures, nature has no discernible voice. Though Edwards spoke more forcefully on the revelatory content of nature than others, it is useful to compare his views with those of other Evangelical emblematic theologians who are also undeniably orthodox. Although Edwards' response to Enlightenment mechanistic philosophy has been referred to as *reenchantment*, referring to a reintroduction

[49]Edwards, "Images of Divine Things" and "Types," in *Typological Writings, WJE,* 11. "Images of Divine Things" is a notebook comprised of 212 entries in which Edwards set out to discover and amplify the correspondences between the natural world and spiritual reality. Volume 11 editor Mason Lowance notes the importance of Edwards' endeavor: "Edwards attempted to free typology from the narrow correspondences of the two testaments without reverting to exaggerated medieval allegory. In the process, he transcended philosophical dualism, linking the natural and the supernatural in a compelling and dynamic unity with God (33)."

[50]David Dawson, "Allegorical Intratextuality in Bunyan and Winstanley," *The Journal of Religion* 70 (1990): 189–212.

[51]"Images of Divine Things," *WJE,* 11:106.

[52]"Images of Divine Things," *WJE,* 11:106.

of wonder, I believe that Edwards' program is better described as reinscripturation due to his efforts to recover the spiritual and distinctly biblical dimension of creation.[53] This study will show that Edwards' reinscripturation of the world is critical to comprehending his distinctively biblical and emblematic world view as expressed in his emblem book "Images of Divine Things."[54]

The next parts will introduce Jonathan Edwards' context and perspective. This will begin with a quick overview of the emblematic world view in the Christian past, as well as how this emblematic vision fared throughout the Protestant Reformation and afterwards, including the genesis of the emblem book genre. It will next be shown that Edwards' emblematic world view, as expressed in the key text "Images of Divine Things," definitely belongs under the emblem book genre. It will be seen that Edwards' preferred vehicle for reinscripturating the universe was the emblem book.

Emblematic World View in the Christian Tradition

The emblematic world view can be traced back to medieval symbolism, an aesthetic world view that had two forms: metaphysical symbolism and universal allegory. Metaphysical symbolism, which was based on Neoplatonism, emphasized God's craftsmanship in the beauty of creation. This viewpoint is held by John Scotus Eriugina and Hugh of St. Victor. A contemplative look at the world will show a theophanic harmony. The beauty of creation reflects the invisible aspects of the Trinity. Man's sensitivity to this aesthetic harmony prompts him to seek explanation in the design and to perceive the universe allegorically, as a book written by the Creator for the creature. According to universal allegory, the universe, like the Bible, was accessible to exegesis.[55]

---

[53]McGilchrist, *The Master and His Emissary,* 389–90. Concerning the enchantment of the world, McGilchrist observes that the shift from rural to urban life, both due to the growth of industry and the Enlightenment's pursuit of an idealized society, caused a collapse of familiar social structures and a feeling of not belonging, with deep-seated consequences for mental life. Science and materialism, on one hand, and bureaucracy on the other, helped to create what Weber referred to as a disenchanted world.

[54]Avihu Zakai, *Jonathan Edwards's Philosophy of History: The Re-Enchantment of the World in the Age of Enlightenment* (Princeton: Princeton University Press, 2003). Avihu Zakai, *Jonathan Edwards's Philosophy of Nature: The Re-Enchantment of the World in the Age of Scientific Reasoning* (New York: T&T Clark, 2010).

[55]Umberto Eco, *Art and Beauty in the Middle Ages,* trans. Hugh Bredin (New Haven: Yale University Press, 1988), 56–59. See also Jaroslav Pelikan, *The Christian Tradition: A History of the Development of Doctrine, Vol. 3: The Growth of Medieval Theology (600–1300)* (Chicago: University Of Chicago Press, 1980), 104–05.

This propensity to investigate the world as a realm of divine allegory and sign was prevalent among Puritans who had a penchant for discovering amazing providences in everyday life. Viewing the world through the eyes of faith was necessary because, while God operates through the established rules of nature, it was a sin comparable to atheism not to look beyond second causes to the divine providence that filled the universe and choreographed every event.[56] Cotton Mather stated in *The Christian Philosopher* his inability to ignore Hugh of St. Victor's appeal to listen to the voice of the creatures. It is highly becoming of a "Christian Philosopher, to fetch Lessons of Piety from the whole Creation of God, and hear what Maxims of Piety all the Creatures would, in the way of Reflection and Similitude, mind us of . . . from all these Thousands of Powerful Preachers" which continually surround us.[57]

Emblematic World View in the Protestant Tradition

The basis for Edwards' reinscripturation scheme was the emblematic world view of the late Renaissance period of the sixteenth and seventeenth centuries, which thought that the Creator filled all particulars in the world with a plethora of hidden meanings and associations.

To have a correct understanding of a specific animal, thing, or event, one must know not only its external appearance, but also what its name means, what proverbs are associated with it, what it symbolizes in various traditions, and what other species it may be similar to. True knowledge of a particular could not be obtained by studying it in isolation from the rest of the world. This style of investigation differs from a study of outer appearances alone.[58] The Enlightenment and the subsequent decline of the emblematic world view have been variously described as a decontextualization of the universe, disenchantment, or desymbolization of nature.[59]

The Reformers

Barbara Lewalski argues in her seminal study *Protestant Poetics and the Seventeenth-Century Religious Lyric* that the Protestant Reformation encour-

---

[56]Robert MiddleKauff, *The Mathers: Three Generation of Puritan Intellectuals 1596–1728* (Berkeley: University of California Press, 1999), 139–40.

[57]Cotton Mather, *The Christian Philosopher,* ed. Winton U. Solberg (Chicago: University of Illinois Press, 1994), 22–23.

[58]William B. Ashworth, Jr., "Natural History and the Emblematic World View," in *Reappraisals of the Scientific Revolution* (Cambridge: Cambridge University Press, 1990), 306.

[59]Ashworth, "Natural History and the Emblematic World View," 318.

aged a "specifically biblical poetics, which revived and further developed these ancient assumptions [of an emblematic world view] under the impetus of Protestant theology and the new literary and philological interests of the period."[60] Both Luther and Calvin admit that the created order has emblematic meaning.

Luther spoke of the Word of God in his lectures on Genesis, in which every creation is a word. The act of creating is a divine communication.[61] As a result, he concludes that in the divine system of language, every bird and any fish are nothing more than nouns.[62] Simply said, the world is God's spoken Word.[63] Luther sees a linguistic quality to creation that is inextricably linked to God's Word. This linguistic dimension extends beyond outward appearances to ontological realities.

John Calvin, too, recognizes the link between creation and the Word of God. Calvin's exposition of the Lord's Supper centered on the appropriate relationship between physical and spiritual things. Calvin observed that the symbol, whether a rock, lamb, dove, ark, or circumcision, precisely depicts the item indicated because God has ordained it to do so. The fundamental nature of creation lends itself to an easy link between physical and spiritual phenomena.[64]

English Protestants

In the sixteenth and seventeenth centuries, Protestants continued to operate on the premise that the "centrality of figurative language to theological truth" had been divinely ordained.[65] Reformers like Wycliffe, Erasmus, Melancthon,

---

[60]Barbara Kiefer Lewalski, *Protestant Poetics and the Seventeenth-Century Religious Lyric* (Princeton: Princeton University Press, 1979), 8. Lewalski observes that "the most important feature identifying the Bible as poetry was its presumed symbolic mode" which rested on the medieval belief that Scripture contained both a literal and historical meaning as well as a spiritual meaning "whereby the things or events signified by the words point beyond themselves to other things or events."

[61]For further reading on Luther's view of creation as a communication see, Johannes Schwanke, "Luther on Creation," *Lutheran Quarterly* 16.1 (2002) 1–20, and Dennis Bielfeldt, "Luther, Metaphor, and Theological Language," *Modern Theology* 6.2 (1990) 121–35.

[62]Martin Luther, *Lectures on Genesis Chapters 1–5*, vol. 1 of *Luther's Works*, ed. Jaroslav Pelikan (St. Louis: Concordia, 1958), 49.

[63]Luther, *Lectures on Genesis Chapters 1–5*, 21–22.

[64]John Calvin, *Institutes of the Christian Religion*, in *The Library of Christian Classics*, ed. John T. McNeill, trans. Ford Lewis Battles (Philadelphia: Westminster, 1960), IV.xvii.20.

[65]Lewalski, *Protestant Poetics and the Seventeenth-Century Religious Lyric*, 78–81.

and Tyndale gave instructions on how to comprehend the poetic and aesthetic features of the Bible, as did Puritans like William Perkins and Richard Baxter, and emblem book writers like George Wither and Francis Quarles.[66]

Puritan clergyman and theologian Richard Baxter (1615–91) stated that people do not view the world spiritually because of their sloth and sensuality.[67] In their devotional pursuit of God, believers, according to Baxter, should ponder on the spiritual meaning and beauty of the natural world.[68] God uses the joy and beauty of creation to arouse spiritual longing and draw his people back to himself, the fountain of all beauty.[69] Edwards' notebooks clearly reflect Baxter's invitation to make full and proper use of nature through devotional activities that contemplate the spiritual importance and beauty of God's creation.

Emblem Books

According to Charles Hambrick-Stowe, the Puritans' devotional writing in the seventeenth century was heavily influenced by previous Roman Catholic meditative literature. The emblem book was a popular subgenre of religious literature—a continuation of the Middle Ages' iconographic tradition, consisting of "visual devotional aids with meditative verse."[70] Anne Bradstreet

[66]Lewalski, *Protestant Poetics and the Seventeenth-Century Religious Lyric,* 78–81.

[67]Richard Baxter, *A Christian Directory,* vol. 1 of *The Practical Works of Richard Baxter,* reprint, 1846 (Morgan, PA: Soli Deo Gloria, 2000), 253.

[68]Belden C. Lane, "Two Schools of Desire: Nature and Marriage in Seventeenth-Century Puritanism," *Church History* 69 (2000): 383. See also Belden C. Lane, *Ravished by Beauty: The Surprising Legacy of Reformed Spirituality* (New York: Oxford University Press, 2011).

[69]Lane, "Two Schools of Desire: Nature and Marriage in Seventeenth-Century Puritanism," 373.

[70]Charles E. Hambrick-Stowe, *The Practice of Piety: Puritan Devotional Disciplines in Seventeenth-Century New England* (Chapel Hill: University of North Carolina Press, 1982), 28–30. Prominent scholarship on emblem books and other emblematic literature include Michael Bath, *Speaking Pictures: English Emblem Books and Renaissance Culture,* Longman Medieval and Renaissance Library (London:Longman, 1994); Peter M. Daly, ed., *The English Emblem and the Continental Tradition,* AMS Studies in the Emblem 1 (New York: AMS, 1988); Mary Cole Sloane, *The Visual in Metaphysical Poetry* (Atlantic Highlands, NJ: Humanities, 1981); International Emblem Conference, 3rd, *Deviceful Settings: The English Renaissance Emblem and Its Contexts: Selected Papers from the Third International Emblem Conference, Pittsburgh, 1993,* eds. Michael Bath and Daniel Russell, AMS Studies in the Emblem 6 (New York: AMS, 1999); Michael Bath, John Manning, and Alan R. Young, eds., *The Art of the Emblem: Essays in Honor of Karl Josef Höltgen,* AMS Studies in the Emblem 9 (New York: AMS, 1993); Ronald Paulson, *Emblem and Expression: Meaning in English Art of the Eighteenth Century* (Cambridge, MA: Harvard University Press, 1975); Bart Westerweel, ed., *Anglo-Dutch Relations in the Field of the Emblem,* Symbola et Emblemata, 8 (Leiden: Brill, 1997); Tibor Fabiny, *The Lion and the Lamb: Figuralism and Fulfilment in the Bible, Art, and Literature* (New York: St. Martin's, 1992); Thomas Heffernan, *Art*

and Edward Taylor were influenced by emblem books, which were popular at English fairs and whose drawings were replicated on funeral broadsides and gravestones in New England. Title pages and chapter headers with iconographic printers' embellishments were only a few examples of how emblem books affected the appearance of future Puritan publications. It's worth noting that the Puritans' devotional use of symbolic and biblical illustrations persisted even though they were hostile to stained glass and other icons.[71]

Francis Quarles, an Anglican poet, was the most important English emblem writer (1592-1644).[72] Following in the footsteps of Jesuit emblem books, Quarles' *Emblemes* successfully captured the religious intensity and ecstasy of the Catholic Counter-Reformation for Protestants in early Stuart England. *Emblemes,* a devotional emblem book that could capture mind, imagination, and emotion, was published together with *Hieroglyphikes of the Life of Man.*[73] Quarles saw the entire universe as a system of holy hieroglyphics.

> An Emblem is but a silent Parable. Let not the tender Eye checke, to see the allusion to our blessed Saviour figured, in these Types. In holy Scripture, He is sometimes called a Sower; sometimes a Fisher; sometimes, a Physician: And why not presented so, as well to the eye, as to the ear. Before the knowledge of letters, GOD was known by hieroglyphics, And, indeed, what are the Heavens, the earth, nay every creature, Hieroglyphics and Emblems of his glory?[74]

and Emblem: Early Seventeenth- Century English Poetry of Devotion (The Renaissance Institute, 1991); Pierre Buhler & Tibor Fabiny, *Interpretation Of Texts Sacred And Secular* (Zurich: Pano Verlag, 1999); Peter M. Daly and Mary V. Silcox, *The Modern Critical Reception of the English Emblem* (München, GER: K G Saur Verlag Gmbh & Co,1992); Peter M. Daly, ed., *Companion to Emblem Studies,* AMS Studies in the Emblem (New York: AMS, 2008).

[71]Hambrick-Stowe, *The Practice of Piety,* 28–30.

[72]*Catalogues of Books, WJE,* 26:195. Quarles was cited twice in Edwards' "Catalogue" of Reading.

[73]Karl Josef Höltgen, *Aspects of the Emblem: Studies in the English Emblem Tradition and the European Context,* with a foreword by Sir Roy Strong, Problemata Semiotica (Kassel, GER: Reichenberger, 1986), 32–33. The authoritative study of Quarles and his emblems is Karl Josef Höltgen, *Francis Quarles (1592–1644) Als Meditativer und Emblematischer Dichter,* Buchreihe der Anglia, Zeitschrift Für Englische Philologie (Tübingen: Niemeyer, 1978).

[74]Francis Quarles Emblems [on-line]; accessed 29 November 2022; available from https://ia600205.us.archive.org/8/items/quarlesemblems00quar/quarlesemblems00quar_bw.pdf; Internet.

The association of creatures with hieroglyphs is echoed in Edwards' "Images of Divine Things" entry 206, as well as in his "Types of the Messiah," where he speculated that the origin of Egyptian hieroglyphics stemmed from "[i]t being so much God's manner from the beginning of the world to represent divine things by types."[75]

Evangelical Writers

Edwards' notebooks show a definite kinship with, and perhaps reliance on, the emblem books of the Evangelical writers. John Bunyan (1628–88), an English nonconformist clergyman and author of *Pilgrim's Progress*, agreed with Quarles that a human may only experience the world correctly when it is considered as a shadowy version of the real, spiritual reality. "I find that holy Writ in many places hath semblance with this method, where the cases do one call for one thing, to set forth another; use it I mean then, and yet nothing smother Truth's golden Beams; Nay, by this method may make it cast forth its rays as light as day," he wrote.[76] Roger Sharrock noticed that Bunyan's imagery was heavily influenced by the realm of emblem books, the most important of which being Quarles' publications.[77] In *Solomon's Temple Spiritualized* (1688), Bunyan clearly conveyed his emblematic world view:

> Since it is the wisdom of God to speak to us ofttimes by trees, gold, silver, stones, beasts, fowls, fishes, spiders, ants, frogs, flies, lice, dust, &c., and here by wood; how should we by them understand his voice, if we count there is no meaning in them?[78]

Ralph Austen (1612–1656), an Oxford Baptist conventicler and renowned cidermaker, provided a comparable example of using creation as a source of

---

[75]"Types," *WJE*, 11:127–28, 202.

[76]John Bunyan, *The Pilgrim's Progress* (Westwood, NJ: Barbour, 1970), xi.

[77]Roger Sharrock, "Bunyan and the English Emblem Writers," *The Review of English Studies* 21 (1945): 105–06.

[78]John Bunyan and George Offor, "Solomon's Temple Spiritualized," in *The Whole Works of John Bunyan* (Grand Rapids: Baker, 1982), 3:500.

emblems.[79] *The Spiritual Use of an Orchard* is a lengthy exercise in gleaning spiritual insights from the art of horticulture.

> The World is a great Library, and Fruit-trees are some of the Bookes wherein we may read & see plainly the Attributes of God his Power, Wisdome, Goodnesse etc. and be Instructed and taught our duty toward him in many things even from Fruit- trees for as trees (in a Metaphoricall sence) are Bookes, so likewise in the same sence they have a Voyce, and speake plainely to us, and teach us many good lessons ... Fruit-trees are a TEXT from which may be raysed many profitable Doctrines, and Conclusions, which may be proved by Scripture, and Experience.[80]

In his *Tropologia* of husbandry and God as husbandman, English Particular Baptist pastor Benjamin Keach (1640–1704) similarly drew thirty-four parallels between the heavenly and earthly husbandmen and their work and relationship to their gardens and orchards.[81]

Reinscripturation: Edwards and the Emblematic Tradition

Jonathan Edwards shared Austen's poetic sensibility and allegorical habit of mind, as did Bunyan, Keach, and others. This sensibility was reflected in their emblem books. Because Scripture, in their opinion, gave the inspiration and bounds for their emblematic theology, these men spoke in a "common tongue." Horticulture is a prominently shared theme. Similarly to Austen, Bunyan, and Keach, Edwards saw fruit trees as powerful symbols of mankind at various phases of conversion and sanctification. In "Images of Divine Things," entry 171, he reflected on the flowering and ripening of fruit trees and other things of that type. According to Edwards, the "puttings forth of the tree [blossoms] in order to make fruit make a great show and

---

[79]For a biographical study of Ralph Austen and a review of his work see Larry J. Kreitzer, "The Gardener: Ralph Austen," in *Seditious Sectaryes: The Baptist Conventiclers of Oxford 1641–1691* (Milton Keynes, UK: Paternoster, 2006), James Turner, "Ralph Austen, an Oxford Horticulturist of the Seventeenth Century," *Garden History* 6, no. 2 (1978), and Belden C. Lane, "Two Schools of Desire: Nature and Marriage in Seventeenth-Century Puritanism," *Church History* 69, no. 2 (2000).

[80]Ralph Austen, *The Spiritual Use of an Orchard* (New York: Garland, 1982), 3, 6.

[81]Benjamin Keach, *Tropologia: A Key to Open Scripture Metaphors..: To Which Are Prefixed, Arguments to Prove the Divine Authority of the Holy Bible: Together with Types of the Old Testament* (London: William Hill Collingridge, 1856), 254.

are pleasing to the eye, but the fruit is then very small and tender." The fruit is increased later, when there is less display.[82] Edwards interprets this horticultural phenomenon as a symbol of conversion and maturity. When a person first becomes a Christian, he is full of blossom and show, emotion and joy. This is the blossom that will fall off soon. Fresh believers, like young fruit, are also highly delicate and easily injured.

Edwards' Emblematic View of Creation

Edwards' understanding of the Spirit's work went well beyond the typical Puritan perception of extraordinary providences and prodigies, which were normally limited to outliers or aberrations in nature. Edwards looked for the rule, not the exception: a comprehensive vision of the world that could address the Enlightenment's mechanistic philosophy.

> If we look on these shadows of divine things as the voice of God, purposely, by them, teaching us these and those spiritual and divine things, to show of what excellent advantage it will be, how agreeably and clearly it will tend to convey instruction to our minds, and to impress things on the mind, and to affect the mind. By that we may as it were hear God speaking to us. Wherever we are and whatever we are about, we may see divine things, excellently represented and held forth, and it will abundantly tend to confirm the Scriptures, for there is an excellent agreement between these things and the Holy Scriptures.[83]

Edwards' emblematic world view of "the whole outward creation" as shadows of spiritual things in which there are thousands of wonderful agreements and correspondences can be described as pansemiotic.[84] Pansemioticism, posits that natural phenomena do not exist in isolation but are connected to each other in a complex web of significations.[85] The emblematic meaning of a thing did not arise from the subjectivity of the beholder but from the fact that the thing depicted an objective meaning that transcended

---

[82]"Images of Divine Things," *WJE,* 11:115.

[83]"Images of Divine Things," *WJE,* 11:74.

[84]Jan C. Westerhoff, "A World of Signs: Baroque Pansemioticism, the Polyhistor and the Early Modern Wunderkammer," *Journal of the History of Ideas* 62, no. 4 (October 2001): 634.

[85]Westerhoff, "A World of Signs," 641–42.

the physical and factual dimensions of its existence. Edwards' emblems and types are a reflection of a pansemiotic world view.[86]

In Edwards' preaching and writing, familiar items such as spiders, arrows, death, the sun, rain, plants, animals, and human events were converted into strong and striking mental imagery. The entire world is a vivid picture of spiritual truth, a true second book of revelation that produces strongly affecting images that are both comforting and terrifying. Edwards agreed with Bunyan that metaphors/ideas of the created order are a type of revelation.

> 'Tis very fit and becoming of God, who is infinitely wise, so to order things that there should be a voice of his in his works instructing those that behold them, and pointing forth and showing divine mysteries and things more immediately appertaining to himself and his spiritual kingdom. The works of God are but a kind of voice or language of God, to instruct intelligent beings in things pertaining to himself. And why should we not think that he would teach and instruct by his works in this way as well as others, viz. by representing divine things by his works, and so pointing them forth, especially since we know that God hath so much delighted in this way of instruction.[87]

"Miscellanies" no. 362 on the Trinity contains a stunning example of Edwards' emblematic world view. "Miscellanies" no. 362 was composed in the second part of 1728, about the time he started composing "Images of Divine Things."

> TRINITY. We have a lively image of this Trinity in the sun. The Father is as the substance of the sun; the Son is as the brightness and glory of the disk of the sun; the Holy Ghost is as the heat and continually emitted influence, the emanation by which the world

---

[86]Westerhoff, "A World of Signs," 639.

[87]"Images of Divine Things," *WJE*, 11:67. Bunyan also notes the appropriateness of such revelation. "And if some better handle can a fly, than some a text, why should we then deny their making proof, or good experiment, of smallest things, great mischiefs to prevent? Wise Solomon did fools to pissmires send, to learn true wisdom, and their lies to mend. Yea, God by swallows, cuckoos, and the ass, shows they are fools who let that season pass, which he put in their hand, that to obtain which is both present and eternal gain. I think the wiser sort my rhymes may slight, but what care I, the foolish will delight to read them, and the foolish God has chose, and doth by foolish things their minds compose, and settle upon that which is divine; great things, by little ones, are made to shine." John Bunyan, *Divine Emblems, or, Temporal Things Spiritualized* (London: Bickers & Son, 1867), xvi.

is enlightened, warmed, enlivened and comforted. The various sorts of rays and their beautiful colors do well represent the various beautiful graces and virtues of the Spirit, and I believe were designed on purpose. And therefore the rainbow is a sign of the covenant: and St. John saw a rainbow round about the throne of God (Rev. 4:3) and a rainbow upon the head of Christ (Rev. 10:1); Ezekiel say a rainbow about the throne (Ezek. 1:28).

For indeed the whole outward creation, which is but the shadows of beings, is so made as to represent spiritual things. It might be demonstrated by the wonderful agreement in thousands of things, much of the same kind as is between the types of the Old Testament and their antitypes, and by spiritual things being so often and continually compared with them in the Word of God. And it's agreeable to God's wisdom that it should be so, that the inferior and shadowy parts of his works should be made to represent those things that are more real and excellent, spiritual and divine, to represent the things that immediately concern himself and the highest parts of his work. Spiritual things are the crown and glory, the head and soul, the very end and alpha and omega of all other works: what therefore can be more agreeable to wisdom, than that they should be as made as to shadow them forth?[88]

According to Edwards, such vision necessitated spiritual understanding. Edwards noticed in "Miscellanies" no. 408 in early 1729, shortly after the start of "Images of Divine Things," the effect spiritual understanding has on one's vision of the natural world.

SPIRITUAL KNOWLEDGE. When the ideas themselves appear more lively, and with greater strength and impression, as the ideas of spiritual things do [to] one that is spiritually enlightened, their circumstances and various relations and connections between themselves and with other ideas appear more. . . Rationination, without this spiritual light, never will give one such an advantage to see things in their true relations and respects to other things and to things in general.

A mind not spiritually enlightened beholds spiritual things faintly, like fainting, fading shadows that make no lively impression on

---

[88]"Miscellanies" no. 362. TRINITY, *WJE*, 13:434–35.

the mind ... A man that sets himself to reason without divine light is like a man that goes in the dark into a garden full of the most beautiful plants, and most artfully ordered, and compares things together by going from one thing to another, to feel of them and to measure the distances; but he that sees by divine light is like a man that views the garden when the sun shines upon it. There is as it were a light cast upon the ideas of spiritual things in the mind of the believer, which makes them appear clear and real, which before were but faint, obscure representations.[89]

Edwards describes spiritually enlightened Christians' ability to perceive the world and spiritual things in entirely new ways, seeing associations and significances that were before concealed or buried.

Central Text of Edwards' Emblematic World View

The "Images of Divine Things" notebook by Edwards has 212 notes of his reflections on the spiritual message found within the created order. Though Edwards eventually settled on the title "Images of Divine Things," he had considered various titles such as "Shadows of Divine Things," "The Book of Nature and Providences," and "The Language and Lessons of Nature."[90] "Images" was a long-term effort of Edwards' that began early in his pastorate at Northampton, around September or October 1728, and ended shortly before he took over as president of Princeton in 1758.[91]

At first glance, "Images of Divine Things" appears to be a charming compilation of things Edwards discovered in nature and everyday experience that he thought may enliven and reinforce his sermon ideas. A closer reading of "Images" and the accompanying notebook "Types" reveals a self-consciousness and hesitancy about the reception of his true design: a systematic exposition and defense of his emblematic world view, which had as its central thesis that God designed all visible creation to "represent spiritual things."[92]

Edwards' acknowledgment of an intertextual relationship between nature and Scripture is evident in "Images of Divine Things," as is his reliance on

---

[89]"Miscellanies" no. 408. SPIRITUAL KNOWLEDGE, *WJE*, 13:469–70.

[90]"Notes on the Manuscript," *WJE*, 11:34–35.

[91]"Notes on the Manuscript," *WJE*, 11:39, 46.

[92]"Editor's Introduction," *WJE*, 11:7.

the Protestant tradition of devotional meditation on the Word, the self, and creation.[93] "Images" is an emblem book, which is a collection of emblems produced in book form for devotional, political, or entertainment purposes. Edwards' added tables and indexes of Scriptures and subjects demonstrate the systematic character of his emblem book project and considerably aid the identification of associations and significances within the created order and the spiritual realm, which is a trademark of the emblem book genre.[94] "Images of Divine Things" is clearly an example of a complex emblem book, based on the logical organization of his notebooks.

Wallace E. Anderson notes that Edwards' varying terminology, like "image, shadow, type, correlation, representation, and symbol," originates from his efforts to define connected occurrences and indicates his readiness to view typology more broadly than his contemporaries and to give it a metaphysical dimension.[95] From the notebook entries below, "emblem" should be added to this shifting list of Edwards' terminology:

> The way of a cat with a mouse that it has taken captive is a lively *emblem* of the way of the devil with many wicked men.[96]

> What is observable in trees is also a lively *emblem* of many spiritual things, as particularly of the dispensations of providence since the coming of Christ. Christ is as it were the trunk of the tree, and all the church are his branches: "I am the vine, ye are the branches," says Christ [John 15:5].[97]

> Indeed, the course of the sap of the tree, from its beginning in the extremities of the roots to its end in the extremity of the branches, is an *emblem* of the whole series and scheme of divine providence, both before and after Christ, from the beginning to the end of the world.[98]

> The waters in Scripture is represented as the place of the dead, the Rephaim, the destroyers; and whales and sea monsters that

[93] Lewalski, *Protestant Poetics and the Seventeenth-Century Religious Lyric,* 155.

[94] Huston Diehl, *An Index of Icons in English Emblem Books, 1550–1700* (Norman, OK: University of Oklahoma Press, 1986), 3.

[95] Edwards, Wallace E. Anderson, Mason I. Lowance Jr., and David H. Watters, *Typological Writings,* 8–9.

[96] "Images of Divine Things," *WJE,* 11:75.

[97] "Images of Divine Things," *WJE,* 11:80.

[98] "Images of Divine Things," *WJE,* 11:81.

swim in the great deep are used in Scripture as *emblems* of devils and the wrath of God. And the miseries of death and God's wrath are there compared to the sea, to the deeps, to floods and billows, and the like.[99]

There is a fish that they call 'Ovos,' the ass-fish, which hath its heart in its belly; a fit *emblem* of a sensual epicure (see Manton on James, p. 535).[100]

At this point we are able to reveal the foundations of *emblematic theology*, by pointing out that it is not the least part of divine wisdom that it established such wonderful harmony and conformity between the visible world and that other, the spiritual world … From this wisdom and marvelous harmony and conformity of all divine works it would be possible for us, with no further effort, to deduce the whole doctrine of *emblematics* …[101]

Edwards' Rationale for Reinscripturation

In the editor's preface to "Images of Divine Things," Anderson observes that Edwards' natural typology was an attack on the materialism of philosophers such as Thomas Hobbes, who recoiled at the idea of an immaterial spiritual realm.[102] Edwards' use of the devotional emblematic world view contrasted with *physico-theology*, which viewed the world as a huge and intricate machine. The emphasis on the complexity and subtleties of creation's visible design had the unintended consequence of decreasing what was invisible. The supernatural was being cast out in favor of the material and practical.[103] The invisible roads of heaven and hell were becoming increasingly obscure. Although Newtonians believed in the miraculous character of the universe's main principles, including gravity, they were skeptical of specific instances of divine intervention. This hesitancy resulted in a diminished emphasis on Christ's person and work.[104]

---

[99]"Images of Divine Things," *WJE*, 11:84–85.

[100]"Images of Divine Things," *WJE*, 11:104.

[101]"Images of Divine Things," *WJE*, 11:128–29.

[102]"Editor's Introduction," *WJE*, 11:13–14.

[103]Roy Porter, *The Creation of the Modern World: The Untold Story of the British Enlightenment* (New York: W.W. Norton & Co., 2001), 297.

[104]Jonathan I. Israel, *Enlightenment Contested: Philosophy, Modernity, and the Emancipation of Man 1670–1752* (New York: Oxford University Press, 2009), 212–13.

As Edwards pointed out in *Religious Affections*, seeing God's overall splendor in magnitude is insufficient to convert an individual. Only the sight of God's glory consisting in the beauty of his holiness is enough to "melt and humble the hearts of men, and wean them from the world, and draw them to God, and effectually change them..." but if the moral beauty of God is hidden, the enmity of the heart will remain in full strength.[105] A single perception of God's boundless magnificence lacks the ability to "enkindle" love in the heart and be effective in gaining the will.[106]

Looking for God's glory in the big world machine, according to Edwards, was nonsense. In an ironic twist, he used the common deistic illustration of a clock to demonstrate that the entire creation has a teleological movement with a devotional purpose. Edwards' approach to the Enlightenment challenge of the mechanized universe is illuminating, rather than enlightening. God created the world with the grand and universal goal of communicating himself. God is a communicative being ... God created the world for his excellency to shine forth and his gladness to pour forth.[107]

> The Book of Scripture is the interpreter of the book of nature two ways: viz. by declaring to us those spiritual mysteries that are indeed signified or typified in the constitution of the natural world; and secondly, in actually making application of the signs and types in the book of nature as representations of those spiritual mysteries in many instances.[108]

This concern for correct interpretation of the cosmos is more proof that "Images of Divine Things" was Edwards' emblem book: the beginnings of a systematically emblematic world view. This volume will explore Edwards' emblematic vision and the intertextual relationship between nature and Scripture that has been missed in earlier analyses of Edwards' notebooks.

---

[105]"Religious Affections," *WJE*, 16:264–65.

[106]"Religious Affections," *WJE*, 16:264–65.

[107]"Miscellanies" no. 332, *WJE*, 13:410. Zakai observes that Edwards' utilization of The Great Chain of Being metaphor in which the entire universe was "structured according to a grand theological teleology ... was Edwards' main strategy in combating" the mechanistic philosophy of the Enlightenment. "World phenomena were thus established as a mode of reality" which emanated or shadowed forth the excellencies of Christ. Avihu Zakai, *Jonathan Edwards's Philosophy of History: The Reenchantment of the World in the Age of Enlightenment*, 119–20.

[108]"Images of Divine Things," *WJE*, 11:106.

Outline of Study

This study will begin with a historical analysis of the emblematic world view and its acceptance by post-Reformation Protestants. This survey is significant because it will introduce the early modern thought-world in which Edwards operated and will support the notion that Edwards maintained an emblematic world view and wrote in the emblem book genre.

The available English emblem books will be canvassed using Huston Diehl's *An Index of Icons in English Emblem Books, 1550–1700* along with source documents available at various online depositories. The works of emblematic Baptists and Puritans will be examined, including Oxford conventicler Ralph Austen, Puritan preacher John Bunyan, Particular Baptist pastor Benjamin Keach, and others. An analysis of these works reveals startling parallels with Edwards' world view and emblematic writing. Their intertextual interpretation of nature and Scripture will be investigated to support the notion that Edwards was writing in the emblem book tradition. The emblematic world view of Edwards in "Images of Divine Things," as well as his typological adaptations and extensions, will be analyzed and compared with the larger emblem tradition using primary and secondary sources, which will further support the thesis that Edwards' "Images of Divine Things" and "Types" notebooks are examples of the emblem book genre.

The second chapter will provide context for Jonathan Edwards and his world view. The developments during the Renaissance that contributed to the rise, and later decline, of the emblematic world view will be examined. The backdrop of the emblematic world view in the Christian tradition will be explored by briefly exploring the previous emblematic world view, how this emblematic perspective fared throughout the Protestant Reformation and afterwards, and its centrality and importance. The emblem book genre will be introduced, and its evolution will be analyzed.

The third chapter will look at the emblematic world view as held by early Evangelicals, as well as the history and evolution of the emblem book genre. It will be demonstrated that the emblematic theology of Bishop Joseph Hall, Ralph Austen, John Bunyan, Benjamin Keach, Cotton Mather, and others has the same goal and scope as Edwards' "Images of Divine Things." To support the thesis of this study, this part will show that the reading of nature with Scripture practiced by Hall, Austen, Bunyan, Keach, Mather, and others differs only in scope and comprehensiveness from Edwards' reading. An examination of *Spiritual Use of an Orchard, A Book for Boys and Girls,*

Tropologia, and *Spiritual Melody,* as well as other emblematic works, will reveal this similarity with Edwards.

The fourth chapter will argue that Edwards' emblematics and his notebook "Images of Divine Things" contain distinguishing characteristics that position them within the emblematic world view of the Renaissance. "Images of Divine Things" will be scrutinized further for similarities and differences with the work of other authors. Along with the poetic quality and Edwards' empirical method, the intertextual nature and doctrinal content of the notebook will be discussed. The role of exegesis and occasional meditation will be examined, as will the discussion around the hazards of subjective readings of nature. It will be seen that in response to the mechanistic philosophy of the Enlightenment, Edwards restored and developed the emblematic world view of the Renaissance.

The fifth chapter introduces Edwards' project of reinscripturating the world. The essential contours of his meditation practice will be examined, as well as characteristics of his embodied encounter with nature. The structure of Edwards' emblematic world view and its universal linguistic quality will be revealed through reconstruction according to creational and theological themes. His mission of reinscripturating the universe is, in essence, the same as the Renaissance quest for meaning through discovering the poetic aspects of the world, with its correspondences and similitudes. Edwards' "Images of Divine Things" will be reconfigured and simplified into theological categories in order to illustrate the doctrinal precision and scope of his vision and ambition.

The study will conclude with a summary of the argument that Jonathan Edwards rehabilitated and refined the Renaissance emblematic view of the world through the emblem book genre in order to reinscripturate creation, and that the central text of his program of reinscripturation is his emblem book "Images of Divine Things." Finally, the significance of "Images of Divine Things" for future study will be discussed.

In light of this preliminary background study of Edwards' world view and notebooks, it is clear that "Images of Divine Things" is an emblem book. This thesis reflects a consensus that Jonathan Edwards' understanding of natural order fits within the emblematic tradition of the Renaissance. It goes on to argue that the intertextual relationship between Scripture and nature in Edwards' theology fits specifically within the emblem book genre. The recognition of some of these intertextual linkages in Edwards is reason enough to believe that there needs to be more close examination and consideration of Edwards' reinscripturation of the world.

CHAPTER TWO: EMBLEMATIC WORLD VIEW

Introduction

EDWARDS' DISCOVERY OF GOD'S LANGUAGE in nature raises, for some people, questions regarding his orthodoxy, originality, and sources of influence. The fundamental point to evaluate is whether or not Edwards was innovative in his emblematic reinscripturation of the world. Edwards uses pagan authors, Hebraists, poets, and others in "Images of Divine Things" to support his emblematic world view.[1] The recognition of these citations and relationships provides context for Edwards' emblematic thought. Avihu Zakai's contribution to *The Cambridge Companion to Jonathan Edwards,* his *Jonathan Edwards's Philosophy of Nature,* and Janice Knight's chapter in *The Princeton Companion to Jonathan Edwards* have all studied the context of Edwards' emblematic and typological world view.[2] Gerald R. McDermott investigated Edwards' typology in *Everyday Glory Jonathan Edwards Confronts the Gods,,* and *The Theology of Jonathan Edwards.*[3]

These articles and books are excellent primers on Edwards' typology. However, it appears that the examination of Edwards' typology is incom-

---

[1]"Images of Divine Things," *WJE,* 11:22, 98, 118.

[2]Avihu Zakai, "The Age of Enlightenment," in *The Cambridge Companion to Jonathan Edwards* (Cambridge: Cambridge University Press, 2007), 80–99. Avihu Zakai, *Jonathan Edwards's Philosophy of Nature: The Re-Enchantment of the World in the Age of Scientific Reasoning* (New York: T&T Clark, 2010). Janice Knight, "Typology," *The Princeton Companion to Jonathan Edwards,* Ed. Sang Hyun Lee (Princeton: Princeton University Press, 2005) 190–209.

[3]Gerald R. McDermott, *Everyday Glory: The Revelation of God in All of Reality* (Grand Rapids, Michigan: Baker Academic, 2018), Gerald McDermott, *Jonathan Edwards Confronts the Gods* (New York: Oxford University Press, 2000), 110–29. Michael J. McClymond and Gerald R. McDermott, *The Theology of Jonathan Edwards* (New York: Oxford University Press, 2012) 116–29.

plete. Tibor Fabiny highlights a considerable possibility for future study of Edwards' typology in a chapter on types. "I have written elsewhere on how Shakespeare's language and imagery were indebted to the emblem tradition," he continues, "which is a special Renaissance genre that combines a motto, a picture, and a text." Although Edwards uses the term emblem as a synonym for types, scholars of typology have yet to identify this relationship.[4] An examination of the Renaissance quest for the significance and meaning of nature through emblems, correspondences, and similitudes will help to clarify the sources of Edwards' emblematic view of reality, as well as reveal the close proximity of the earlier emblematic world view to Edwards' project of reinscripturating a world that had suffered from de-inscription (or description) during the Enlightenment.[5]

Recent studies on Edwards' typology in scripture interpretation have overlooked this broader conceptual background, especially his emblematic world view/project. According to Gerald McDermott, "Edwards made considerable use of the age-old Christian tradition of typology to interpret the Old Testament foreshadowings ("types") of New Testament fulfillments ("antitypes"). However, he broadened that traditional interpretation to include the entire 'system of nature' as the "voice of God to intelligent creatures."[6] According to McDermott, this development represents a considerable divergence from Edwards' Puritan typological background. Edwards was confident that the reading of natural types was permitted by Scripture. In addition to Scripture, much of the created order bears witness to the sense of divine and morality in nature. The world's analogical structure and appearance demand that meaning be discerned. These analogies manifest not only in similarities between animals and people, as well as between plants and animals, but also in a hierarchical system, a vast chain of being that extends from heaven to hell. Edwards also emphasizes the essential ontological link between language and moral ideas. Finally, the teleology and beauty of creation argue for an intelligible system.[7]

[4]Tibor Fabiny, "Edwards and Biblical Typology," in *Understanding Jonathan Edwards: An Introduction to America's Theologian,* ed. Gerald McDermott (New York: Oxford University Press, 2008), 101.

[5]James J. Bono, *The Word of God and the Languages of Man: Interpreting Nature in Early Modern Science and Medicine, Science and Literature* (Madison: University of Wisconsin Press, 1995), 84.

[6]McClymond and McDermott, *The Theology of Jonathan Edwards,* 116.

[7]McClymond and McDermott, *The Theology of Jonathan Edwards,* 120–22.

For Edwards, then, Scripture overflows with a surplus of meaning. It points from Old Testament to New Testament realities, and is the guidebook to a world full of divine signs. Amidst what others would call the discordances of life, Edwards found persistent symmetry. Scripture and nature were finally harmonious in his system, as were secular and sacred history, even the history of religions. The key to seeing this intricate system of signs displaying cosmic harmony was typology.[8]

While McDermott mentions Luther and the Reformers' use of typology, he does not address Fabiny's invitation to investigate the larger heritage of emblematics.[9] McDermott shows admiration for Fabiny's understanding into the convergence of thinking among Luther, Shakespeare, and Edwards in his answer to Fabiny's essay in *Understanding Jonathan Edwards*.[10] Nonetheless, McDermott makes no mention of broadening horizons in his work with Michael McClymond on Edwards' typology. Edwards' shared debt to Shakespeare's emblem tradition remains largely uninvestigated.[11] McDermott defers to future Edwardsean scholars: "This is a way of seeing [typological or emblematic world view] that, I hope, will be more fully explored by theologians who build upon this Edwardsian foundation. They will, I trust, look through Edwards's typological model to see even more of the Trinity's footprints in life and history."[12]

Edwards' thought regarding the created order's linguistic capacity was a refinement and amplification, not a novel one. Zakai notes that Edwards' concern in associations and relationships within the created order, as well as his disdain for mechanical philosophy, resonate powerfully with the Renaissance quest for a symbolic system of knowledge: a world that delivers meaning, not just the how, but the why.[13] This introduction to the emblematic world view will provide a quick overview of the emergence and eclipse of the emblem tradition.

---

[8]McClymond and McDermott, *The Theology of Jonathan Edwards,* 129.

[9]McClymond and McDermott, *The Theology of Jonathan Edwards,* 118.

[10]Gerald McDermott, "Alternative Viewpoint: Edwards and Biblical Typology," in *Understanding Jonathan Edwards: An Introduction to America's Theologian,* ed. Gerald McDermott (New York: Oxford University Press, 2008), 110.

[11]Fabiny, "Edwards and Biblical Typology," 101.

[12]McDermott, "Alternative Viewpoint: Edwards and Biblical Typology," 112.

[13]Zakai, *Jonathan Edwards's Philosophy of Nature: The Re-Enchantment of the World in the Age of Scientific Reasoning,* 243–45.

Development of the Emblematic World View

The emblematic vision of reality is considerably different from the empirical perception of the world held by a modern person. The concept that particulars of this universe can be endowed with meaning through layers of connections and significances not immediately available to scientific equipment is regarded as exotic at best and decidedly strange at worst. The paradigm shift in perception from the emblematic world view was dramatic. What were ducks in the scientist's world before the revolution are now rabbits, as Thomas Kuhn observed of scientific revolutions.[14] Perspective and authority have a strong influence on how we perceive and understand the world. The scientist has no recourse other than what he sees with his eyes and instruments. If there was some higher authority to whom his perspective could be proved to have transferred, that authority would become the source of his data.[15] As a result, it is not surprising that empiricism considers the emblematic or enchanted world view to be the domain of fiction rather than reality. Such fantastic world views belong in J.R.R. Tolkien's *Lord of the Rings* or C.S. Lewis' *Chronicles of Narnia,* not in the humdrum, matter-of-fact world of pragmatic modern man.[16] Such juvenile conceptions are set aside by the mature man. McGilchrist relates a Tolkien story that illustrates this point:

> For some reason, people feel much happier nowadays talking about creativity than they do talking about the I-word, imagination. This may be because creativity is thought to be dealing with possible realities in a way that imagination is not. There is a story told of a Fellow of Merton College, a mathematician, who was irritated by the attention paid to J.R.R. Tolkien, a Fellow of the same Oxford college, by the fawning guests of other Fellows. One day in the Common Room yet another guest was introduced to the great man, and gushed: "Oh, Professor Tolkien, I do so admire your writing, it's so—so full of imagination!" The mathematician could bear it no longer, and from behind a newspaper

---

[14]Thomas S. Kuhn, *The Structure of Scientific Revolutions,* (Chicago ; London: The University of Chicago Press, 2012), 111–12.

[15]Kuhn, *The Structure of Scientific Revolutions,* 114.

[16]George M. Mardsen, *Jonathan Edwards: A Life* (New Haven: Yale University Press, 2003), 137. Marsden notes the alien quality of Edwards' universe and the similarity it bears to a number of our modern day epics such as *Lord of the Rings* and *Star Wars*. Not only was reality an epic struggle between light and darkness, but even the particulars of creation spring to life and become players in this grand epic. In a sense, Edwards was a world creator.

was heard to snort indignantly: "Imagination? Imagination?! Made it all up." From the left hemisphere's point of view, imagination, like metaphor and myth, is a species of lying: from the right hemisphere's point of view, it is, like metaphor and myth, necessary for access to truth.[17]

When Jonathan Edwards wrote the following, he clearly sensed this tension:

> I expect by very ridicule and contempt to be called a man of a very fruitful brain and copious fancy, but they are welcome to it. I am not ashamed to own that I believe that the whole universe, heaven and earth, air and seas, and the divine constitution and history of the holy Scriptures, be full of images of divine things, as full as a language is of words; and that the multitude of those things that I have mentioned are but a very small part of what is really intended to be signified and typified by these things.[18]

This enchanted view of creation did not come to Edwards by chance. The emblematic world view has a lengthy history that has been traced back to Egyptian hieroglyphics and to the Garden of Eden.[19] However, the more immediate setting and historical backdrop provided much inspiration for his world view.

According to James Bono, W.B. Ashworth's work "Natural History and the Emblematic World View" has made the emblematic world view an integral aspect of the Scientific Revolution's historiography.[20] According to Ashworth,

---

[17] McGilchrist, *The Matter With Things*, 1178–79.

[18] "Types," *WJE*, 11:152.

[19] "Images of Divine Things," *WJE*, 11:127–28. Edwards quoting Andrew Ramsay's *The Philosophical Principles of Natural and Revealed Religion* writes: "It is certain, that the word 'hieroglyphics,' which the Greeks made use of to design these symbolical characters (used by the ancients), signifies a sacred graving or sculpture ... to preserve and transmit to posterity some idea of the mysteries of religion ... [and] to represent intellectual and spiritual truths."

[20] William B. Ashworth, Jr., "Natural History and the Emblematic World View," in *Reappraisals of the Scientific Revolution* (Cambridge: Cambridge University Press, 1990), 303–32. Bono notes that a consideration of the history of the "emblematic world view" best begins with the scholar who coined the phrase. William B. Ashworth Jr. is an associate professor of history at the University of Missouri-Kansas City and specializes in Science, the Renaissance, and Early Modern Europe. James J. Bono, "From Paracelsus to Newton: The Word of God, the Book of Nature, and the Eclipse of the 'Emblematic World View'," in *Newton and Religion: Context, Nature, and Influence*, International Archives of the History of Ideas, vol. 161 (Dordrecht ; Boston: Kluwer Academic, 1999), 46.

looking through the eyes of a Renaissance man reveals an entirely new cosmos in which animals, symbols, and emblems are all components of a complex and interwoven language of correspondences and similitudes. When one studies Jonathan Edwards' vision of a world of types, images, and divine language in "Images of Divine Things," the question of origin and influence arises. It appears that Renaissance man's and Jonathan Edwards' eyes saw something pretty similar. As a result, a reading of Ashworth's and Bono's well-known studies on the changing world views of the Renaissance and Scientific Revolution is needed.

The 'emblematic world view,' according to Ashworth, was "the single most important factor in determining the content and scope of Renaissance natural history."[21] The heart of this view is the belief that everything in the universe "has myriad hidden meanings and that knowledge consists of an attempt to comprehend as many of these as possible," he continues.[22] The blossoming of the emblematic world view took place between 1550 and 1650, and it declined abruptly with the introduction of the Scientific Revolution and mechanical philosophy.[23]

Ashworth lists six advances in sixteenth-century natural history that culminated in the "emblematic world view." Despite the fact that the number six is "not intended to be canonical," he neatly categorizes the developments as "hieroglyphic, antiquarian, Aesopic, mythological, adagial, and emblematic."[24]

First, there was a resurgence of interest in hieroglyphics in the early fifteenth century, owing chiefly to the discovery and translation of the *Hieroglyphics* of Horapollo in 1505. *Hieroglyphics* is a symbolic dictionary in which animal symbols play an important role. Pigs signified pernicious people, weasels represented frailty, flies indicated impudence, and so on. The humanist *ad fontes* impulse rejoiced in the new horizons given by this Platonic language. A revelatory language of symbols enabled direct seeing and understanding of reality, analogous to the divine perspective. In essence, using this symbolic and global language, conventional language, including vernacular, might be bypassed. This hieroglyphic revival had a seismic impact. A new

---

[21] Ashworth, "Natural History and the Emblematic World View," 305. Further elaboration of the world views of the Renaissance period and the transitions toward the Enlightenment can be found in Lorraine Daston and Katharine Park, *Wonders and the Order of Nature, 1150–1750* (New York: Zone Books, 2001).

[22] Ashworth, "Natural History and the Emblematic World View," 312.

[23] Ashworth, "Natural History and the Emblematic World View," 305.

[24] Ashworth, "Natural History and the Emblematic World View," 307.

world view emerged in which the particulars of creation "became part of a visual language; they were symbols, but more importantly, they were Platonic ideas, whose meaning the mind could immediately perceive." In God's words, the creatures were "living characters." Those who were unable or unwilling to observe the world in this way missed Nature's essential nature.[25]

As will be discussed later, Luther, who was aware of advancements in natural history, sensed new discoveries of linguistic marvel in the world and chastised Erasmus for failing to see the communicative character of the created order.[26] "The entire world is deaf . . ." Luther wrote. They have ears but cannot hear and eyes but cannot see.[27] "The whole earth is filled with speaking."[28] Luther noted that Pythagoras testified of the constellations' "lovely consonance and harmony," but that due to dullness and boredom, people no longer paid attention. Similarly, Luther's contemporaries overlooked the beautiful creatures that surrounded them. They would become oblivious to the familiar.[29]

Second, the Renaissance's interest in symbols and hieroglyphics coincided with an increase in the antiquarian impulse. In the fifteenth century, the discovery of ancient Roman coins featuring portraits on one side and a symbolic image on the other heightened interest in numanistics. By the mid-century, antiquarian treatises were being written, which largely consisted of plates of symbols and mottoes with animals prominently featured. These treatises on ancient coins proved valuable sources for humanists whose interest in *ad fontes* pushed them beyond written histories and into the study of artifacts. Antiquarianism began to emerge as a distinct discipline and way of investigating the past.[30]

The humanist fascination with symbolic language was a natural fit for the third tradition, Aesop's tales, which appeared in varied forms and lengths during the Renaissance. Humanist naturalists eager to comprehend the

---

[25] Ashworth, "Natural History and the Emblematic World View," 307–8.

[26] Oswald Bayer, *Martin Luther's Theology: A Contemporary Interpretation,* trans. Thomas H. Trapp (Grand Rapids: Eerdmans, 2008), 94.

[27] Martin Luther, *Schriften,* vol. 46 of *D. Martin Luthers Werke: Kritische Gesamtausgabe* (Weimar: Hermann Böhlaus Nachfolger, 1912–21), 495. Cited in Bayer, *Luther's Theology,* 107.

[28] Martin Luther, *Tischreden,* vol. 5 of *D. Martin Luthers Werke: Kritische Gesamtausgabe* (Weimar: Hermann Böhlaus Nachfolger, 1912–21), 225. Cited in Bayer, *Luther's Theology,* 107.

[29] Bayer, *Luther's Theology,* 107

[30] Ashworth, "Natural History and the Emblematic World View," 308.

significance of animals such as the peacock, nightingale, fox, and others relied on the Aesopic corpus. Along with Aesop's fables, the rediscovery of classical mythology was a fourth development that contributed to the sixteenth century's sophisticated world view. Classical mythology extensively featured animals and had a crucial influence, along with Horapollo's *Hiero-glyphics*, in bolstering the belief that the natural world held a plethora of associations and messages that amounted to a visual language bordering on extravagance.[31]

For Renaissance natural historians, nature was already suspended in an intertextual web of meaning, and the religious quest that led to the Refor-mation enormously enhanced the tapestry of meaning. Johannes Reuchlin (1455–1522), a famous Hebraist concerned with the restoration of correct knowledge of biblical Hebrew, was also interested in resurrecting the Cabala for Christians and Jews.[32] Reuchlin, a forerunner of and influence on Paracel-sus, contributed to an exegesis of the Book of Nature based on illumination and faith combined with esoteric rituals. According to Reuchlin, access to the Book of Nature's secret qualities could only be obtained through the Word of God.[33]

The fifth key development in Renaissance natural history and world view was the adagial tradition, which reveals the increasing link between the Book of Nature and the Word of God. Desiderius Erasmus was the most famous name linked with this practice (1466-1536). Erasmus was concerned with recovering the biblical Greek of the New Testament, as Reuchlin was with recovering the Hebrew language. Despite Erasmus's lack of interest in occult characteristics or the textual dimension of creation, his study for the Greek language made unintentional contributions to Renaissance natural history and the emblematic world view.

Erasmus' *Adages*, a significant collection of proverbial sayings drawn mostly from the *Greek Anthology*, a body of ancient epigrams initially gath-ered in the thirteenth century and published in Greek in the late fifteenth century, was a byproduct of his attempt to understand the Greek language. Erasmus' *Adages* had a wide influence during the sixteenth century and inspired notable naturalist Conrad Gesner.[34]

---

[31]Ashworth, "Natural History and the Emblematic World View," 309–10.

[32]William R. Estep, *Renaissance and Reformation* (Grand Rapids: Eerdmans, 1986), 54.

[33]Bono, *The Word of God and the Languages of Man: Interpreting Nature in Early Modern Science and Medicine,* 124–28.

[34]Ashworth, "Natural History and the Emblematic World View," 309–10.

The emblematic tradition was the sixth and climactic tradition that emerged during the Renaissance. Andrea Alciati is credited with creating the Renaissance emblem (1492-1550). Alciati's original intention was "to devise epigrams that were especially enigmatic, so that readers would get a sudden and pleasing illumination when they figured them out, with the help of a commentary; an accompanying image was not intended."[35] *Emblemata* (1531), Alciati's emblem book, was supplemented with woodcut drawings, which swiftly became an intrinsic part of emblematics.[36] The resulting emblem book genre can be described as follows:

> [A] collection, or anthology, of individual emblems. Each emblem in a typical emblem book combines an enigmatic motto, either in Latin or in the vernacular; a symbolic picture or icon; and an epigram or verse commentary. The motto and picture pose a riddle or an enigma which the epigrams solves or explains. Ideally, the three parts of an emblem are interdependent. Together motto, icon, and epigram revealed that emblem's meaning, a meaning that was initially concealed by the enigmatic nature of the motto and icon. Separated, however, each part is inadequate to express the larger significance of the emblem.[37]

During the Renaissance, the expansion of schools and universities and improved literacy, along with the invention of print in the mid-fifteenth century, led to a shift in what people read. This period also saw the rediscovery of classical antiquity, discovery of the New World, the Reformation, and the Copernican Revolution, as well as a renewed interest in mysticism and symbolism, resulting in the emergence of new and novel literary genres. One of the most successful of these genres was the emblem book, which first appeared at the beginning of the sixteenth century and was one of Europe's best-selling literary genres for the next two hundred years.

---

[35] Ashworth, "Natural History and the Emblematic World View," 310–11. Alciati, an Italian, lived for a time in France teaching law at the University of Bourges, which was a significant center for reform activity. Among his students was John Calvin. Though Alciati never left the Roman church, he was a supporter of religious reform and the early publications of his emblem book in Augsburg and Paris corresponded with outbursts of reform activities in both cities. Huston Diehl, "Graven Images: Protestant Emblem Books in England," *Renaissance Quarterly* 39, no. 1 (1986): 52.

[36] Diehl, "Graven Images: Protestant Emblem Books in England," 52.

[37] Huston Diehl, *An Index of Icons in English Emblem Books, 1550–1700* (Norman, OK: University of Oklahoma Press, 1986), 3.

Born in 1492 to a prestigious family with the elk as their heraldic mark, Andrea Alciati was a celebrated legal scholar who was recognized early on for his brilliance. At the age of 24, he earned his doctorate in law from Ferrara and went on to teach law in Avignon in 1518.[38] Francis I then invited Alciati to teach at the University of Bourges in 1529. After returning to Italy in 1534, he held teaching positions at Pavia, Bologna, Ferrara, and Pavia until his death in early 1550, leaving behind a remarkable career.[39] Alciati was renowned for his interpretations of Roman law, for which he was highly praised by Erasmus and other scholars, noting, "he was the most jurisprudent of orators, and the most eloquent of lawyers."[40] He is also remembered most famously for his *Emblematum liber,* or *Book of Emblems.*

Alciati was the author of the first emblem book, which he named *Emblemata* and circulated among his learned friends and colleagues in manuscript form. Heinrich Steyner, an Augsburg printer-publisher, printed the book in 1531 with illustrations. The book was an instant success. Alciati's *Emblemata* is considered the ideal emblem book. Its subject matter ranged from classical myth and allegory to biblical and Christian tradition, medieval nature lore, Horapollo and hieroglyphics, heraldry and devices, and literary conceits.[41]

Most of the emblems in the early editions were sourced from ancient allegories and proverbs and were intended primarily as entertainment. The force of the genre is largely based on its bi-mediality, which effectively combines moral, religious, or political ideas with visual images. This combination captivates the reader's and viewer's attention and provides them with both aesthetically pleasing visuals and meaningful messages.[42] The emblem is frequently built on a literal or implied comparison, connecting even the most disparate objects to the personal, public, moral, social, ethical, physical, spiritual, or monetary realm. Animals, plants, and other elements of nature can all take on symbolic meanings, expressing human values, feelings, and ideas. The world itself is transformed into a literary device, a rhetorical tool, to explore these meanings. While they may be scholarly in nature, the emblems are always relevant to the realities of life. Alciato praises the sound

---

[38]Henry Green, *Andrea Alciati and His Books of Emblems a Biographical and Bibliographical Study* (New York: B. Franklin, 1965), 3–5.

[39]Green, *Andrea Alciati and His Books of Emblems,* xvi.

[40]Green, *Andrea Alciati and His Books of Emblems,* 30.

[41]Daly, *Literature in the Light of the Emblem,* 8.

[42]Karl A.E. Enenkel, et al., *Emblems and the Natural World* (Leiden: Brill, 2017), 1–2.

and virtuous, while condemning the ill and wicked.[43] The area covered by a single emblem may be limited to a couple of pages; however, its capacity to educate is powerful.[44] Alciato's emblem book was soon translated into various languages and appeared in hundreds of editions and spawned thousands of other titles, with 1.5 million emblem books in circulation by the 1620s.[45]

The Renaissance period was characterized by a unique sense of history, looking back to the Middle Ages and re-appropriating the rich legacy of moralized allegory and typological exegesis of history that had been handed down.[46] This was exemplified by the bestiaries, collections of folk-wisdom tales, and the notion of a meaningful universe created by God to reveal himself and his divine plan to mankind. This interpretive undertaking was typically addressed to the "Book of Nature." Thomas à Kempis explained the still ongoing meditative practice in his *Imitatio Christi*: "If your heart is upright, then every creature [and object] is like the mirror of life, and it serves you as a book of holy doctrine." The Renaissance was a "rebirth" of the golden age of classical antiquity, which retained the similitudes and correspondences of the medieval period. Alciati inherited and built upon this pre-Renaissance tradition.[47]

The decline of the emblematic world view and its literary genre occurred long before Jonathan Edwards' life, raising the question of why Edwards would embrace a world view that was already outdated and on its way to being invalidated by Enlightenment philosophy. Edwards' imagination and emotions were captivated by the harmony and beauty of the emblematic world view.

---

[43] Manning, *The Emblem*, 55.

[44] Enenkel, et al., *Emblems and the Natural World*, 2.

[45] Enenkel, et al., *Emblems and the Natural World*, 1–2.

[46] McGilchrist, *The Master and His Emissary*, 312–13. The Renaissance had a sense of the interconnectedness of knowledge and understanding, and the need for the broadest context for knowledge. The metaphysical poets, such as Donne, Herbert and Traherne, were captivated by the connection between ourselves and a world that had depth. They used images, like the glass in the window, the mirror's flat surface, and the reflective surface of a pool of water, to explore the idea of contact with a realm beyond what is seen. The world is not just a fact, but something akin to a myth or metaphor, semi-transparent, with its own meaning, yet hinting at something more. Seeing things in context involves a depth of space, time, and even metaphysics, recognizing the existence of multiple levels, as is seen in myth and metaphor.

[47] Andrea Alciati, *A Book of Emblems: The Emblematum Liber in Latin and English*, translated and edited by John F. Moffitt (Jefferson, N.C.: McFarland & Co., c2004), 5–6.

Reformers and Natural History

According to George Marsden, Edwards believed that both Scripture and nature reveal the mysteries of God to rational creatures in a systematic way, and that "God had built into Scripture, as he had into nature and the rest of history, elaborate harmonies all resolved in the grand theme of Christ's love."[48] As previously mentioned, both Luther and Calvin recognize the Renaissance harmonies and emblematic significances within the established order.[49] Luther observes in his commentary on the Genesis creation's verbal act,

> [A]ttention must also be called to this, that the words "Let there be light" are the words of God, not of Moses; this means that they are realities. For God calls into existence the things which do not exist (Rom. 4:17). He does not speak grammatical words; He speaks true and existent realities. Accordingly, that which among us has the sound of a word is a reality with God. Thus sun, moon, earth, Peter, Paul, I, you etc.–we are all words of God, in fact only one single syllable or letter by comparison with the entire creation. We, too, speak, but only according to the rules of language; that is, we assign names to objects which have already been created. But the divine rule of language is different, namely: when He says: "Sun, shine,: the sun is there at once and shines. Thus the words of God are realities, not bare words ... For what else is the entire creation than the Word of God uttered by God, or extended to the outside?"[50]

Luther's understanding of the particulars of creation as letters and sylla-bles of a heavenly language reveals the world's emblematic and linguistic nature. This emblematic understanding of nature was later carried forward by Wolfgang Franzius (1564–1628), provost of Wittenberg and professor of

---

[48] Mardsen, *Jonathan Edwards: A Life,* 478–79.

[49] McGilchrist, *The Master and His Emissary,* 314. McGilchrist might be surprised by their recognition of the depth of creation. McGilchrist sees the nailing of Luther's *Ninety-Five Theses* at Wittenberg in 1517, the beginning of the Reformation, as a rejection of the right hemisphere's world, which had declined from metaphoric understanding of rituals and ceremonies into empty forms of repetition. Rather than a revival of metaphoric understanding, he believes the Reformation brought an outright dismissal of it.

[50] Martin Luther, *Lectures on Genesis Chapters 1–5,* vol. 1 of *Luther's Works,* ed. Jaroslav Pelikan (St. Louis: Concordia, 1958), 21–22.

theology, who published *Historia animalium sacra* in 1612. This book was widely read and had many editions until 1671, with an English translation published in 1670 as *The history of brutes, or, A description of living creatures : wherein the nature and properties of four-footed beasts are at large described.*[51] Johannes Cyprianus, professor of physics and later of theology in Leipzig, wrote extensive commentaries on the work which were reprinted until 1712. The preface of the book, 'to the pious reader', explains the plan of the work and the relationship between the animal world and theology. *Historia animalium sacra* was created with the intention of providing a theological resource for priests and teachers. By drawing comparisons between animals and religious doctrine, it enables a simple audience to better visualize and understand.[52] The book is filled with parables and similes that can be used to illustrate theological truths.[53]

Luther's adversary, the "Satan of Allstedt," Thomas Muntzer, recognized the linguistic nature of the universe as well. Muntzer's *Vindication and Refutation* contains at least ninety separate images, according to Peter Matheson.[54] Muntzer took many of his emblems from ordinary life as well as from Scripture.

> [F]rom patching garments, sleeping, waking, and even defecating; or from the workshop of the tanner, the cobbler, the butcher, the refiner; many refer to cooking or eating: to roasting or stewing food, to tasty dishes, tough meat, to fake sausages made of fox meat, to drinking, wining and dining, gobbling, smearing the mouth with honey; many of the parts of the body figure: the eyes, the ears, the nose, the mouth, the beard, the cheeks, the fists; fighting, crime and war provide many analogies; a whole menagerie of animals is presented as actors in the carnival: domestic farmyard hens, roosters, and pigs; wild, and predatory

[51] Wolfgang Franz, The History of Brutes, or, A Description of Living Creatures : Wherein the Nature and Properties of Four-Footed Beasts Are at Large Described (London: Printed by E. Okes, for Francis Haley, 1670).

[52] A current application of this pedagogy can be found in Scott Steltzer, "Equipping People for Biblical Meditation on Creation at St. Paul's Evangelical Presbyterian Church in Somerset, Pennsylvania," DEdMin Project (Louisville, KY: The Southern Baptist Theological Seminary, 2022), 4–6.

[53] Vibeke Roggen, "Biology and Theology in Franzius's Historia Animalium Sacra (1612)," in *Early Modern Zoology: The Construction of Animals in Science, Literature and the Visual Arts (Intersections)* (London: Brill, 2007), 121, 129. See also Karl A.E. Enenkel, *The Invention of the Emblem Book and the Transmission of Knowledge, Ca. 1510–1610* (Leiden: Brill, 2019), 204–13.

[54] Peter Matheson, *The Rhetoric of the Reformation* (Edinburgh: T. & T. Clark, 1998), 148.

animals as the lion, wolf, and bear, and mythical creatures like the dragon.[55]

Muntzer aimed to enchant or resignify reality. Everywhere a person looked ,and every experience they had, was associated with Muntzer's apocalyptic viewpoint. Muntzer's main target was Luther. Luther is a crow who pecks out people's eyes so they cannot see the truth. He is a cunning fox who raids the hen house. "He is Esau, Goliath, Saul, and Caiaphas: personifications of greed, violence, envy, and hypocrisy." He comes as an angel of light.[56]

> It is quite clear then, that Doctor Liar does not dwell in the house of God, Psalm 15, since he does not despise the godless, but denounces many God-fearing men as devils or rebellious spirits in order to serve the interests of the godless. The black crow knows this very well. He pecks out the eyes of the pigs to turn them into carrion, he blinds these pleasure-loving people. For he is indulgent about their faults in order to eat his fill of their wealth and honors and especially of the fine-sounding titles at their disposal.[57]

Noah's crow is transformed in this passage from the wily crow of the ark to the scholar robed in black, to a crow who flatters the self-indulgent swine in order to get close enough to peck out their eyes, blinding them so he can enjoy all their wealth and honor.[58] In the minds of Muntzer's disciples, Luther's identification with a crow established an emotive association. Because the crow feeds on dirty things, it is inedible. The crow is cunning and must be watched closely should it devour a good crop. Nonetheless, the image of a lovely dove evokes pleasant ideas and associations. Doves are kind and gentle. Because they only eat clean foods, their meat is sweet. The

---

[55]Matheson, *The Rhetoric of the Reformation*, 148.

[56]Matheson, *The Rhetoric of the Reformation*, 148–49. Some of the most striking images that flowed from Muntzer's linguistic brush depicted Luther as a crow, as soft-living flesh, and as a fox. Luther is painted as the "wily black crow" that Noah released from the ark. By contrast, Muntzer casts himself as the innocent dove who, according to Psalm 68, has wings covered with silver and a guilded back. Luther the crow does not return to the ark, but instead is satisfied to perch on the carrion which he loves. Muntzer the pure dove will have none of Luther's filth.

[57]Thomas Muntzer, Peter Matheson, ed., "Vindication and Refutation," in *The Collected Works of Thomas Muntzer* (Edinburgh: T. & T. Clark, 1988), 333.

[58]Matheson, *Rhetoric of the Reformation,* 150.

dove, above all, represents the Holy Spirit. Muntzer could not have selected finer images to highlight the disparities between Luther and himself.

Muntzer spoke to the common people in a language they immediately understood. It was a visual, almost hieroglyphic language. The wild and disturbing images resembled graffiti scrawled on the sides of buildings.[59] The use of Scripture by Muntzer reflects its subsidiary role in his mystical theology.[60] The fundamental shortcoming of Muntzer's rhetoric, according to Matheson, was a lack of systematic Scripture exposition. Muntzer did not so much expound Scripture as he did paint with it. There was no intertextual link between Scripture and the created order.

Calvin, on the other hand, observed the appropriate relationship between the created particulars of the world and the spiritual significance allotted to them in Scripture.

> It remains for us, therefore, to admit that, on account of the affinity which the things signified have with their symbols, the name of the thing was given to the symbol– figuratively, indeed–but not without a most fitting analogy ... I say that this expression is a metonomy, a figure of speech commonly used in Scripture when mysteries are under discussion. For you could not otherwise understand such expressions as "circumcision is a covenant" [Gen. 17:13], "the lamb is the passover" [Ex. 12:11], "the sacrifices of the law are expiations" [Lev. 17:11; Heb. 9:22], and finally, "the rock from which water flowed in the desert" [Ex. 17:6], "was Christ" [I Cor. 10:4], unless you were to take them as spoken with meanings transferred. Not only is the name transferred from something higher to something lower, but, on the other hand, the name of the visible sign is also given to the thing signified: as when God is said to have appeared to Moses in the bush [Ex.3:2]; the Ark of the Covenant is called God and God's face [Ps. 84:8; 42:3]; and the dove, the Holy Spirit [Matt. 3:16]. For though the symbol differs in essence from the thing signified (in that the latter is spiritual and heavenly, while the former is physical and visible), still, because it not only sym-

---

[59]Matheson, *The Rhetoric of the Reformation*, 155. For an extended study on the role of imagination in the Reformation see Peter Matheson, *The Imaginative World of the Reformation* (Minneapolis: Fortress Press, 2001).

[60]Peter Matheson, "Thomas Muntzer's Vindication and Refutation: A Language for the Common People?" *The Sixteenth Century Journal* 20, no. 4 (1 December 1989): 605.

bolizes the thing that it has been consecrated to represent as a bare and empty token, but also truly exhibits it, why may its name not rightly belong to the thing? Humanly devised symbols, being images of things absent rather than makes of things present (which they very often even falsely represent), are still sometimes graced with the titles of those things. Similarly, with much greater reason, those things ordained by God borrow the names of those things of which they always bear a definite and not misleading signification, and have the reality joined with them. So great, therefore, is their similarity and closeness that transition from one to the other is easy.[61]

According to Calvin, God has structured creation in such a way that there is a "definite and not misleading" correlation and significance between the physical and the spiritual. Calvin's works are described by Peter Huff as a "veritable bestiary of Christian doctrine," with frequent references to creatures of the sea, land, and air.[62] "In Calvin's mind, the world of nature is never separated from the realm of divine revelation."[63]

The emergence of natural history coincided with the Reformation.[64] Natural history's contribution in the Scientific Revolution is generally dated no earlier than 1660, with the advent of physico-theology and the work of individuals such as John Ray. However, the impact of natural history may be traced back a century to the work of Swiss physician Conrad Gesner (1516–65).[65] Gesner's *Historiae Animalium* (1551–87) is a Renaissance zoological encyclopedia, although it is not what one would anticipate from a zoology text.[66] Instead, Gesner's book spans five volumes in which he explores a plethora of beasts, both real and mythical, and expounds the matrix of

---

[61] John Calvin, *Institutes of the Christian Religion,* in *The Library of Christian Classics,* ed. John T. McNeill trans. Ford Lewis Battles (Philadelphia: Westminster, 1960), IV.xvii.20.

[62] Peter A. Huff, "Calvin and the Beasts: Animals in John Calvin's Theological Discourse," *Journal of the Evangelical Theological Society* 42, no. 1 (1999): 68.

[63] Huff, "Calvin and the Beasts: Animals in John Calvin's Theological Discourse," 68. Huff notes that Calvin conceived of the created order as having a far greater theological significance than a mere setting for the drama of human redemption.

[64] Natural history is the study of the natural world, including living things, minerals and fossils, natural phenomena and their various relations with each other.

[65] Ashworth, "Natural History and the Emblematic World View," 303, 305.

[66] Conrad Gesner, *Historiae Animalium,* (1551–87), [online]; accessed 30 November 2022; available from https://www.biodiversitylibrary.org/page/52773824; Internet.

associations found within "history, mythology, etymology, and the rest of the animal kingdom, indeed with the entire cosmos."[67]

Whereas a modern naturalist limits his research to measurable declarations of fact and regulates his results through empiricism and objectivity, Foucault observes that in the sixteenth century,

> To search for meaning is to bring to light a resemblance. To search for the law governing signs is to discover the things they are like. The grammar of beings is in an exegesis of these things. And what the language they speak has to tell us is quite simply that the syntax is that binds them together. The nature of things, their coexistence, the way in which they are linked together and communicate is nothing other than their resemblance. And that resemblance is visible only in the network of signs that crosses the world from one end to the other... The face of the world is covered with blazons, with characters, with ciphers and obscure words — with 'hieroglyphics'... [68]

The sources for Gesner's numerous associations stem from classical authors such as Aristotle and Pliny, as well as others such as Erasmus, Horapollo, and Alciati. Gesner broadened the scope of natural history to include the most recent humanist scholarship: adagial writings, hieroglyphics, and emblematics.[69]

Gesner's world view is distinct from the "medieval" world view, while there are some outward similarities between *Historiae Animalium* and medieval bestiaries whose animal symbolism had a distinctively Christian foundation. Gesner's work is informed by ancient and modern humanist sources, as well as well-known traditions from the Middle Ages. The lack of moral messages in his writing distinguishes it from anything medieval. There is also no overt emphasis on magic. The widespread absence of morality and magic characterizes Gesner's world view as a widely emblematic approach that sought knowledge and meaning in relationships rather than isolation.[70] Gesner's natural history claimed that knowledge was discovered in the broad

---

[67] Ashworth, "Natural History and the Emblematic World View," 306.

[68] Michel Foucault, *The Order of Things; an Archaeology of the Human Sciences* (New York: Vintage Books, 1973), 27.

[69] Ashworth, "Natural History and the Emblematic World View," 306.

[70] Ashworth, "Natural History and the Emblematic World View," 313.

sweep of relationships rather than the microscopic perspective of individual particulars.

Ulisse Aldrovandi, a lesser-known sixteenth-century naturalist, published a much more comprehensive natural history than Gesner. Aldrovandi (1522–1605) created an encyclopedic book that took thirteen folios as opposed to Gesner's five.[71] Aldrovandi expanded not only the length of his articles, but also the web of associations. Gesner's paper on the peacock was eight pages lengthy and divided into eight sections. Aldrovandi's peacock article was nearly thirty-one pages long, with thirty-three subtopics. Between Gesner and Aldrovandi, the emblematic universe expanded significantly in terms of breadth of linkages and depth of perspective.[72] The incorporation of the ever-expanding research resulting from the six developments: hieroglyphics, antiquarianism, Aesopic tales, myth, and adages contributed to the wide scope of Aldrovandi's emblematic world view. Though Gesner includes myth, etymology, and tradition in his *History*, he wrote before the emergence of interest in hieroglyphics, antiquarianism, Aesopic fable tradition, and emblematics.[73]

The emblematic world view remained popular long into the mid-seventeenth century. The works of Gesner and Aldrovandi inspired a number of imitators, notably Edward Topsell. Topsell's *Historie of Four-Footed Beastes* (1607) was significantly influenced by Gesner's work, to which he added hieroglyphic and emblematic literature.[74] His taxonomy of animals was distinctly semiotic, with "every living beast being a word, every kind being a sentence, and all [sic] of them togither [sic] a large history, containing admirable knowledge & learning, which is, which shall continue, (if not

---

[71] Ashworth, "Natural History and the Emblematic World View," 313.

[72] Ashworth, "Natural History and the Emblematic World View," 313–14.

[73] Ashworth, "Natural History and the Emblematic World View," 313–14. For further discussion of the development of Renaissance natural history see Ogilvie, Brian W. *The Science of Describing: Natural History in Renaissance Europe.* Chicago: University of Chicago Press, 2006.

[74] Edward Topsell, *The Historie of Fovre-Footed Beastes. Describing the True and Liuely Figure of Euery Beast, with a Discourse of Their Seuerall Names, Conditions, Kindes, Vertues (Both Naturall and Medicinall) Countries of Their Breed, Their Loue and Hate to Mankinde, and the Wonderfull Worke of God in Their Creation, Preseruation, and Destruction. Necessary for All Diuines and Students, Because the Story of Euery Beast is Amplified with Narrations Out of Scriptures, Fathers, Phylosophers, Physitians, and Poets: Wherein Are Declared Diuers Hyerogliphicks, Emblems, Epigrams, and Other Good Histories, Collected Out of All the Volumes of Conradvs Gesner, and All Other Writers to This Present Day.* London, Printed by William Iaggard and 1607, The English Experience, Its Record in Early Printed Books Published in Facsimile, no. 561 (Amsterdam: Theatrum Orbis Terrarum; New York: Da Capo Press, 1973).

forever) yet to the world's end."[75] Topsell and Edwards are quite similar in this regard. Concerning the universe's semiotic character, Edwards speculated, "that there is room for persons to be learning more and more of this language and seeing more of that which is declared in it to the end of the world without discovering it all."[76]

Topsell's exegetical method gave rise to the concept of animals or things as pages in what has come to be known as the Book of Nature. These portions of the Book of Nature featured analogies and symbols that required interpretation. A symbolic literalism evolved, obliterating the boundary between the metaphorical and literal. "Material things themselves came to be seen as symbolic and as constituting an elaborate tropological network linked together by intersecting, and metaphorical conceived, relationships in which the distinction between the"metaphorical" and the "literal" was continually eroded." The various approaches to exegeting the Book of Nature changed depending on the exegetes' specific circumstances and their interpretation of the Fall, the loss of Adamic language at Babel, and the restoration of a universal language at Pentecost.[77]

Paracelsus provided a story of the Fall that may provide some light on the interpretation of the Book of Nature and the quest for Adamic wisdom.[78] He claimed that the unfallen Adam could detect the inner essence of things and precisely encapsulate its nature in its name.[79] Adam did not choose names at random.

> [T]he signatory art teaches how to give true and genuine names to all things. All of these Adam the Protoplast truly and entirely understood. So it was that after the Creation he gave its own proper name to everything, to animals, trees, roots, stones, minerals, metals, waters, and the like, as well as to other fruits of the earth, of the water, of the air, and of the fire. Whatever names he imposed upon these were ratified and confirmed by God.

---

[75] Edward Topsell, *The History of Four-Footed Beasts.* Cited in Ashworth, "Natural History and the Emblematic World View," 316.

[76] "Types," *WJE*, 11:152.

[77] James J. Bono, "From Paracelsus to Newton: The Word of God, the Book of Nature, and the Eclipse of the Emblematic World View," in *Newton and Religion: Context, Nature, and Influence,* International Archives of the History of Ideas, vol. 161 (Boston: Kluwer Academic, 1999), 52–53.

[78] Bono, "From Paracelsus to Newton," 53.

[79] Bono, "From Paracelsus to Newton," 54.

Now these names were based upon a true and intimate foundation, not on mere opinion, and were derived from a predestined
knowledge, that is to say, the signatorial art. Adam is the first
signator.[80]

Fallen man lacks perfect understanding and competence to practice the
ars signata (signatory art). Despite the significant noetic consequences of
the Fall, Paracelsus felt that man retained the freedom to choose the path
of wisdom. However, this path must be walked piously and with God's
assistance.[81]

Aldrovandi's way of reading the Book of Nature was textual exegesis
of fables, adages, and emblematic sayings, but Paracelsus' method was
metaphorical and experiential. Both methodologies were intertwined in
emblematic natural history. The first Adamic language, which was associated
with God's Word, left symbolic traces or symbols inside the established order.
Humans who are sufficiently motivated can read these divine vestiges.[82] In
their revelatory role, the Word of God, human language, and the Book of Nature are closely linked. As James Bono points out, this is an original privilege
of being formed in the image of God:

> Adam's perfect understanding of the names of things depends on
> his ability to grasp, through direct experience, signs that reveal
> to the able practitioner of the ars signata the innermost secrets,
> hidden properties, occult virtues, and hence the true nature
> of things. By freely and accurately reading such signs, Adam
> exercises his privilege as unfallen imago dei and microcosm to
> rule over all other creatures . . . The Adamic names thus bear a
> direct and univocal relationship to the Word of God."[83]

The Historie of Foure-Footed Beastes by Edward Topsell is a classic example
of this emblematic world view. Topsell believed that by studying creatures in
depth, man may reclaim lost Adamic wisdom, reverse the tangle of tongues

---

[80]Paracelsus, *The Hermetic and Alchemical Writings of Aureolus Philippus Theophrastus Bombast,
of Hohenheim, Called Paracelsus the Great.* Now for the First Time Faithfully Tr. Into English. Ed.
with a Biographical Preface, Elucidatory Notes, a copious Hermetic vocabulary and index by
Arthur Edward Waite (London: J. Elliott and co., 1894), 188.

[81]Bono, "From Paracelsus to Newton," 56.

[82]Bono, "From Paracelsus to Newton," 59–60.

[83]Bono, "From Paracelsus to Newton," 55–56.

that occurred at Babel, and recreate the ideal language that reunites men's languages with the Word of God.[84] Topsell believed that the animals preserved on Noah's ark were saved not so much for God's kindness toward the creatures, but so that man "might gain out of them much devine knowledge, such as is imprinted in them by nature, as a tipe or spark of that great wisdome whereby they were created."[85] Topsell felt that the Scriptures taught about the creatures' revelatory function. The Bible "likens the Divell to a Lyon; false prophets to Wolves; heretics and false preachers to Scorpions."[86] Thus, the natural histories of Gesner, Aldrovandi, and Topsell, as well as other emblematic works, are part of a restorationist drive to reclaim the universal, Adamic language.[87] Until the seventeenth century, there existed a significant primitivist trend in natural history.[88] In the eighteenth and later centuries, instances of the emblematic world view and quest for God's language in nature were "atypical."[89] Edwards' acceptance of the emblematic world view appears to mark him as both atypical and archaic.

Decline of the Emblematic World View

"The bottom . . . suddenly dropped right out of the emblematic cosmos" with the publication of Johannes Jonston's *Natural History* (1650).[90] Jonston's encyclopedia was a watershed moment in natural history. A comparison of Gesner's, Aldrovandi's, and Jonston's peacock articles is instructive. Whereas Aldrovandi stretched Gesner's eight-page article to thirty-one pages, Jonston reduced his peacock article to only two pages. Jonston did so by removing any references to embems, adages, and hieroglyphics. According to Ash-

---

[84] Bono, *The Word of God and the Languages of Man: Interpreting Nature in Early Modern Science and Medicine*, 182.

[85] Edward Topsell, *The History of Four-Footed Beasts*. Cited in Bono, *The Word of God and the Languages of Man: Interpreting Nature in Early Modern Science and Medicine*, 183.

[86] The similarities with Edwards' "Images of Divine Things" are striking.

[87] Bono, *The Word of God and the Languages of Man: Interpreting Nature in Early Modern Science and Medicine*, 183.

[88] McGilchrist, *The Master and His Emissary*, 328. During the Renaissance, there was imitation of, and intense attention to, the natural world and for the knowledge of those who lived in earlier times. According to McGilchrist, this commitment to understanding the world in its fullness and interconnectedness reflects the way of thinking of the right hemisphere.

[89] Bono, *The Word of God and the Languages of Man: Interpreting Nature in Early Modern Science and Medicine*, 183–84.

[90] Ashworth, "Natural History and the Emblematic World View," 317.

worth, Jonston's *Natural History* represents the world's decontextualization, disenchantment, and desymbolization.[91]

The discovery of new species of animals in the New World, as well as the advent of empiricism, have both contributed to the abrupt decline of the emblematic world view. The ages produced a web of associations consisting of myth, tradition, adages, and hieroglyphics, and the similarities and similitudes were limited to animals found in the Old World. However, natural historians were now confronted with animals such as anteaters and sloths that had no historical or mythological associations. Other than local stories, the only data provided were physical descriptions, diet, habitat, and other observed habits. The animals in the New World wore no garments, and the effort of building a new emblematic world proved too difficult. Animals would rarely wear their emblematic robes after Jonston's *Natural History*.[92]

The realization of flaws in the natural histories of the day was another aspect in the decontextualization of nature and the downfall of the emblematic world view. With his *Pseudodoxia epidemica* or *Vulgar Errors*, Thomas Browne (1605-82) hoped to rid natural history of false notions (1646).[93] Popular ideas, such as a salamander's capacity to survive in fire and the natural antagonism between toads and spiders, were challenged. Experimentation demonstrated that such folk ideas were false.[94]

Browne's view of nature contrasted with Aldrovandi's emblematic and aphoristic. Browne was not opposed to the emblematic world view. He simply dismissed anything that could not be demonstrated to be real.[95] The literary tradition of natural history, like antiquarianism, came to be subject to the test of empiricism. "With this new understanding of what constitutes natural history, the entire emblematic tradition fell apart — or, to be more precise, became irrelevant." Animal symbolism, according to Browne, was no longer a part of the study of nature because it had no basis in truth."[96]

Francis Bacon dealt another blow to the emblematic world view. Bacon believed that imagination had no role in natural history. What matters is

---

[91] Ashworth, "Natural History and the Emblematic World View," 317–18.

[92] Ashworth, "Natural History and the Emblematic World View," 319.

[93] Thomas Browne, *Pseudodoxia Epidemica, or, Enquiries Into Very Many Received Tenents and Commonly Presumed Truths by Thomas Browne* (London: Printed by T.H. for E. Dod, 1646).

[94] Ashworth, "Natural History and the Emblematic World View," 319.

[95] Ashworth, "Natural History and the Emblematic World View," 320.

[96] Ashworth, "Natural History and the Emblematic World View," 322.

not what folks think about the world, but what is actually there.[97] The emblematic world view, with its web of associations and correspondences, eventually obscures the fundamental essence of reality. Similarly, the world cannot be viewed as a code that, when deciphered, reveals divine attributes. Bacon departed from a Platonic conception of reality in which "words and things were all of a piece, and the entire world of objects, letters, signs, and symbols was part of one language, the meaning of which was built in by God."[98] Bacon argued, in Aristotelean fashion, that words and things only have the meaning that men ascribe to them. If human language is arbitrary, this strongly suggests that there is no universal language of nature. As a result, "How can the Book of Nature shed light on God's plan if the language of that book is devoid of meaning?"[99]

Although the influence of Baconianism cannot be directly linked to Jonston and Browne's separate work, their diverse reasons for the insufficiency of the emblematic world view demonstrate a similarity. Even before the development of Baconianism and Cartesian mechanical philosophy, the downfall of the emblematic world view was underway.[100]

Bacon's rejection of the natural world as God's language, based on his notion of language as an arbitrary human fabrication, and his reservations about the Book of Nature's meaningful content are significant. The shift in perspective drastically impacted the narrative framework of the emblematic world view. Natural historians began to focus on the distinctions between animals and plants after removing the "correspondences and similitudes that [bound] them into an analogical and symbolic network."[101]

The paradigm shift away from the emblematic world view resulted in a second collapse, known as the Fall of Nature. A creation narrative in which the Logos visibly stamped the archetypes within God's mind on the creature was lost. Nature was no longer God's language or image. This Fall of Nature was also associated with a weakened image of man as a "privileged

[97]Brian W. Ogilvie, *The Science of Describing: Natural History in Renaissance Europe* (Chicago: University of Chicago Press, 2006), 258–59.

[98]Ashworth, "Natural History and the Emblematic World View," 323.

[99]Ashworth, "Natural History and the Emblematic World View," 323.

[100]Ashworth, "Natural History and the Emblematic World View," 324.

[101]Bono, *The Word of God and the Languages of Man: Interpreting Nature in Early Modern Science and Medicine,* 180.

reader of the text of nature."[102] As language lost "its status as the originary source of knowledge," the hermeneutical hunt for Adamic language faded, as did attempts to get information through ciphers engraved on the created order.[103]

Creation Deinscribed

The rejection of symbolic hermeneutics and the emblematic world view was not a rejection of nature as a text in general, but only as a text that mirrored God's image and ideas. Furthermore, this alternative viewpoint did not deny the existence of a natural language. The communicative bond between nature and God was denied. Nature came to be regarded as different from God, despite originating from him. Nature's order and regularity were the only genuine evidences of God's creative activity. "Early modern authors turned toward this nonsymbolic text of nature... Constructing new hermeneutic practices aimed at *de-in-scribing* nature, that is, describing the order and regularity of God's visible text," Bono writes.[104] Galileo's world view is a wonderful example of nature *de-in-scribed*. Galileo believed that the Book of Nature's text or language was mathematical:

> Philosophy is written in this grand book, the universe, which stands continually open to our gaze. But the book cannot be understood unless one first learns to comprehend the language and read the letters in which it is composed. It is written in the language of mathematics, and its characters are triangles, circles, and other geometric figures without which it is humanly impossible to understand a single word of it; without these, one wanders about in a dark labyrinth.[105]

In the early seventeenth century, the Scientific Revolution picked up speed, having blossomed out of the Renaissance. This was evidenced by

---

[102] Bono, *The Word of God and the Languages of Man: Interpreting Nature in Early Modern Science and Medicine,* 180.

[103] Bono, *The Word of God and the Languages of Man: Interpreting Nature in Early Modern Science and Medicine,* 180.

[104] Bono, *The Word of God and the Languages of Man: Interpreting Nature in Early Modern Science and Medicine,* 193. Jonathan Edwards re-in-scribed, or reinscripturated nature.

[105] Galileo Galilei, *Discoveries and Opinions of Galileo,* translated with introduction and notes by Stillman Drake (Garden City, NY: Doubleday, 1957), 237–38.

Galileo's *Dialogue* in 1632. The Renaissance spirit of admiration for the natural world gave way to a focus on empirical observation, which allowed for the flourishing of both the arts and sciences, which were not yet separate entities.[106] Galileo retains the concept of a Book of Nature, but alters its nature from one that required interpretation to one that is entirely open to anybody who can mathematically decode it.[107]

Previously considered a "polysemous text written in symbolic and divine language that required etymological, symbolic, allegorical, cosmological, or moral exegesis," Galileo saw the Book of Nature "as a stubborn but self-revealing text that did not require human agency to construct its meaning."[108] Galileo fully reversed the emblematic world view, voiding it of poetry or any linguistic turn.[109] Those who attempted to read the Book of Nature were only given a literal interpretation.[110] The *why* issue of theology would no longer be asked or answered. When approaching the Book of Nature, the only legitimate question was *how*. The only valid questions that may be asked are how nature is structured and organised and how its pieces are geometrically related.[111]

According to Galileo, the Book of Nature can only convey a literal message to its readers. It solely speaks of itself and nothing greater, such as God's will, future intentions, or the heavenly realm. To learn about these subjects, the reader must turn to a more specific revelation, the Scriptures.[112]

---

[106] McGilchrist, *The Master and His Emissary,* 327.

[107] Bono, *The Word of God and the Languages of Man: Interpreting Nature in Early Modern Science and Medicine,* 195. Bono calls this decoding de-in-scription. Jonathan Edwards agenda was to use Scripture to reinscript, or reinscripturate nature.

[108] Bono, *The Word of God and the Languages of Man: Interpreting Nature in Early Modern Science and Medicine,* 196.

[109] Galilei, *Discoveries and Opinions of Galileo,* 237–38.

[110] McGilchrist, *The Matter With Things,* 1533. Galileo claimed that the universe is written in a language of mathematics, with symbols of triangles, circles, and other geometrical figures necessary to comprehend it. However, McGilchrist observes that the universe is composed of patterns, and mathematics is just one way to view them. These patterns are not only the predictable patterns of Platonic philosophy, but also patterns that cannot be expressed mathematically.

[111] Bono, *The Word of God and the Languages of Man: Interpreting Nature in Early Modern Science and Medicine,* 197. For further reading on early scientific interpretations of nature see, Fernand Hallyn, *The Poetic Structure of the World: Copernicus and Kepler,* trans. Donald M. Leslie (New York: Zone Books, 1990).

[112] Bono, *The Word of God and the Languages of Man: Interpreting Nature in Early Modern Science and Medicine,* 198.

Nature, according to Galileo, offers no invitations or accommodations and is unwilling to divulge its secrets to the common man:

> For the Holy Scripture and nature derive equally from the God-head [Verbo divino], the former as the dictation of the Holy Spirit and the latter as the most obedient executrix of God's orders; moreover, to accommodate the understanding of the common people it is appropriate for Scripture to say many things that are different (in appearance and in regard to the literal meaning of the words) from the absolute truth; on the other hand, nature is inexorable and immutable, never violates the terms of the laws imposed upon her, and does not care whether or not her recondite reasons and ways of operation are disclosed to human understanding.[113]

A dilemma arises when one gets beyond the emblematic world view and into Newtonian physics. Newton helped to shape a world view based on fixed natural laws of motion and gravity. What happens to Newton's interests, such as alchemy, after the proverbial apple falls? Are they consistent with his mathematical cosmos, or are they aberrations, outliers to be ignored, anachronistic vestiges that may be safely snipped off? The widely accepted account of a simple transition from an emblematic to a mechanistic world view ignores the critical religious context in which this transition occurred. The world's relationship with God's Word was not broken, but rather redefined. The universe no longer represented the divine Word's essence, only its force, grandeur, and providence.[114]

This reconfiguration helps to explain the difficult interaction between science and religion that evolved prior to the eighteenth century with Boyle and Newton. Boyle, like Newton, continued to be fascinated by theology and biblical languages, as well as the new philosophy devoid of emblematic connotations. Newton's fascination with the Scriptures, prophecy, and the chronology and significance of the broad biblical narrative was not separate from his scientific interests in the Book of Nature. They were, rather, signs of a growing reconfiguration of the relationship between the Book of Nature and the Word of God.[115]

---

[113]Maurice A. Finocchiaro, "Galileo's Letter to the Grand Duchess Christina (1615)," in *The Galileo Affair: A Documentary History,* California Studies in the History of Science (Berkeley: University of California, 1989), 93.

[114]Bono, "From Paracelsus to Newton," 72–73.

[115]Bono, "From Paracelsus to Newton," 73–74.

Newton's rejection of the emblematic world view was also motivated by theological concerns. He was convinced that the emblematic world view was essentially idolatrous. Newton also believed that the *prisca theologia* was tainted as biblical patriarchs were identified with celestial bodies and then transposed into Egyptian hieroglyphic symbols. These same hieroglyphics became a source of polytheism. Newton wanted to preserve the distinction between the creation and its Creator.[116]

The Calvinist habit of reading signs in nature and the devotional activity of "occasional meditations" on creation and human events will be described later, but both disciplines follow a pattern of reconfiguration similar to Newton and others. The Paracelsian Protestants, such as Oswald Croll, recognized divine signals in nature but believed they were only contingent expressions with no intrinsic relationship to God's unchanging nature.[117] Newton's view of reality is based on a divinely ordained order of both the universe and its history that is wholly distinct in substance and image from the Creator.[118]

Conclusion

To summarize, the burst of natural history that occurred with the New World discoveries overwhelmed and tended to delegitimize the web of correspondences and symbols that served as the foundation for the emblematic world view. Diversity in both natural history and language became troublesome for the textual hermeneutic hunt for the original Adamic language. The flood of textual and symbolic information proved too great to absorb into a story of originative unity. As a result, and for the numerous reasons indicated above, the search for nature's language eventually began to embrace a demystified universe.[119] The world has become estranged from God's Word. This *de-inscription* of the world is the impetus for Jonathan Edwards' *rein-scripturation* of the world and the Word. Newton and others continued the deinscription of the world while reading the Book of Nature and the Word of God in a reconfigured manner.

---

[116]Bono, "From Paracelsus to Newton," 74.

[117]Stephen H. Daniel, *The Philosophy of Jonathan Edwards, A Study in Divine Semiotics* (Bloomington: Indiana University Press, 1994), 75–77.

[118]Bono, "From Paracelsus to Newton," 74–75.

[119]Bono, "From Paracelsus to Newton," 171.

Religious persons with a devotional disposition and contemplative practice found the shift away from an emblematic world with a linguistic stamp and toward a world of purely mathematical expression unacceptable. A descripted reality had nothing to communicate to the beholder. A scripted universe was valuable because it had meaning. Furthermore, a world inscribed with the Bible had biblical meaning, which Edwards and other creative Evangelical theologians desired.

CHAPTER THREE: EMBLEMATIC THEOLOGY

Introduction

THE PRECEDING CHAPTER EXAMINED the numerous causes that contributed to the growth and demise of the emblematic world view. The Renaissance's *ad fontes* quest fueled the rediscovery of classics of literature and art, as well as the original text of the Scriptures. However, the quest for the fountain sparked an interest in hieroglyphics, mythology, fables, adages, and other subjects. This culminated in the emblem tradition, which brought the numerous threads together to form a holistic world vision: the emblematic world view. The emblematic world view of signs, text, poetry, correspondences, and similitudes was deinscripted with the emergence of empiricism, science, and mathematics for the reasons stated previously. A descripted universe, in which the world is mostly described, was a revolution in world view. The true language of nature was supposed to be mathematical and geometrical, while the emblematic world was more significant for religious meditative purposes. The ancient emblematic world, on the other hand, was distinctly linguistic and communicative because it was inscribed with the Word of God. It became clear that the world's deinscription, which presented an external, demystified, and merely descriptive depiction of reality, did not satisfy everyone. There were a number of religious people who maintained (and developed) the emblematic world view. To counter the freshly described universe of Bacon, Galileo, and Newton, they offered a meditative and devotional version of the emblematic world view.

Though Edwards' notebook "Images of Divine Things" contained a very sophisticated system of emblems, he was not alone in his embrace of an ascriptive emblematic world view. Prior to him, the Anglican Bishop Joseph Hall, the Oxford horticultural and Baptist conventicler Ralph Austen, John

Bunyan, Benjamin Keach, and even Cotton Mather all understood the instructional value of creation and shared Edwards' emblematic world vision. The created order loomed large for these men, so much so that their vision of nature could be regarded as "God-haunted." A comparison and investigation of their devotional and meditative interpretations of the Book of Nature, particularly regarding fruit trees, reveals their theological affinity. This chapter will establish Edwards' place among the emblematic theologians who carried on the emblematic enterprise during the Enlightenment, and it will lay the groundwork for a closer examination of Edwards' emblematics in subsequent chapters. We shall begin with a quick overview of some of the religious developments that led to the restoration of the Renaissance's emblematic world vision within early Evangelicalism.

Religious Developments

Because of the connection with "medieval habits of allegory and biblical exegesis," the application of Renaissance emblems to represent theological truths and religious experience was not a wholly new development.[1] The Word of God and the Book of Nature serve as objects of contemplation in a variety of meditative emblems in England, the most significant of which is that they are subjects of reflection.[2] Although the traditional domain of exegesis was the Word of God, and allegory was used to expound the Book of Nature, "the spiritual or meditative emblem frequently takes a biblical text as its starting point, using traditional exegetic techniques. . . [and] spiritual emblems meditating the Book of the creatures."[3]

Emblems and their associated meditations all have a sensory origin. The emblems engage the body's eye, while the meditations engage the soul's eye, providing spiritual sight. The purpose of a meditative act that engaged both body and spirit was to elicit an affective response that shifted the will toward God and away from sin. The affective and emotive religious response arising from such meditative techniques has frequently been classified as

[1] Michael Bath, *Speaking Pictures: English Emblem Books and Renaissance Culture,* Longman Medieval and Renaissance Library (New York: Longman, 1994), 160. Michael Bath notes that the "precise relationship between meditation and emblem has not, however, been systematically studied."

[2] Bath, *Speaking Pictures: English Emblem Books and Renaissance Culture,* 160.

[3] Bath, *Speaking Pictures: English Emblem Books and Renaissance Culture,* 161. It can be difficult to distinguish clearly whether emblems are exegetical or allegorical because the Bible employs allegorical signs, as noted by Augustine.

Puritanism, despite the fact that this art of meditation has its roots in the Catholic Counter-Reformation's effort to "harness sensuous imagery for spiritual ends."[4] To be sure, meditative traditions steeped in nature can be traced back to St. Bonaventure and Hugh St. Victor. Though early English Protestants were opposed to anything Catholic, sectarian and polemical struggle in England appeared to have a great influence on contemplative practices as a means of rediscovering a vibrant piety among Protestants. Joseph Hall was the most important proponent of this form of meditation and the eventual development of the English devotional emblem.

Bishop Hall

The founder of Protestant occasional meditation, who is also listed in Edwards' *Catalogues of Books,* is Bishop Joseph Hall.[5] Hall was an exemplar of this devotional practice in which meditations are taken from the "Book of Creatures." He defined the meditation on this book as a way to learn something from every creature, as well as from the things God has allowed man to create. He used the term "creatures" to include more than just animals, flowers, and rain, but also man and the things man has created. Through this meditation, Hall believed one can learn about the power and wisdom of the infinite Creator, and use the creatures as a way to observe duty and occasion for devout thoughts.[6]

> Every herb, flower, spire of grass, every twig and leaf, every worm and fly, every scale and feather, every billow and meteor,[7] speaks the power and wisdom of their infinite Creator. Solomon sends the sluggard to the ant; Isaiah sends the Jews to the ox

[4]Bath, *Speaking Pictures: English Emblem Books and Renaissance Culture,* 161–62.

[5]Edwards and Thuesen, *Catalogues of Books,* 63, 221, 411.

[6]Frank Livingstone Huntley, "Bishop Joseph Huntley and Protestant Meditation," *Studies in the Literary Imagination* 10, no. 2 (Fall 1977): 67–68.

[7]Celestial objects have received less attention in emblem studies than other elements of the natural world. On the whole, the sun, moon and stars seem to make only scattered appearances in emblem books. A remarkable exception is the *Meteorologia philosophico-politica* (1698), composed by the Linz Jesuit theologian Franz Reinzer, in which, being both an emblem book and a traditional meteorological treatise, celestial objects were an important issue in the text as well as in the illustrations. The publication has been described as a compendium of meteorology, a didactic emblem book, a moralising mirror of princes and an academic disputation. See Sabine Kalff, "Comets—Celestial Objects in the Emblem Tradition of the Late Seventeenth and Early Eighteenth Century," in *Emblems and the Natural World* (Leiden: Brill, 2017), 321.

and the ass; our Saviour sends his disciples to the ravens, and to the lilies of the field. There is no creature of whom we may not learn something. We shall have spent our time ill in this great school of the world, if, in such store of lessons, we be nonproficients in devotion ... And indeed, wherefore serve all the volumes of natural history but to be so many commentaries upon the creatures wherein we may read God? ... Who can be so stupid as not to take notice of the industry of the bee, the providence of the ant, the cunning of the spider, the reviving of the fly, the worm's endeavour of revenge, the subtlety of the fox, the sagacity of the hedgehog, the innocence and profitableness of the sheep, the laboriousness of the ox, the obsequiousness of the dog, the timorous shifts of the hare, the nimbleness of the deer, the generosity of the lion, the courage of the horse, the fierceness of the tiger, the cheerful music of birds, the harmlessness of the dove, the true love of the turtle, the cock's observation of time, the swallow's architecture; shortly—for it were easy here to be endless—of the several qualities and dispositions of every one of those our fellow creatures with whom we converse on the face of the earth? and who that takes notice of them cannot fetch from every act and motion of theirs some monition of duty and occasion for devout thoughts?[8]

Bishop Hall (1574–1656) was a major influence on Protestants and the flowering emblematic literature of the seventeenth and eighteenth centuries. Hall wrote *The Art of Divine Meditation* (1606), the first Post-Reformation systematic treatment of devotional meditation, in an attempt to integrate Calvinism with traditional Catholic contemplative practice. According to emblem scholar Karl Höltgen, Hall supported kinds of meditation that were respected by both Catholics and Protestants, including self-analysis, Bible meditation, and occasional meditation on creation.[9] Hall prayed in his treatise *The Invisible World* that God would wash the clay from his eyes with

---

[8]Huntley, "Bishop Joseph Huntley and Protestant Meditation," 67–68.

[9]Karl Josef Höltgen, *Aspects of the Emblem: Studies in the English Emblem Tradition and the European Context,* with a foreword by Sir Roy Strong, *Problemata Semiotica* (Kassel, GER: Reichenberger, 1986), 39–40.

the waters of Siloam and anoint them with salve, allowing him to view the exquisite marvels of creation.[10] Hall thought that with improved vision,

> Every action, every occurance shall remind me of those hidden and better things: and I shall so admit of all material objects, as if they were so altogether transparent, that through them I might see the wonderfull prospects of another world. And certainly, if we shall be able to withdraw our selves from our senses, we shall see, not what we see, but what we thinke ... and shall make earthly things, not as Lunets, to shut up our sight, but Spectacles to transmit it to spiritual objects.[11]

When viewed through the "spectacles" of faith, Hall's adoption of the intelligibility of the world shows an emblematic world view that parallels the symbolic metaphysics and universal allegory of the medievals John Scotus Eriugina and Hugh of St. Victor.[12] Hall's Protestant contemplative techniques are divided into two categories: formal and occasional. The formal meditations adhere to the broad strokes of Ignatius' *Spiritual Exercises*.[13] In contrast, occasional meditations had no systematic framework and were

---

[10]Joseph Hall, "The Invisible World," in *The Works of the Right Reverend Joseph Hall, D. D.* (Oxford: Oxford University Press, 1863), 8:180–81. Edwards used a similar emblem of dirt in the eyes: "145. If persons have dirt in their eyes, it exceedingly hinders their sight. This represents how much it blinds men when their eyes are full of dirt or full of earth. In order to the clearness of our sight, we had need to have our eyes clear of earth, i.e. our aims free from all things belonging to this earthly world, and to look only at those things that are spiritual, agreeable to what Christ says: 'If thine eye be single, thy whole body shall be full of light. But if thine eye be evil, thy whole body shall be full of darkness' [Matthew 6:22–23]." *WJE*, 11:101.

[11]Hall, "The Invisible World," 215–16.

[12]Umberto Eco, *Art and Beauty in the Middle Ages*, trans. Hugh Bredin (New Haven: Yale University Press, 1988), 56–59. See also Jaroslav Pelikan, *The Christian Tradition: A History of the Development of Doctrine, Vol. 3: The Growth of Medieval Theology (600–1300)* (Chicago: University Of Chicago Press, 1980), 104–05.

[13]Bath, *Speaking Pictures: English Emblem Books and Renaissance Culture,* 163. Another Anglican with ideas similar to those of Bishop Hall was the influential English emblem writer and poet Francis Quarles (1592–1644). Quarles is cited twice in Edwards' "Catalogue" of reading. WJE, 26:129, 232. Quarles's *Emblems* followed the pattern of Jesuit emblem books and successfully captured the religious emotion and ecstacy of the Catholic Counter-Reformation for Protestants in early Stuart England. *Emblems,* published together with *Hieroglyphics of the Life of Man,* was "a striking, new type of devotional emblem book that could capture mind, imagination, and emotions." Höltgen, *Aspects of the Emblem: Studies in the English Emblem Tradition and the European Context,* 32–33. Quarles viewed all of nature as a system of divine hieroglyphics: "An Emblem is but a silent Parable. Let not the tender Eye check, to see the allusion to our blessed Saviour figured, in these Types. In holy Scripture, He is sometimes called a Sower; sometimes a Fisher; sometimes, a Physician: And why not presented

mostly spontaneous contemplative responses to random thoughts, events, and accidents. The occasional meditation can be the development of an idea or proverb, or it can be a created object that is interpreted allegorically for spiritual goals. This reconstruction of the medieval symbolic universe for English Protestant meditative activities was possibly Hall's most significant contribution to the emblem tradition in the seventeenth century.[14]

> There is nothing, that we can see, which doth not put us in mind of God: what creature is there, wherein we do not espy some footsteps of a Deity? Every herb, flower, leaf, in our garden; every bird, and fly in the air; every ant and worm, in the ground; every spider in our window; speaks the omnipotence, and infinite wisdom of their Creator. None of these may pass us without some fruitful monition of acknowledging a Divine Hand.[15]

In the preceding paragraph, the Augustinian sentiment conveys an emblematic plenitude within creation. Though Hall did not include images in his meditations, the titles were emblematic: "Upon the Sight of Gold Melted," "Upon the Sight of a Tree Full Blossomed," "Upon the View of the Heaven and the Earth," "Upon the Occasion of a Redbreast Coming into his Chamber," "Upon the Occasion of a Spider in his Window," "Upon the Sight of a Rain in the Sunshine," and many others.[16] On the subject of spiritual growth, Hall discovers a rich emblem in tree blossoms:

> Here is a tree overlaid with blossoms. It is not possible that all these should prosper; one of them must needs rob the other of moisture and growth. I do not love to see an infancy over-hopeful; in these pregnant beginnings one faculty starves another

so, as well to the eye, as to the ear. Before the knowledge of letters, GOD was known by Hieroglyphics, And, indeed, what are the Heavens, the Earth, nay every Creature, Hieroglyphics and Emblems of his Glory?" Francis Quarles, Emblems, divine and moral, together with Hieroglyphics of the life of man [on-line]; accessed 29 November 2022; available from https://ia600205.us.archive.org/8/items/quarlesemblems00quar/quarlesemblems00quar_bw.pdf; Internet.

[14]Bath, *Speaking Pictures: English Emblem Books and Renaissance Culture,* 163–64.

[15]Joseph Hall, "The Remedy of Profaneness," in *The Works of the Right Reverend Joseph Hall, D. D.* (Oxford: Oxford University Press, 1863), 8:339.

[16]Frank Livingstone Huntley, *Bishop Joseph Hall and Protestant Meditation in Seventeenth-Century England: A Study with Texts of The Art of Divine Meditation (1606) and Occasional Meditations (1633),* Medieval & Renaissance Texts & Studies, vol. 1 (Binghamton, N.Y.: Center for Medieval & Early Renaissance Studies, 1981), 128–31.

and at last leaves the mind sapless and barren. As therefore we are wont to pull off some of the too-frequent blossoms, that the rest may thrive, so it is good wisdom to moderate the early excess of the parts or progress of over-forward childhood. Neither is it otherwise in our Christian profession: a sudden and lavish ostentation of grace may fill the eye with wonder and the mouth with talk but will not at the last fill the lap with fruit. Let me not promise too much nor praise too high expectations of my undertakings. I had rather men should complain of my small hopes than of my short performances.[17]

In "Images of Divine Things," Edwards similarly mentions pruning as a spiritual emblem. He notices that the best time to prune a tree is when the sap is low, at the end of winter, and just before it blooms in the spring. This pruning method is analogous to how God prunes his people right before seasons of grace and blessing.[18] The parallel between Hall's occasional view of a fully flowered tree and Jonathan Edwards' "image" of a fruit tree's abundance of blossoms is striking.

That of so vast and innumerable a multitude of blossoms that appear on a tree, so few come to ripe fruit; and that so few of so vast a multitude of seeds as are yearly produced, so few come to be a plant; and that there is so great a waste of the seed of both plants and animals, but one in a great multitude ever bringing forth any things, seem to be lively types: how few are saved out of the mass of mankind, and particularly how few are sincere, of professing Christians, that never wither away but endure to the end, and how, of the many that are called, few are chosen.[19]

Hall's contribution to emblematically interpreting the world is quite illuminating. He uses Moses as an example to explain the art of seeing the invisible, spiritual, and divine. Hall believes that the world is divided into three parts: perceptible, intelligible (rational), and spiritual. "[B]y the eye of sense, he saw Pharaoh's court and Israel's servitude; by the eye of reason, he saw the mysteries of Egyptian learning; and by the eye of faith, he saw

[17]Huntley, *Bishop Joseph Hall and Protestant Meditation in Seventeenth-Century England,* 129.

[18]"Images of Divine Things," *WJE,* 11:116.

[19]"Images of Divine Things," *WJE,* 11:70.

him who is invisible," Moses said.[20] The unreflective animal realm can only observe through sight or passive observation. Humans also have the ability to reason. However, only the redeemed and angels have access to a spiritual perspective of reality.[21]

Although the concept of spiritual sight and understanding has a long history, Hall's merger of spiritual meditation with the Book of Nature had "consequences for the emblem and for theories of perception in the visual arts in England which have not been widely recognized."[22] The brief introductory paragraph to Hall's *Occasional Meditations* reveals his doctrine of plenitude.

> I have heedlessly lost, I confess, many good thoughts. These few my paper hath preserved from vanishing, the example whereof may perhaps be more useful than the matter. Our active souls can no more forbear to think than the eye can choose but to see when it is open; would we but keep our wholesome notions together, mankind would be too rich. To do well, no object should pass us without use. Everything that we see reads us new lectures of wisdom and piety. It is a shame for a man to be ignorant or Godless under so many tutors. For me, I would not wish to live longer that I shall be better for my eyes, and have thought it thankworthy thus to teach weak minds how to improve their thoughts upon all like occasions. And if ever these lines shall come to the public view, I desire and charge my reader, whosoever he be, to make me and himself so happy as to take out my lesson and to learn how to read God's great book by mine.[23]

Hall's *Occasional Meditations* has 140 entries. Later, editor Frank Livingstone Huntley created an index that divided the meditations into eight sections based on the Genesis creation account: The Heavens, Gen. 1:8; The Earth and the Waters, Gen. 1:9-10; The Grass, Flowers, Shrubs, and Trees, Gen. 1:11-12; The Birds, Gen. 1:20; The Animals, Gen. 1:24; The Insects,

---

[20] Joseph Hall, "The Remedy of Profaneness," 6:329–30.

[21] Joseph Hall, "The Remedy of Profaneness," 6:329–30.

[22] Bath, *Speaking Pictures: English Emblem Books and Renaissance Culture,* 165.

[23] Huntley, *Bishop Joseph Hall and Protestant Meditation in Seventeenth- Century England,* 123. Edwards also notes that saints need to exercise "great care" and should endeavor to become fluent in reading the Book of Nature. "Images of Divine Things," *WJE,* 11:67; "Types," *WJE,* 11:151.

Gen. 1:25; Man, Gen, 1:26; Man-made Objects, Gen 22:22.[24] Despite having just recorded a few meditations on the Book of Nature, Hall said that "everything that we see reads [sic] us new lectures of wisdom and piety."[25]

Ralph Austen

In his book *Seditious Sectaryes: The Baptist Conventiclers of Oxford 1641–1692,* Larry Kreitzer examines the fascinating and somewhat enigmatic life and convictions of early Baptist conventicler Ralph Austen. Austen, who was born about 1612 in Leek, Staffordshire, grew up without a formal university education but served as the Deputy Registrar to the Parliament Visitors for several years.[26] Austen established a nursery in 1652 and began his mission to "apply his horticultural principles to society so as to create the kingdom of God on earth."[27] Austen aimed to expand "on the Biblical image of the Garden of Eden," regarding human beings as followers of their divinely set work of managing the garden, tilling the earth, and other agricultural pursuits, similar to our distant forefather, Adam.[28]

Austen first sought the assistance of Samuel Hartlib, a well-known educationalist and philanthropist.[29] Austen requested Hartlib's feedback and suggestions, and Hartlib agreed. Both individuals saw the economic and scientific opportunities that widespread cultivation of fruit trees could pro-

---

[24] Huntley, *Bishop Joseph Hall and Protestant Meditation in Seventeenth- Century England,* 215–19.

[25] Huntley, *Bishop Joseph Hall and Protestant Meditation in Seventeenth- Century England,* 123.

[26] James Turner, "Ralph Austen, an Oxford Horticulturist of the Seventeenth Century," *Garden History* 6, no. 2 (1978): 39.

[27] Larry J. Kreitzer, *Seditious Sectaryes: The Baptist Conventiclers of Oxford 1641–1691* (Milton Keynes, UK: Paternoster, 2006), 1:222.

[28] Kreitzer, *Seditious Sectaryes,* 1:222.

[29] A. Rupert Hall, *The Revolution in Science, 1500–1750* (New York: Longman, 1983), 216–17. Hartlib (1600–1662) was a German Protestant immigrant who influenced the formation of the British Royal Society. A polymath, Hartlib had a wide variety of interests which ranged from astronomy to botany. He was a promoter of educational reform and was friends with Czech educational pioneer, John Amos Comenius, who was no stranger to emblematics. Comenius' renowned and influential pictorial dictionary, the *Orbis sensualium pictus,* was published in 1658. The woodcuts in the book were designed for young viewers. They included a title similar to the motto, a picture that mirrored the icon, but not as intricate as normal emblems, and a bilingual or even multilingual dictionary that explained the illustration and taught the children a large amount of vocabulary in a fun way. See Sonja Schreiner, *"Orbis Pictus* for Boys—Emblematics for Men: Some Remarks on Learning by Studying Pictures and Interpreting Riddles," in *Emblems and the Natural World* (Leiden: Brill, 2017), 631–32.

vide for the country. According to Turner, Austen "believed that a massive nationalized program of fruit-tree plantations, supplied by his nurseries and guided by his text-books, could solve the nation's economic and social problems."[30] Hartlib was so taken with Austen's *Treatise on Fruit-trees* that he championed it in his own work, which was published the same year.[31] Austen's first book was *A Treatise on Fruit-trees Shewing the Method of Grafting, Setting, Pruning, and Ordering of Fruits … With the Alimental and Physical Use of Fruits* (1653). Though the government never supported his program, his publications boosted his nursery business, and his theories drew the attention of notables such as Robert Boyle and Isaac Newton.[32] Austen included a theological study titled *The Spiritual Use of an Orchard, or Garden of Fruit-trees,* with the first printing. Though the spiritual application of an orchard affected Austen, he withdrew it from the 1656 edition on the advice of Boyle and for the purpose of general acceptance.[33] Austen did not abandon the theological dimension of an orchard, according to Kreitzer, and in the year he died, he published *A Dialogue, or Familiar Discourse, and Conference between the Husbandman, and Fruit-trees in his Nurseries, Orchards, and Gardens* (1656).[34] Austen finally gained admission to the Royal Society in 1656, but by the time Isaac Newton attempted to contact him, Austen had died.[35]

Austen lays out his understanding of the proper use of creation, namely an orchard of fruit trees, in the preface to *The Spiritual Use of an Orchard.*

> When we have gone through all the workes and labours to be performed in the Orchard, & have received thereby a rich recompense of Temporall Profits & Pleasures in the use of the Trees and Fruits, we may (besides all that) make a Spirituall use of them, and receave much Profit and Pleasure thereby.[36]

> The World is a great Library, and Fruit-trees are some of the Bookes wherein we may read & see plainly the Attributes of God his Power, Wisdome, Goodnesse etc. and be Instructed and

[30]Turner, "Ralph Austen, an Oxford Horticulturist of the Seventeenth Century," 40.

[31]Kreitzer, *Seditious Sectaryes,* 1:222–23.

[32]Turner, "Ralph Austen, an Oxford Horticulturist of the Seventeenth Century," 40, 42.

[33]Kreitzer, *Seditious Sectaryes,* 1:228.

[34]Kreitzer, *Seditious Sectaryes,* 1:228.

[35]Kreitzer, *Seditious Sectaryes,* 1:241.

[36]Ralph Austen, *The Spiritual Use of an Orchard* (New York: Garland, 1982), 3.

taught our duty toward him in many things even from Fruit-trees for as trees (in a Metaphoricall sence) are Bookes, so likewise in the same sence they have a Voyce, and speake plainely to us, and teach us many good lessons ... The Ancients were skilled in this kind of Learning, in teaching by SIMILITUDES, and one of them observes, that God sent us the Booke of Nature, before he sent us the Booke of Scriptures ... One says, as Windows are to a house, so are SIMILITUDES to a Discourse: they both let in light. Fruit-trees are a TEXT from which may be raysed many profitable Doctrines, and Conclusions, which may be proved by Scripture, and Experience.[37]

The seventeenth century saw a surge in interest in horticulture, landscaping, orchards, botanic gardens, and parks. Though predominantly an aristocratic concern, there was a commensurate growth in Puritan millenarianism. The desire for primeval purity, which normally accompanies millennial expectations, found concrete form in the ambition of re-creating Eden in England.[38] The millennial anticipation and environmental concern found a common voice in Austen's single volume, *Treatise on Fruit-trees and Spiritual Use of an Orchard.* For Austen, the created order was a large library, and he recommended the book of fruit trees as one of the best books, because they metaphorically talk to us and offer "many good lessons."[39] Not only fruit trees, but all of God's creations (including inanimate nature and events) are to be studied as books, and such books are particularly beneficial to those "who cannot read a line in any printed book [but] may read many good lessons in the Book of the Creatures."[40]

Fruit-trees though they are dumb companions, yet (in a sense) we may discourse with them: The works of God speak to the mind as his word does to the ear: Mr. Boulton says Our eyes (especially on the Sabbath day) ought as little bees fall upon several objects, and from them (as from so many flowers) gather honey,

---

[37]Ralph Austen, *The Spiritual Use of an Orchard,* 3–6.

[38]Werner Hüllen, *English Dictionaries 800–1700: The Topical Tradition* (New York: Oxford, 2006), 235.

[39]Austen, *The Spiritual Use of an Orchard,* 3.

[40]Austen, *The Spiritual Use of an Orchard,* 3.

and bring it into the hive; That is; Sweet heavenly wholesome meditations for magnifying the Creator in all his attributes.[41]

According to Psalm 19, "even inanimate creatures have a voice and speak loudly to men, and it is our duty to learn their language and listen to them." Because God bends down and takes heed of our inadequate communications, we "must be content to stoop to their way and manner of teaching," because "dumb creatures speak virtually and convincingly, to the mind and the conscience."[42] Edwards is convinced that an emblematic picture of the world will be highly efficient for instructing, impressing, and altering the mind of the certainty of Scripture. "By that we may as it were hear God speaking to us. Wherever we are and whatever we are about, we may see divine things excellently represented and held forth."[43] Austen shares the same conviction that a spiritual use of the world will draw the attentive student closer to God:

> If we make use of creatures to serve our turn only in reference to our outward man, we make not half that use of them as we ought, we should study the creatures & learn from them to bring us nearer the Creator, climbing up by them, as by steps, or stairs, till we ascend to the highest good.[44]

According to Austen, the Ancients welcomed this type of learning, and God sent the Book of Nature before the Book of Scripture. Isaac's meditations in the fields undoubtedly offered numerous insights from the Book of Nature "[t]eaching by similitudes is the most plain way of teaching, and makes dark things more clear to the understanding, and best to be retained in the memory. Our blessed Saviour (the great Prophet and teacher of his Church, who spake as never a man spake) he taught much by similitudes."[45] Austen enumerated twenty propositions in the 1653 edition that he considered were "shadowed out unto us by observations in nature, and cleared by Scripture and experience."[46] His twenty propositions are classified as follows:

[41] Austen, *The Spiritual Use of an Orchard*, 4–5.

[42] Austen, *The Spiritual Use of an Orchard*, 4.

[43] "Images of Divine Things," *WJE*, 11:74.

[44] Austen, *The Spiritual Use of an Orchard*, 4.

[45] Austen, *The Spiritual Use of an Orchard*, 6.

[46] Austen's rich emblematic reading of fruit trees compares favorably to Edwards exegesis of the rainbow in Gen. 9:12-17 from which he extracts sixteen doctrinal teachings including the

God's election and providence are addressed in the first five proposi-tions. 1) He begins by noting that the notion of God's sovereign election is shown by his function as Husbandman, who chooses and refuses plants at his discretion.[47] 2) God is gentler with weak Christians than with mature and strong Christians.[48] 3) The Husbandman inspects fruit carefully and distinguishes between good and bad.[49] 4) Grafts and stocks of contrary or opposing natures will not thrive together or yield healthy fruit. Many couples who are unequally yoked in marriage have this unfortunate experience.[50] 5) God usually calls and grafts in his people while they are young and tender.[51] The first five propositions proclaim God's sovereignty and electing grace. Yet, Austen finds God's loving care and sympathy toward his weaker children in the work of a husbandman. Pastoral concerns are clear in the encouragement to marry within the faith for unity and peace, as well as the hope of growing grace and delight in God.

The following three propositions address what are known as seasons of the Spirit. 6) When the Holy Spirit departs, the spiritual plants endure a period of dormancy and seeming fruitlessness.[52] 7) Spiritual trees that focus on external appearances (blossoms=works) frequently have little energy left over to create true fruit.[53] 8) The fruit of a spiritual tree can be identified.[54] 9) Some people, like blooms, make a profession for a time before falling off

persons and work of the Trinity, the nature of man, and the work of redemption. "Notes on Scripture," *WJE*, 15:329–35. See also entries 55 and 58 in "Images of Divine Things," and "Miscellanies" 362 and 370.

[47] Austen, *The Spiritual Use of an Orchard*, 1–2.

[48] Austen, *The Spiritual Use of an Orchard*, 2–4.

[49] Austen, *The Spiritual Use of an Orchard*, 4–5.

[50] Austen, *The Spiritual Use of an Orchard*, 5–6.

[51] Austen, *The Spiritual Use of an Orchard*, 6–11.

[52] Austen, *The Spiritual Use of an Orchard*, 11–15. Edwards observes the same emblem in entry 108 of "Images of Divine Things." "Now this is remarkable of wheat and other bread-corn: that it is sown and grows before winter, and then is as it were killed, and long lies dead in the winter season, and then revives in the spring and grows much taller than before, and comes to perfection and brings forth fruit; which is a lively image of the resurrection of saints— as well the grain's being first buried in the earth and dying there before it comes up— and that often comes to pass, concerning the saints in this life, that is livelily represented by it. After their conversion they have falling away, and long continue in a cold and dead carnal state, and then revive again and grow much taller than before, and never fail again till they bring fruit to perfection." "Images of Divine Things," *WJE*, 11:91–92.

[53] Austen, *The Spiritual Use of an Orchard*, 16–17.

[54] Austen, *The Spiritual Use of an Orchard*, 17–19.

and becoming nothing.[55] Austen sees fruit trees as teaching lessons on the saint's absolute dependence on God's grace, as well as the futility of relying on past experiences of grace for present comfort and strength. Saints can expect periods when God appears to hide his face and gracious comforts, and they should spiritually prepare for such spiritual winters. Not mere rituals, but a genuine religion of the heart, should be prioritized. One's limited time and energy should be directed on producing fruit.

The following four propositions take spiritual struggle and walking with God principles from fruit trees. 10) We must aim our wants and wills toward the best fruits and graces.[56] 11) While our spiritual nature is strong, our flesh is weak.[57] 12) The closer a tree's branches are to its root, the stronger it is.[58] 13) Just as the two natures of the tree and graft coexist as long as they live, the sin nature lives on in a believer until he dies.[59] Austen recognizes that the road of faith necessitates perseverance and efforts to walk closely with God, seeking the highest gifts and graces, and maintaining constant vigilance against fleshly temptations. "Let us labor for the increase of Grace, for as that grows, Corruption wasteth, or is kept under."[60]

In the next two propositions, Austen emphasizes that true glory is found in the image of God. As one grows into the likeness of Christ, one grows in excellency. 14) The worth of a fruit tree is determined not by its appearance or the spread of its branches and leaves, but by its ability to produce fruit (holiness).[61]

> 15) In material fruit-trees there is a close, and firm knot between the stock, and the graft, whereby they are joined fast together, and made one body; which knot, and conjunction continues, and holds fast, as long as the tree lives.

> This observation shadows out unto us that there is a firm and constant union between Christ and every believer.[62]

---

[55] Austen, *The Spiritual Use of an Orchard,* 19–20.

[56] Austen, *The Spiritual Use of an Orchard,* 20–22.

[57] Austen, *The Spiritual Use of an Orchard,* 22–24.

[58] Austen, *The Spiritual Use of an Orchard,* 24–25.

[59] Austen, *The Spiritual Use of an Orchard,* 25–26.

[60] Austen, *The Spiritual Use of an Orchard,* 26.

[61] Austen, *The Spiritual Use of an Orchard,* 26–27.

[62] Austen, *The Spiritual Use of an Orchard,* 27–28.

Austen had harsh words for "University men" while living in Oxford. Austen compares an educational institution to a nursery, noting that 16) fruit trees do not get old in nurseries, and that Christians should mature and go out in service of the church, rather than selfishly seeking out "Fellowships in Colledges" for life.[63] He also notices in observation 17) that fruit trees never lose their innate nature, but rather keep it for the rest of their lives. Men, similarly, do not lose God's grace once it has been bestowed.[64] 18) God, as Husbandman, prefers to employ sharp tools but discards dull ones.[65] A sharp (well-prepared) and devoted saint brings the Lord gladness.

The latter two propositions inspire the saint to find solace in God's ultimate purposes. Though mysterious, the difficulties of this life are eventually for our good. 19) For the benefit and fruitfulness of his spiritual trees, God prunes them.[66] Finally, 20) just as a stock and graft become one, Christ becomes one with those who are ingrafted into him.[67] Being a partaker of the divine nature is the highest privilege a Christian has this side of heaven, and it should serve as a strong incentive to yield fruit abundantly.

Austen closes with a hint of a far larger number of parallels, over a hundred, but he believed it best to make his initial analysis brief and discuss only the necessary.[68] Edwards' exegesis of the rainbow reveals a parallel of similar profundity to Austen's depth of vision into fruit trees as a single volume in the vast library of creation.[69]

John Bunyan

John Bunyan is probably the most well-known evangelical adherent to the emblematic world view. Bunyan was born into a humble family, received no formal education, and followed in his father's footsteps as a tinker. Bunyan joined the Parliamentary Army at the age of sixteen and served from 1644 until 1647. Bunyan married his first wife shortly after leaving the army. From

---

[63] Austen, *The Spiritual Use of an Orchard*, 28–31.

[64] Austen, *The Spiritual Use of an Orchard*, 31–35.

[65] Austen, *The Spiritual Use of an Orchard*, 35–36.

[66] Austen, *The Spiritual Use of an Orchard*, 36–38.

[67] Austen, *The Spiritual Use of an Orchard*, 38–40.

[68] Austen, *The Spiritual Use of an Orchard*, 41.

[69] "Notes on Scripture," *WJE*, 15:329–35.

1649 to 1655, they lived in Elstow until his wife died. He then moved from Elstow to Bedford, where he married his second wife in 1659.

Bunyan was baptized by immersion into the Baptist church in Bedford in 1653. He clearly had ministerial potential, and he immediately began to serve as a deacon and occasional preacher. Bunyan's ministerial efforts were a resounding success. Though the authorities tolerated Bunyan's preaching, he was convicted in 1658 for not having a legal license and imprisoned from 1660 to 1672.

During his confinement, Bunyan was able to compose some of his most famous works. *Grace Abounding to the Chief of Sinners* (1666), his spiritual autobiography, was written during his first imprisonment, and part one of *Pilgrim's Progress* (1678) was begun in 1676 during a second brief imprisonment. Despite the fact that Bunyan penned a number of books and treatises, *Pilgrim's Progress* was his most successful work.

Bunyan, like Ralph Austen, saw the Word, the world, and experience as revelatory.[70] According to Bunyan, a human can only correctly comprehend the world when it is viewed as a shadowy version of the real world to come:

> I find that holy Writ in many places hath semblance with this method, where the cases do one call for one thing, to set forth another; use it I mean then, and yet nothing smother Truth's golden Beams; Nay, by this method may make it cast forth its rays as light as day.[71]

Physical birth, for example, is a type of true spiritual birth. Valleys, hills, castles, swamps, caves, chained lions, spiders, dust, water, cages, battles, rivers, and many more elements in this visible world all represented spiritual reality in *Pilgrim's Progress*. Roger Sharrock, a noted Bunyan scholar, noticed that Bunyan's iconography was heavily influenced by the realm of

---

[70]Thomas H. Luxon, *Literal Figures: Puritan Allegory and the Reformation Crisis in Representation* (Chicago: University of Chicago Press, 1995), 141–42 "Bunyan uses allegory to present his experience of Scripture, what would otherwise be "other mens words," as particular instances of Scripture speaking directly to him. Bunyan presents his knowledge of Scripture in *Grace Abounding* as a knowledge attained not by reading, nor by hearing, but by unuttered and unutterable revelations. And his favorite allegorical model for such experience is physical violence, often imaged as painful physical violence. . .The iconoclastic attitude Calvin reserves for images Bunyan extends to language itself, and so finds himself thrust into, or as he put it in *The Pilgrim's Progress*, fallen into, the imagistic language of allegory."

[71]John Bunyan, *The Pilgrim's Progress* (Westwood, NJ: Barbour, 1970), xi.

emblem books, the most important of which being Quarles' publications.[72] In *Solomon's Temple Spiritualized* (1688), Bunyan stated unequivocally that it is the wisdom of God to communicate with us often through trees, gold, silver, stones, animals, birds, fish, spiders, ants, frogs, flies, lice, dust and wood.[73] Bunyan, like Edwards, believes that emblems within the created order are revelatory.

> 'Tis very fit and becoming of God, who is infinitely wise, so to order things that there should be a voice of his in his works instructing those that behold them, and pointing forth and show-ing divine mysteries and things more immediately appertaining to himself and his spiritual kingdom. The works of God are but a kind of voice or language of God, to instruct intelligent beings in things pertaining to himself. And why should we not think that he would teach and instruct by his works in this way as well as others, viz. by representing divine things by his works, and so pointing them forth, especially since we know that God hath so much delighted in this way of instruction.[74]

Bunyan's reference to the language of Canaan in *Pilgrim's Progress* sheds light on the importance of metaphorical knowledge and discourse.

> And as they wondered at their apparel, so they did likewise as their speech; for few could understand what they said; they naturally spoke the language of Canaan; but they that kept the Fair were the men of this World: So that from one end of the Fair to the other, they seemed barbarians each to the other.[75]

The language of Canaan was understood to be the prophetic and metaphor-ical language of the Bible, which God's elect used to speak of God's kingdom

---

[72]Roger Sharrock, "Bunyan and the English Emblem Writers," The *Review of English Studies* 21 (1945): 105–6.

[73]John Bunyan and George Offor, "Solomon's Temple Spiritualized," in *The Whole Works of John Bunyan* (Grand Rapids: Baker, 1982), 3:500.

[74]"Images of Divine Things," *WJE*, 11:67. Bunyan also notes the appropriateness of such revelation. "And if some better handle can a fly, than some a text, why should we then deny their making proof, or good experiment, of smallest things, great mischiefs to prevent? . . . I think the wiser sort my rhymes may slight, but what care I, the foolish will delight to read them, and the foolish God has chose, and doth by foolish things their minds compose, and settle upon that which is divine; great things, by little ones, are made to shine." John Bunyan, *Divine Emblems, or, Temporal Things Spiritualized,* (London: Bickers & Son, 1867) xvi.

[75]Bunyan, *The Pilgrim's Progress,* 100.

and its eschatological realization. The people, events, and experiences in the Bible correspond to the personal experiences of living believers in a true way. Increase Mathers' exposition of the City of God in his book *A Discourse Concerning Faith and Fervency in Prayer and the Glorious Kingdom of the Lord Jesus Christ* (1710) is an example of this metaphorical and emblematic language. Mason Lowance observes that Mather used a figural sensibility to bring Scripture into current relevance.[76]

> They of the City, viz., the Citizens of Jerusalem, who are a synec-doche put forth for all the Subjects of the Kingdom, Shall Flour-ish Like the Grass of the Earth, they shall increase and become very numerous and very happy. All these Expressions are used Emblematically to set forth the success of the Gospel, and the wonderful growth and flourishing of Christ's Kingdom.[77]

Traditionally, the language of Canaan was limited to the confines of Scripture alone, which served as a source of figurative and literal examples and illustrated God's providential intervention in human affairs.[78] There was no license to discover emblems in the created order, as Bunyan, Hall, Austen, and Edwards had argued. The biblical matrix established historical continuity between biblical events and the Puritan experience.[79]

Bunyan had amassed enough emblems at the end of his life to warrant the printing of an emblem book. Bunyan opens *Divine Emblems, or, Temporal Things Spiritualized,* also known as *A Book for Boys and Girls,* by warning the

---

[76]Mason I. Lowance, *The Language of Canaan: Metaphor and Symbol in New England from the Puritans to the Trancendentalists* (Cambridge: Harvard University Press, 1980), 144.

[77]Increase Mather, *A Discourse Concerning Faith and Fervency in Prayer and the Glorious Kingdom of the Lord Jesus Christ,* (1710), 14. Cited in Lowance, *The Language of Canaan,* 144.

[78]Samuel Mather, *The Figures or Types of the Old Testament* (London: Printed for N. Hillier, 1705). Mather notes that "[s]ometimes the types are not explicitly taught, but implyed; and then a thing may be known to be a type by diligently observing and comparing the phrase of the prophets in the Old Testament, and of the apostles in the New. Men must not indulge their own fancies, as the Popish writers use to do, with their allegorical senses, as they call them; except we have some Scripture ground for it. It is not safe to make anything a type meerly upon our own fancies and imaginations; it is God's prerogative to make types (55)." See also Thomas M. Davis, Sacvan Bercovitch, ed., "The Traditions of Puritan Typology," in *Typology and Early American Literature* (Amherst: University of Massachussetts Press, 1972), 11-45.

[79]Lowance, *The Language of Canaan,* 61. "[W]riters and thinkers like Samuel Mather, Increase Mather, Benjamin Keach, and John Davenport attempted to hold together a world view, a method of exegesis, a way of reading history, and an epistemology in their monumental efforts to assert the efficacy of typology and biblical figuralism in a period that was falling away from a belief in the active relevance of Scripture for its own historical circumstances."

reader that, while his emblem book's intended audience is "boys and girls,"
he must add a caveat or two:

> They're boys and girls, of all sorts and degrees,
> From those of age to children on the knees.
> Thus comprehensive am I in my notions,
> They tempt me to it by their childish motions.
> We now have boys with beards, and girls that be
> Huge as old women, wanting gravity.[80]

> They do not blame me, I thus describe 'em,
> Flatter I may not, left thereby I bribe them
> To have a better judgment of themselves,
> That wise men have of babies on shelves.
> Their antic tricks, fantastic modes and way
> Shew they like very boys and girls do play
> With all the frantic fooleries of the age,
> And that in open view, as on a stage;
> Our bearded men do act like beardless boys,
> Our women please themselves with childish toys ...[81]

> Wise Solomon did fools to pismires send,
> To learn true wisdom, and their lives to mend.
> Yea, God by swallows, cuckows, and the ass,
> Shews they are fools, who let that season pass,
> Which he put in their hands, that to obtain,
> Which is both present and eternal gain.[82]

Some of Bunyan's emblems are particularly striking, such as when he
compares the mole to a worldly person who is entirely focused on earthly
concerns.

---

[80]Rosemary Freeman writes that "Bunyan published a set of emblems intended not for adult readers but for the amusement and the moral and religious instruction of the young." Yet Bunyan explicitly targets foolish adults, and cites Solomon's exhortation to seek wisdom from ants as a biblical precedent and authorization for using the Book of Nature. Rosemary Freeman, *English Emblem Books* (New York: Octagon Books, 1966), 204.

[81]Pleasure and delight, according to Edwards, are experienced by God when he communicates emblematically. "God hath so much delighted in this way of instruction." "Images of Divine Things," *WJE,* 11:67.

[82]John Bunyan, *Divine Emblems, or, Temporal Things Spiritualized* (London: Bickers & Son, 1867), iii, v.

OF THE MOLE IN THE GROUND

The mole's a creature very smooth and slick,
She digs i' th' dirt, but 'twill not on her stick;
So's he who counts this world his greatest gains,
Yet nothing gets but's labour for his pains.
Earth's the mole's element, she can't abide
To be above ground, dirt heaps are her pride;
And he is like her who the worldling plays,
He imitates her in her work and ways.
Poor silly mole, that thou should'st love to be
Where thou nor sun, nor moon, nor stars can see.

But O! How silly's he who doth not care
So he gets earth, to have of heaven a share![83]

Bunyan's emblem of a fruit tree corresponds to both Edwards' and Austen's ideas. The fundamental points are the same: a large number of blooms, those that fall away, and those that ripen with good works.

UPON THE PROMISING FRUITFULNESS OF A TREE

A comely sight indeed it is to see
A world of blossoms on an apple-tree:
Yet far more comely would this tree appear,
If all its dainty blooms young apples were.
But how much more might one upon it see,
If all would hang there till they ripe should be.
But most of all in beauty 'twould abound,

---

[83] Bunyan, *Divine Emblems, or, Temporal Things Spiritualized*, 39. Edwards includes a brief entry on the mole. "Images of Divine Things," *WJE*, 11:118. Edward's entry is actually a brief quote from John Spencer's *Things Old and New*. "Tostatus observeth out of Pliny, that the mole, after he hath long lived under ground, beginneth to see when he dieth: *oculos incipit aperire moriendo, quos clauso habuit vivendo* : he beginneth to open his eyes in dying, which he always had shut whilst he lived. This is the true state of a wicked earthly-minded man, he neither seeth heaven, nor thinketh of hell: tell him that the wicked shall be turned into hell, and all that forget God; it is but as *brutum fulmen*, a mere scare-crow, he feareth not God nor man all his life-time, till he approacheth to judgment, and then too soon he beginneth to feel that which he could not be brought to believe." In a footnote Spencer cites Psa 9:17 and English emblem writer, Andrew Willet. John Spencer, *Things New and Old: Or, A Storehouse of Similes, Sentences, Allegories, Apophthegms, Adages, Apologues, Divine, Moral, Political, &c., with Their Several Applications. Collected and Observed from the Writings and Sayings of the Learned in All Ages to This Present* (London: William Tegg, 1869) 125–26.

If then non worm-eaten should there be found.
But we, alas! do commonly behold
Blooms fall apace, if mornings be but cold.
They to, which hang till they young apples are,
By blasing winds and vermin take despair,
Store that do hang, while almost ripe, we see
By blust'ring winds are shaken from the tree,
So that of many, only some there be,
That grow till they come to maturity.

Comparison

This tree a perfect emblem is of those
Which God doth plant, which in his garden grows,
Its blasted blooms are motions unto good,
Which chill affections do nip in the bud.
Those little apples which yet blasted are,
Show some good purposes, no good fruits bear.
Those spoiled by vermin are to let us see,
How good attempts by bad thoughts ruin'd be.
Those which the wind blows down, while they are green,
Show good works have by trials spoiled been.
Those that abide, while ripe upon the tree,
Show, in a good man, some ripe fruit will be.
Behold then how abortive some fruits are,
Which at the first most promising appear.
The frost, the wind, the worm, and time doth show,
There flows, from much appearance, works but few.[84]

Bunyan's emblem book deviated from the emblem book genre in some ways. It was a "blind" emblem book because it lacked pictures.[85] "Images of Divine Things" by Edwards follows the same design as a blind emblem book, albeit it has not been classified as such to date. However, as previously said, Edwards' notebook compares favorably to Joseph Hall's *Occasional Meditations,* which is regarded as a source of Protestant emblematic reflection. The world offered the emblems for Hall, Austen, Bunyan, and Edwards,

[84]Bunyan, *Divine Emblems, or, Temporal Things Spiritualized,* 45–47.

[85]Huston Diehl, *An Index of Icons in English Emblem Books, 1550–1700* (Norman, OK: University of Oklahoma Press, 1986), 3.

while the books provided the explication and interpretation based on the Scriptures and the analogy of faith.

Benjamin Keach

Keach was an emblematic theologian as well as a Particular Baptist pastor in seventeenth-century England. Keach is best known for his pioneering contributions to Baptist hymnody, but he was also a prolific producer of polemical works on a wide range of doctrinal topics in Baptist theology and practice. His contributions to emblematic studies have been highlighted in a work by Tibor Fabiny and a PhD dissertation by James Holmes.[86]

Tropologia

Tropologia (1681), Keach's magnum opus, is practically a systematic theology in its scope.[87] The emblematic aspect of Keach's work merits more investigation. James Leo Garrett acknowledges in his *Baptist Theology: A Four Century Study,*

> Like and even prior to Bunyan, he [Keach] employed allegory and his imagination in the writing of books on the Christian life ... produced a detailed study of Jesus' parables, coauthored a study of biblical metaphors, and refuted Quakers, the Roman Catholic Church, and the sabbatarian teaching of Seventh-Day Baptists ... The theological significance, however, of Keach's work is to be found chiefly in three areas: Baptist ecclesiology, Calvinistic soteriology, and congregational hymn singing.[88]

However, when one analyzes the pedagogical connection between *Tropologia* and his hymnal *Sacred Melody*, it is reasonable to reconsider the significance of Keach's emblematic theology.

Keach, like Austen, emphasized the revelatory richness of horticulture. Keach identifies four characteristics of a husbandman in *Tropologia*. "A

---

[86]Tibor Fabiny, "Edwards and Biblical Typology," in *Understanding Jonathan Edwards: An Introduction to America's Theologian,* ed. Gerald McDermott (New York: Oxford University Press, 2008). James Christopher Holmes, "The Role of Metaphor in the Sermons of Benjamin Keach, 1640–1704" (Ph.D. diss., The Southern Baptist Theological Seminary, 2009).

[87]Holmes, "The Role of Metaphor in the Sermons of Benjamin Keach, 1640–1704," 93.

[88]James Leo Garrett, Baptist Theology: A Four-Century Study (Macon, Ga.: Mercer University Press, 2009), 83–84.

Husbandman must have ground to work upon." He must have "a stock to defray the charges and requisite to manage it." He must have the "[s]kill and knowledge to perform it." And he must have "[i]nstruments, and whatsoever else is needful for such an undertaking, or employment."[89]

Keach concluded that God is a husbandman because "he is a rich Husbandman; for all the world is his—'the earth is the Lord's,' and so on." God is also a "great and honorable Husbandman; for all bow before him." The Father is a "skillful and wise Husbandman; for no neglect can be charged against him," as well as a "skilful and wise Husbandman; for none can teach him." Finally, God is described as a "generous and liberal Husbandman, for all partake of his bounty."[90]

Keach pulls thirty-four specific illustrations from the life and work of a husbandman and his relationship to his orchards and gardens from the overall metaphor of God as husbandman. The following is an example of a metaphor and its analogies.

METAPHOR

A Husbandman takes much pains to weed his gardens and prune his trees, and if he finds the weeds come up thick, especially such as are of a hurtful and mischievous kind, he uses all the way and proper means to destroy them, lest they should spoil the fruit of his garden, field, or vinyard, &c. Yet, notwithstanding, some relics of the old roots are left, which are apt to spring up afresh, unless continually cropt off and kept short.[91]

PARALLEL

The heavenly Husbandman bestows much pains that he may destroy the weeds of indwelling sin and corruption in his people. He uses various means, as his Word and Holy Spirit, trials, afflictions, &c., in order to that end; by these he digs up those weeds by the roots, as worldly-mindedness, unbelief, and sensual lusts, which else would choke the good seed. Though some remains of them that are left behind, (to keep us humble and watchful) such

---

[89]Benjamin Keach, *Tropologia: A Key to Open Scripture Metaphors..: To Which Are Prefixed, Arguments to Prove the Divine Authority of the Holy Bible: Together with Types of the Old Testament* (London: William Hill Collingridge, 1856), 254.

[90]Keach, *Tropologia*, 254.

[91]In addition, Edwards sees an appropriate time to weed (practice church discipline): after it has rained (an outpouring of the Holy Spirit) when the ground is soft, the weeds can be safely pulled up without damaging the good plants. "Images of Divine Things," *WJE*, 11:127.

ill weeds grow apace, and are ready to spring up when the least liberty is given. Heb. Xii. 15. By these also this blessed Husbandman prunes and pares off suckers or superfluous branches, which feed upon that sap which should nourish his tender plants, such are, carnal divisions, strife and unnecessary contention among saints, busying themselves about idle and unprofitable notions, or matters of slender consequence, neglecting in the mean time those serious and practical parts of Christianity which are of absolute and undoubted necessity: these are the spiritual suckers of our time, and are the cause that so many lean and barren souls are found in this spiritual vineyard.[92]

Keach continues his series of metaphors about God as a husbandman with a number of corollaries. First, Keach argued that the metaphor emphasized God's "wonderful condescension of the great and almighty God in comparing himself to an Husbandman, an employment of great toil and very hard labour, yet profitable and honest." Second, the metaphor reveals the church's tremendous dignity and privilege as the "plantation of God, in which he takes great delight; the rest of the world being like a barren and howling wilderness to it—'Woe is me that I sojourn in Mesech and dwell in the tents of Kedar,' Psal. Cxx. 5." Third, the metaphor emphasizes the "necessity of being grafted into this vineyard: a bare profession will not do, as in the foolish virgin's case— He has a quick eye, and will soon find out such as bear no fruit, or are rotten at heart, such he cuts down and burns." Fourth, Keach sees the metaphor as a "cause of joy to those that are truly implanted into Jesus Christ, they are under his special care and watch, they shall flourish, and bring forth fruit in old age—walled in on every side, and so very safe, John xv. 2, Psalm. Xcii. 13, 14."[93]

Sacred Melody

Keach, most recognized for his involvement in the emergence of hymn-singing, also utilized songs to teach his figurative theology. Keach writes in his letter to the reader of *Spiritual Melody*,

It may not be unnecessary if I acquaint thee with the chief design of my publishing these Sacred Hymns . . . Such who like

[92]Keach, *Tropologia,* 257.

[93]Keach, *Tropologia,* 260.

and approve of Books in Verse which treat Divine Things, and would gladly have a little help in order to the understanding of Metaphorical Scripture; who cannot also well spare so much Money as to purchase larger Volumes; the Folio I put forth some years ago, call'd, *A Key to open Scripture Metaphors*, being near Twenty Shillings price, comes into but a very few Peoples hands: Besides, the Impression will soon be gone (as far as I can gather) and tis not like to be reprinted any more. Now in this small Tract I can assure you is contained great part of the principal things under divers Metaphors opened in that Book, though they are there more largely insisted on.

Parents and Masters of Families, I am persuaded, with the Blessing of God, this Book may prove of great advantage to their Children, who generally are taken with Verse, and are much addicted to learn such Songs and Ballads which generally to to corrupt Youth; and 'tis a shame to godly Christians they should suffer their Children to learn many of them; but since Singing is God's Ordinance, I mean, to sing Psalms, and Hymns, and Spiritual Songs, 'tis doubtless their duty to instruct them therein, as well as to teach them to read; and by learning Sacred Hymns, they may be taken, before their Parents are aware, with the Matter therein contained (as divers have, through the Blessing of God, as I have been oft inform'd, by reading that smal Poem, called *War with the Devil,*) and some others. Youth are generally inclin'd to Poetry, and as one of the Ancients excellently observes, The Holy Ghost seeing the Souls of Mankind strugling in the way of Godliness, and being inclined to the Delights of this Live, hath mixed the power of his Doctrine with sweet Singing, that whilst the Soul was melted with the sweetness of the Verse, the Divine Word might the better be grafted with profit.

Now these Hymns being short, Children will soon get them by heart, as also full of varieties, and if instructed to sing, they may be the more affected with the matter, and receive the greater advantage.[94]

Keach noted the human love of poetry, metaphors, and song, as well as their teaching potential. It was a brilliant idea to merge figurative (emblem-

---

[94]Benjamin Keach, *Spiritual Melody* (London: Printed for John Hancock in Castle-Alley, 1691), 2–5.

atic) theology and singing into an economically accessible form, a hymn book, and use it for the building up of the church.

Cotton Mather

Cotton Mather (1663–1728) is an example of an emblematicist encountering the early Enlightenment. Cotton Mather's synthesis of John Flavel's spiritualizing of nature and a conservative biblical typology, according to Mason Lowance, contributed to his "sense that underneath the natural universe there lies a spiritual significance that wants explanation."[95] Lowance suggests Mather laid the groundwork for Edwards to "make full use of the synthesis between natural and scriptural relevation."[96] As a result, a quick consideration of Mather's sense of the spiritual meaning of the natural cosmos will be beneficial, especially since Mather, like Joseph Hall, practices occasional meditation.[97]

Cotton Mather believed that Christ, God's Wisdom, exists as the archetype of all wisdom shown throughout creation. "Whenever we see the Wisdom of God admirably shining before us, we are invited to such a thought as this; this glory is originally to be found in thee, O our Emmanuel!"[98] Creation functions as a teacher in Christ's school. Mather goes on:

> When in a way of occasional Reflection I employ the Creatures as my Teachers, I will by the Truths wherein those ready Monitors instruct me, be led to my glorious JESUS; I will consider the Truths as they are in JESUS, and count my Asceticks deficient, till I have some Thoughts of HIM and of His Glories awakened in me... If we mind Heaven whilst we live here on Earth, this Earth will serve to conduct us to Heaven, thro the Merits and Mediation of the Son of God, who was made the Son of Man, and came thence on purpose into this lower World to convey us up thither.[99]

[95] Lowance, *The Language of Canaan*, 176–77.

[96] Lowance, *The Language of Canaan*, 177.

[97] Mather's occasional reflections on fire compare strikingly with those of Edwards and others found in Part Two of this volume. See Mather's "Meditations on Fire" in Cotton Mather, et al., *A Cotton Mather Reader* (New Haven: Yale University Press, 2022), 23–38.

[98] Cotton Mather, *The Christian Philosopher*, ed. Winton U. Solberg (Chicago: University of Illinois Press, 1994), 315.

[99] Mather, *The Christian Philosopher*, 317.

Mather's short treatise on sacred thunder is a great example of his spiritual sense of nature. In 1695, Mather published *Brontologia Sacra* anonymously. This treatise on thunder demonstrates a careful approach to natural providences in that the phenomenon of thunder is closely linked to a scriptural exegesis. The treatise was inspired by the abrupt onset of a thunderstorm during a time of worship. Mather, moved by the idea of making devotional use of the storm, threw aside his prepared lecture and "ventured upon an extemporaneous contemplation of the thunder."[100] "Thunder was directed by the God of Heaven to fall with very tearing, tho'no killing effect, upon his own house,"[101] he decided at the same time. Because of the event's providential timing, his audience "found a sensible edge" to his reflections. "The Thunder being a thing that often entertains us," Mather writes, "it was thought that it would be no disservice unto the Church of God, if a few such reflections were offered unto the publick for the entertainment of the serious."[102]

Mather draws the attention of his audience to Psalm 29:3, "The Voice of the Lord is upon the Waters, and the God of Glory Thundereth." Mather felt it was appropriate to draw spiritual teachings about God's voice in nature from this passage. "What is the voice of the glorious God in thunder?"[103] he asks. During this meditation, Jesus expounds on several distinct divine voices that can be heard amid a thunderstorm. First and foremost, Mather acknowledges that thunder is a truly magnificent work of God. Having said that, he admits that thunder is a natural event governed by the "Common Laws of Matter and Motion."[104] Mather acknowledges that God may utilize the agency of angels to create thunderstorms because they are described in the Bible as flames of fire. Though angels may be involved in thunder, they are merely tools in God's hands. Whether through the instrumentality of angels or directly from the mouth of God, thunder should not strike fear in those who are in covenant with God. Mather tells the story of a "Profane Persecutor" who was terrified by a thunderstorm while traveling. Noticing his Christian wife's lack of fear, he questioned her why she was not terrified,

---

[100] Cotton Mather, *Brontologia Sacra: The Voice of the Glorious God in Thunder* (London: Printed by John Astwood, 1695), i.

[101] Mather, *Brontologia Sacra*, i.

[102] Mather, *Brontologia Sacra*, i–ii.

[103] Mather, *Brontologia Sacra*, 5.

[104] Mather, *Brontologia Sacra*, 5.

to which she replied, "I know 'tis the voice of my Heavenly Father; and shall a Child be afraid of a Kind Father's Voice?"[105] Mather observes:

> Thunder also declares the glory and power of God. With thunder God routes armies, shakes the mountains, and strikes down the proud. No man can stand against the thunder of the Lord. Thunder also carries a message of God's wrath. People most often experience fear of thunderstorms because they may suspect their own Souls to stand before and Angry God. Their Consciences tell them that their Sins are yet unpardoned, that their Hearts are yet unrenewed, that their Title to Blessedness is yet unsettled, and that if the next Thunder-clap shoud strike them Dead, it had been good for them that they had never been Born.[106]

God's thunder is an unequivocal invitation to repentance and rebirth. Mather told his audience about a miraculous event that occurred thirteen years before. There was a loud clap of thunder in the middle of a storm. A mariner's compass he kept in his house responded strangely to the clap. The arrow, which normally pointed north, abruptly changed direction and has been pointing south ever since.[107]

"It is a vulgar Error, that the Thunder never kills any who are asleep,"[108] Mather adds. He exhorts his audience to recognize that thunder calls people to remember their sins and to fear the possibility of sudden execution, as Nadab and Abihu, Uzzah, Korah, and others did. Thunder strikes horror into the soul, serving as a potent reminder to fear and follow God. It is also important to remember to thank God that thunder and lightning cause no more harm than they do. God is kind and withholds his anger from time to time, but this will not always be the case. Satan, like the angels, can play a role in the creation of thunder.[109]

Mather's "Barbarism"

The cathedral of the world encompasses not only the heavens above and the earth beneath, but also horrible things that are better hidden beneath the

[105]Mather, *Brontologia Sacra*, 7.

[106]Mather, *Brontologia Sacra*, 9.

[107]Mather, *Brontologia Sacra*, 11.

[108]Mather, *Brontologia Sacra*, 12.

[109]Mather, *Brontologia Sacra*, 12–14.

earth. A comparison of Edwards' and Cotton Mather's meditations reveals similar insights but a major difference in sensitivities. According to Richard Lovelace, Mather's occasionally flawed poetic imagination "would often emerge with similes and tropes that were unconsciously grotesque."[110] Edwards demonstrated a sophisticated poetic sensibility to the point of genius, forcefully proposing a parabolic vision of nature shared by Jesus himself.[111] Edwards' reflections on the same subject of human filth and baseness show evidence of this refinement:

> The inside of the body of man is full of filthiness, contains his bowels that are full of dung, which represents the corruptions and filthiness that the heart of man is naturally full of. See [no.] 115.[112]

> Man's inwards are full of dung and filthiness, which is to denote what the inner man, which is often represented by various parts of his inwards—sometimes the heart, sometimes the bowels, sometimes the belly, sometimes the veins—is full of: spiritual corruption and abomination. So as there are many foldings and turnings in the bowels, it denotes the great and manifold intricacies, secret windings and turnings, shifts, wiles and deceits that are in their hearts. See [no.] 109; Prov. 20:27, 18:8, 26:22, 20:30 and 22:18.[113]

Edwards' observation is not exceptionally insensitive or obnoxious. He does not allude to himself or dive into superfluous explanations; rather, he simply states facts, perceives correspondences, and concludes that the inward twisting of the intestines and the nasty stuff carried is emblematic of man's deceitful and filthy inward nature. Mather, unlike Edwards, had a less delicate way of conveying spiritual truths, and he usually erred on the side of earthiness. One example from Mather's diary on the same topic as Edwards' notebook entries above is from July 1700:

> From my Youth it has been my Frequent, my Daily practice, to make occasional Reflections, or, from Occasions which I have

---

[110]Richard F. Lovelace, *The American Pietism of Cotton Mather: Origins of American Evangelicalism* (Grand Rapids, MI: Christian University Press, 1979), 120.

[111]Lovelace, *The American Pietism of Cotton Mather*, 120.

[112]Images of Divine Things," *WJE*, 11:92.

[113]Images of Divine Things," *WJE*, 11:95.

seen in Occurrences before me, to raise Thoughts of Piety, and these mostly by finding Similitudes to assist and excite such Thoughts in those Occurrences.

These occasional Reflections do not only serve me very commonly, to carry on useful Conferences, made savoury with some little sort of Witt, when I am in Company; but they are also a delightful Entertainment unto me, when I am alone.

But at length, I saw, I had one Opportunity every Day for such occasional Reflections, as it might not be amiss for me, to oblige myself, rarely to lett pass me, without them. I was once emptying the Cistern of Nature, and making Water at the Wall. At the same Time, there came a Dog who did so too, before me. Thought I; "What mean, and vile Things are the Children of Men, in this mortal State! How much do our natural Necessities abase us, and place us in some regard, on the same Level with the very Dogs!"

My Thought proceeded. "Yett I will be a more noble Creature; and at the very Time, when my natural Necessities debase me into the Condition of the Beast, my Spirit shall (I say, at that very Time!) rise and soar, and fly up, towards the Employment of the Angel."

Accordingly, I resolved, that it should be my ordinary Practice, whenever I step to answer the one or other Necessities of Nature, to make it an Opportunity of shaping in my Mind, some holy, noble, divine Thought; usually, by way of occasional Reflection on some sensible Object which I either then have before me, or have lately had so: a Thought that may leave upon my Spirit, some further Tincture of Piety!

And I have done according to this Resolution!

Be sure, the loathsome and filthy Nature of SIN, and the Method of Deliverance from it, must make an Article, in some Thousands of Thoughts, on these Occasions.[114]

---

[114]Cotton Mather, *Diary of Cotton Mather* (New York: Frederick Ungar Publishing Co., 1957), 1:356–57. Mather describes his rational for the timing and method of his devotional practices: "There are with me, in common with all the Children of Men, the usual Evacuations of Nature, to be daily attended. I would not only improve the Time which these call for, to form some Thoughts of Piety, wherein I may differ from the Brutes, (which in the Actions themselves I do very little) and this I have usually already done; but I would now more particularly

His theological insights on man's kinship with creatures include a kernel of truth, but the style of meditation is rather earthy. A comparison of Mather and Edwards demonstrates that their conclusions are substantially the same, yet Edwards is far more convincing in communicating spiritual truths since he is more fluent in the language of parables and types than Mather. Both Edwards and Mather use a mundane event as the focus of their meditation, but Edwards is more graceful, precise, and economical with words. Edwards' remark of "barbarous expressions that fail entirely of the proper beauty of the language, that are very harsh in the ears"[115] is exemplified by Mather's emblematic and occasional pondering. Edwards' aesthetic sensitivity was most likely influenced by his upbringing in a female environment. According to George Marsden, "some of his sisters' affections and piety may have been early lessons in his own cultivation of such sensibilities."[116]

Mather's Retreat

Mather lived during the shift from a medieval to an enlightened world view, and he experienced a sharp tension between his religious tradition and modern scientific discoveries. This was a trying time for men who wanted to be respected by both the Royal Society and their Puritan contemporaries.[117] Enthusiasm was a charge to be avoided at all costs. *The Lord's Loud Call to England* (1660) by Henry Jessey is an example of such zeal that perceived God's judgments in earthquakes, lightning, whirlwinds, toads, flies, and sudden deaths.[118] Because motives influenced interpretation, the employment of wonders in the service of politics raised more issues than it solved.

---

study that the Thoughts I form on these Occasions, may be of some abasing Tendency. The Actions themselves carry Humiliations in them; and a Christian ought alwayes to think humbly of himself, and be full of self-abasing and self-abhorring Reflections. By loathing of himself continually, and Being very sensible of what are his own loathsome Circumstances, a Christian does what is very pleasing to Heaven. My Life (above any Man's) ought to be filled with such Things: and now I contrive certain Spotts of Time, in which I shall be by Nature itself invited unto them" (369).

[115]"Types," *WJE,* 11:150–51.

[116]George M. Mardsen, *Jonathan Edwards: A Life* (New Haven: Yale University Press, 2003), 19.

[117]Mather was eventually admitted to the Royal Society, and Edwards had in his youth sought from them the publication of his "Spider Letters."

[118]Henry Jessey, *The Lord's Loud Call to England* (London, 1660). Both in England and New England such stories embodied a "mentality that united the learned and the unlearned. Being so pervasive, and so widely credited as reality, these stories readily became, as well, weapons in a complex game of politics." David D. Hall, *Worlds of Wonder, Days of Judgment* (New York: Alfred A. Knopf, 1989), 94–95.

What was true and what was an illusion, or worse, delusion? Aside from the possibility of human deception, the order of the universe defied discernment for much of the time.[119] Edwards, ironically, acknowledges the inscrutability of providence with a reading of nature:

> There is a wonderful analogy between what is seen in RIVERS: their gathering from innumerable small branches beginning at a great distance one from another in different regions, some on the sides or tops of mountains, others in valleys, and all conspiring to one common issue, all after their very diverse and contrary courses which they held for a while, yet all gathering more and more together the nearer they come to their common end and ultimate issue, and all at length discharging themselves at one mouth into the same ocean. Here is livelily represented how all things tend to one, even to God, the boundless ocean, which they can add nothing to, as mightiest rivers that continually dis-embogue themselves into the ocean add nothing to it sensibly ... The innumerable streams, of which great rivers are constituted, running in such infinitely various and contrary courses, livelily represent the various dispensations of divine providence.[120]

With all of his questions and doubts about providence, Mather could not shake his innate proclivity for recognizing divine marvels. Cotton Mather reminds his audience in *Touching Prodigies in New England*, an appendix to Mather's book *The Wonderful Works of God Commemorated*, of recent, surprising events that served as portents from heaven and the finger of God, such as odd-shaped cabbages, red snow, gunfire, and flaming swords in the sky that defied meteorological laws.[121]

---

[119] Hall observes an additional difficulty of discerning divine intent: "[T]hat which adds to the wonderment, is, in that the works of God sometimes seem to run counter with his word: so that there is dark and amazing intricacie in the ways of providence." Hall, *Worlds of Wonder, Days of Judgment*, 94.

[120] "Images of Divine Things," *WJE*, 11:77. See further comparison between Mather and Edwards in Michael P. Clark, "The Eschatology of Signs in Cotton Mather's Biblia Americana," in *Cotton Mather and Biblia Americana, America's First Bible Commentary: Essays in Reappraisal* (Grand Rapids, Mich.: Baker Academic, 2011), 431–36.

[121] Cotton Mather, *The Wonderful Works of God Commemorated* (Boston: Published by S. Green & sold by Joseph Browning, 1690). David Hall notes that seventeenth-century New Englanders inhabited an enchanted world of wonders frequented by nocturnal ghostly visitations, armies battling in the sky on a cloudless day, voices from heaven, deformities of nature, and devastating weather phenomena. God was a wonder-working God providentially ordering all of creation

When Mather took on the mantle of physico-theologian and began writing as a scientist, he made considerable departures from his inherited Puritan world view, which was filled with wonders and omens.[122] *The Christian Philosopher* (1721) was one of Mather's works in which he attempted to integrate Newtonian science into his inherited Puritan beliefs. He began to shift away from occasional meditations, essays on prodigies and omens, and reflections on witchcraft and the invisible realm in this work. Instead, he concentrated on observed physical nature, relegating theology to a secondary role. Devotion and speculation gave way to objective and firm empiricism.[123] Mather rarely spiritualized or allegorized nature in this work, instead emphasizing the providential ordering and intelligent design of the universe.[124]

to speak of his will. (Hall, *Worlds of Wonder, Days of Judgment,* 72). This enchanted world view had its origins in a number of intellectual traditions: The meteorology of the Greeks and Romans, astrology, apocalyptic prophecy, and natural history. Yet the wonder-filled world view depended primarily on the doctrine of the providence of God. God was the ever-present force behind all occurrances in this world. There is no substance without a cause . . . no such thing as chance. The regularity of the world was due to the exercise of God's sovereign will as was the surprising interruptions of nature from its usual course. (Hall, 77–78).

[122] Jeffrey Jeske, "Cotton Mather: Physico-Theologian," *Journal of the History of Ideas* 47, no. 4 (December 1986): 586.

[123] Jeske, "Cotton Mather: Physico-Theologian," 587.

[124] Contributing to the decline of providences and prodigies were the attacks of John Spencer. Spencer was a Hebraic scholar and master of Corpus Christi College at Cambridge. In 1660 Spencer was responding to a number of publications, like Jessey's *Loud Call,* which marshalled prodigies as evidences of Divine displeasure at the Restoration Settlement which signaled the end of Puritanism as political force. William E. Burns, " 'Our Lot Is Fallen Into an Age of Wonders': John Spencer and the Controversy Over Prodigies in the Early Restoration," *Albion: A Quarterly Journal Concerned with British Studies* 27, no. 2 (Summer 1995): 239. Michael Winship concludes that, "Spencer's purpose was to delegitimate the appropriation of the natural world for political purposes by the losers in the recent conflict. . . There was little new in Spencer's arguments, but in the uneasy time of the Restoration, they struck a fresh and resonant cord." He contended that it was in the interest of peace that prodigies be abandonded, and that men would become more manageable by the state authorities once they cast aside their superstitions. Michael Winship, "Prodigies, Puritanism, and the Perils of Natural Philosophy: The Example of Cotton Mather," *The William and Mary Quarterly* 51, no. 1 (1994): 98. The promise of peace strengthened his argument. Spencer also noted that a disposition toward the fear of God is connected to belief in prodigies, and fearing God is an inappropriate emotion. God is a benevolent and reasonable being in which wrathful prodigies have no place. God is glorified through his beneficient and wonderfully regular governence of nature. Prodigies are simply beneath his majesty. Burns, " 'Our Lot Is Fallen Into an Age of Wonders'," 244–45. Part of Spencer's success was due to the fact that he was not a persecutor of Dissent, therefore his audience broadened and eventually reached New England. Spencer was even visited by Increase Mather around the time of Mather's completion of *Essay on Illustrious Providences.* Evidently the interview caused Increase to review his own understanding of the prodigious, and the following year he first expressed his doubts concerning prodigies. Winship, "Prodigies, Puritanism, and the Perils of Natural Philosophy: The Example of Cotton Mather," 99. The younger Mather was

Conclusion

An intertextual reading of the world and Scripture was a feature shared by Hall, Austen, Bunyan, Keach, and the younger Mather. This quality was lacking in Bacon's, Galileo's, Newton's, and others' descripted world views. A purely descriptive and mechanical understanding of the cosmos could show a distant, providential clockwinder but not the God who was near. According to Zakai, mechanical philosophy denied the concept of divine immanence in nature by "rejecting the classical and medieval notion of nature as an organic being, or as an organism of active bodies."[125]

These men read "all of reality . . . according to patterns generated by the prior realistic, typological unified reading of Scripture."[126] The world, in their opinion, was a poetic composition that, when viewed through the eyes of Christian faith, provided believers with a distinctively Christian world vision. The Bible offered the overarching themes, storylines, and emblems that allow for an intertextual reading of the Book of Nature and the Word of God while maintaining the authority of Scripture.[127] The following chapter will look at the details of Edwards' devotional answer to the Enlightenment challenge, as well as the resonance of his emblematics with the emblematic world view of the Renaissance.

---

faced with a dilema. In his commentaries on the Bible, he had cited Spencer numerous times and considered him a noted authority. Spencer did not rule out God's supernatural presence or intervention in the natural order, nor did he rule out demonic activity. In part because of these features of Spencer's view, Mather was comfortable to consider Spencer's understanding of prodigies. Mather concluded that Spencer was correct, and came to treat prodigies as the dividing line between the superstitious masses and the educated few. Jerome Friedman, "The Battle of the Frogs and Fairford's Flies: Miracles and Popular Journalism During the English Revolution," *The Sixteenth Century Journal* 23, no. 3 (Autumn 1992): 424.

[125]Zakai, *Jonathan Edwards's Philosophy of History*, 103.

[126]Dawson, "Allegorical Intratextuality," 190.

[127]Dawson, "Allegorical Intratextuality," 190.

Chapter Four: Emblematics & Edwards

Introduction

E DWARDS, LIKE MANY OF HIS IMMEDIATE predecessors, saw a world filled with divine communication. The preceding chapter demonstrated how the Renaissance's emblematic world view found new life with early Evangelicals during the Enlightenment. The emblematic world view, augmented by devotional meditation on the creatures, gave rise to the practice of occasional meditation and a sub-genre of Evangelical emblem literature. Creation filled with unique spiritual truths for those with ears to hear and eyes to see in the worlds of men like Hall, Austen, Bunyan, Keach, and Edwards. According to Richard Baxter, it is critical to recognize the spiritual significance of the created order:

> Doest thou not first separate it from God, who is the life, and glory, and end, and meaning of every creature? Thou killest it, and turnest out the soul, and thinkest only on the corpse ... The World is Gods book, which he set man at first to read; and every Creature is a Letter, or Syllable, or Word, or Sentence, more or less, declaring the name and will of God. There you may behold his wonderful Almightiness, his unsearchable Wisdom, his unmeasurable Goodness, mercy and compassions; and his singular regard of the sons of men! ... Those that with holy and illuminated minds come thither to behold the footsteps of the Great and Wise and bountiful Creator, may find not only matter to employ, but to profit and delight their thoughts.[1]

---

[1] Richard Baxter, *A Christian Directory*, vol. 1 of *The Practical Works of Richard Baxter*, reprint, 1846 (Morgan, PA: Soli Deo Gloria, 2000), 253.

In this revelation-filled universe, nature was a book of wonders and marvels. Every tiny aspect of the created order added to the great drama of redemption. Nature, according to Edwards, was not only a silent emblematic language, but it also spoke audibly—sometimes praising the Creator, sometimes groaning for redemption, but always communicating. A mere description of the world is deaf to nature's speech. By linking the Book of Nature to the Book of Scripture, Edwards' emblematic world view contrasts with the descripted picture of the Enlightenment. This chapter will delve deeper into Edwards' emblematic world view, which he shared with Hall, Austen, Bunyan, Keach, Mather, and others. It will be shown that Edwards' spiritual world view displays clear traces of the emblematic Renaissance world view, and that his notebook "Images of Divine Things" falls within the emblem book genre. In the face of the Enlightenment challenge, Edwards' reinscripturation attempt was a continuation and development of traditional emblematic and occasional devotional meditation.

A Contrast in Views

Edwards supported an emblematic world view and rejected a mechanistic world view by adopting an organic view of the universe, alive with God's immanent presence.[2] He writes the following in his "Miscellanies":

> EXISTENCE OF GOD. There is just the same sort of knowledge of the existence of an universal mind in the world from the actions of the world, and what is done that is objected to our senses or that is effected by this mind, as there is of the existence of a particular mind in an human body from the observation of the actions of that, in gesture, look and voice. And there wants nothing but a comprehensive view, to take in the various actions in the world and look on them at one glance, and to see them in their mutual respects and relations, and these would as naturally, as quick, and with as little ratiocination, and more assuredly, intimate to us an universal mind, than human actions do a particular.[3]

[2] Avihu Zakai, *Jonathan Edwards's Philosophy of History: The Reenchantment of the World in the Age of Enlightenment* (Princeton: Princeton University Press, 2003), 103.

[3] "Miscellanies" no. 124, *WJE*, 13:288. In "Miscellanies" no. 383, Edwards continues the comparison of God's animating presence in the world to the human soul and body. He concludes that the relationship between the human soul and body is the best shadow of God's relationship

Edwards observes a universal mind that not only animates the world, but also acts and communicates through "mutual respects and relations."[4] According to Edwards, this viewpoint necessitates three components: A quick glance that does not rely heavily on reason, a broad perspective, and an eye toward relationships. A broad or panoramic perspective, as established in chapters one and two, and attention to relationships, correspondences, and similitudes are trademarks of the emblematic world view. A narrow concentration on the world's external appearance misses the spiritual nature of things.[5] Edwards writes in "Miscellanies" no. 123, "Spiritual Sight," that one's eyes must be open in order to perceive the world in its entirety. Spiritual things are "mental motions, energies, and operations" that defy even the most precise explanations.[6] Knowledge is incomplete without experience. Edwards uses the rainbow as an example of something that is difficult to describe to someone who has never seen it yet is simple to define.[7]

Poetic Sensibility

In that both are characterized by perceptions of correspondences and similitudes within the creation that impart meaning, Edwards' viewpoint coheres with the Renaissance emblematic world view. Each aspect of the created order serves as a page of text in the larger Book of Nature. In contrast to the abstract mathematical computations of the Enlightenment, the emblematic approach is literary and invites us to pick up and read.

Though reading the world as a text necessitates a massive shift in perspective for modern man, Edwards identifies a key to interpreting the world symbolically in "Miscellanies" no. 251. He claims that the authors of the Scriptures, in the Psalms and elsewhere, were inspired by a "poetical genius

with the world, because "[m]an's soul influences the body, continues its nature and powers and constant regular motions and productions, and actuates it, as the supreme principle does the universe (451–52).

[4]"Miscellanies" no. 124, *WJE,* 13:288.

[5]McGilchrist notes that divergent thinking is about discovering connections and forms that can guide thinking by analogy: broadening a field that has become too restricted, or finding different ways of looking at something that has become too familiar. All literature on creativity in any field makes the same point: recognizing unseen parallels, recognizing shapes that others have missed, taking a step back and looking at the bigger picture, not focusing on the same small field and consulting the rulebook. "Talent hits a target no one else can hit; genius hits a target no one else can see." McGilchrist, *The Matter With Things,* 363.

[6]"Miscellanies" no. 123, *WJE,* 13:286.

[7]"Miscellanies" no. 123, *WJE,* 13:286.

and fire, excited and invigorated by an extraordinary exercise of grace and a holy and evangelical disposition, in which excitations there was the afflatus of God's Spirit."[8] According to Edwards, the poetic quality of Scripture necessitates that the reader be poetically disposed or prepared in order to have a full comprehension of the types and shadows intended by the Spirit of God. He states:

> For there is a most wonderful analogy and natural correspondence between one and the other; which one will see the more, the more they have of a poetical and gracious disposition, and clear and comprehensive understanding of these matters. The affairs of the Jewish church are so much of a shadow, that a mind so prepared and exercised would naturally be led to the substance, for a poetical and hyperbolical representation. The Spirit of God excited those extraordinary flames in their minds, and they were likewise (it is probable) subject to his special direction; for he intended that gospel things should be represented by them, and that they should hereafter be used in the church for such representations.[9]

Edwards observes that in order to recognize and appreciate the poetic and emblematic quality of Scripture and the world, the human mind must be exercised and spiritual blindness restored. One must submit to God's wisdom in creating a world that intelligent beings can understand. According to Edwards, the fact that God created an understandable universe should come as no surprise because he "hath so much delighted in this way of instruction."[10] Edwards notices a 'fitness' to God's aim of communicating in an emblematic manner, especially because the emblems and shadows confirm rather than contradict Scripture. In his "Images" journal, he notes,

> If we look on these shadows of divine things as the voice of God, purposely, by them, teaching us these and those spiritual and divine things, to show of what excellent advantage it will be, how agreeably and clearly it will tend to convey instruction to our minds, and to impress things on the mind, and to affect the mind. By that we may as it were hear God speaking to us. Wherever

[8]"Miscellanies" no. 252, *WJE,* 13:363.

[9]"Miscellanies" no. 252, *WJE,* 13:363–64.

[10]"Images of Divine Things," *WJE,* 11:67.

we are and whatever we are about, we may see divine things excellently represented and held forth, and it will abundantly tend to confirm the Scriptures, for there is an excellent agreement between these things and the Holy Scriptures.[11]

Edwards knows that studying this emblematic language demands the same dedication as learning any other human language. Mastering idioms is one of the most difficult aspects of learning a foreign language. Similarly, God's language of types is very idiomatic and is not naturally acquired by fallen man, but must be learned.

> [B]y much use and acquaintance together with a good taste or judgment, by comparing one thing with another and having our senses as it were exercised to discern it (which is the way that adult persons must come to speak any language, and in its true idiom, that is not their native tongue).[12]

A purely grammatical understanding of the emblematic language will not be sufficient because the meaning of a language is found in the comparison of idioms, which are based on associations, correspondences, and similitudes by definition. God's language in Scripture and across the earth is poetic in character, both beautiful and harmonious.[13]

Pedagogy and the Imagination

The function of the imagination and associative processes in discovering meaning in the world was essential for the emblematic world view. Similitudes, riddles, natural jokes, and a general poetic sensibility (things inherent in human thought processes) were crucial in the perception of reality. Edwards' 1728 sermon, *Profitable Hearers of the Word* outlines the pedagogical advantages of allegory, such as its ability to engage the imagination, its use of analogy and comparison, and the mental exercise it provides.[14] As he points out, God clearly enjoys the parabolic, as evidenced by Christ's teaching ministry and the regularity with which it appears in the Scriptures.[15]

[11]"Images of Divine Things," *WJE,* 11:74.

[12]"Types," WJE, 11:150–51.

[13]"Types," WJE, 11:150–51.

[14]*WJE,* 14:243–77.

[15]*WJE,* 14:247.

Reality is riddled with mysteries. The Bible is a collection of exciting true stories. Nature and Scripture have been designed to engage humans in the most effective way possible. In a nutshell, revelation has been adapted to the human condition.

In his apology for *Pilgrim's Progress*, Bunyan emphasizes the importance of appealing to the human desire for entertainment in order to connect with the audience and effectively communicate his message.

> Behold how he [the fisherman] engageth all his Wits. . .
> Yet Fish there be, that neither Hook, nor Line,
> Nor Snare, nor Net, nor Engine can make thine;
> They must be grop't for, and be tickled too,
> Or they will not be catch't, what e're you do.[16]

Edwards also understood the value of capturing the imagination via entertainment, story, and song. He was well aware that the way to comprehension did not involve rote memory and repetition, but rather "familiar" speech incorporating stories and images.[17] The main enemy of education was boring and uninteresting lessons. The affections were important to Edwards' educational process. The teacher's goal was to instill a hunger or desire for understanding. If the learner had a desire to learn, he or she would not be forced to pick up a book and read.[18]

Edwards, like Keach, was acutely aware of the power of music to mold the affections, in addition to "familiar discourse" and storytelling.[19] "Music, especially sacred music, has a powerful efficacy to soften the heart into tenderness, to harmonize the affections, and to give the mind a relish for objects of a superior character."[20]

Edwards as Emblematicist

It is useful to compare Edwards' interpretation of fruit trees with Austen and Keach in order to determine Edwards' place among emblematic theologians.

[16] John Bunyan, *The Pilgrim's Progress* (Westwood, NJ: Barbour, 1970), vii.

[17] Kenneth Minkema, " 'Informing of the Child's Understanding, Influencing His Heart, and Directing Its Practice': Jonathan Edwards on Education," *Acta Theologica* 31, no. 2 (2011): 164, 168.

[18] Ibid., 165.

[19] Minkema, "Jonathan Edwards on Education," 167.

[20] *Letters and Personal Writings, WJE,* 16:794. This was also recognized by Benjamin Keach.

Tropologia, by Keach, has been compared to Edwards' typological studies.[21] Both Edwards and Keach are possibly hermeneutically related to Solomon Glassius' *Philologia sacra* (1620).[22] The first section of *Tropologia* is a translation of Glassius' work by Keach's colleague, Thomas Delaune.[23] Edwards most likely used *Philologia sacra* because Yale's library possessed a copy.[24] Solomon Glassius is cited by Bernard Ramm as a proponent of a moderate school of typology. Glassius distinguished between two types: "innate and inferred ... An innate type is a type specifically declared to be such in the New Testament ... [whereas an] inferred type is one that, not specifically designated in the New Testament is justified for its existence by the nature of the New Testament materials on typology."[25] This school's adherents include Keach (whom Ramm particularly named) and Jonathan Edwards.[26]

Fruit trees, according to Edwards, were striking emblems of persons at various phases of conversion and sanctification. It is no surprise that Austen, Keach, and Edwards find the connection between men and fruit trees so rich.[27] Edwards wrote about "the blossoming and ripening of fruit trees and other things of that nature" in "Images of Divine Things" entry 171.[28] According to Edwards, the "puttings forth of the tree [blossoms] in order

[21]Tibor Fabiny, "Edwards and Biblical Typology," in *Understanding Jonathan Edwards: An Introduction to America's Theologian,* ed. Gerald McDermott (New York: Oxford University Press, 2008), 98.

[22]Keach was a popularizer of Glassius. Richard A. Muller, *Post-Reformation Reformed Dogmatics: The Rise and Development of Reformed Orthodoxy, Ca. 1520 to Ca. 1725* (Grand Rapids: Baker Academics, 2003), 118.

[23]James Christopher Holmes, "The Role of Metaphor in the Sermons of Benjamin Keach, 1640–1704" (Ph.D. diss., The Southern Baptist Theological Seminary, 2009), 86.

[24]James E. Mooney, Eighteenth-Century Catalogues of the Yale College Library (New Haven: Beinecke, 2001), A26.

[25]Bernard Ramm, *Protestant Biblical Interpretation: A Textbook of Hermeneutics* (Grand Rapids: Baker, 1980), 219–20.

[26]Ramm, *Protestant Biblical Interpretation,* 220.

[27]Even non-believers perceive the informational power of metaphor. George Lakoff and Mark Turner, professors of linguistics/cognitive science and English respectively, recognize that people are viewed as plants on a number of counts, but primarily as pertains to the life cycle. People are blossoms that go through various stages—"burgeons, and then withers or declines." Their use of Psalm 103 is a prime biblical example. "As for man, his days are as grass: as a flower of the field, so he flourisheth." Stages of a plant's development and decline are commonly used to describe a person's season of life. A young child is referred to as a sprout, a young adult is said to be in full bloom, and a person in his last days is said to be withering away. George Lakoff and Mark Turner, *More Than Cool Reason: A Field Guide to Poetic Metaphor* (The University Of Chicago Press, 1989) 6.

[28]"Images of Divine Things," *WJE,* 11:115.

to make fruit make a great show and are pleasant to the eye, but the fruit then is very small and tender. Afterwards, when there is less show, the fruit is increased."[29] He draws an emblem of conversion and maturity out of this horticultural truth. When a person first becomes a Christian, he is full of blossom and show, emotion, and delight. That is the blossom that will fall off soon. Fresh believers, like young fruit, are also highly delicate and easily injured.[30]

He also notices that fruit that hangs from a tree or vine is not permanent. It is constantly maturing, and its function is not to remain on the end of the branch or vine, but rather to be harvested when ripe.[31] Similarly, believers must constantly grow in Christian maturity and look forward to the time when they will be snatched from this world and taken to live with their Husbandman.

"Many kinds of fruit have a great deal of bitterness and sourness while green, and much that is crude and unwholesome, which as it ripens becomes sweeter, the juices purer, the crude parts are removed,"[32] Edwards writes. This happens during the summer heat when the sun beats down on the fruit. "So young converts have a remaining sourness and bitterness. They have a great mixture in their experiences and religious exercises, but as they ripen for heaven they are more purified."[33] This is accomplished by "afflictions, persecutions and occasions of great self-denial, or in one word, by the cross of Christ. Whereas these trials bring hypocrites to nothing."[34]

Finally, Edwards adds, "Green fruit hangs fast to the tree, but when it is ripe it is loose and easily picked. Wheat, while it is green in the field, sucks and draws for nourishment from the ground, but when it is ripe, it draws no more."[35] This is a divine emblem of saints who have been weaned from this world and are ready for heaven.

[29]"Images of Divine Things," *WJE,* 11:115.

[30]"Images of Divine Things," *WJE,* 11:115.

[31]"Images of Divine Things," *WJE,* 11:115.

[32]"Images of Divine Things," *WJE,* 11:115.

[33]"Images of Divine Things," *WJE,* 11:115.

[34]"Images of Divine Things," *WJE,* 11:115.

[35]"Images of Divine Things," *WJE,* 11:116.

Exegesis and Meditation

Edwards' perception of the depth of creation was not without criticism. Editor Wallace Anderson writes in the introduction to "Images of Divine Things" that Edwards' Reformed critics would undoubtedly object to Edwards' extensive typologizing of nature.[36] They would argue that there are a limited number of legitimate correspondences to Christ in the created order, but to conclude that all of creation speaks of Christ may be taking things too far.[37] Wallace gives some examples that may go beyond what was considered conservative typology:[38]

> In the manner in which birds and squirrels that are charmed by serpents go into their mouths and are destroyed by them, is a lively representation of the manner in which sinners under the gospel are very often charmed and destroyed by the devil. The animal that is charmed by the serpent seems to be in great exercise and fear, screams and makes ado, but yet don't flee away. It comes nearer to the serpent, and then seems to have its distress increased and goes a little back again, but then comes still nearer than ever, and then appears as if greatly affrighted and runs or flies back again a little way, but yet don't flee quite away, and soon comes a little nearer and a little nearer with seeming fear and distress that drives 'em a little back between whiles, until at length they come so [near] that the serpent can lay hold of them: and so they become their prey.[39]

> Just thus, oftentimes sinners under the gospel are bewitched by their lusts. They have considerable fears of destruction and remorse of conscience that makes 'em hang back, and they have a great deal of exercise between while, and some partial reformations, but yet they don't flee away. They won't wholly forsake their beloved lusts, but return to 'em again; and so whatever warnings they have, and whatever checks of conscience that may exercise 'em and make [them] go back a little and stand off for a while, yet they will keep their beloved sin in sight, and won't

---

[36] Anderson, "Editor's Introduction," *WJE,* 11:31.

[37] At least thirty of the entries in "Images of Divine Things" are explicit images of Christ.

[38] Anderson, "Editor's Introduction," *WJE,* 11:32.

[39] "Images of Divine Things," *WJE,* 11:71.

utterly break off from it and forsake [it], but will return to it again and again, and go a little further and a little further, until Satan remedilessly makes a prey of them. But if anyone comes and kills the serpent, the animal immediately escapes. So the way in which poor souls are delivered from the snare of the devil is by Christ's coming and bruising the serpent's head.[40]

The late invention of telescopes, whereby heavenly objects are brought so much nearer, and made so much plainer to sight, and such wonderful discoveries have been made in the heavens, is a type and forerunner of the great increase in the knowledge of heavenly things that shall be in the approaching glorious times of the Christian church.[41]

Water in artificial waterworks rises no higher than the spring from whence it comes, unless by a super-added strength from some other cause. So nothing in man can rise higher than the principle from whence it comes. Nature can't be improved by men themselves so as to bring them to any qualification higher than natural principles more excellent in their kind than self-love, etc.[42]

Edwards discovers spiritual truths vividly represented not only in nature, but also in human invention and fluid mechanics in these three notebook entries. According to Anderson, Edwards was attempting to amplify "biblical, natural, and historical examples of correspondences between the material and natural world," and that this was "an important innovation" that would "free typology from the narrow correspondences of the two testaments without reverting to exaggerated medieval allegory."[43] The notion that Edwards is wholly novel is mitigated by the fact that Hall, Austen, Bunyan, and Keach all expanded typology beyond Scripture into the natural world.[44]

---

[40]"Images of Divine Things," WJE, 11:71–72.

[41]"Images of Divine Things," WJE, 101.

[42]"Images of Divine Things," WJE, 11:107.

[43]Anderson, "Editor's Introduction," WJE, 11:32–33.

[44]Though Austen limited his meditations to fruit trees (admitting that they were only one volume in the library of creation), he finds in them an analogy and resemblance of the Son of God: "How much of the goodnes & excellencies of God doe Fruit-trees shew forth when they (in their seasons) flourish with Leaves Blossomes & Fruits, especially considered not only as they appear beautifull to the eye, but also with all their inward beautyes, and perfections,

Furthermore, the arrangement, style, and subject matter of Hall's *Occasional Meditations* resemble Edwards' "Images of Divine Things."

These parallels, together with Hall's recognized involvement in the construction of a Protestant meditation tradition within the emblematic world view, show that Edwards' "Images of Divine Things" is not a departure from, but rather a development of the Renaissance emblematic world view. Instead of developing a new typological view of reality to confront the Enlightenment's mechanical disenchantment, Edwards set out to restore, refine, and extend the Renaissance's and his Protestant forefathers' powerful earlier emblematic world view. "Images of Divine Things" by Edwards is a crystallization and systematization of an emblematic world view.

Controversial

Edwards expected his views to be met with scorn, if not by his peers, then by the intellectual world at large. Access to hidden mysteries, signs, providences, and any knowledge that was less than empirical was regarded as dubious during the Age of Enlightenment and reason. Such knowledge claims were dismissed as enthusiastic, superstitious, and positively medieval. Edwards was acutely aware that his opinions would not be met with acclaim. He fully expects to be mocked and despised.[45] However, if Edwards had a "fruitful brain and a copious fancy," he was not alone in his ailment. Edwards alludes to a pamphlet titled *Creation, the Foundation of Revelation* (1750) in a comment after the preceding entry.

Wallace Anderson identifies the author of the pamphlet, Andrew Wilson, in a footnote to the Yale edition. Wilson contends that the material world was created to correspond to the spiritual realm.[46] The Adamic language was ideal for expressing the intrinsic essence, goodness, and function of all aspects of creation. Wilson is convinced, writing, "Who can doubt but that the Creator is carrying on, and supporting a spiritual economy, every way

---

their vertues, and uses in the life of man. Both in Alimentall and Physicall respects; but most of all, as they are SIMILITUDES, and beare the figure, and resemblance of many high and great Mysteries in the Word of God, the Analogie and resemblance in very neere in many things to the most noble visible Creature MAN, Fruit-trees beare the Figure and resemblance of what is of highest esteeme with God, his People, his Jewells, his Adopted Sons, yea of his Naturall Sonne, as we frequently find in Scripture." Ralph Austen, The Spiritual Use of an Orchard (New York: Garland, 1982), "Preface to Reader."

[45] "Types," *WJE*, 11:152.

[46] "Types," *WJE*, 11:152.

answerable to the material one?"[47] Anderson attributes Wilson's view of language and nature to Lockean concepts, but further reading of Wilson's pamphlet reveals ideas that resonate strongly with Renaissance interest in Adamic language, hieroglyphics, the spiritual purpose of the world, and even hints at the rise of the emblematic world view in the ancient world—"the rise of hieroglyphics, fables, mythology, etc."[48]

In entries 206 and 207 of the "Images" notebook, Edwards also mentions hieroglyphics and emblematic theology, mentioning authors who, like Wilson, endorse his beliefs.[49] Along with Wilson, Edwards contends that discerning spiritual truths in the natural world requires wisdom: "The wise man argues from an image in the natural world, Ecclesiastes 1:7, 'All the rivers run into the sea; yet the sea is not full.'"[50]

It is understandable to expect to be charged with an overactive imagination, but why did Edwards anticipate this reaction? According to Anna Svetlikova, the most contentious component of Edwards' viewpoint is the task of distinguishing genuine from false types. Which types were divinely ordained, and which were the result of human imagination?[51] Nonetheless,

---

[47] Andrew Wilson, *The Creation, the Ground-Work of Revelation, and Revelation the Language of Nature. Or, a Brief Attempt to Demonstrate, That the Hebrew Language is Founded Upon Natural Ideas, and That the Hebrew Writings Transfer Them to Spiritual Objects* (Edinburgh, 1750), 24.

[48] Wilson, *The Creation, the Ground-Work of Revelation*, 20, 26, 29. Lockean influence is evident, but Wilson notes its limits: "The medium by which the spiritual powers in man are roused, is his senses. His understanding is instructed, and explains itself by the perceptions his senses transmit, so that, with all the capacity he has, he can make no progress in matters higher than sense, unless he takes the creation for his lesson, and the omniscient Creator for his preceptor" (22). Wilson echoes the sentiment of Austen, Baxter, Bunyan, Edwards and others in advocating the spiritual use of creation. "That we derive all our knowledge from the operations of matter, is evident, so that if we were to divest ourselves of the perceptions depending upon it, we would not leave ourselves masters of one conception we now have of spiritual affairs. It is from the influences of the sun, diffusing a vital principle through nature, that we owe our notions of life; from operations of force and impulse, we derive our conceptions of power; the variety, subtilty, intricacy and arrangement of material operations, are inseparably connected with our apprehensions of wisdom; the stability of the frame of nature, and the certainty of its effects, furnishes us with the apprehension of unchangeableness and truth. Light stands for knowledge and understanding, and darkness for ignorance" (22). Wilson rebukes as wicked those who would "desert such a wise and kind instructor [God] . . . and set [himself] up for an independent discovery" (22). "But if we submit, with humility, to be instructed by God, we shall find him making all the works of nature correspond with a spiritual administration of his efficacious powers unto a spiritual world"(23).

[49] "Images of Divine Things," *WJE*, 11:127–28.

[50] "Images of Divine Things," *WJE*, 11:57.

[51] Anna Svetlikova, "Jonathan Edwards' Typology as Language," Theologica Wratislaviensia 7 (2012), 163.

the comprehensiveness of Edwards' system of images and shadows appears to negate the issue of subjectivity. A look at the "Scriptures" series at the back of the "Images" notebook reveals forty-five images that Edwards appears to identify as having specific correspondence with Scripture:

> [44.] SPIDER'S WEB, of the rest, the confidence or dependence, possessions and glory of wicked men. Job 8:14.[52]

> [39.] STORMS, of the wrath of God. The storms that brought on the Flood (see also Joshua 10:11); and the storm in the time of the battle against Sisera [Judges 4]; and the storm of rain, thunder and lightning at the Red Sea [Exodus 14:12]. See Psalms 77.[53]

> [11.] WOOL, SILK, SKINS. The clothes of animals, by their death, [a] type of Christ's righteousness, Genesis 3:21.[54]

The primary debate can be better understood by situating Edwards within his Enlightenment culture and the dominant reliance on reason. Edwards was most likely connecting the accusations of having an uncontrolled imagination with the broader charge of enthusiasm or his reliance on a discredited world view, rather than mere subjectivity. According to Edwards, it is not irrational to suppose that the entire universe is God's language. He is certain that "it is rational to suppose that Scripture abounds with types," as does the entire created order.[55] Edwards takes a Martin Luther-like stance when he states, "[T]hey are welcome to it. I'm not ashamed . . ."[56] Edwards believed that the revelation he found in the Books of Scripture and Nature was divinely inspired, complementary, and authoritative. He writes,

> For such a system (or Bible) of the word of God is as much the work of God as any other of his works, the effect of the power, wisdom and contrivance of a God whose wisdom is unsearchable and whose nature and ways are past finding out. And as the

---

[52]"Images of Divine Things," *WJE,* 11:135.

[53]"Images of Divine Things," *WJE,* 11:134.

[54]"Images of Divine Things," *WJE,* 11:132.

[55]Robert E. Brown, *Jonathan Edwards and the Bible* (Bloomington: Indiana University Press, 2002), 148. Brown notes that Edwards was not alone in his response to rationalistic natural religion, but was part of a much larger international movement to reform religious epistemology and typology.

[56]"Types," *WJE,* 11:151–52.

system of nature and the system of revelation are both divine works, so both are in different senses a divine word. Both are the voice of God to intelligent creatures, a manifestation and declaration of himself to mankind. Man's reason was given him that he might know God and might be capable of discerning the manifestations he makes of himself in the effects and external expressions and emanations of the divine perfections.[57]

Though Edwards sees nature and the Bible as sources of revelation, it is Scripture that contains the interpretive key to unlocking nature's grammar and meaning.[58] "The book of Scripture is the interpreter of the book of nature," Edwards says.[59] Nature's images and shadows are indecipherable without the authoritative Word that originated and sustains all things.

A Revolution of Mind

It is difficult to estimate the mental revolution that would be required of a twenty-first-century person in order to recapture Edwards' emblematic world view, or even whether such a revolution would be desirable because it may be seen as contradictory to the practical achievements of empiricism, science, and technology.[60] The accusation of enthusiasm (an overheated imagination) was one that Edwards' contemporaries desired to avoid at all costs.

Yet the world view of Deists, let alone materialists, was riddled with flaws and failed to grasp the inherently spiritual nature of humans and the need for a God who is close.[61] A providential (or fictitious) deity operating a massive machine of "wheels, levers, and pulleys" could not bridge the gap between

---

[57]"Miscellanies" no. 1340, *WJE*, 23:374.

[58]Brown, *Jonathan Edwards and the Bible*, 149.

[59]"Types," *WJE*, 11:106.

[60]McGilchrist notes that a revolution of mind would require a rethink of the main components of the universe: time, space, breadth, motion, matter, awareness, singularity, beauty, goodness, truth, purpose, and the concept of a God's presence or absence—huge topics that have been discussed by the most brilliant minds for ages. He is convinced that the hemisphere hypothesis provides a new and compelling counter to the popular view—which is largely based on reductionism—and its potential impact on the world's troubles and our culture in the West. McGilchrist, *The Matter With Things*, 19–20.

[61]Not only the rise of Pietism and the awakenings that followed, but also the rise of Romanticism give evidence to the impoverished world view of Deism and Rationalism.

general and special revelation.[62] As a result, concentrating on nature's external appearance and mechanism had the unintended consequence of decreasing the invisible aspects of reality.[63] The spiritual constitution of the world was lost in the absence of the Book of Scripture interpreting the Book of Nature. Spiritual mysteries no longer existed, and the invisible paths to heaven and hell were readily forgotten with the passing of the emblematic world view.

Though many people in Edwards' day believed in the miraculous nature of the general laws of the cosmos, particularly gravity, there was a rising trend to avoid specific instances of divine intervention. This hesitancy led in a deemphasis of Christ's person and work.[64] Yet, according to Edwards, looking for God's glory in a descripted, mechanistic world view is useless. According to Edwards, God is a clockmaker, but the movement of His clock is of a completely different nature and order than that of the mechanical philosophers.[65] Edwards elaborates on the devotional design of the world in "Miscellanies" tt. Devotion:

> To illustrate it by example: if the highest end of every part of a clock is only mutually to assist the other parts in their motions, that clock is good for nothing at all; the clock in general is altogether useless, however every part is useful to turn round the other parts. So, however useful all the parts of the world are to each other, if that be their highest end, the world in general is

---

[62]Jonathan I. Israel, *Radical Enlightenment: Philosophy and the Making of Modernity 1650–1750* (New York: Oxford University Press, 2002), 463.

[63]Roy Porter, *The Creation of the Modern World: The Untold Story of the British Enlightenment* (New York: W.W. Norton & Co., 2001), 297.

[64]Jonathan I. Israel, *Enlightenment Contested: Philosophy, Modernity, and the Emancipation of Man 1670–1752* (New York: Oxford University Press, 2009), 212–13.

[65]Edwards was not the only one who realized the threat posed to vital religion by the mechanical philosophy of the Enlightenment. Reginald Ward notes that early Evangelicalism was awash with ideas and paths that promised true religion. Caballa, Paracelsianism, radical mysticism, and other schools of religious thought were regularly tapped by Pietists and other in an effort to discover the essence of vital religious experience. W. R. Ward, *Early Evangelicalism: A Global Intellectual History, 1670– 1789* (New York: Cambridge University Press, 2006), 6–23. "The vitalism that characterized the whole alchemical tradition was a clear attraction to men like Arndt and the Pietists of a later generation who were seeking to recover religious vitality, but it had other virtues as well. It seemed, as it seemed much later to Newton, to be an answer to the perceived weaknesses of a mechanical or materialist philosophy" (11). It was plain to many, including Edwards, that a mere atomistic world view could simply not account for the complexity and beauty of life. Typological exegesis seemed to hold the key for making Christian sense of the world (12).

altogether useless. I am sure there is the same reason for one as for the other. Yea it is a contradiction and nonsense to say, the highest end of a particular part of the world is to be useful to the rest; for if that is the highest end, they are not useful. So it is nonsense to say of a machine whose highest end is to have one part move another, that the parts of the engine are useful to move the rest; for the whole is useless, and so every part, however they correspond together.[66]

Edwards contended that the entire universe, like the gears and motions of a clock, works toward the ultimate purpose of encouraging man to glorify God. In other words, there is a teleological process with a devotional aim in creation. According to Edwards, those who label such thinking enthusiasm "talk very unphilosophically."[67] In his "enthusiasm," he was not alone. This devotional perspective on the world was not unique; since the Middle Ages, the universe has been viewed as:

[A] vast cathedral in which both the whole architecture and the smallest details of decoration were designed with hidden theological referents... By [Cotton] Mather's [and later Edwards's] time the enterprise of cracking the code of nature through meditation on its parabolic detail, which he calls 'occasional reflections,' had become a standard took in Puritan methodology.[68]

Below are some examples of Edwards' emblematic reading of nature. The parallel with Mather's experience of God's voice through thunder is striking. This voice, according to Edwards, extended throughout the cathedral of the world, from base things like human waste to beautiful things like rainbows and flowers.

Edwards and Thunder

When Edwards heard the voice of God in thunder during meditation, he experienced spiritual sight, a comprehensive view, and sensitivity to mutual relationships. Following his evangelical conversion, Edwards experiences

[66]"Miscellanies" no. tt. DEVOTION, *WJE,* 13:190. Edwards' view of the highest end of creation reflects the same sentiments as those of Hall, Austen, Baxter, and others.

[67]"Miscellanies" no. tt. DEVOTION, *WJE,* 13:191.

[68]Richard F. Lovelace, *The American Pietism of Cotton Mather: Origins of American Evangelicalism* (Grand Rapids, MI: Christian University Press, 1979), 118–19.

a spiritual view of creation in what appears to be a devotional practice comparable to that of Bishop Hall.

> God's excellency, his wisdom, his purity and love, seemed to appear in everything; in the sun, moon and stars; in the clouds, and blue sky; in the grass, flowers, trees; in the water, and all nature; which used greatly to fix my mind. I often used to sit and view the moon, for a long time; and so in the daytime, spent much time in viewing the clouds and sky, to behold the sweet glory of God in these things: in the meantime, singing forth with a low voice, my contemplations of the Creator and Redeemer. And scarce anything, among all the works of nature, was so sweet to me as thunder and lightning. Formerly, nothing had been so terrible to me. I used to be a person uncommonly terrified with thunder: and it used to strike me with terror, when I saw a thunderstorm rising. But now, on the contrary, it rejoiced me. I felt God at the first appearance of a thunderstorm. And used to take the opportunity at such times, to fix myself to view the clouds, and see the lightnings play, and hear the majestic and awful voice of God's thunder: which often times was exceeding entertaining, leading me to sweet contemplations of my great and glorious God. And while I viewed, used to spend my time, as it always seemed natural to me, to sing or chant forth my meditations; to speak my thoughts in soliloquies, and speak with a singing voice.[69]

Not only did Edwards discern God's voice in thunder and other natural phenomena, but he also appeared to believe in the potential of a providential occurrence (defined as the motion of the world animated by God) bearing the authority of the Lord's Word.[70] According to Edwards:

---

[69]"Personal Narrative," *WJE*, 16:794. Harold Simonson compares Edwards view of creation with Calvin's. Noting Calvin's commentary on Acts 7:55–56 and the experience of Stephen seeing Christ in the heavens, Simonson concludes that, "For both Edwards and Calvin the miracle of vision belongs to the regenerate. All others live in the darkness of nature where unmediated paradoxes leave the human soul fractured and sight distorted. The heart, says Edwards, is the faculty that leads to synthesis, and the redeemed heart brings the beatific vision of true wholeness." Harold P. Simonson, *Jonathan Edwards, Theologian of the Heart* (Grand Rapids: Eerdmans, 1974), 89.

[70]This is a point of debate. In *Jonathan Edwards's Philosophy of History*, 74, Avihu Zakai, commenting on entry 57 of "Images of Divine Things," believes that Edwards held nature authoritative since it is a voice of God. In a review of this position, Michael McClymond

'Tis observed by the prophet Jeremiah (Jeremiah 32:8), concerning only a common providential occurrence, that it "was the word of the Lord," that is, that it was designedly ordered to be a special signification of God's mind and will, as much as his Word. By which it appears that God don't think this a thing improper, or unbecoming of his wisdom, thus designedly to contrive his works and to dispose things in the common affairs of the world in such a manner as [to] represent divine things and signify his mind as truly as his Word.[71]

Edwards' emblematic world vision comprised not just the particulars of the created order, but also history. If interpreted correctly, the motion of the present moment has the potential to be a revelation from God. In Edwards' mind, Providence, God's movement in the universe, linked the Book of Nature to the Book of Scripture.[72]

Mather's impression of God's voice in thunder is comparable to Edwards' thoughts in his "Personal Narrative." Though not in narrative form, Edwards heard comparable messages in the thunderous voice: God's grandeur, fierceness, might, anger, and hatred of pride. The following entries from the "Images" journal differ little in content from Mather's *Brontologia Sacra*, however Edwards' notes are noticeably shorter:

As thunder, and thunder clouds, as they are vulgarly called, have a shadow of the majesty of God, so the blue sky, the green fields and trees, and pleasant flowers have a shadow of the mild attributes of goodness, grace and love of God, as well as the beauteous rainbow.[73]

The extreme fierceness and extraordinary power of the heat of lightning is an intimation of the exceeding power and terribleness of the wrath of God.[74]

---

disagrees: "A related problem is Zakai's claim that Edwards showed "an exaltation of nature to a level of authority co-equal with revelation" (p. 74)—a statement that overlooks Edwards's criticisms of the Deists and their reliance on natural theology." Michael J. McClymond, review of *Jonathan Edwards's Philosophy of History,* by Avihu Zakai, *The Journal of Religion* 85:1 (2005): 121–23.

[71]"Images of Divine Things," *WJE,* 11:125.

[72]Zakai, Jonathan Edwards's Philosophy of History, 74.

[73]"Images of Divine Things," *WJE,* 11:58.

[74]"Images of Divine Things," *WJE,* 11:59.

> That high towers and other high things are commonly smitten with thunder, and mountainous places more subject to terrible thunder and lightning, shows how that pride and self-exaltation does peculiarly excite God's wrath. See Isaiah 2:11–17.[75]

Despite the fact that Edwards perceived the same message in thunder, his entries in "Images of Divine Things" make no mention of an occasion or event surrounding the sight. Edwards might have easily stretched each item into a broader narrative if he had provided details about how he discovered many of his emblems. However, the absence of a specific event or narrative does not rule out the possibility that the entries were the result of meditation, as Edwards clearly describes the practice of meditating on the creation in his "Personal Narrative." Because occasional meditation or thought was a regular Puritan devotional practice, many of Edwards' entries in the "Images" notebook are most likely derived from his meditations.[76]

Edwards and the Rainbow

Along with thunder, one of Edwards' most significant emblems is the rainbow. The rainbow is a 'chapter' in the Book of Nature, full with soteriological meaning. In his commentary on Revelation 4:3, Edwards notes that the rainbow that surrounded the throne had the color of an emerald. The color green in the rainbow was established by God as a covenantal sign after the Flood as a "emblem of divine grace."[77] Green is the predominate hue of flourishing flora and fauna, according to Edwards, and it is "the color of joy and gladness." The fields are believed to sing and shout for delight since they are a cheery green.[78] In his notes on Genesis 9:12-17, Edwards presents an extended emblematic exegesis of the rainbow. He identifies a variety of features that are emblematic of spiritual and doctrinal truths while meditating on the numerous characteristics of the rainbow: The rainbow's brightness is pleasant and lovely, expressing hope, comfort, pleasure, grace,

---

[75]"Images of Divine Things," *WJE*, 11:91.

[76]Charles E. Hambrick-Stowe, *The Practice of Piety: Puritan Devotional Disciplines in Seventeenth-Century New England* (Chapel Hill: University of North Carolina Press, 1982), 163–64, 273.

[77]"Notes on Scripture," *WJE*, 15:224-25. For a full discussion of Edwards' integration of theology with Newtonian optics see: Stephen J. Stein, "Jonathan Edwards and the Rainbow: Biblical Exegesis and Poetic Imagination," *The New England Quarterly* 47.3 (Sept 1974): 440–56.

[78]"Notes on Scripture," *WJE*, 15:225. On creation shouting and singing see Edwards' sermon on Romans 8:22: "Creation Groans," *WJE Online*, Volume 52.

love, peace, and sweetness.[79] A rainbow appears amid a disintegrating cloud, representing both nourishing rain and Christ's weak human nature. The cloud is sacrificed to make raindrops, which symbolise the saints who reflect God's glory.[80] The church is represented by the bow. If finished, the bow would form a complete circle (as in Revelation 4:3) around the Sun, which is Christ. Saints who are still living are symbolized by a half bow, whereas saints who have died are represented by an unseen bow. The ascension of the rainbow from earth to heaven represents the pilgrimage and sanctification of saints on their way to heaven.[81] Each rainbow drop represents a different spiritual gift, which is a grace reflected from the Sun.[82] After the darkness and storm, a rainbow appears, symbolizing the law's threat before the kindness and forgiveness of the wonderful Gospel.[83] Individual men are insignificant, unstable, dissolving, and of ephemeral life, as represented by raindrops. Those light-filled drops signify saints who reflect the light of the sun: a mingling of fire and water that represents the believers' flesh and Spirit nature.[84]

Edwards and Flowers

Edwards not only detected divine communications in the world-cathedral's heavenly vaults, but he also discerned divine emblems when he looked outward and downward. Edwards expounds Job 14:2, "He cometh forth like a flower, and is cut down," in the 1741 sermon "Youth is Like a Flower Cut Down," later updated and preached at the death of his daughter Jerusha. He considers this text "fit" and "applicable" for young people who look to be far from death but are suddenly cut down in their youth. He writes:

> As some such are endowed with those qualifications that [are] peculiarly pleasant and promising. A flower is the most beautiful, pleasant and fragrant part of the plant, that is most commonly put forth in the spring, the pleasantest part of the year, as was observed before. And it is also the most promising part of the

---

[79]"Notes on Scripture," *WJE*, 15:329.

[80]"Notes on Scripture," *WJE*, 15:329–31.

[81]"Notes on Scripture," *WJE*, 15:331–33.

[82]"Notes on Scripture," *WJE*, 15:333.

[83]"Notes on Scripture," *WJE*, 15:333–34.

[84]"Notes on Scripture," *WJE*, 15:334–35.

plant, promising fruit. And it may be observed of many flowers, that the time of their opening themselves is in the morning; in the afternoon they shut up.

This therefore is a fit emblem of a young person in the bloom of life, with amiable, pleasant and promising qualifications, not only with a blooming body but mind also; with desirable natural and moral endowments, rendering comfortable, pleasant and agreeable now to those that are round about, and giving hopes of much fruit hereafter to be brought forth, of much future serviceableness in the world.

Such as these are sometimes cut down by death in their youth, as a pleasant flower in the spring and morning is cut down by the scythe of the mower. And sometimes this is done suddenly— not by fading as a leaf in the fall of the year, but as a flower that is cut down by the scythe. It is done at one stroke."[85]

The characteristics that make a flower cut down a "fit emblem" of a person's death, particularly of a young person, are their beginning and their end.[86] A flower is emblematic of a young man in that they are both lovely and hopeful, and they both bloom swiftly. A flower's bloom is the most beautiful, pleasant, and fragrant part of the plant, just as a young person's bloom of body and mind, with both natural and moral character, is his beauty. The flower is the most promising component of the plant, as it produces fruit. This corresponds to the blossoming of a young person's body and mind, which has great promise. Many flowers bloom in the morning and close in the afternoon, just as most individuals blossom in their youth and lose youthful vigour of body and mind as they age. The flower fades after fully blossoming, and the wind blows its petals away. Similarly, after reaching the pinnacle of his grandeur and might, a man fades away. Flowers are often cut down abruptly before they mature and fade normally in the fall season. Though everyone dies in the end, some young people die in their prime.

If arranged in a table format, Edwards' arrangement of the correspondences look quite similar to the entries in Keach's *Tropologia*. There is a significant horticultural connection between Edwards' emblems and those of Austen and Keach. According to Edwards:

---

[85] "Youth is Like a Flower that is Cut Down," *WJE*, 22:329.

[86] "Youth is Like a Flower that is Cut Down," *WJE*, 22:322, 329.

Husbandmen are wont to PRUNE their trees after the dead time of winter, a little before the spring, when the time approaches for them to put forth and blossom with new life and rejoicing. So God is wont to wound his saints a little before he revives them, after falls and long seasons of deadness, and to purge them and prepare them for revival and comfort. So he is wont to wound and purge his church, and to lead them into sorrows. He will bring them into the wilderness and speak comfortably to them [Hosea 2:14].[87]

The job of a husbandman in his garden or orchard is familiar to these men, who reach the same conclusions about the meaning of what they see in the world's cathedral or library.

Voice of the Creatures

Edwards held that emblems engaged not only the eye, but the ear—speaking pictures, if you will. There is a voice in creation, but there is also the voice of creation, and both are intelligible for those that have ears to hear.

In addition to the voice of God in creation, "Images," nos. 57 and 70, we find Edwards focusing on the voice of the creatures in "Images," no. 110, and Sermon no. 445—the crowing of the rooster, the singing of spring birds, and the groaning of an abused creation.

The cock's crowing is emblematic of the introduction of the day of the church by ministers preaching the Gospel. This is analogous to Peter's awakening out of his deep sleep, brought to repentance by the crowing of the cock at break of day, which is representative of the awakening of the church and the rousing of the wise virgins from their slumbering and backsliding state, through the preaching of the Gospel, to usher in the morning of the glorious times. "The introducing of the spring by the voice of spring birds signifies the same thing."[88]

In a sermon on Romans 8:22, Edwards reasons that when creatures or things of the natural world are used to serve sin, they are being abused and debased—they are worthy of being used for better purposes. God made the visible creation and its elements very good, and therefore they should be improved to good uses, rather than being subjected to sin. He further states

---

[87]"Images of Divine Things," *WJE*, 11:116.

[88]"Images," no. 110.

that when these things are used to serve men's lusts, it is a debasement of them, as men's lusts are viler than the vilest of the beasts.

> What a vile use is that men put such a noble fabric as God hath built, in the upper stories of it adorned with sun, moon, and stars, and below with beautiful trees, herbs, and flowers, and filled with riches and treasures of his goodness, that they should turn it into a meat kitchen for Satan's drudgery shop of sin or a kitchen wherein to do Satan's drudgery, making use of the several parts of it to no other purpose.

He concludes by noting that the whole creation is represented as groaning under such abuse and is being held in bondage.[89]

Praise of the Creatures

Godfrey Goodman (1582–1656), an Anglican Bishop of Gloucester, wrote *The Creatures Praysing God* (1622), which can add to Edwards' idea of the voice of the creatures—especially their prayers and praise.

> Thus, as they were ordained for man's natural use, for his food, clothing, and labor, so it should seem they were appointed for his spiritual use, to serve him in the nature of Chaplains; that they should honor and praise God, while their master, sinful and wretched man, dishonors Him. Yet, their service might seem to be done by his appointment.[90]

> Now listen a while to their prayers: here every creature hath its sound and its voice, *Vox naturae inclamautis Dominum naturae,* The voice of nature calling upon the God of nature. Nature is not foolish, that she should babble and talk to herself, nor is there any other nature, with whom she might have conference; she is no more idle and superfluous in her words, than in her works: *Natura nihil fecit frustra, natura nihil dicet frustra.* Then undoubtedly in these cries, she offers up her prayers to her Maker.

---

[89] Sermon no. 445 on Romans 8:22, *WJEO* 52.

[90] Godfrey Goodman, *The Creatures Praysing God: Or, The Religion of Dumbe Creatures* (London: Printed by Felik Kingston, 1622), 3.

Now would you know the meaning and sense of these prayers? Surely I conceive them to be to this or the like purpose: *Venite, iubilemus Deo nostro, quifecit nos, exultemus & laetemur in ipso* (the very beginning of our Morning Service): O all ye works of the Lord, praise ye the Lord, bless him, and magnify him for ever. Do you yet require some more particular notice, what they request in their prayers? Truly they pray in a strange tongue, I never learnt their language; yet this I can say for a truth, in my own experience:

That according to the diversity of occasions, you shall find a difference in their prayers: in their joy and mirth, you may discern their pleasant notes[91] of thankfulness; in their grief and heaviness, you shall hear their sorrowful sighs, and groans of complaints. Then it should seem that nature becomes a petitioner: and to whom should she petition, but to that higher power which sits above nature? Though the dumb Creatures have neither speech nor language among them, yet their sound is gone out into all quarters: though their cries be inarticulate, and insignificant to us, yet are they understood of their Maker; he that sees the secrets of our hearts, can much more easily discern the intent of their prayers.[92]

Occasional Meditation

Edwards' meditations on nature, recorded in a notebook of divine emblems or shadows, are consistent with the convergence of a devotional and emblematic tradition, "for both meditation and spiritual emblem reflect on two objects ... The book of scripture and the book of nature."[93] Though a long-standing devotional practice, concentrating on God's voice in nature was losing favor in the seventeenth and eighteenth centuries. Meditation, spiritual sight, and religious enthusiasm complicated the initial humanist

---

[91]McGilchrist, *The Master and His Emissary,* 105–6. On this "note," McGilchrist observes that dogs use a form of "musilanguage" that combines body language with intonation to interact with humans. Some of the most intelligent animals, such as bonobos, whales, and dolphins coordinate their social lives and behaviors through what could be considered a form of music. This language of pitch, intonation, and temporal relation reveals that music can be a flexible and extensive means of communication.

[92]Goodman, *The Creatures Praysing God,* 23–24.

[93]Michael Bath, *Speaking Pictures: English Emblem Books and Renaissance Culture,* Longman Medieval and Renaissance Library (New York: Longman, 1994), 160.

ethos of Alciato's and others' emblems.[94] In an Enlightened age, unregulated meditation on the created order to hear God's voice or detect providences and prodigies was a source of humiliation and ill repute.[95] This is most likely why Edwards anticipated the charge of enthusiasm for his emblematic world view. Not only was the realm of similitudes and correspondences out of vogue, but hearing God's voice was the domain of the delusional. Edwards had ample reason to be concerned about the charge. Cotton Mather's life exposes not only some of the pillars of Edwards' emblematic reading of nature, but also the pitfalls of reading providences and prodigies in natural events and occasions.

Edwards' Advance

Nevertheless, we do not find Edwards retreating from a spiritualized nature in his "Types" notebook. He cites 1 Corinthians 13:2 as proof that "[t]here were [an] abundance of mysteries then not understood." Divine truths wrapped up in shadows and enigmatic representations are specifically referred to as "mysteries."[96] He then argues for a balance between "those who cry down all types and those who are for turning everything into nothing but allegory."[97] Edwards cites scriptural examples of a dove, rushing wind, and tongues of fire as emblems of the Holy Spirit, as well as small instances of silence in Scripture, such as details of Melchizedec's birth and death, as having major typological value.[98] In the following paragraphs, he claims that the entire universe is "full of images of divine things, as full as a language is of words," and that:

> To say that we must not say that such things are types of these and those things unless the Scripture has expressly taught us that they are so, is as unreasonable as to say that we are not to interpret any prophecies of Scripture or apply them to these and those events, except we find them interpreted to our hand, and must interpret no more of the prophecies of David, etc. For by

---

[94]Bath, *Speaking Pictures,* 161.

[95]For an extended treatment of the decline of the spiritual world view see, Leigh Eric Schmidt, *Hearing Things: Religion, Illusion, and the American Enlightenment* (Cambridge: Harvard University Press, 2000).

[96]"Types," *WJE,* 11:151.

[97]"Types," *WJE,* 11:151.

[98]"Types," *WJE,* 11:151.

the Scripture it is plain that innumerable other things are types that are not interpreted in Scripture (all the ordinances of the Law are all shadows of good things to come), in like manner as it is plain by Scripture that these and those passages that are not actually interpreted are yet predictions of future events.[99]

Edwards most likely pondered the historically difficult nature of providences and prodigies that engaged Cotton Mather and others, in addition to the immediate issue on the extent of legitimate types. It is worth noting that Edwards' emblematic world view is mainly devoid of prodigies and amazing providences. Rather than looking for God's voice in exceptions and aberrations of the natural order, Edwards was tuned in to the symphonic harmony of all creation. This emphasis on harmony is consistent with the emblematic world view of correspondences and similitudes.

Characteristics of Edwards' Emblematic World View

Several elements of Edwards' emblematics situate him within an emblematic world view quite close to that of Renaissance natural historians such as those outlined earlier. If his philosophical idealism, which is absent from "Images of Divine Things," is excluded, Edwards' thought contains some prominent themes that are essential to Renaissance emblematics and later developments.

Agreement, Consent, and Excellency

Edwards, like the emblematic Renaissance world view, sees a connection or agreement between the spiritual and material constitutions of the universe, and alludes to occasional meditation as a way to discern the divine message in the natural order. "Wherever we are and whatever we are about, we may see divine things excellently represented and held forth, and it will abundantly tend to confirm the Scriptures, for there is an excellent agreement between these things and the Holy Scriptures," he writes.[100] He even believes that meditating on the inhabitants of this planet reveals the spiritual realm's inhabitants and their respective habitations. The physical structure of this world corresponds precisely to the spiritual structure:

[99]"Types," *WJE*, 11:152.

[100]"Images of Divine Things," *WJE*, 11:74.

There are three sorts of inhabitants of this world inhabiting its three regions, viz. the inhabitants of the earth, and the animals that inhabit the waters under the earth, and the fowls of heaven that inhabit the air or firmament of heaven. In these is some faint shadow of the three different sorts of inhabitants of the three worlds, viz. earth, heaven and hell. The birds represent the inhabitants of heaven. These appear beautiful above the beasts and fishes; many of them are decked with glorious [plumage]. Whereas others do but go on the earth or move in the waters, these fly with wings and are above all kinds of animals; employ themselves in music, many of them as it were sweetly praising their Creator. The fishes in the waters under the earth represent the inhabitants of hell. The waters in Scripture is represented as the place of the dead, the Rephaim, the destroyers; and whales and sea monsters that swim in the great deep are used in Scripture as emblems of devils and the wrath of God. And the miseries of death and God's wrath are there compared to the sea, to the deeps, to floods and billows, and the like.[101]

Edwards is considering a wide-angle view of creation, recalling commonplace notions such as "up" is good, "down" is evil, and "middle" is a gray area or indeterminate. No Scripture is quoted in this entry, though he does state that the Scriptures do represent this overall system. Non-doctrinal features of these three zones demonstrate "fitness" for human life. Humans cannot breathe underwater, and in fact, humans are food for the devourers who live in the depths (sharks, etc.). Humans can live where birds live, and flight (which humans have always desired) reflects the freedom of heaven. Thus, there is a comprehensive and widespread agreement or "fitness" to the divine system.[102]

The harmony perceived by emblematicists such as Hall, Austen, and others between the natural and spiritual worlds corresponds with Edwards' perception of excellency. During the Enlightenment, a wide range of theologians and philosophers were interested in the theme of excellency. Though Edwards argues philosophically about beauty at times, he comes to the same conclusion as non-philosophical types like Austen and Bunyan: there is an appointed harmony and correlation between the created order and spiritual reality.

[101]"Images of Divine Things," *WJE,* 11:84–85.

[102]"Images of Divine Things," *WJE,* 11:67.

Edwards observes that the traditional explanation of excellency, "harmony, symmetry, or proportion," is insufficient.[103] "There has nothing been more without a definition than excellency, although it be what we are more concerned with than anything else whatsoever. Yea, we are concerned with nothing else. But what is this excellency?"[104] He finds that excellency in nature consists in equalities:[105]

> And so in every case, what is called correspondency, symmetry, regularity and the like, may be resolved into equalities; though the equalities in a beauty in any degree complicated are so numerous that it would be a most tedious piece of work to enumerate them. There are millions of these equalities. Of these consist the beautiful shape of flowers, the beauty of the body of man and of the bodies of other animals. That sort of beauty which is called "natural," as of vines, plants, trees, etc., consists of a very complicated harmony; and all the natural motions and tendencies and figures of bodies in the universe are done according to proportion, and therein is their beauty. Particular disproportions sometimes greatly add to the general beauty,[106] and must necessarily be, in order to a more universal proportion— so much equality, so much beauty—though it may be noted that the quantity of equality is not to be measured only by the number, but the intenseness, according to the quantity of being. As bodies are shadows of being, so their proportions are shadows of proportion.[107]

Edwards observes that beauty or perfection is made up of complex harmonies of symmetry and correspondence, which are shadows of being. He goes on to add that, as great as natural harmonies are, spiritual harmonies are far deeper and more complicated. Perception of these parallels and

[103]"The Mind," *WJE*, 6:332.

[104]"The Mind," *WJE*, 6:332.

[105]"The Mind," *WJE*, 6:332.

[106]McGilchrist notes that animals may have a preference for symmetry in a mate, yet humans appear to lack such inclinations. Even if symmetry is seen as healthier, it is still not seen as attractive. Symmetry in living faces is often perceived as eerie, which is likely the motivation behind Blake's "fearful symmetry" of the tiger. This sentiment is echoed in Enlightenment portraiture, which is so symmetrical it is easily forgotten. McGilchrist, *The Master and His Emissary*, 343.

[107]"The Mind," *WJE*, 6:335.

differences is an acquired ability or taste, akin to a cultivated liking for music. Harmony and quality in simple tunes are easily discernible at a basic level.[108] The notes come together in their speed and rhythm with an easy pleasantness. The same pleasantness can be found in proportionate bodies and symmetrical features. The opposite side of a body or face corresponds to the opposite side. A lack of symmetry is often regarded as a malformation that disrupts the beauty or harmony of the object in question, whether it be a person, plant, animal, or building. According to Edwards, humans are hardwired to search out patterns, similarities, and correspondences:

> How exceedingly apt are we, when we are sitting still and acci-
> dentally casting our eye upon some marks or spots in the floor
> or wall, to be ranging of them into regular parcels and figures;
> and if we see a mark out of its place, to be placing of it right
> by our imagination—and this even while we are meditating on
> something else. So we may catch ourselves at observing the rules
> of harmony and regularity in the careless motions of our heads
> or feet, and when playing with our hands or walking about the
> room.[109]

The human proclivity or disposition to identify patterns in random locations on the wall through imagination can be applied to various forms of associations and systems. The desire for order and harmony drives all fields of research, discovery, and creation. Humans crave beauty and expect harmony and order. The unavoidable use of metaphor in everyday conversation demonstrates a similar leaning toward correspondences and relations. Something is explained in terms of something else. All communication and reality are inextricably linked. The study of harmony and regularity in our human body's insignificant motions is easily extended to things outside the body, beyond spots on the floor or wall to patterns in occurrences, providences, and signs. It is only a short step from stains on the floor to an emblematic world view. According to Edwards, plurality is required for harmony, proportion, and excellency. Harmony and proportion cannot exist in solitude.[110] Similarly, excellence does not happen in isolation, "because there can be no such thing as consent or agreement." True being, according to Edwards, is

[108]"The Mind," *WJE*, 6:335–36.

[109]"The Mind," *WJE*, 6:336.

[110]"The Mind," *WJE*, 6:337.

spiritual, and material bodies are shadows of being. The more the proportion, likeness, and harmony of bodies, the more they shadow or correspond
to greatness or true being. There is thus agreement or accord between the
natural and the spiritual. The more excellent or beautiful anything is, the
more it resembles or corresponds to God.[111]

Edwards' idea that the Old Testament is full of types and shadows of
things that find correspondence and fulfillment in the New Testament exemplifies the drive for harmony. The harmony of the two testaments demonstrated their superiority. The harmony between the two testaments even
flowed over into the created order, as demonstrated by Edwards' notebook
"Images of Divine Things." This notebook contained his observations and
expositions of agreement between the created order and the Scriptures: a
harmony between the shadowy material world and that which is real and
spiritual.[112] There is a compatibility or agreement between the shadow and
the thing shadowed. With shadow, the phrases emblem and image can be
used interchangeably. Correspondences between the two testaments can be
perceived, but the testaments themselves expressly point out the correspondence between the created order and the spiritual realm. Man, as a created
being, was created in God's image (shadow, emblem). The incarnate Christ is
the exact representation of the Father. Edwards' philosophical consideration
of excellency is based on proportion, harmony, correspondence, and consent,
and it is anchored in the emblematic and representative composition of the
created order as acknowledged by earlier Evangelicals such as Hall, Austen,
Bunyan, and others.[113]

Primacy of Scripture

Edwards' emblematic world view is based on scriptural precedent and is
subject to its authority. In many cases, the Bible identifies and applies
spiritual mysteries discovered to be a part of the created world.[114] This is

---

[111]"The Mind," *WJE*, 6:337.

[112]E. Brooks Holifield, "Edwards as Theologian," in *The Cambridge Companion to Jonathan Edwards* (New York: Cambridge University Press, 2007), 147.

[113]Hall, "The Invisible World," in *The Works of the Right Reverend Joseph Hall, D. D.*, 8:180–81. Austen, *The Spiritual Use of an Orchard*, 3–6. Bunyan, "Solomon's Temple Spiritualized," in *The Whole Works of John Bunyan*, 3:500.

[114]"Images of Divine Things," *WJE*, 11:106.

especially noticeable in the "Scriptures" series, which follows his 212 "Image" entries.[115] He insists that

> The book of Scripture is the interpreter of the book of nature two ways, viz., by declaring to us those spiritual mysteries that are indeed signified and typified in the constitution of the natural world; and secondly, in actually making application of the signs and types in the book of nature as representations of those spiritual mysteries in many instances.[116]

Edwards adhered to the authority of Scripture throughout his vast typology of nature. Though Edwards extols nature, it is nowhere near an autonomous source of revelation. The communication constrains the created order's communicative nature. The message's objective is to bring God glory. According to Robert Brown, the discovery of types in nature is warranted by the Bible's use of types "because it, not the vague and meager reflections of unaided reason, gave them voice, and because creation was fundamentally structured to communicate the history of redemption."[117] The Scriptures supply the governing paradigm, which is "strictly rule-governed through an authoritative precedent."[118] Outside the interpretive authority of the Bible, nature has no clear voice.

Similitudes and Correspondences

The analogous nature of the natural world is closely tied to the natural world's agreeableness to the spiritual world. Edwards uses the terms analogy and similitude to describe two characteristics of the Renaissance world view. Entry 86 is quite similar to entry 82, except that entry 82 emphasizes the world's three-story structure, whereas entry 86 emphasizes similitudes and gradation or chain of being:

> As it is in the analogy that is to be observed in the works of nature, wherein the inferior are images of the superior, and the analogy holds through many ranks of beings, but becomes more and more faint and languid (thus, how many things in brutes are

---

[115]"Images of Divine Things," *WJE*, 11:131–35.

[116]"Images of Divine Things," *WJE*, 11:106.

[117]Brown, *Jonathan Edwards and the Bible,* 151.

[118]Brown, *Jonathan Edwards and the Bible,* 151.

analogous to what is to be observed in men: in some the image is more lively, in others less, till we come to the lowest rank of brutes, in whom it is more faint than others; but if we go from them to plants, still the analogy and similitude holds in many things, and in different degrees in different plants, till we come to metals and some other inanimate things, wherein still is to be seen some very faint representations of things appertaining to mankind); so it is with respect to the representations there are in the external world, of things in the spiritual world. Thus the visible heavens are a type of the highest heavens, but in a lower degree mountains are types of heaven. The great deep under the earth is a type of hell, but in a lesser degree valleys, and the water that is in valleys, is so. The stars are types of saints in glory, and in a fainter degree the singing birds that fly in the firmament of heaven are so And so in innumerable instances; and the same is to be observed of the types of Scripture.[119]

Edwards' usage of the term "emblem" is telling. It is in his vocabulary, but not as frequently as his favorite terms, type and shadow. Nonetheless, in his exposition of Jonah, he employs the terms "emblem," "type," and "represents" interchangeably. The gourd has been described as a type, representation, and emblem. His use of "emblem" is identical to his use of "type" or "shadow."[120] There are several examples of his use of "emblem," but the following is representative:

Hence the Scripture symbol of the Holy Ghost is a dove, which is the emblem of love, and so was continually accounted (as is well known) in the heathen world, and is so made use of by their poets and mythologists, which probably arose partly from the nature and manner of the bird, and probably in part from the tradition of the story of Noah's dove, that came with a message of peace and love after such terrible manifestations of God's wrath in the time of the deluge. This bird is also made use of as an emblem of love in the Holy Scriptures; as it was on that message of peace and love that God sent it to Noah, when it came with

---

[119]"Images of Divine Things," *WJE,* 11:85–86.

[120]The synonymous usage of these terms with "emblem" goes to Fabiny's point that the emblematics of Edwards needs to be viewed in a wider context. Tibor Fabiny, "Edwards and Biblical Typology," in *Understanding Jonathan Edwards: An Introduction to America's Theologian,* ed. Gerald McDermott (New York: Oxford University Press, 2008), 101.

an olive-leaf in its mouth, and often in Solomon's Song: Cant. i. 15—"Thou hast doves' eyes:" Cant. v. 12—"His eyes are as the eyes of doves:" Cant. v. 2—"Open to me, my love, my dove," and in other places in that song.[121]

Edwards is alluding to the ancient pagan world, mythology, and poetry in addition to the term "emblem." This is typical of the Renaissance's emblematic world view's search for a specific's meaning inside a web of associations. Entry 125 of "Images" contains a nearly identical reference to the relationship between the Spirit and a dove. Edwards refers to love in action rather than love itself: shelter, warmth, heat, brooding, feeding, and nourishment:

> There are many things between the young birds in a nest and a dam, resembling what is between Christ and his saints. The bird shelters them; so Christ shelters his saints, as a bird does her young under her wings. They [are] brought forth by the dam; so the saints are Christ's children. They are hatched by the brooding of the dam; so the soul is brought forth by the warmth and heat and brooding of Christ, by the Heavenly Dove, the Holy Spirit. They dwell in a nest of the dam's providing, on high out of the reach of harm, in some place of safety; so are the saints in the church. They are feeble and helpless, can neither fly nor go, which represents the infant state of the saints in this world. The manner of the dam's feeding the young, giving every one his portion represents the manner of Christ's feeding his saints. When the dam visits the nest, all open their mouths wide together with a cry, and that is all that they can do. So should the saints do, especially at times when Christ makes special visits to his church by his Spirit. They don't open their mouths in vain. So God says, "Open thy mouth wide and I will fill" [Psalms 81:10]. The birds grow by this nourishment till they fly away into heaven to sing in the Firmament. So the saints are nourished up to glory.[122]

Edwards draws an explicit correspondence between nature and spiritual excellencies, but its perception requires discernment and feeling: "And there

---

[121]"Documents on the Trinity, Grace and Faith," *WJE Online*, Vol. 37.

[122]"Images of Divine Things," *WJE*, 11:96.

is really an analogy, or consent, between the beauty of the skies, trees, fields, flowers, etc. and spiritual excellencies; though the agreement is more hid and requires a more discerning, feeling mind to perceive it ..."[123] The harmony between the natural and the spiritual seems "strange," but it exists:

> [N]atural in such frames of mind to think of them, and fancy ourselves in the midst of them. Thus there seems to be love and complacency in flowers and bespangled meadows; this makes lovers delight so much in them. So there is a rejoicing in the green trees and fields, [and] majesty in thunder beyond all other noises whatever ... And doubtless this is a reason that Christ is compared so often to those things and called by their names; as, the sun of righteousness, the morning star, the rose of Sharon and lily of the valleys, the apple tree amongst the trees of the wood, a bundle of myrrh, a roe, or a young hart. By this we may discover the beauty of many of those metaphors and similes, which to an unphilosophical person do seem so uncouth.[124]

Developmental Features

The above-mentioned elements of Edwards' emblematic world view: agreement, fitness, harmony, Scripture, similitudes and correspondences, gradation of being, and analogy all set Edwards' thought at variance with a mechanical world view. This is widely acknowledged. Nonetheless, as previously stated, his emblematic viewpoint has been considered as innovative at times. When one considers Edwards' references to hieroglyphics, mythology, poets, ancient pagan beliefs, and the adagial tradition (John Spencer's *Things New and Old*), it is evident that he is reviving and refining the Renaissance emblematic world view.

Emblem Book

The emblem book, as mentioned in Chapter Two, was the pinnacle of these Renaissance developments. Though emblem books typically featured a three-part format consisting of a motto, a symbolic image, and a riddle that was solved when viewed in connection with an epigram or commentary beneath, there was great latitude within the genre. Some emblem books were "blind"

---

[123]"Miscellanies" no. 108, *WJE,* 12:278.

[124]"Miscellanies" no. 108, *WJE,* 12:278–80.

or "naked," with no graphics like Bunyan's, however they "refer[ed] to imagined visual images."[125]

The subject matter of emblem books varied as much as the structure, which included all of the developmental features mentioned above: hiero-glyphics, mythology, poetry, ancient pagan beliefs, beast and plant lore, adages, and biblical and theological topics.[126] Given that Edwards' notebook "Images of Divine Things" bears the above marks, was intended for eventual publication as part of his "Rational Account of the Main Doctrines of the Christian Religion Attempted,"[127] and lacks pictures, it is convenient to clas-sify it as a subcategory of the "naked" or "blind" emblem book genre, similar to Bunyan's *Book for Boys and Girls*, which drew its images from the created order.

Critique

It should be emphasized that Edwards' emblems are not without criticism. The emblematic world view and reinscripturation have both advantages and disadvantages. On the plus side, Edwards takes pains in the Scripture tables and indexes of "Images of Divine Things" to demonstrate scriptural precedence to his typology of nature.[128] He also takes precautions. This is evidenced by the fact that the notebook remained a thin volume of only 212 entries, despite the fact that he actively wrote in it for twenty-eight years. He was careful not to "give in to a wild fancy," but rather to find justification "by some hint in the New Testament of its being the true interpretation, or a lively figure and representation contained or warranted by an analogy to other types that we interpret on sure grounds."[129] It has been noted that

---

[125] Diehl, *An Index of Icons in English Emblem Books, 1550–1700*, 3.

[126] Diehl, *An Index of Icons in English Emblem Books, 1550–1700*, 3.

[127] "Outline of A Rational Account," *WJE*, 6:396.

[128] "Images of Divine Things," *WJE*, 11:131–35, 141–42.

[129] "Types," *WJE*, 11:148. Edwards also noted that the use of "understanding and invention" was necessarily used by the OT saints as they searched into the meaning of types given to them. They had to search for meaning and fulfillment of types outside of Scripture. "If we may use our own understandings and invention not at all in interpreting types, and must not conclude anything at all to be types but what is expressly said to be and explained in Scripture, then the church under the Old [Testament], when the types were given, were secluded from ever using their understanding to search into the meaning of the types geven to 'em; for God did, when he gave 'em, give no interpretation" (150). He was concerned to "show how there is a medium between those that cry down all types, and those that are for turning all into nothing but allegory" (151).

Edwards anticipated criticism, yet he expressed confidence despite it.[130] This is owed, no doubt, to his faith in the Scripture warrant, but also to his position in an Evangelical emblematic tradition that is consistent with Scripture and experience.

Another advantage, according to Avihu Zakai, is Edwards' thought's continued relevance: "Edwards' emblematic, symbolic view of the world of nature, the typological reading of created order, is not radically opposed to certain trends in modern physics regarding the essential nature of reality."[131] "[M]odern science rather tends again to the re-enchantment of the world of nature ... Within this new metaphysical context,[132] Edwards' re-enchantment of the world resonates clearly and powerfully," says the author of the metaphysical shift in physics.[133]

However, there are risks associated with Edwards' project. The issue expressed earlier about purging natural histories of mistakes must also be addressed to Edwards' emblems. Serpents do not entice their prey into their mouths, and moles do not open their eyes at the end of their lives.[134] The emblem's accuracy is dependent on the accuracy of scientific information. Though such flaws do not affect the extrapolated scriptural truth, they do pose the risk of appearing antiquated, out-of-date, or obsolete. To Edwards' credit, such errors are rare; but, the possibility of exegeting an entire universe of emblems and emblematic human experience presents substantial challenges due to the immense (and ever-expanding) web of information and correspondences.

Further complexities arise when one considers Edwards' natural language's idiomatic and fluid aspect, which, as a true language, frequently resists literal interpretation or singular definition.[135] In addition to the aforementioned difficulties, the language of nature is insufficient for clear communication. Just as images can improve a book's text, so can creation enhance the text of Scripture. However, without the text of Scripture, creation only conveys the idea of the story. Though Edwards realized this, man's fallen nature tends to put the creature above the Creator. Idolatry and

---

[130]"Types," *WJE,* 152.

[131]Avihu Zakai, "An Interview with Avihu Zakai." [on-line]; accessed 29 November 2022; available from https://www.jesociety.org/an-interview-with-avihu-zakai/; Internet.

[132]Ibid.

[133]Ibid.

[134]"Images of Divine Things," *WJE,* 11:54, 71, 118.

[135]"Types," *WJE,* 11:150–51.

overheated imaginations that go beyond the analogies of faith are always a risk.

Conclusion

Based on what has been discussed thus far, it is easy to place Edwards' "Images of Divine Things" in the emblem book genre. The emblematic world view dates back to the medieval period and earlier, and it evolved in book form, both in terms of insight and expression, from Alciati to Edwards.[136] Natural historians, Paracelsians, and Evangelicals all contributed throughout the intermediate stages. Edwards' "Images of Divine Things" is definitely a notebook of emblems, and it shares a strong topical resonance with John Bunyan's Evangelical emblem book, *A Book for Boys and Girls*, and Joseph Hall's emblematic book, *Occasional Meditations*. These three representative works mix occasional meditation with an emblematic world perspective. Edwards, Bunyan, and Hall all used everyday objects as meditation objects, and they all published 'blind' emblem books with no illustrations. Wilson Kimnach's description of the "Images" notebook only adds to these views of Edwards' place within the emblem book genre:

> From a literary point of view, the notebook is at least an impressive collection of images or word pictures designed to give key doctrinal points the utmost vividness, immediacy, and mnemonic vitality without sacrificing (as is the rule with richly suggestive images or symbols in poetry) one jot of doctrinal precision ...Whether or not Edwards had discovered the hieroglyph of Deity in Nature, or like Newton had perceived the consistent principle within the event, he had certainly isolated, largely in the commonplaces of human experience, a suprarational confirmation of his doctrine that combined the functions of exposition and illustration, and that fixed the attention through the perception of analogy becoming symbol.[137]

As a work of literature, Edwards' work exhibits all of the hallmarks of an emblem book thoroughly within the emblematic world view: visuals and word pictures, mnemonic life, hieroglyphs, Deity in Nature, consistent

---

[136]It is an interesting coincidence that Alciati's emblem book had 212 entries, as did Edwards' "Images of Divine Things." See Green, *Andrea Alciati and His Books of Emblems*, 22.

[137]Kimnach, "Editor's Introduction," *WJE*, 10:45.

principle, commonplaces, analogy, and symbol. What remains to be seen is Edwards' application of the emblematic world view and his emblem book, "Images of Divine Things," to his ambition of reinscripturating the universe. The following chapter will show Edwards' efforts to bring both the Renaissance and the Evangelical emblematic world views to a crescendo by directly (and more explicitly than ever before) identifying the correspondences between the Book of Scripture and the Book of Nature.

CHAPTER FIVE: REINSCRIPTURATED WORLD

Introduction

EDWARDS' "IMAGES OF DIVINE THINGS," as seen in previous chapters, is a book of emblems that incorporates his systematic observation and meditation on a three-story universe that perfectly corresponds to the spiritual world. Edwards' brief entries have been described as "brief moral allegory" by John Gatta.[1] Each entry's brevity is the product of Edwards' skilled meditation and economy of words in his pursuit of theological accuracy. "Images of Divine Things" was written in a "plain style," with little consideration for the adornment and flourish that were generally associated with symbolic works. In his precision, however, Edwards does not sacrifice comprehensiveness. He wants to capture a "comprehensive view, to take in the various actions in the world and look on them at one glance, and to see them in their mutual respects and relations."[2] This panoramic view provided him, and any other intelligent being with eyes to see, with "an opportunity to complete God's creation through the spiritualization of nature ... re-attaching the material and spiritual in accordance with the design of the Creator."[3] The purpose of this chapter is to look at Edwards' theological encounter with nature. It shall be shown that reorganizing Edwards' views on nature in his "Images" journal reveals a doctrinal comprehensiveness in his world. His re-attachment of the natural order to the Scriptures may be referred to as

---

[1] John Gatta, *Making Nature Sacred: Literature, Religion, and Environment in America from the Puritans to the Present* (New York: Oxford University Press, 2004), 64.

[2] "Miscellanies" no. 383. BEING OF GOD, *WJE*, 13: 451–52.

[3] William Kimnach, "General Introduction," *WJE*, 10:45–46.

reinscripturation, because he seeks to undo the Enlightenment's deinscripted, mechanical world view and make the world a text of revelation once more.[4]

Uniqueness of Edwards

Several factors surrounding this comprehensive view and spiritual reattachment must be explored in order to comprehend Edwards' objective. Edwards' emblematic world view harkens back to the Renaissance's inscribed world view, which was rich with correspondences and similitudes. However, Gesner and Aldrovandi's Renaissance emblematic world view was insufficient on its own to offer intentional meaning. A purely emblematic approach that sought significance in a wide range of associations, myths, tales, histories, and so on led nowhere. If the correspondences of the emblematic world view did not point beyond themselves and motivate the discerning observer to devotion, they were no more useful than the metaphorical wheels and gears of the mechanical world view. "So it is nonsense to say of a machine whose highest end is to have one part move another, that the parts of the engine are useful to move the rest; for the whole is useless, and so every part, however they correspond together,"[5] Edwards stated of the numerous correspondences in the world. Harmony as an aim in itself is without purpose or direction. This teleological dilemma is solved by Edwards by making the Word of God clear in its correspondences with the world. The three-story universe is like a cathedral or commonplace that everyone inhabits. The illuminated representations of the world, like a cathedral, serve as windows into spiritual reality. Even the simplest features of architecture and art, as in many cathedrals, are infused with spiritual and biblical importance. Edwards' objective, an explicit re-attachment of Scripture to the world in accordance with the Creator's purpose, results in the renewal of the natural order. Edwards takes us back to an inscripturated world, not just an inscribed world. A reinscripturation is the restoration of unity between the Book of Scripture and the Book of Nature.

---

[4]I arrived at the terms *reinscriptured, reinscripturate,* and *reinscripturation* in an effort to describe Edwards' reinscription of the world, not as a general text, but one with specific correspondences to Scripture.

[5]"Miscellanies" tt. DEVOTION, *WJE,* 13:190.

Renaissance Emblematics

Edwards' efforts to reinscripturate the world are a continuation and refinement of the Renaissance endeavor to uncover meaning in the world by reading it like a book. The drive to uncover correspondences and similitudes was eventually pushed to great lengths by the Paracelsian hunt for the *ars signata* as a medieval impulse to find oneness everywhere.[6] Edwards believed in the immediate relationship between the Word of God and creation, as seen by his theology of continual creation and the linguistic and emblematic structure of the created order.[7] Another factor emphasizing the significance of Edwards' technique was the purported collapse or fall of the emblematic world view prior to the seventeenth century.

Evangelical Emblematics

With John Bunyan, the world of correspondences, similitudes, and emblems (as well as the emblem book genre) died. By Bunyan's day, the emblem book genre had devolved into children's entertainment, unworthy of serious literary, let alone theological, attention.[8] However, Bunyan's emblematic correspondences were reaching new heights in his emblem book, *A Book for Boys and Girls,* at the same time. Bunyan's emblematic works, *Pilgrim's Progress* and *A Book for Boys and Girls,* are outstanding instances of "a particular way way of reading Scripture and . . . a particular way of reinterpreting the world in accordance with the patterns of. . . prior Scripture reading."[9] Bunyan is writing in the language of Canaan, a language exclusive to believers.

It is significant that Edwards resurrected the emblematic world view and put it explicitly in service of Scripture. He was well aware of the Enlightenment's challenges. More significant is his belief in the comprehensiveness of theological revelation in nature. "Images of Divine Things" contains Edwards' musings on the abundance of revelation in creation. There is also a substantial allusion to Erasmus's *adagial* tradition. This is evident in the title page

[6]E. M. W. Tillyard, *The Elizabethan World Picture* (New York: Vintage, 1959), 83–84.

[7]"Things to be Considered an[d] Written fully about," *WJE,* 6:241–42.

[8]Rosemary Freeman, *English Emblem Books* (New York: Octagon Books, 1966), 206.

[9]David Dawson, "Allegorical Intratextuality in Bunyan and Winstanley," *The Journal of Religion* 70 (1990): 189.

comment, where Edwards wrote "See Spencer's *Similes and Sentences.*"[10] This work is a classic collection of adages that begins with a comprehensive list of all authors, ancient and modern, who are cited. Edwards' reference to this work hints at the importance he placed on the proverbial tradition, which was central to the emblematic Renaissance world view. He actually mentioned Spencer twice. Spencer inspired one of Edwards' most animated images:

> It is observed of the CROCODILE that it cometh of an egg no bigger than a goose egg, yet grows till he is fifteen cubits long; Pliny says thirty. He is also long- lived and grows as long as he lives. (See Spencer's Similes and Sentences, p. 68.) And how terrible a creature does he become, how destructive, and hard to be destroyed.

> So sin is comparatively easily crushed in the egg, taken in its beginning; but if let alone, what head does it get, how great and strong, terrible and destructive does it become, and hard to kill, and grows as long as it lives.

> So it is with sin, or Satan's interest in particular persons; and so it is with his interest in towns, countries and empires, and the world of mankind. How small was Satan's interest in the old world, beginning in Cain's family, but what did it come to before the Flood. How small was idolatry, in its beginnings after the Flood, but how did it carry the world before it afterwards, and hold it for many ages, growing stronger and greater, and worse and worse. So it was with the kingdom of Antichrist, and so it was with Satan's Mahometan kingdom, and so it will probably be with the last apostasy before the end of time.[11]

This entry is brimming with Renaissance wisdom: natural history, a reference to an ancient author, and spiritual precepts. Despite its origins in Spencer's work, it sounds rather Edwardsean when compared to the other entries in the "Images" notebook. The crocodile and his egg get a new voice in Edwards' reinscripted world, neatly filed in the "Images" notebook between entries "177. A HOG" and "178. The wheels of a WATCH or a

---

[10]"Images of Divine Things," *WJE*, 11:50. This is a reference to John Spencer's work, *Things New and Old: or, A Large Storehouse of Similes, Sentences, Apologues, Allegories, Apophthegms, Adages, Divine, Moral, Political, &c, with their Several Applications* (1658).

[11]"Images of Divine Things," *WJE*, 11:118.

CLOCK."[12] If nature's voice speaks of nothing higher than itself, then nature has no purpose other than itself: nature exists for the sake of nature, not for the sake of God. Crocodiles and the rest of creation are silent save for their bellows and other audible noises. A skewed perspective of nature underscores the issue raised by Edwards in "Miscellanies" no. tt. on the devotional aim of the world.[13]

Edwards' Response

When confronted with the challenges of a described world and empiricism, Edwards took a direct path, attempting to avoid the mistakes of the past and embrace an observational method through which he sought a biblically legitimatized correspondence between the Book of Scripture and the Book of Nature. He built an emblematic world view on an overtly scriptural base that was unaffected by legitimate scientific discovery. Rainbows, thunder, lightning, flowers, spiders, and all the other details of the created order captivated Edwards as both a theologian and a natural scientist. He was able to manage the deluge of correspondences and similitudes in the natural and spiritual worlds by boiling most of it down to commonplaces and corresponding ideas.

Edwards' acceptance of his firsthand observations of nature has been attributed to naiveté.[14] As a creature and intellectual participant in nature, Edwards relied on surface (or first) impressions to decipher meaning. However, the plethora of consents and agreements in nature were so interwoven and complex that a systematic exposition of the correspondences was a laborious and nearly impossible effort.[15] Despite this, Edwards continued to write in his "Images" journal for nearly three decades. A world that 'fit' with spiritual truth drew him in with an irresistible pull.

Edwards was not the only one who saw parallels between natural and spiritual phenomena. Yet, perceiving a world of analogies, correspondences, and similitudes did not necessarily entail adoption of Edwards' philosophical

---

[12]"Images of Divine Things," *WJE,* 11:116–18.

[13]"Miscellanies" no. tt. DEVOTION, *WJE,* 13:190.

[14]Clyde Holbrook, *Jonathan Edwards, The Valley and Nature, An Interpretive Essay,* (Lewisburg: Bucknell University Press, 1987), 33–34. Anna Svetlikova, "Jonathan Edwards' Typology as Language," Theologica Wratislaviensia 7 (2012), 163.

[15]Holbrook, *Jonathan Edwards, The Valley and Nature,* 45, 77.

idealism.[16] As mentioned in previous chapters, other Evangelicals such as Hall and Bunyan had comparable experiences to Edwards. Their interaction with nature had a tangible impact on them and elicited spiritual emotion.[17] Nature and intuition, not ratiocination, transformed everyday occurrences into signs pointing to spiritual reality.[18] In comparison, Edwards' connection with nature differs little from his Protestant forefathers' customary modes of occasional meditation. The contemplative union of Scripture and earthly experiences yielded "sublime truths."[19] It is not surprising that Edwards' emblematization of the natural world occasionally exceeded the confines of conservative typology. His anticipation of the accusation of zeal shows that he was aware he was typologizing "at the end of the rope."[20] Edwards' method was similar to allegories, similes, and correspondences of the Renaissance's emblematic world view. The question of Edwards' audience is raised by his journey into the older world view. In "Images," he refers to ancient wisdom, hieroglyphics, and commonplaces known by both elect and nonelect. The correspondences and similitudes that comprise the meaningful world appear to be part of a general revelation, rather than being dependent on divine and supernatural light. This would make much of Edwards' emblematic world view available to the wider public.[21]

An Embodied Encounter with Nature

Because his encounter with nature is spatiotemporal, Edwards' emblematic world view is widely accessible.[22] The fact that Edwards' direct experience is an embodied experience is significant. His experience of a three-story reality is not abstract, but rather tangible. Heaven, the source of all good, is up. Hell, the abode of all evil, is down. Edwards' use of the up-down spatial orientation metaphor extends to happy-sad, life-death, conscious-unconscious, more-less, and virtue-depravity.[23] The up-down metaphor,

---

[16]Holbrook, *Jonathan Edwards, The Valley and Nature,* 49–50.

[17]Holbrook, *Jonathan Edwards, The Valley and Nature,* 53.

[18]Holbrook, *Jonathan Edwards, The Valley and Nature,* 72.

[19]Holbrook, *Jonathan Edwards, The Valley and Nature,* 75–76.

[20]Holbrook, *Jonathan Edwards, The Valley and Nature,* 78.

[21]Holbrook, *Jonathan Edwards, The Valley and Nature,* 95–97.

[22]Holbrook, *Jonathan Edwards, The Valley and Nature,* 55.

[23]George Lakoff and Mark Johnson, *Metaphors We Live By* (Chicago: University of Chicago Press, 1980), 15–16.

as well as the linked good-bad, are critical to comprehending Edwards' three-story universe presented in "Images of Divine Things." Rather than Edwards arbitrarily generating categories and emblems, as Holbrook claims, his design has a universally known intuitive structure based on his firsthand experience with nature.[24]

Edwards' emblematic world view is distinguished by well-known folk metaphor. Pigs, lions, foxes, dogs, cats, and a wide range of other animals are frequently connected with human behavior and features.[25] Pigs are filthy, lions are brave, foxes are cunning, dogs are devoted, cats are finicky, and so on. Human instincts and behavior, in turn, are commonly defined in terms of animal instincts and behavior. "That kid's a pig." "That soldier had the bravery of a lion." "The lawyer is as shrewd as a fox." When Edwards portrays the laziness of grasshoppers who do not save food for the winter in the summer, he is transferring the human attribute of laziness onto a grasshopper that is merely responding instinctively.[26]

In addition to projecting human characteristics onto the animate and inanimate worlds, Edwards projects both the divine and the satanic onto created objects. The higher a creature or object ascends in the great chain of being, the more similar it is to divine and heavenly things. The lower anything is on the great chain of being, the more it resembles diabolical things. The three-story world of heavens, earth, and deep is rich of parallels and projections. However, the expected qualities have limitations. Divine correspondences are rarely seen in the deep in Edwards' theory. The abyss and depths are where the damned live.[27] There are some exceptions, such as water, that are endowed with both divine and diabolical traits, but Edwards' emblematic framework generally follows the up-down orientational metaphor.[28] Similarly, evil correspondences are uncommon in high places. However, there is tremendous overlap of divine and diabolical correspondences in the terrestrial realm. The tension in earthly correspondences, which may be seen in water, heights, birds, insects, and other things, demonstrates that the creation is not in a fixed and final condition. In Scripture,

[24]Holbrook, *Jonathan Edwards, The Valley and Nature,* 81.

[25]George Lakoff and Mark Turner, *More Than Cool Reason: A Field Guide to Poetic Metaphor* (The University Of Chicago Press, 1989), 194.

[26]"Images of Divine Things," *WJE,* 11:90.

[27]"Images of Divine Things," *WJE,* 11:56.

[28]The up-down orientation to Edwards' emblematic world view can be seen in numerous places in his "Images" notebook: Entries 3, 7, 12, 13, 15, 21, 22, 27, 28, 29, 71, 77, 111, 117, 155, 161, 196.

the lion, who represents both Christ and the devil, does not yet lie down with the lamb.

The flexibility of several of Edwards' visuals raises concerns about stability. Is it possible to make an image signify anything? No, it is not. The plasticity of an image has limits. Certain aspects of creation are so established in their natures and instincts that correspondences rarely vary. Doves and rocks, for example, are emblems of purity and solidity, respectively. Water's fluidity of correspondence had previously been recognized, but when one looks closer at Edwards' images, it becomes clear that moving water is good and stagnant water is bad. It is worth noting that the new heaven and new earth will no longer have a sea, but will instead have a river. A thing's or creature's core nature or instinctual activity is what gives it significance or voice. Like the dove, an unchanging emblem of peace and purity, spiders are emblematic of the wicked and diabolical. These emblems are diametrically opposed in nature and meaning. A spider does not have the flexibility observed in water correspondences. Spiders are never pleasant. That is an absurd concept since the repulsive spider's instinctive nature does not allow for flexibility.

The organisms' correspondences are fundamentally stable due to their unchanging nature. The meaning of organisms and things can be found in their instinctual behavior. Their voice is their significance. "Images of Divine Things" by Edwards is a record of the voices in nature created by God to resonate with the voice of the Scriptures. Edwards writes about the relationship between the two voices::

> The Book of Scripture is the interpreter of the book of nature two ways: viz. by declaring to us those spiritual mysteries that are indeed signified or typified in the constitution of the natural world; and secondly, in actually making application of the signs and types in the book of nature as representations of those spiritual mysteries in many instances.[29]

Edwards accomplished reinscripturation by re-mapping Scripture onto the world in the original design of the Creator.[30] Scripture is replete with images and figures that correspond to and elaborate on the world's general

---

[29]"Images of Divine Things," *WJE*, 11:106.

[30]William Kimnach, "General Introduction," *WJE*, 10:46. An alternative metaphor, in keeping with the *Types Explorer* software project would be *reinstalling* Scripture in the world. The operating system or underlying code that runs the world is the Word. The icons and interface come alive when running the right operating system. "Images of Divine Things" is a theological

and popular folk metaphors. A reinscripturated world is the product of special revelation (the Scriptures with their explicit pictures and figures) mixed with general revelation (the world and folk metaphors based on the world). Throughout this approach, Edwards discovers God's voice or language in the created order. The species' set instincts and natures become significations, even words, acknowledged by all human societies. Because of the enormous number of creatures with fixed instincts, Edwards concluded that Scripture had established the precedent, provided a grammar and norms of interpretation, and effectively commissioned man to acquire this language.[31] Edwards' use of commonplaces and folk metaphors, as well as his interest in hieroglyphics and ancient wisdom, indicate that he was operating firmly within the emblematic world view of correspondences and similitudes, and that his emblem book "Images of Divine Things" was his field guide to a God-haunted world. For these reasons, Edwards' notebook requires deeper examination to explain how he applies Renaissance ideas to theological purposes.

Analysis of Images

The notebook "Images of Divine Things" contains 212 entries, followed by 45 brief entries titled "Scriptures," which detail specific species and what they represent, as well as a reference to the scriptural basis for the association. As an example, consider the following:

> FLIES represent evil spirits and wicked men. The prince of the devils is called "Baalzebub," i.e. the lord of the flies [Matt. 12:24].

> A great RIVER, with its various branches, represents the course of divine providence; thus Christ, when he appeared as the Lord and Superintendent of the course of things in providence, is represented in Daniel once and again as standing in the river Hiddekel [Dan. 10].

> VALLEYS, in which is WATER, represents hell, or a state of death: so when it is said in Job, "the clods of the valley shall be sweet

---

interface to an enchanted world. Edwards' images are like interactive computer icons that represent different facets and functions of the divine system.

[31]"Types," WJE, 11:150–52.

to him," or rather, "shall sweetly devour him." The word in the original also signifies "brook" (Job 21:33).[32]

Following the "Scriptures" series is a "Subject Index" of the 212 creatures.[33] A "Scripture Index" of the Scripture texts cited in the 212 entries follows the "Subject Index."[34] Edwards appears to have indexed "Images of Divine Things" in an attempt to establish order and highlight explicit and implicit connections between the Word of God and the Book of Nature. Edwards' indexes, albeit more thorough, serve the same purpose as Huntley's. "Images" is a notebook with periodic comments on the spiritual purpose of creation, in addition to indexing.

> 'Tis very fit and becoming of God, who is infinitely wise, so to order things that there should be a voice of his in his works instructing those that behold them, and pointing forth and showing divine mysteries and things more immediately appertaining to himself and his spiritual kingdom. The works of God are but a kind of voice or language of God, to instruct intelligent beings in things pertaining to himself. And why should we not think that he would teach and instruct by his works in this way as well as others, viz. by representing divine things by his works, and so pointing them forth, especially since we know that God hath so much delighted in this way of instruction?[35]

Edwards' attention to detail and arrangement has a scientific quality to it, similar to the observational notebooks of natural historians of the time. This comes as no surprise given his "Spider Letter" and other scientific writings. As will be seen later in this chapter, Edwards' emblems are drawn from everyday objects, events, and experiences.[36] Though Edwards' entries in the "Images" notebook lack the first-person tone of occasional meditations, it is simple to distill an occasional meditation into one of Edwards' notebook entries. Edwards felt that he had just seen a glimmer of reality's symbolic

---

[32]"Images of Divine Things," *WJE*, 11:131.

[33]"Images of Divine Things," *WJE*, 11:136–41.

[34]"Images of Divine Things," *WJE*, 11:141–42.

[35]"Images of Divine Things," *WJE*, 11:57.

[36]William Kimnach, "General Introduction," *WJE*, 10:194. Kimnach notes that Edwards' "improvement" of commonplaces was a long held interest among Puritans, and that such interests fit well with the views of Locke and the Cambridge Platonists.

nature, and that all the time in the world would be insufficient to delve into the depths of the divine language of creation. "There is room for persons to be learning more and more of this language and seeing more of that which is declared in it to the end of the world without discovering all."[37]

Organization of Hall's Meditations

Bishop Hall's occasional meditations on blossoms, spiders, storms, rain, sunshine, flies, spring water, and a variety of other topics have striking similarities to entries in Edwards' notebook.[38] Frank Livingstone Huntley developed an index, with highlighted keywords, according to the Genesis creation account in order to uncover major emphases in *Occasional Meditations*. He noted the view of this design "in light of the background of interest in the Genesis story."[39]

What follows in this chapter is inspired in part by Huntley's index to Hall's *Occasional Meditations*. Huntley's index provides a doorway into Hall's thoughts as well as a measure of analysis. Hall had provided a basic table for his 140 meditations, which Huntley considered sorting alphabetically initially. He felt that alphabetizing the meditation subjects would be cumbersome and ultimately ineffective. His creation account index of the meditations reveals the emphasis upon man's dominion and artifacts.[40]

Organization of Edwards' "Images"

Similarly, arranging Edwards' "Images of Divine Things" according to creational categories and theological themes will highlight his "key doctrinal points" and "doctrinal precision."[41] It will be seen that Edwards tamed the emblematic world view and emblematic book genre in order to reinscripturate the entire world.

---

[37]"Types," *WJE*, 11:152.

[38]Frank Livingstone Huntley, *Bishop Joseph Hall and Protestant Meditation in Seventeenth-Century England: A Study with Texts of The Art of Divine Meditation (1606) and Occasional Meditations (1633)*, Medieval & Renaissance Texts & Studies, vol. 1 (Binghamton, N.Y.: Center for Medieval & Early Renaissance Studies, 1981), 129, 131–32, 140–41, 145, 149.

[39]Huntley, *Bishop Joseph Hall and Protestant Meditation in Seventeenth-Century England*, 215.

[40]Sixty-eight of the one hundred forty entries.

[41]William Kimnach, "General Introduction," *WJE*, 10:45. Kimnach's observation of the doctrinal precision in Edwards' "Images of Divine Things" is further reason for a theological analysis of his notebook.

A reorganization of the contents of Edwards' "Images" notebook is helpful in discovering theological themes. As Huntley pointed out in his review of Hall's *Occasional Meditations*, a basic alphabetized index of themes would be ineffective. Nonetheless, by the end of "Images," that is the largest of Edwards' tables. Both the "Subject" index and the "Scriptures" series include duplicate entries.[42]

Huntley's concept of organization based on the creation account was a promising starting point. As a result, I divided Edwards' "Subject" index into eight categories: 1) Heavens, 2) Earth and Waters, 3) Grass, Flowers, Shrubs, and Trees, 4) Birds, 5) Animals, 6) Insects, 7) Man, and 8) Man-Made Objects and Activities Each category was then subdivided into Good and Bad using the up-down orientational metaphor. Finally, each Good and Bad category's qualities were examined. For example, good insects are characterized by NOURISHMENT and SACRIFICE, whereas evil insects are characterized by FILTHY, DECEIT, TRAP, FOOLISH, and EXCESS. This strategy of grouping the good and bad in each category was used throughout. Edwards' reconfigured "Images" are the result, organized by creation category, the up-down/good-bad orientational metaphor, and annotated with first impression attributes. This basic rubric aids in visualizing the structure of Edwards' three-story universe.

This approach has the advantage of providing a systematic structure to Edwards' emblematic theology. "Images of Divine Things" is not a treatise, but rather a collection of occasional entries enumerated solely for indexing purposes. The entries can be rearranged and regrouped to determine patterns, themes, and doctrinal emphases without affecting Edwards' content or message.

Bishop Hall's metaphor of "spectacles of faith" is particularly apt for describing firsthand encounters with this emblematic world view.[43] Individuals can now view a virtual world or augmented reality thanks to modern technologies. Smart phones with GPS and accelerometers, for example, can allow a person to aim the phone to the sky and "see" the precise position

---

[42]"Images of Divine Things," *WJE*, 11:131-41. "Sleeping with garments put off, 121," "Garments, put off in sleep, 121," "Clothes off in sleep, 121," "Lancing a wound, 39," "Wound, its cure, 39," "Searching a wound, 39," "Bridle, natural to two members of the body, 104" "Tongue, 120; its natural bridle, 104," "[Body and head, 193]," "Head, 24; [and body, 193]," "Carcass, 1, 51, 61," "Corpse, 1, 51, 61," "Putrefaction, 1, 51, 61," Harvest, succeeded by winnowing, 94," "Winnowing follows the harvest, 94," "Wood that grows without root, 194," "Trees or wood growing without root, 194," and many other occurrences.

[43]Joseph Hall, "The Invisible World," in *The Works of the Right Reverend Joseph Hall, D. D.* (Oxford: Oxford University Press, 1863), 215–16.

of planets, stars, and constellations in broad daylight. Other types of augmented reality enable the tagging of things and places with commentary and information. Simply pointing the phone at the targeted object and seeing through the screen unlocks an entirely new world. As a result, using Bishop Hall's "spectacles of faith," we shall examine Edwards' enlarged, emblematic world view.

Holbrook offers a useful difference between Edwards' firsthand and secondhand views of nature.[44] His firsthand contact with nature could elicit an emotional and religious response. A secondhand experience prompted more introspection and analysis. His scientific writings, as well as his emblematic writing, were inspired by his secondhand encounters and reflections. The "Images" notebook demonstrates much thought on the patterns of the established order and their correspondences with creatures and with Scripture. It should be emphasized that the "Images" notebook lacks philosophical and scientific analysis. This is not to suggest that such factors were not present in Edwards' thinking while he penned his entries, but they are not apparent in the notebook's design.

Firsthand Encounter with Nature

As previously noted, the notebook appears simple, which has been attributed to a naive acceptance of first impressions of nature. The piece has an enchanted, Bunyan-like wonder to it. Reading Edwards' "Images" is like spending weeks in *Pilgrim's Progress'* Interpreter's House. Despite the apparent naivety and simplicity, there is a daunting intricacy of correspondences that is better effectively explained with nonlinear diagrams than with paragraphs of words. A map better describes the overlapping and interwoven links, the spatial nature of the three-story cosmos, and the variety of creatures within categories that are further divided according to a fundamental up-down metaphor.[45] The various regions of creation and its inhabitants are the most

---

[44]Holbrook, *Jonathan Edwards, The Valley and Nature,* 34.

[45]This is further complicated when one attempts to overlay Edwards' emblematic world doctrinally. Despite the difficulty, due to the slippery nature of metaphors and the complex weave of the correspondences and similitudes, it is profitable to further reconfigure "Images of Divine Things," beyond the creational categories of Huntley, according to a theological scheme. This is something that Edwards did not live to do.

appropriate starting point for gazing through Edwards' (previously Hall's) spectacles of faith.[46]

The Heavens are the first creational category and the highest on the analogical scale of existence. Edwards' images and entries in this area include light, stars, the creation of the world, the height of heaven, the visible heavens (sky), the sun, moon, and rainbow, as well as weather events and night. The Heavens are separated into good and terrible, with unreflective firsthand experiences and the basic feelings they elicit: light, beauty, color, height, violence, heat, darkness, hope, comfort, certainty, doubt, and terror.[47]

The Earth and Waters are the second category. Rivers, springs, wells, seas, waves, rain, floods, cataracts, fish, mountains, hills, valleys, caverns, volcanoes, fire and brimstone, dirt, precious metals, and jewels all fall under this group. Height, largeness, depth, movement, sustenance, value, worth, heat, death, filth, smallness, silence, violence, dread, and darkness are the first impressions formed by these objects.[48]

Grass, Flowers, Shrubs, and Trees make up the third group. The images mostly depict trees, plants, flowers, fruits, grains, their life cycles and usefulness or inutility, as well as the effort involved in cultivation and harvesting. Green, sustenance, maturity, life, value, providence, transience, lack of depth, pain, disease, excess, unfruitfulness, and worthlessness are the firsthand impressions associated with these things.[49]

Birds are in the fourth category. Doves, crowing roosters, young birds and their mothers, singing birds, ravens, crows, eagles, vultures, and owls are among the occupants of this category. These creatures' firsthand impressions range from pleasantness, peace, hope, love, height, white, and day to violence, death, black, night, and filth.[50]

Animals are the fifth category. Sheep, milk, wool, skins, conception, embryo, miracles, lions, tigers, crocodiles, foxes, cats, mice, serpents, swine, whales, dragons, and all toxic and predatory animals fall within this category.

---

[46]I have used the creational categories by which Huntley organized Hall's occasional meditations to uncover basic emphases and impressions in the 212 entries of Edwards "Images" notebook.

[47]"Images of Divine Things," *WJE,* 11:52, 58, 65–69, 74–77, 91, 96–97.

[48]"Images of Divine Things," *WJE,* 11:54–58, 72–74, 77–80, 84–85, 94, 101, 105–07, 114–15.

[49]"Images of Divine Things," *WJE,* 11:62–63, 64, 70, 86, 87, 93, 96, 105–06, 107–13, 116, 123, 127.

[50]"Images of Divine Things," *WJE,* 11:70, 92–93, 96–97, 127, 132–33.

Nourishment, warmth, curiosity, life, death, violence, terror, night, deception, and worthlessness are the firsthand impressions linked with the animals.[51]

Insects populate the sixth category of creation. Bees, silkworms, grasshoppers, flies, spiders, and all other insects fall within this category. Their firsthand characteristics span from nutrition and sacrifice to folly, excess, filth, deception, and traps.[52]

Man is the seventh category of creation. Breath, blood, body, heart, tongue, tears, head, posture, love, marriage, children, parenting, government, celebrations, games, judgment, names, sleep, garments, nakedness, bowels, inwards, excrement, death, putrefaction, dirt, corpse, and embalming are the aspects of man's body and life that populate this category. Discipline, leadership, love, privilege, life, sight, birth, growth, provision, and purpose are all firsthand impressions, as are vulnerability, filth, disease, and death.[53]

Man-made Objects and Activities comprise the ninth category. Lamps, candles, oil, balm, mining, wine, bread, fire, food, processing, coins, hieroglyphics, plowing, clothes, towers, bubbles, bait, sailing, and ships are all included in this category. These items generate the following firsthand impressions: fuel, light, foundation, depth, refinement, sustenance, significance, value, privilege, health, heat, pride, height, deceit, uselessness, and destruction. Science and Technology and Intelligent Perception are subsets of this seventh category. Edwards' entries on Newtonian physics (gravity, acceleration, and color theory), machines, and telescopes, as well as observations on the analogical and shadowy composition of the world as perceived by intelligent beings, fall under these categories.[54]

These categorized creation categories assist in imagining the meaningful and dimensional structure of the world, as well as the related firsthand impressions, that would be available to the spectator if he or she possessed Hall's spectacles of faith. Because it is an intuitive, embodied sensation, firsthand encounters with nature are difficult to convey in words. The secondhand encounter is more detached and introspective, allowing for easier description and analysis.

---

[51]"Images of Divine Things," *WJE*, 11:52, 60, 61, 71–72, 75–76, 93–94, 98, 117–18, 120, 122–23, 127.

[52]"Images of Divine Things," *WJE*, 11:59, 63, 90, 100–01, 107, 119–20, 124.

[53]"Images of Divine Things," *WJE*, 11:51–52, 53, 55, 58, 59, 61, 67, 70–71, 72, 89, 90, 91, 92, 94–96, 98, 101, 116, 119, 123, 133.

[54]"Images of Divine Things," *WJE*, 11:53, 55–56, 62, 64, 65, 67–70, 73, 76, 81, 86, 91, 99, 101, 102–03, 107–08, 113–14, 120–21, 123, 127–28.

The firsthand and secondhand encounter processes correspond to the right hemisphere and left hemisphere processes outlined by McGilchrist. The right hemisphere's world sends something (a firsthand encounter) to the left hemisphere's world to be processed, only to be returned to the right hemisphere's world for a new synthesis (a secondhand encounter).[55]

Secondhand Encounter with Nature

A secondhand encounter with creation is distinguished from a firsthand encounter by the presence of focused observation, reasoning, and contemplation.[56] Although this is typically linked with a scientific approach, same characteristics equally apply to occasional meditation. Occasional meditation necessitates being a ready, keenly attentive observer at all times, meditating on the attributes and context of the item under observation and determining its place in a larger system of correspondences and similitudes. In "Images of Divine Things," Edwards' meditations on the created order indicate an observational intensity of mind that reveals a dependence on occasional meditation, but larger in depth and scope. "Images" entries, devoid of any personal or narrative material, highlight the theological substance of the natural order. Edwards seeks to convey the instinct, essence, or "voice" of God's creatures and things. The "Images" journal rewrites the creation, bringing the Book of Nature and the Book of Scripture back together. As indicated by its subject tables and Scripture index, Edwards' emblem book is more extensive and methodical than Hall's or Bunyan's publications. The most natural way to examine the theological content of "Images" is to reconstruct the entries according to theological categories: Revelation, God the Creator and Father, God the Son, God the Holy Spirit, Humanity, Church, and Last Things, along with various subcategories.

Revelation

The "shadows of divine things" and the Scriptures, according to Edwards, have a complementary relationship. He attempted to 'enhance' the mundane things and experiences of life by the practice of occasional meditation so that "wherever we are and whatever we are about, we may see divine things

---

[55]McGilchrist, *The Master and His Emissary,* 195–96.

[56]Holbrook, *Jonathan Edwards, The Valley and Nature,* 33–34.

excellently represented."[57] The voice of God "purposefully" instructs the believer through this emblematic approach and verifies the teachings of Scripture to those who are ready and listening.[58] In turn, the divine types and shadows identified in the created order are interpreted and applied in the Scriptures.[59] In the created order, emblematic revelation finds scriptural precedence for reading analogies and providences.

Though occasional meditation on nature and Scripture is the way to discover the world's emblematic constitution, the frequency of discoveries is far from 'occasional.' Shadows and emblems are the norm rather than the exception throughout the world. This world's things were created to represent spiritual reality. Vines, light, and bread, for example, all point to Christ, who is the true Vine, the true Light, and the true Bread from heaven (John 1:9; 6:32; 15:1).[60] Milk is a specific biblical example. It is general knowledge that newborn infants are completely dependent on their mother's milk. Milk symbolizes the Word of God because of its pure white color, delicious taste, and nourishing benefits to newborn believers.[61] Edwards also observes that the Word is closely related to providential occurrences that merit pause and consideration.

> 'Tis observed by the prophet Jeremiah (Jeremiah 32:8), concerning only a common providential occurrence, that it "was the word of the Lord," that is, that it was designedly ordered to be a special signification of God's mind and will, as much as his Word. By which it appears that God don't think this a thing improper, or unbecoming of his wisdom, thus designedly to contrive his works and to dispose things in the common affairs of the world in such a manner as [to] represent divine things and signify his mind as truly as his Word.[62]

He obviously leaves the door open for reading providences and prodigies in this entry. Edwards was well aware of an uncontrolled imagination's

---

[57]"Images of Divine Things," *WJE,* 11:74.

[58]"Images of Divine Things," *WJE,* 11:74.

[59]"Images of Divine Things," *WJE,* 11:106.

[60]The emblematic constitution of the created order is referred to frequently in his "Images" notebook. See entries 7, 8, 12, 16, 21, 26, 30, 41, 43, 45, 55, 57, 70, 86, 95, 118, 130, 132, 135, 156, 164, 168, 169, 170, 199, 203, 206, 207, 210.

[61]"Images of Divine Things," *WJE,* 11:93–94.

[62]"Images of Divine Things," *WJE,* 11:125.

passionate predisposition. "Observe the danger of being led by fancy," he observes, "as he who looks on the fire or on the clouds, giving way to his fancy, easily imagines he sees images of men or beasts in those confused appearances."[63] An imaginative view of the world, including its particulars and occurrences, must submit to the interpretation and application of Scripture.[64]

Nonetheless, patterns within the created order are discernible. In this world, there is a clear analogical link between lower and higher forms of life. Animals' physiological constitution is similar to that of humans, while plants' regenerative processes are similar to that of animals. The comparison also applies to the physical and spiritual worlds. Edwards observes the world's fundamentally analogical structure:

> As it is in the analogy that is to be observed in the works of nature, wherein the inferior are images of the superior, and the analogy holds through many ranks of beings, but becomes more and more faint and languid (thus, how many things in brutes are analogous to what is to be observed in men: in some the image is more lively, in others less, till we come to the lowest rank of brutes, in whom it is more faint than others; but if we go from them to plants, still the analogy and similitude holds in many things, and in different degrees in different plants, till we come to metals and some other inanimate things, wherein still is to be seen some very faint representations of things appertaining to mankind); so it is with respect to the representations there are in the external world, of things in the spiritual world. Thus the visible heavens are a type of the highest heavens, but in a lower degree mountains are types of heaven. The great deep under the earth is a type of hell, but in a lesser degree valleys, and the water that is in valleys, is so. The stars are types of saints in glory, and in a fainter degree the singing birds that fly in the firmament of heaven are so And so in innumerable instances; and the same is to be observed of the types of Scripture.[65]

Everything in the universe, from outer space to the depths of the ocean, serves as a guidepost to spiritual reality. The analogical nature of this world

[63]"Images of Divine Things," *WJE,* 11:116.

[64]"Images of Divine Things," *WJE,* 11:106.

[65]"Images of Divine Things," *WJE,* 11:85–86.

is echoed by Paul in his comparison of saints and bright stars: Philippians 2:15, "[S]o that you may become blameless and pure, children of God without fault in a crooked and depraved generation, in which you shine like stars in the universe." Both Scripture and intuition indicate that God created the physical world to guide the observing mind toward spiritual truths.[66] The hieroglyphics of the ancients, who saw all things in this world as signs and shadows of the spiritual realm, provided further support of Edwards' emblematic world view.[67] Though Edwards expected such views to be met with surprise and controversy, he responds, "And why should we not think that he would teach and instruct by his works in this way as well as others, viz. by representing divine things by his works, and so pointing them forth, especially since we know that God hath so much delighted in this way of instruction?"[68]

God the Creator and Father

The doctrine of revelation assumes a gracious God who reveals himself. From the heavens and atmospheric phenomena to the fields, from providential provision to the medical disciplines, the Father's and Creator's delight is expressed. The entire creation is replete in emblems of God's various attributes and beneficent nature. The storm reveals his ferocious majesty and anger. His tenderness and lovingkindness can be seen in the rainbow and the fields that bloom after a shower. The winding course and nourishing effects of rivers demonstrate His providential sovereignty and provision. Edwards writes in an entry that recalls his "Personal Narrative":

> As thunder, and thunder clouds, as they are vulgarly called, have a shadow of the majesty of God, so the blue sky, the green fields and trees, and pleasant flowers have a shadow of the mild attributes of goodness, grace and love of God, as well as the beauteous rainbow.[69]

The sun, which illuminates the rainbow in the heavens, is a symbol of the Creator's faithfulness and loving care. The inexhaustible nature of its beneficent light and heat attest to his eternal goodness and abundant

[66]"Images of Divine Things," WJE, 11:55–56, 69–70, 85–86.

[67]"Images of Divine Things," WJE, 11:127.

[68]"Images of Divine Things," WJE, 11:67.

[69]"Images of Divine Things," WJE, 11:58.

provision for his beings. However, the deep places, along with thunder and lightning, dreadful ocean storms, and deadly river cataracts, represent Almighty God's wrath and the horrible torments of hell.[70] According to Edwards:

> The waves and billows of the sea in a storm and the dire cataracts there are of rivers have a representation of the terrible wrath of God, and amazing misery of [them] that endure it. Misery is often compared to waters in the Scripture— a being overwhelmed in waters. God's wrath is compared to waves and billows (Psalms 88:7, Psalms 42:7). Job 27:20 "Terrors take hold as waters." Hosea 5:10, "I will pour out my wrath upon them like water." In Psalms 42:7, God's wrath is expressly compared to cataracts of water: "Deep calleth unto deep at the noise of thy waterspouts." And the same is represented in hail and stormy winds, black clouds and thunder, etc.[71]

Rivers, as emblems of both providence and provision, that endlessly pour into the ocean without raising its level, represent God's unlimited benevolence via provision and care, which, in turn, tend back to Him as unending worship. It is impossible to enlarge the infinite God, but all things must flow toward Him.[72] The bond between parent and child reflects God's love and correction of His children. God is humanity's Deliverer and Savior. As a parent, he clothed the naked to remove their shame. He provides food and drink to those who are hungry or thirsty rather than eliminating the need for sustenance. He gives breath by breath rather than independent life. He provides medicine rather than long-term health. God supplies not only the essentials of life, but also many joys. Similarly, God the Father provides believers not only forgiveness of sin and freedom from hell, but also the blessings and glory of Heaven through Christ.[73]

Every component of this world demonstrates a dependent nature.[74] This implies that everything exists only by the grace of God. Hurricanes, tornadoes, blazing wildfires, thunder, lightning, searing heat of the sun,

[70]"Images of Divine Things," *WJE*, 11:54, 59, 97.

[71]"Images of Divine Things," *WJE*, 11:58.

[72]"Images of Divine Things," *WJE*, 11:54–55, 77.

[73]"Images of Divine Things," *WJE*, 11:121–22.

[74]"Images of Divine Things," *WJE*, 11:107, 121–22.

and other terrible events are all emblems of God's wrath. These symbols of mercy and wrath should compel each to raise their eyes to ponder the unfathomable grandeur of the universe and the enormous size of the planets, stars, and galaxies, as well as the infinite nature of God.[75]

Creation

Edwards was convinced that because the natural world's analogical nature was "agreeable" to God's "method of working" in similitudes, it is only rational to conclude that the physical world points to spiritual reality. Even the chaotic and dark beginnings of this world foreshadow what it would later become: a realm of vanity, confusion, and darkness.[76] The earth and everything on it point to the spiritual world. There are numerous emblems of spiritual reality in creation. Edwards' three-story world cathedral was brimming with various emblems of spiritual reality.[77] Above these, in the heavens, the dazzling stars and planets of distant space represent the saints' and angels' magnificent state. The insignificance of the world in comparison to the vastness of space indicates the absence of worldly grandeur and wealth in comparison to that of Heaven. The entire universe, however vast and majestic, is simply a shadow of God's splendor. The link between Christ and his saints is represented by the sun and the moon. Saints simply reflect the Son's glory. The moon also denotes the waxing and waning of worldly pride and riches, as well as its absence and unexpected eclipses.[78]

The earth, natural law, and the entire universe are all subservient to the spiritual world. This is demonstrated by the parting of the Red Sea during Moses' time, the sun standing still during Joshua's time, and several other documented examples of unusual providences and miracles. The ephemeral nature of worldly prosperity, fame, and pleasures is mirrored in the fading of leaves, grass, and flowers. Only Heaven's riches are eternal. If a person is satisfied with the bliss that simple earthly life provides, the earth will swallow him eternally, never allowing that person to experience the resurrection of saints. Spring, on the other hand, heralds a time when the world will be spiritually restored.[79]

---

[75] "Images of Divine Things," *WJE*, 11:58, 59, 64, 97.

[76] "Images of Divine Things," *WJE*, 11:60–70, 74–75, 125.

[77] "Images of Divine Things," *WJE*, 11:11:84–85.

[78] "Images of Divine Things," *WJE*, 11:52, 60, 64, 65–66, 86–87, 96, 99, 123, 129–130.

[79] "Images of Divine Things," *WJE*, 11:61, 96, 98, 99, 106, 120, 123.

For his emblematic understanding of the world, Edwards consistently invokes scriptural precedent. In Ecclesiastes 1:7, for example, Solomon employs a river running into the sea as a symbol of the vain pursuit of earthly good. The river never stops flowing to the sea, just as people can never find true satisfaction in the things of this world. The wisest of men, Solomon, derived spiritual realities from nature. Nature's types can only be correctly comprehended in the light of Scripture, because Scripture holds the spiritual truths that nature's illustrations are based on.[80]

Providence and Purpose

River and stream courses, according to Edwards, are emblems of God's providential rule over creation. Though rivers and streams eventually discharge into the ocean, seeing this from the ground is difficult or impossible. Rivers appear to flow away from the ocean at times, and streams appear to flow away from rivers at other times. Occasionally, streams that eventually discharge into the same river flow in opposite directions. The similar idea may be seen in the inner workings of machinery and gears.

> Tis because the providence of God is like a wheel, as a machine composed of wheels, having wheels in the midst of wheels, that 'tis so ordered in the constitution of nature and in the dispositions of God's providence, that almost all the curious machines that men contrive to do any notable things or produce any remarkable effect, are by wheels, a compage of wheels, revolving round and round, going and returning, representing the manner of the progress of things in divine providence.[81]

Some wheels and gears turn at different rates and in opposite directions, yet the machine accomplishes its goal: the engine starts and the clock strikes twelve. Rivers and machines are both emblems of God's providence. Though difficulties appear to obstruct the advancement of his kingdom, and people and events in the church appear to act in opposition, all things will eventually work together to accomplish God's plan and glory. Even commonplace providences and activities can be revelatory.[82] Familiar farm animals such as horses, cows, and sheep are examples of divine purpose

---

[80]"Images of Divine Things," *WJE,* 11:57, 106, 107.

[81]"Images of Divine Things," *WJE,* 11:86.

[82]"Images of Divine Things," *WJE,* 11:77–80, 80–81, 86, 104–5, 118, 124, 125.

obedience. Horses transport riders, cows produce milk, and sheep produce wool. Despite its filthy nature, the pig serves a purpose: slaughter. Pigs are symbolic of rebellious men who fail to fulfill their destiny of carrying God's image and giving glory to him.[83]

Suprahuman Beings

The influence of the stars on this world and its inhabitants, according to Edwards, correlates to the angelic administration of this world.[84] God asks Job, "Can you bind the beautiful Pleiades? Can you loose the cords of Orion? Can you bring forth the constellations in their seasons or lead out the Bear with its cubs? Do you know the laws of the heavens? Can you set up [God's] dominion over the earth? (Job 38:31– 33)."

The diabolical spirits correlate with ravens, who symbolise demons, in the lower heavens. The raven, a popular emblem or omen of evil, feeds on dead corpses, which represent the souls of those who have died. Ravens are instinctual scavengers who feed on the dead, just as Satan eventually devours the souls of the wicked when God consigns them to hell after death.

> Ravens don't prey on the bodies of animals till they are dead; so the devil has not the souls of wicked men delivered into his tormenting hands and devouring jaws till they are dead. Again, the body in such circumstances, being dead and in loathsome putrefaction, is a lively image of a soul in the dismal state it is in under eternal death.[85]

The black color of the raven depicts the Prince of Darkness. Snakes and spiders are also fitting emblems since they discreetly track their prey and remain unseen until they attack and inject their venom. Bottled-up spiders depict devils in their last state; incapable of hunting men (flies), they hunt each other.[86] In his "Scriptures" series, Edwards notes that: "1. FLIES represent evil spirits and wicked men. The prince of the devils is called "Baalzebub," i.e. the lord of the flies [Matthew 12:24]."[87]

---

[83] "Images of Divine Things," *WJE,* 11:117–18.

[84] "Images of Divine Things," *WJE,* 11:100, 104–5, 120.

[85] "Images of Divine Things," *WJE,* 11:70.

[86] This is reminiscent of C.S. Lewis's Screwtape Letters, and the final conversation between Screwtape and Wormwood.

[87] "Images of Divine Things," *WJE,* 11:131.

The haunting voices of owls and other night creatures represent devils. Their cries are the cries of devils and lost souls condemned to eternal darkness.[88] Evil spirits, like many beasts of prey, work at night. Animals such as cats, lions, tigers, and crocodiles are also used to depict Satan.[89] Cats mock their prey, giving it false hope of escape before consuming it. Lions, tigers, and crocodiles instill fear into the hearts of the defenseless. The curse placed on the snake in Genesis 3:14 (going on its belly and eating dust) is quite emblematic because it explicitly points to the curse placed on Satan.[90]

God the Son

Edwards discovers in Malachi 4:2 that the brightness of the sun is an explicit representation of Christ's power and influence in the heavens.

> The beams of the sun can't be scattered, nor the constant stream of their light in the least interrupted or disturbed, by the most violent winds here below; which is a lively image of what is true concerning heavenly light, communicated from Christ, the Sun of Righteousness, to the soul. 'Tis not in the power of the storms and changes of the world to destroy that light and comfort; yea, death itself can have no hold of it. The reasons why the sun's light is not disturbed by winds is two-fold: first, the light is of so pure and subtle a nature that that which is so gross as the wind can have no hold of it; and second, the sun, the luminary, is far above, out of the reach of winds. These things are lively images of what is spiritual.[91]

The earth's storms cannot prevent the sun from shining since the sun is out of reach. Similarly, the dark clouds and storms of this life cannot change Jesus Christ's unchanging power and love who is exalted in the heavens. The stars disappearing as the sun rises symbolizes the end of the Jewish dispensation with the advent of the Gospel.[92] The sun, like Christ in his

---

[88] Dawkins, *The God Delusion*, 87. Dawkin's shares an account of a friend who on an overnight camping trip was terrified by the voice of the devil, and was driven to be ordained. The sound turned out to be the diabolical sounding call of the Manx Shearwater. The parallels with Martin Luther's call to take monastic vows are striking.

[89] "Images of Divine Things," *WJE,* 11:70, 97, 102, 107, 127, 129.

[90] "Images of Divine Things," *WJE,* 11:70, 71–72, 75–76, 86, 88, 98, 118, 119.

[91] "Images of Divine Things," *WJE,* 11:88.

[92] "Images of Divine Things," *WJE,* 11:60, 88, 129.

judgment of those who reject Him, is a consuming fire. When Christ was crucified, the sun lost its light, and Christ rose with the sun. When the sun rises, the evil creatures that stalk the night return to their dens. The devils who roar like lions will be imprisoned to the bottomless pit when the Son of Righteousness rises.[93]

The union of Adam and Eve foreshadowed Christ and his church. Marriage between a man and a woman represents Christ's close bond with his church, as well as his limitless jealousy of all competitors. The authority of the head over the physical body symbolizes Christ's authority over His mystical body, as well as the body's cooperation with the head. As the head of the body, Jesus Christ bore God's wrath and atoned for sin. The body mystically participates in the death and resurrection of Christ, the head of the body, and shares in His inheritance. In His final hours of suffering Christ was not only clothed in purple, but also in scarlet garments stained with His own blood. These royal colors signify that Christ is king over all.[94]

Plants, insects, animals, and birds all display signs of Christ's benevolence. Because the leaves and branches are dependent on the root and trunk, which is Christ, a tree and its branches represent Christ and his church. Christ's incarnation is symbolized by His entering the barren tree of humanity and making it fruitful. The labor of the silkworm and the lamb, which create white silk and wool respectively, reflects Christ's atonement.

> The silkworm is a remarkable type of Christ. Its greatest work is weaving something for our beautiful clothing, and it dies in this work. It spends its life in it, it finishes it in death, as Christ was obedient unto death; his righteousness was chiefly wrought out in dying. And then it rises again, a worm, as Christ was in his state of humiliation, but a more glorious creature. When it rises, it leaves its web for our glorious clothing behind, and rises a perfectly white [butterfly], denoting the purity from imputed grace with which He rose as our surety, for in His resurrection He was justified.[95]

These garments are emblematic of the saints and their robes of righteousness.[96] A bird with its nest of young ones symbolizes Christ's caring

[93]"Images of Divine Things," *WJE*, 11:58, 81–84, 97, 120, 129.

[94]"Images of Divine Things," *WJE*, 11:52, 53, 57, 59, 60–61, 64, 67, 93, 98, 103, 121, 124.

[95]"Images of Divine Things," *WJE*, 11:100.

[96]"Images of Divine Things," *WJE*, 11:59, 63, 76, 80–81, 100, 109–13, 124.

for believers. Both the mother bird and Christ provide brooding, hatching, nurturing, protection, and provision until the young are ready to leave the nest and fly into the heavens.[97]

The heavens, trees, animals, and human customs all have correspondences to Christ's mediatorial ministry of incarnation, atonement, and conferring of inheritance. Christ is referred to as the Branch in the Scripture (Zech 3:8). The ingrafting of a branch represents the incarnation of Christ. Christ gladly gave up his heavenly splendor to be grafted into the wicked tree of mankind. Christ assumed human nature yet bore fruit.[98] The rising of the sun and the crowing of a rooster represent the beginning of a new day, a proclamation of the coming of the Kingdom, in which men must awaken, repent, and believe the Gospel of Jesus Christ.

> [O]ftentimes sinners under the gospel are bewitched by their lusts. They have considerable fears of destruction and remorse of conscience that makes 'em hang back, and they have a great deal of exercise between while, and some partial reformations, but yet they don't flee away. They won't wholly forsake their beloved lusts, but return to 'em again; and so whatever warnings they have, and whatever checks of conscience that may exercise 'em and make [them] go back a little and stand off for a while, yet they will keep their beloved sin in sight, and won't utterly break off from it and forsake [it], but will return to it again and again, and go a little further and a little further, until Satan remedilessly makes a prey of them. But if anyone comes and kills the serpent, the animal immediately escapes. So the way in which poor souls are delivered from the snare of the devil is by Christ's coming and bruising the serpent's head.[99]

Though the serpent has charmed its prey and sinners have succumbed to their own lusts, there is still hope. They are unable to run because they are helpless and paralyzed by contradicting fear and desire. However, deliverance comes through Jesus Christ, who bruises the serpent's head.[100] This deliverance is made possible by divine sacrifice. The famous balm of

---

[97]"Images of Divine Things," *WJE,* 11:96.

[98]"Images of Divine Things," *WJE,* 11:109–13.

[99]"Images of Divine Things," *WJE,* 11:71–72.

[100]"Images of Divine Things," *WJE,* 11:60, 66, 71–72, 92–93.

Gilead, which heals all wounds, depicts Christ's healing blood. Just as the tree must be wounded to obtain the healing balm, Christ was pierced for his blood, which heals the world's sins. Edwards also believed that the red sunset represented Christ's blood. The setting of a blood red sun predicts good weather, and Christ, whose earthly life ended in blood and anguish, rose again to bring God and humanity peace. Fruit trees also represent Christ. Red, ripe fruit signifies Christ's blood, because they are only ready to be eaten when they turn red.[101]

Among the animals, Edwards noticed a scripturally plain symbol of sheep being sheared to offer their fleece to men as clothes. Similarly, Christ, the Lamb of God, clothed believers in garments of righteousness to cover their guilt. The silkworm also relates to Christ's work by producing silk that is sewn into luxurious garments. Edwards observed that the worm appears to die in the course of its labor, only to be resurrected as a beautiful white moth, and that this death and resurrection are emblematic of Christ. Human activities such as meal preparation are emblematic of Christ's redeeming mission. The way wheat must be beaten into flour to make bread and grape juice must be brutally crushed out of the vine to make wine indicates the agony that Christ had to endure in order to be nourishment for those who believe.[102] The human practice of leaving an inheritance to children depicts believers who get an inheritance as a result of Christ's death, according to Heb 9:15-17.[103]

God the Holy Spirit

Edwards observes emblems of the Holy Spirit in the heavens, the earth, and humanity. The Spirit is represented through emblematic color and diversity. The colors of light in a rainbow, precious stones, and the color white, which includes all colors, depict the Holy Spirit and his beauty. The harmony of the numerous hues observed in white depicts the various operations of the one Spirit.[104] Breath represents the creature's constant reliance on God's Spirit. Physical life is sustained by continuous respiration, just as the believer's soul is sustained by the unceasing exertions of the Holy Spirit. The Holy Spirit

[101]"Images of Divine Things," *WJE*, 11:76, 81–82, 93.

[102]"Images of Divine Things," *WJE*, 11:52, 63, 73, 100.

[103]"Images of Divine Things," *WJE*, 11:100.

[104]"Images of Divine Things," *WJE*, 11:67–69. See also "Miscellanies," nos. 362 and 370. *WJE*, 13:434–35, 441–42.

gives life to the soul, just as breath gives life to the body.[105] Edwards wrote about the Spirit as a dove:

> There are many things between the young birds in a nest and a dam, resembling what is between Christ and his saints. The bird shelters them; so Christ shelters his saints, as a bird does her young under her wings. They [are] brought forth by the dam; so the saints are Christ's children. They are hatched by the brooding of the dam; so the soul is brought forth by the warmth and heat and brooding of Christ, by the Heavenly Dove, the Holy Spirit. They dwell in a nest of the dam's providing, on high out of the reach of harm, in some place of safety; so are the saints in the church. They are feeble and helpless, can neither fly nor go, which represents the infant state of the saints in this world. The manner of the dam's feeding the young, giving every one his portion represents the manner of Christ's feeding his saints. When the dam visits the nest, all open their mouths wide together with a cry, and that is all that they can do. So should the saints do, especially at times when Christ makes special visits to his church by his Spirit. They don't open their mouths in vain. So God says, "Open thy mouth wide and I will fill" [Psalms 81:10]. The birds grow by this nourishment till they fly away into heaven to sing in the Firmament. So the saints are nourished up to glory.[106]

Edwards also found parallels between earthly things and the operation of the Holy Spirit in revival. Confusion and darkness frequently precede a significant move of God's Holy Spirit in an individual's, the church's, or the world's life. Spiritual awakening is analogous to the creation of the world from the dark, chaotic deep. It might also be compared to rekindling a nearly extinguished fire. Revival times are like the rejuvenated earth after a rain shower or downpour. When the Spirit is poured out in a season of grace, the earth's creatures respond by flowering and shouting praises to their Creator. A shower or downpour of rain on a parched and thirsty land symbolizes the Holy Spirit's life-giving impact when poured forth on an individual, church, community, or country. Ezekiel's vision of the dry bones in Ezekiel 37:9-14

---

[105]"Images of Divine Things," *WJE*, 11:55, 70–71, 129.

[106]"Images of Divine Things," *WJE*, 11:96–97.

and Christ breathing the Holy Spirit on his followers in John 20:22 are biblical examples.[107]

Humanity

Humans, through their physiology and actions, furnish Edwards with a wealth of correspondences. "Man is made with his feet on the earth, and with his posture erect, and countenance towards heaven, signifying that he was made to have heaven in his eye and the earth underfoot. See Mr. Henry on Genesis 1:1."[108] The most evident correlation or emblem is that man was created in the image of God. In contrast to humans, most animals have their heads pointed down at the earth. Man, on the other hand, is unique in that his head is directed toward heaven. This exemplifies how man can find his greatest fulfillment only in heaven, not on earth with the rest of the beasts. Another biblical image is that, like Caesar's image on coins, God has stamped His image on humans and claims ownership.[109]

According to Edwards, because man carries the image of God, the lower creation and man share many features. Trees, flames, vapors, mists, and swine all have natural and scriptural correspondences with human nature and experience. Good men are like fruitful trees, whereas wicked men bear no fruit and are only useful as fuel. The life of man is like a little flame or mist. Both are readily extinguished or blown away by a small gust of air. The ease with which a candle's flame can be snuffed out represents the frailty of life: "Yet how often is the lamp of the wicked snuffed out? How often does calamity come upon them, the fate God allots in his anger? (Job 21:17)." A candle can be extinguished by its own fuel or revived by another candle. Everything in existence is dependent on God's providential care, including breath, which represents the Spirit of God supporting the soul.[110] If humans do not fulfill their created purpose of worshiping God, whose image they carry, during their brief time on earth, they are like a fattened pig whose sole purpose is to be slaughtered.[111] The names of people in the Bible are frequently emblematic of their personalities. Similarly, God has designed the

---

[107]"Images of Divine Things," *WJE,* 11:74–75, 99, 105–6.

[108]"Images of Divine Things," *WJE,* 11:88.

[109]"Images of Divine Things," *WJE,* 11:72, 88, 98, 99.

[110]"Images of Divine Things," *WJE,* 11:53, 55, 65, 70–71, 121–22, 129.

[111]"Images of Divine Things," *WJE,* 11:65, 98, 100, 116–18.

natural world to disclose spiritual reality.[112] The human body, in its different parts and functions, depicts the activity of the church, the mystical body of Christ, as a sign of this scriptural ordering (1 Cor 12:12–13).[113]

The marriage relationship between husband and wife, as well as the law of gravity, represent Christ's love. Gravity is an unseen, all-pervasive force that holds everything together. Gravity is essential to life, just as God's love is essential to all existence.[114]

> The whole material universe is preserved by gravity, or attraction, or the mutual tendency of all bodies to each other. One part of the universe is hereby made beneficial to another. The beauty, harmony and order, regular progress, life and motion, and in short, all the well-being of the whole frame, depends on it. This is a type of love or charity in the spiritual world.[115]

God established marriage as a symbol of the union of Christ and His church. Christ and the church were typified by Adam and Eve.[116] As a result, Edwards concludes that since God ordained marriage as a symbol of the union between Christ and his church, there are undoubtedly many more things found in ordinary humans, society, and the world in general that point to spiritual realities.[117]

From the cradle to the grave, Edwards discovered emblems. The manner in which infants are born into this world mirrors their spiritual state: they are born unclean, face-down, with their backs to God, and crying.[118] They are born naked as well. The shame of nakedness shows a sinful state, while clothing represents a covering of righteousness provided by God through Christ.

> When persons lay themselves down to sleep in the night, they are wont to put off their garments. So it is when persons fall into a spiritual sleep. Therefore it is said, "Blessed is he that watches

---

[112]"Images of Divine Things," *WJE,* 11:58, 98.

[113]"Images of Divine Things," *WJE,* 11:98.

[114]"Images of Divine Things," *WJE,* 11:59, 81.

[115]"Images of Divine Things," *WJE,* 11:81.

[116]"Images of Divine Things," *WJE,* 11:52, 53, 67.

[117]"Images of Divine Things," *WJE,* 11:12, 89.

[118]"Images of Divine Things," *WJE,* 11:54, 57, 96.

and keepeth his garments" (i.e. by keeping them on) "lest he walk naked and they see his shame" [Revelation 16:15]. So when God's people were building Jerusalem in troublous times, they did not put off their clothes (Nehemiah 4:23).[119]

The emblems of nakedness and covering can be found throughout Scripture history, from Adam and Eve in the garden to the saints who wear robes washed white in the blood of the Lamb (Rev 7:14).[120] Edwards discovers an emblem in green twigs that is instructive for parenting. Tender twigs represent young children since their growth is easily bent and directed.[121]

Temptation, Sin, and Death

Temptation and sin are universal human experiences that correspond to common events and activities. Hunting, fishing, and trapping reveal temptation and death. To entice the prey, enticing bait is used. The hunter's strategy is a shadow of how the enemy uses individual flaws and addictions to lure mankind into disaster.[122] The predators, represented by highly trained hunters such as spiders and snakes, sneak in dark, concealed areas and strike with deadly venom without warning. Darkness can also be caused by blindness. Dirt is also an image of lust for the world since it obstructs vision when it gets in the eyes.

> If persons have dirt in their eyes, it exceedingly hinders their sight. This represents how much it blinds men when their eyes are full of the world or full of earth. In order to the clearness of our sight, we had need to have our eyes clear of earth, i.e. our aims free from all things belonging to this earthly world, and to look only at those things that are spiritual, agreeable to what Christ says: "If thine eye be single, thy whole body shall be full of light. But if thine eye be evil, thy whole body shall be full of darkness" [Matthew 6:22–23].[123]

The crocodile represents both sin and predator in its beginning and end. Sin is easier to defeat in the beginning because it is easier to step on a

---

[119]"Images of Divine Things," *WJE*, 11:95–96.

[120]"Images of Divine Things," *WJE*, 11:63.

[121]"Images of Divine Things," *WJE*, 11:59.

[122]"Images of Divine Things," *WJE*, 11:54, 106–7, 113–14.

[123]"Images of Divine Things," *WJE*, 11:97, 101.

crocodile egg than to try to kill it when it has completely grown. Similar to the gradual growth of sin is an emblem of its gradual conquest: Sin is like a snake that swallows its victim a little at a time and not all at once. The serpent's tongue signifies the venomous power of the human tongue (Ps 140:3; Rom 3:13; Jas 3:6–6). The teeth act as a barrier to keep it in check. According to Edwards, the entire world is filled with images of temptation and immorality. Because there is dirt everywhere, the earth itself is emblematic of a sinful world. There is nowhere to go to get away from its temptations and filth.[124]

A dead body, according to Edwards, represents the spiritual second death. Similarly, sleep is a form of death, but it is also a state of spiritual unpreparedness (Rev 16:15).[125] The filth and waste within a human body are a fitting representation of the radical corruption and filth that permeates the human heart. The twists and turns of the intestines represent the heart's labyrinth. The dirt that is found all around the world pollutes the soul with worldliness. While rivers of water signify good things, still waters represent deception and unhappiness. They reflect heavenly beauty and charm the viewer by mirroring himself and the wonderful nature around him.

> It is like sin in its flattering appearance. How smooth and harmless does the water oftentimes appear, and as if it had paradise and heaven in its bosom. Thus when we stand on the banks of a lake or river, how flattering and pleasing does it oftentimes appear, as though under were pleasant and delightful groves and bowers, or even heaven itself in its clearness, enough to tempt one unacquainted with its nature to descend thither; but indeed, it is all a cheat. If we should descend into it, instead of finding pleasant, delightful groves and garden of pleasure, and heaven in its clearness, we should meet with nothing but death, a land of darkness, or darkness itself, etc. See Proverbs 5:3–6.[126]

When a person enters the waters, the promise vanishes, and instead of dazzling skies, he discovers a nether world of darkness and death. Any prospect of salvation necessitates God's intervention. An unbroken prosperity with no reprimand or discipline is analogous to an endless summer in which insects thrive and reproduce at an exponential rate. To eliminate them and

---

[124]"Images of Divine Things," *WJE*, 11:59, 74, 90–92, 95, 104, 106, 118, 119–20, 123–24, 129.

[125]"Images of Divine Things," *WJE*, 11:95–96.

[126]"Images of Divine Things," *WJE*, 11:94–95.

control the numbers, a harsh winter is required. Seasons of humiliation are also required to destroy the evils that multiply in the soul.[127] Lightning's affinity to high things, such as steeples, represents God's wrath, which will fall on everyone who is prideful. He will strike them and knock them down. As a consequence, fear of heights should teach individuals to be afraid of pride. People of influence and authority, like tall buildings, require strong foundations to prevent them from toppling.[128]

The Christian Life

For Edwards, the voyage of a believer from calling and new birth to sanctification and perfection was a field rich with emblematic gems. Peter's repentance upon hearing the rooster crow symbolizes the Gospel's proclamation. Roosters are divine representations of preaching that awakens individuals from their guilty slumber. Wheat sown before winter represents revival in the life of a believer. It grows before winter, then appears to die as the cold sets in. It remains dormant until spring, when it awakens and thrives until it bears fruit. Edwards saw this as a metaphor for the spiritual decline that many believers undergo following conversion. They fall into deadness, just to rise again to live a glorious Christian life. The metaphor applies to both the church and the individual. Revival frequently occurs quickly after God prunes the church, just as blooms and new life follow the pruning of a fruit tree.[129]

True Religion

True religion and stirring up grace are analogous to believers waking up from a deep sleep. True grace emphasizes humanity's powerlessness in questions of redemption. Edwards observes, using a hydrolic picture, that water lacks the potential to rise higher than its source. This reflects humans' inability to advance above their natural talents without from God's supernatural grace. Precious metals and jewels were also symbols of real religion: "True grace is like true gold: it will bear the trial of the furnace without diminishing. And it is like the true diamond: it will bear a smart stroke of the hammer and will not break."[130]

---

[127]"Images of Divine Things," *WJE*, 11:65, 92, 94–95, 119–20.

[128]"Images of Divine Things," *WJE*, 11:76, 91, 107.

[129]"Images of Divine Things," *WJE*, 11:91–93, 99, 116.

[130]"Images of Divine Things," *WJE*, 11:107.

It is in the natural world as it is in the spiritual world, in this respect: that there are many imitations of, and false resemblances
of, those things that are the more excellent in the natural world.
Thus there are many stones that have a resemblance of diamonds,
that are not true diamonds. There are many ways of counter-
feiting gold. The balm of Gilead, and many others of the most
excellent medicines, are many ways sophisticated. So is grace
counterfeited.[131]

There are numerous counterfeits of true religion, just as there are of
money, jewels, and other valuable items. The absence of restraining grace
allows all manner of evil to flourish. Just as many predators and dangerous
insects operate at night, the same occurs when the light of grace is gone and
the soul is susceptible to the powers of darkness.[132]

When the Holy Spirit is poured out in a season of revival, hypocrites
thrive alongside true saints. When the rain stops, the hypocrites, like puddles
and streams without a living source, dry up and vanish. When spectacular
outpourings of the Spirit cease, there is a sharp falling away of imposters.
Those who are most proud of their religion accelerate when they are dropped.
When hypocrites and backsliders fall from tremendous heights of knowledge and reputation, they fall hard and create a deep hole for themselves.
Hypocrites are like dead wood on the ground. They sprout in the spring but
shrivel up in the summer heat because they have no root.[133]

The moon represents the elect, a genuine recipient of grace. It reflects
the sun's light and illuminates a dark world, just as the elect saints reflect
Christ's light into spiritual darkness. In contrast, the vast majority of flowers
on a tree that do not bear fruit are symbolic of the majority of people who
make a public profession of faith in Christ but eventually abandon it. A true
work of grace is analogous to Caesar's image being permanently stamped on
his coins: God's image is imprinted on his cherished elect.[134]

The New Birth

The pains that a woman goes through during childbirth represent the
church's suffering as she labors to give new life to believers, as well as

[131]"Images of Divine Things," *WJE,* 11:114–15.

[132]"Images of Divine Things," *WJE,* 11:99, 107–9, 114–15, 120.

[133]"Images of Divine Things," *WJE,* 11:105–6, 107, 108–9, 114–15, 123.

[134]"Images of Divine Things," *WJE,* 11:65–66, 70, 99.

the difficulties that an individual goes through as Christ is formed in him or her. A believer's new life is propelled by a new, spiritual heart that beats incessantly as it strives for spiritual growth. Conception in the womb and the development of a fetus into a fully formed baby, then into an adult, represent this spiritual life.[135] Life's dependence on rain, sunlight, warmth, and so on depicts the soul's reliance on God and the outpourings of the Holy Spirit. Saints are symbolized by fledgling birds in a nest, their mouths open, awaiting nourishment from their mother. Similarly, believers must ready to accept blessing, especially when the Holy Spirit visits the church during times of revival and awakening.[136]

Adversity

Climbing a mountain or high hill is a difficult task that demands perseverance and sacrifice, while the body calls out for rest and relief. It is far easier to descend than it is to climb. Climbing a mountain or steep hill signifies a believer's commitment to spiritual disciplines and self-denial.

> When we travail up an hill 'tis against our natural tendency and inclination, which perpetually is to descend; and therefore we can't go on ascending without labor and difficulty. But there arises a pleasant prospect to pay us for our labor as we ascend, and as we continue our labor in ascending, still the pleasantness of the prospect grows. Just so is a man paid for his labor and self-denial in a Christian course.[137]

The ascent is arduous and painful at first, but with perseverance, one can reach the summit. The benefits of holiness and communion with God much outweigh the sufferings of self-denial. However, the hypocrite's and backslider's aversion to exertion causes them to retreat down the mountain. The fair blossoms that fall from a tree exhibit the same downward inclination. Hypocrites appear promising at first but bear no fruit in the end. They resemble noisy, flowing gullies of water during a rainstorm that appear to run forever but soon dry up once the rain has stopped.[138]

---

[135] "Images of Divine Things," *WJE*, 11:55, 122–23.

[136] "Images of Divine Things," *WJE*, 11:54, 96–97.

[137] "Images of Divine Things," *WJE*, 11:58.

[138] "Images of Divine Things," *WJE*, 11:58, 70, 88, 105–6, 108–9, 115–16.

Adversity and discipline are fundamental components of Christian sanctification. The continual cycle of day and night is an image that reminds believers that they should not expect continuous good fortune in this life, but rather alternating periods of prosperity and adversity. Earthly parents correcting their children represent God's discipline of those he loves. Weeding is a symbol similar to pruning:

> The time for WEEDING a GARDEN is when it has newly rained upon it. Otherwise, if you go to pull up the weeds, you will pull up the good herbs and plants with them. So the time for purging the church of God is a time of revival of religion. It can't be so well done at another time; the state of the church of God will not so well bear it. It will neither so well bear the searching, trying doctrines of religion in their close application, nor a thorough ecclesiastical administration and discipline; nor will it bear at another time to be purged from its old corrupt customs, ceremonies, etc.[139]

A garden can only be successfully weeded after a rain shower has softened the ground. Similarly, for discipline to be effectively received, the heart must be softened by the Holy Spirit. Weeding as a symbol of necessary difficulties and trials in the Christian life is analogous to a refining process. Metals must be refined using high temperatures. Similarly, God purifies and prepares believers for service via tribulation. Adversity and trial are also emblems of God's omnipotent anger, which will burn away the world's sinful impurities. His great prize is the precious metals and stones that remain. They are the redeemed.[140]

Similarly, birthing pain and the harsh effect of winter on wheat represent the hardship and persecution that precede fruit in the spiritual life. Humiliation, pain, and persecution all promote fruitfulness. Knowing that spring will come after winter is emblematic of a believer's hope. Thorns on roses, refining fires, labor and birth pangs, winnowing chaff, grinding grain, and baking are all emblems of suffering, according to Edwards. All of these are necessary steps that result in the desired result: a rose, pure gold, a child, grain, flour, and bread. Suffering is meant to shape a believer into the likeness of Christ.[141]

---

[139]"Images of Divine Things," *WJE*, 11:127.

[140]"Images of Divine Things," *WJE*, 11:58, 89, 97, 116, 127.

[141]"Images of Divine Things," *WJE*, 11:52, 55, 58–59, 64, 86–87, 107–8, 120–22, 124.

Ease and Prosperity

The ease with which items can be disassembled corresponds to the downward inclination of falling objects and backsliders: Moral slackness leads to disaster. The seasons of prosperity and misfortune in this life are symbolized by day and night, summer and winter. Long affluence and ease may appear ideal, yet they do not bring desired results. Edwards contrasts long prosperity to the symbol of endless summers, which would allow insects and other plagues to multiply uncontrollably. Sharp winter seasons of humiliation are required to eliminate the evil impulses of the soul in order for sanctification to occur. Plants wither in the absence of sunlight, much as light and comfort without humility will infect a heart with pride. The acceleration of falling things, according to Edwards, is a symbol of the arrogant who fall.

> The higher anything is raised up in the air, the more swift and violent is its fall. The higher the place is that anyone falls from, the more fatal is his fall. And the higher any body falls from, if it falls into water, the more violently and deeply is it plunged. Thus it is in religion. Thus it is with backsliders and hypocrites and them that are raised high in knowledge, wealth and worldly dignity, and also in spiritual privileges and in profession, and religious illuminations and comforts.[142]

Edwards observes, using an architectural analogy, that a building that is built very high must first have a foundation that sinks very low. Before he was glorified, Christ was as low and humble as an unsightly caterpillar before it transforms into a beautiful butterfly. Before reaching the mountaintop of spiritual elevation, believers must first descend into the valley of humility.[143]

Sanctification and Perfection

Sanctification is analogous to a child maturing into an adult. The transition from infancy to maturity does not happen overnight, but rather at a slow and steady pace. According to Edwards, this indicates a believer's spiritual growth. Obstacles, hardships, and struggles are associated with "putting away childish things" (1 Cor 13:11). Immature Christians react to obstacles and persecutions in the same way that a shallow stream does to rocks and trees: loud and erratic. However, after time, believers become as deep as

---

[142]"Images of Divine Things," *WJE*, 11:107.

[143]"Images of Divine Things," *WJE*, 11:85, 87, 89, 91, 94, 100, 103, 119–20.

a river and flow over obstacles without making a sound. Young fruit also illustrates the sanctification process. It is in its proper place on the tree branch, but it is green and unfit for human consumption. However, as it is exposed to the sun's heat, it ripens and reaches perfection. The growth of an embryo represents the process of regeneration and sanctification. The new heart will continue to beat incessantly until the new creature is fully formed. The same is true for a new believer. The new heart, indwelt by the Holy Spirit, propels the saint forward in sanctification until perfection is attained.[144]

The Church

The sun and moon represent Christ and the church, respectively. The life of a tree, from seed to sprout, sapling to maturity, and the several seasonal phases it goes through, is a direct representation of the church. Wheat, corn, and other grains are analogous to the church. Food processing and cooking symbolizes God purifying his chosen people in order to prepare them for himself. A garden is emblematic of the church because it is safest to eliminate weeds after a rain shower has softened the ground. Thus, when the Holy Spirit is poured out in revival, rigorous preaching of difficult doctrines and the application of church discipline become easier.[145] God created man with the power to love a woman so passionately that it becomes a clear reflection of Christ's love for the church. Similarly, when the woman he loves turns to another, a man can experience extremely violent jealousy. This is a representation of Christ's love for his bride, the church.[146]

Last Things

The invention of telescopes, which allowed for a far clearer view of the heavens, was understood by Edwards as a symbol of the enormous growth in heavenly knowledge in the final days. Tears of grief represent the anguish felt by people who see God (Isaiah 6:1, 5; Luke 5:8).[147] Grasshoppers and insects that do not plan for the future and are destroyed by winter are images of sinners who have no regard for eternity or judgment. He also notices

[144]"Images of Divine Things," *WJE*, 11:61, 64, 74, 122–23.

[145]"Images of Divine Things," *WJE*, 11:52, 89, 91–92, 101, 122, 127.

[146]"Images of Divine Things," *WJE*, 11:59.

[147]"Images of Divine Things," *WJE*, 11:101, 116.

that the steady change from winter to summer corresponds to the church's gradual progress. An abrupt change would be disastrous. Small beginnings of grace, according to Edwards, are paralleled by sin. In this world, sin is like a crocodile that starts out as a little egg but grows into a monster. Great, solemn gatherings, processions, and royal coronations hint at what it will be like in Heaven's court on Judgment Day for both good and evil.[148]

Death, Resurrection, and Eternity

Physical death, with all of its agony and pain, foreshadows eternal death. With the exception of those in Christ, going into the grave and rotting represents the finality of the second death. Sleep is also a form of death, and waking from a deep sleep represents the resurrection. Because of Christ's death, believers can experience victory over death and receive everlasting life. Those in Christ are gloriously resurrected, just as the silkworm is resurrected as a beautiful butterfly. Death is the final and necessary stage in the sanctifying fires. Death, however, has no sanctifying effect on graceless people. Carnal men who refuse to serve God in life shall serve Him as pigs to the slaughter in death. The earth will devour their body in the same way that worldliness devours their soul.[149] Worldly men are likened to huge bubbles. The bubble expands to enormous proportions and shimmers with brilliant hues just before it bursts and vanishes. Similarly, when men grow in success and worldly happiness, they approach a sudden and irreversible destruction. Death comes to saints as well, but as ripe fruit that falls from the tree willingly, ready to leave this world for Heaven.[150]

A kernel of corn dying in the ground and rising to a more splendid existence symbolizes resurrection. The rising sun also denotes new life after a period of darkness and death. Another symbol of resurrection is waking up from a deep slumber. Because men are prone to forgetting about the life to come, these signs are repeated constantly.[151] The sun's never-ending radiance signifies eternity, with no apparent limit to its light and heat. Rivers, by flowing into the ocean and never running dry, similarly represent eternity. Trees by a river symbolize the saints' never-ending source of the Holy Spirit. A

---

[148]"Images of Divine Things," *WJE*, 11:90, 91–92, 93, 99, 101, 103–4, 118, 119, 120.

[149]"Images of Divine Things," *WJE*, 11:51–52, 59, 60–61, 65, 94–95, 106, 107–8, 116–18, 123, 124.

[150]"Images of Divine Things," *WJE*, 11:123.

[151]"Images of Divine Things," *WJE*, 11:57, 64, 66, 86–87, 95, 100, 101.

buried body with no power to rise from the grave represents hell's unending miseries.[152]

Judgment

Physical death, unprepared insects, and bottled-up spiders symbolize the pain and judgment that await demons and unbelievers who are unprepared for God's coming judgment. Large crowds of important people are occasionally present at the trial and execution of a great criminal. Such solemn gatherings are only foreshadowings of the grand and ultimate judgment, in which sinners will be officially condemned to eternal torment. It will be a magnificent day, like the sun rising. The rising Son of God will drive away darkness and cast Satan into the bottomless pit.[153]

Heaven

On a tranquil day, the beauty and serenity of the heavens represent the peaceful state of those who have now entered paradise. The limitless height of the heavens above the earth reveals the immeasurable disparity between heaven's and earth's splendor. High mountains represent heaven and the difficulty of reaching it. As there is lowliness at the foot of a mountain before exaltation, so there is humiliation of the soul before exaltation. Things appear smaller and smaller when one approaches the summit of a mountain. Similarly, those who draw near to heaven regard things on earth as being increasingly insignificant. When mountain climbers reach the summit, they experience peace and tranquillity. Those who make it to heaven will be in ecstasy for all eternity.[154]

Birds that soar beautifully over the sky are symbolic of people who reside in heaven. The sky's unfading blue reflects the eternal splendors of heaven. The stars that shine from generation to generation represent heaven's everlasting and eternal grandeur. Green fruit is difficult to pick, but ripe fruit readily comes off the branch. Similarly, when a saint is ready for heaven, he effortlessly leaves the world behind. Even the highest point on the earth cannot reach heaven. Similarly, nothing on this earth can provide true contentment. When viewed from space, the world's enormous mountains and valleys appear quite little. This is an illustration of how a heavenly

---

[152]"Images of Divine Things," *WJE,* 11:51–52, 54–55, 87.

[153]"Images of Divine Things," *WJE,* 11:51–52, 90, 107, 119, 129.

[154]"Images of Divine Things," *WJE,* 11:56, 72–73, 94, 96, 103.

perspective will make the world's sparkling wealth and honor appear small and dim. The glory and prosperity of this world pale in comparison to the eternal rewards of heaven.[155]

The heavens are much higher than the world's tallest building or mountaintop. This signifies the unfathomably greater joy of paradise in comparison to the happiness of this world. Even those who hold the highest positions in this world find happiness elusive. Citizenship in Rome was emblematic of heavenly citizenship. It was conceivable to be a free citizen of Rome and enjoy all the benefits that came with it while living distant from the city. The same is true of heaven's citizenship. Even if believers live far from paradise and travel through many foreign nations as aliens and pilgrims, they have full citizenship in heaven. True happiness, which we seek, cannot be found in this world. The thorns of a rose bush represent the trials and tribulations that the believer must face in this life. The rose is the last to bloom. It refers to the final reward.[156]

Hell

Worms devouring a rotting body with no possibility of rising to life represent hell's eternity, terrors, and torments. The splendors of the heavens stand in stark contrast to the earth's dark caves and deep recesses. This demonstrates the enormous difference in experience between those who live in heaven and those who are condemned to hell. Hell's inhabitants are as loathsome and repulsive as a rotting corpse (Isa 66:24). Hell is a flood of destruction and a lake of fire, similar to the Flood that destroyed the earth in Noah's day. The denizens of the deep are emblems of hell's devils who live to destroy and execute God's wrath. Volcano eruptions that pour liquid fire on entire cities presage God's last retribution. Hell's occupants are like swarms of spiders that devour one other when confined together. Animals that scream and wail in the middle of the night symbolise the agonizing cries of people tormented in hell.[157]

[155]"Images of Divine Things," *WJE*, 11:64, 84–85, 97, 100–1, 115–16, 123.

[156]"Images of Divine Things," *WJE*, 11:52, 87, 96, 98.

[157]"Images of Divine Things," *WJE*, 11:51–52, 56, 65, 72, 84–85, 107, 127.

Conclusion: A Reinscripturated World

As seen above, Edwards' complex matrix of correspondences between worldly and spiritual things provided in "Images of Divine Things" is doctrinally comprehensive. Edwards is operating on a much larger scale than Hall, Austen, Bunyan, or Keach, yet he is doing the same thing in principle: finding scriptural significance in the correspondences and correlations of the world. He comments in "Miscellanies" no. 124 that a panoramic initial impression or glance is all that is required to see the character of the world:

> [T]here wants nothing but a comprehensive view, to take in the various actions in the world and look on them at one glance, and to see them in their mutual respects and relations, and these would as naturally, as quick, and with as little ratiocination, and more assuredly, intimate to us an universal mind, than human actions do a particular.[158]

The presence of the universal mind communicating with intelligent beings through an emblematic world of similitudes and correspondences informed and interpreted by Scripture seems beyond imagination. Yet, according to Baxter, Hall, Bunyan, Austen, Keach, and others, a sanctified imagination is exactly what is needed to make the most use of this God-haunted world. In his notebook, "Images of Divine Things," Edwards set out to achieve a broad and imaginative reflection and meditation on the world and Scripture. This secondhand experience with nature was a large and ambitious project. The doctrinal content that arose from Edwards' efforts to re-attach the Book of Nature to the Book of Scripture was comprehensive, to the point where his undertaking might be rightly referred to as a *reinscripturation* of the world.

---

[158]"Miscellanies" no. 124, *WJE*, 13:288.

CHAPTER SIX: CONCLUSION

Edwards' ambition of reinscripturating the world might be seen as a culmination of the Renaissance's emblematic world view. The Book of Nature is replete with analogies and correspondences that echo and illustrate the Book of Scripture which guides the interpretation of creation's content. Nature's revelation is sublime, ominous, and emblematic, full of parables, riddles, and links.

The world of Jonathan Edwards is a God-haunted place, where behind every bush, and under every rock, and within every tree, creature, and event is a voice of wisdom for those who have ears to hear and eyes to see. The voice or language of God in creation is faithfully submitted to Scripture according to not only Edwards, but other creative Evangelical theologians like Bishop Hall, Ralph Austen, John Bunyan, and others.

Thesis

This study argues that Edwards' *reinscripturation* of the world is critical to comprehending his distinctively biblical and emblematic world view as expressed in his emblem book "Images of Divine Things." The preceding chapters explored Jonathan Edwards' context and world view, beginning with a brief overview of the Christian tradition's emblematic world view and its development throughout the Protestant Reformation, as well as the emblem book genre that resulted. It was demonstrated that Edwards' emblematic world view, as expressed in the core text "Images of Divine Things," clearly belongs within the emblem book genre, and that the emblem book was the literary vehicle via which Edwards communicated his reinscripturated world view.

Emblematic World View

Tibor Fabiny's suggestion that Edwards' typology be considered in the context of the Renaissance and Reformation required a survey of the emblematic world view. The conclusions of this investigation into the origins of the emblematic world view were fascinating, especially when compared to Edwards' "Images of Divine Things" and his desire to discern nature's voice as it aligns with the Word of God. The recovery of ancient wisdom and literature was fueled by the emergence of the emblematic world view during the Renaissance, which was driven by the *ad fontes* quest. Incidental to Erasmus's collection of adages, was the discovery of literature which expounded all types of plants and animals. The recovery of adages, Aesopic tales, mythology, artifacts, and hieroglyphics aided in the development of natural history that described and explained species in the contexts of their mythology, legend, hearsay, and common folklore. Creation took on an emblematic aspect, with each creature having a unique significance or voice. During the *ad fontes* movement, creation became a poetic text.

The effort of monitoring the ever-growing correspondences and similitudes grew unbearable as natural histories expanded. Simultaneously, as empiricism grew, an endeavor to rid natural histories of errors essentially decontextualized the world. The animals were no longer defined by their relationships and correspondences. The world gradually lost its literary nature. The invention of the scientific method, and the subsequent successful Scientific Revolution, effectively described the world. The subsequent orderly and mechanical world view was purged of divine mystery.

Creative Evangelical Theology

Though many hailed the deinscription of the world, there were many who maintained the emblematic world view while acknowledging the scientific view's triumphs. Bishop Hall, Ralph Austen, John Bunyan, Benjamin Keach, and other evangelicals revived the emblematic world view for devotional purposes. Their emblematic devotional works became quite influential among those seeking religious renewal. The creatures of the world were reconfigured as emblems for occasional meditation. According to Bishop Hall, when one put on the glasses of faith, the invisible world became visible. When considered spiritually, the creation reinforced Scripture's teachings. The emblem book tradition inspired an Evangelical emblem book genre, culminating in the work of John Bunyan. When compared to Hall, Austen, Bunyan, and Keach's emblematic work, Edwards' work is strikingly similar.

Edwards' Emblematic Distinctives

Edwards has numerous things in common with these creative emblematic theologians. 1) He possessed a keen poetic sensibility. As previously noted, he regarded this sensibility necessary for accurately reading the world because he felt that the author of both the world and the Word was poetic. 2) Edwards was concerned with religious rebirth and the experience of a near God. His meditative activities, as seen in the "Personal Narrative," are occasional and resonate with the meditations recorded and prescribed by Hall. 3) He was concerned with the truth of doctrine and religion. Roman Catholicism's scripturally undisciplined allegories were to be avoided. In his natural typology, he was concerned with striking a balance between the priority of Scripture and the emblematic nature of the created world. Edwards not only possessed these fundamental characteristics, but his emblematic reading of nature shares numerous similarities with Hall, Austen, Bunyan, and Keach.

Edwards also shared several important features with the previous emblematic world view. His well-known doctrine of excellency includes agreement, fitness, harmony, Scripture, similitudes and correspondences, gradation of being, and analogies. In light of these discoveries, his emblematic view was not novel. Rather, when one studies Edwards' use of hieroglyphics, mythology, poets, ancient pagan beliefs, and the adagial work of John Spencer's *Things New and Old,* among other things, one can see his dependence on, and rehabilitation of, the Renaissance emblematic world view.

Reinscripturation: World and Scripture Re-attached

The Renaissance's emblematic world view, as well as the devotional emblematic developments of creative Evangelical theologians, set the stage for Edwards' aim of re-attaching the Book of Nature to the Book of Scripture. This project is referred to as *reinscripturation.* Edwards' reinscripturation of the world was a large-scale undertaking to record a "comprehensive view, to take in the various actions in the world and look on them at one glance, and to see them in their mutual respects and relations."[1] A quick look through

---

[1] "Miscellanies" no. 383. BEING OF GOD, *WJE,* 13: 451–52.

his notebook "Images of Divine Things" reveals a plethora of emblematic observations that Edwards had begun to index. Yet Edwards's indexing efforts have some shortcomings. There is an unnecessary redundancy in his indexes. More critically, there is no doctrinal index. The most evident flaw is the lack of theological organization, given that Edwards' notebook is a theological exploration of the created order.

This absence of doctrinal analysis, combined with the notebook's free-form layout, made doctrinal categorization and rearrangement both easy and desired. A quick examination of Edwards' first and secondhand interactions with the three-story universe revealed that his embodied experience of the world was, for the most part, available to all of humanity. The notebook contained common orientational metaphors as well as well-known folk metaphors. Because of the presence of these metaphors in Scripture, Edwards was able to map the world theologically. In his journal, Edwards used commonplaces, folk analogies, hieroglyphics, and old wisdom. Edwards' field guide to such a God-haunted world was "Images of Divine Things." The presence of these features in Edwards' notebook necessitated more investigation to demonstrate how he employs Renaissance themes for theological purposes. When "Images of Divine Things" was rearranged and summarized into theological categories, it was discovered that it provides a comprehensive theological picture of the world, with the major divisions of a systematic theology present. Although similar in substance, Edwards' achievement is a substantial step forward from the work of previous Evangelical emblematicists.

Future Studies

Edwards was undaunted by the possibility that some people would regard his opinions as enthusiastic and unwarranted. When one considers Edward's twenty-eight years on the notebook, a life-long quest, one must contemplate Gerald McDermott's wish that future researchers build on Edward's foundation. McDermott says:

> [T]here are ways to look at life in which we see signs of Christ and his redemption showing up everywhere—in the daily routine, in nature, in the course of history, and in nearly every dimension of existence. This is a way of seeing that, I hope, will be more fully explored by theologians who build upon this Edwardsian foundation. They will, I trust, look through Edwards's typological

model to see even more of the Trinity's footprints in life and history.[2]

Edwards' emblematic world view has been largely forgotten today and, as a result, the church's faith has been significantly impoverished. It is my hope that this study will help believers experience a re-enchantment of the world and a reinvigoration of devotional meditation for the glory of God.

If we look on these shadows of divine things as the voice of God, purposely, by them, teaching us these and those spiritual and divine things, to show of what excellent advantage it will be, how agreeably and clearly it will tend to convey instruction to our minds, and to impress things on the mind, and to affect the mind. By that we may as it were hear God speaking to us. Wherever we are and whatever we are about, we may see divine things excellently represented and held forth, and it will abundantly tend to confirm the Scriptures, for there is an excellent agreement between these things and the Holy Scriptures.[3]

---

[2] Gerald McDermott, "Alternative Viewpoint: Edwards and Biblical Typology," in *Understanding Jonathan Edwards: An Introduction to America's Theologian,* ed. Gerald McDermott (New York: Oxford University Press, 2008), 112.

[3] "Images of Divine Things," *WJE,* 11:74.

PART TWO:
LANGUAGE AND LESSONS OF NATURE

*A Selection of Emblems**

*In Part Two, the selections from Edwards' notebook "Images of Divine Things" have been paraphrased and modernized for easier reading. Alciati's *Emblematum liber* has been translated into English and compared with Andrea Alciati, *A Book of Emblems: The Emblematum Liber in Latin and English,* translated and edited by John F. Moffitt (Jefferson, N.C.: McFarland & Co., c2004) and Andrea Alciato, "Alciato's Book of Emblems: The Memorial Web Edition in Latin and English," https://www.mun.ca/alciato/index.html.

ABYSS

The sublime and glorious beauty of the heavens, visible in the tranquil air, is heightened by the colors and scattered clouds. This serves to remind us of the immense distinction between the blessedness of the heavenly inhabitants and the dismal abyss of the damned. It is a stark reminder of the ineffable joy of the one and the unendurable despair of the other.

— "Images," no. 21

Abyss

ANALOGY

Once again, it is evident that God has a pattern of working in His creations. The visible world offers a great resemblance of effects, with a harmony between one thing and another. This suggests that the material world has been made to imitate the spiritual world, with the less perfect being an image of the more perfect. We can see this in the way that beasts are made after men, plants after animals, and minerals after plants. It follows, then, that the corporeal and visible world is designed to be similar to the spiritual, real world, in accordance with the way God works.

— *"Images," nos. 8, 59*

Analogy

ASCENDING AN HILL

As one ascends a steep hill, it is a struggle against one's natural inclination which is to go downwards. Yet, there is a reward for the effort—the prospect grows more pleasant with each step taken. This is much like the journey of a Christian, who is rewarded for their labor and self-denial. With each step, they gain a better view and, eventually, reach a place of serenity and calm beyond the clouds and winds. This should encourage Christians to continue their climb up the Christian hill, a journey that is much like reaching the heavenly state on a high mountaintop.

— *"Images," nos. 29, 67*

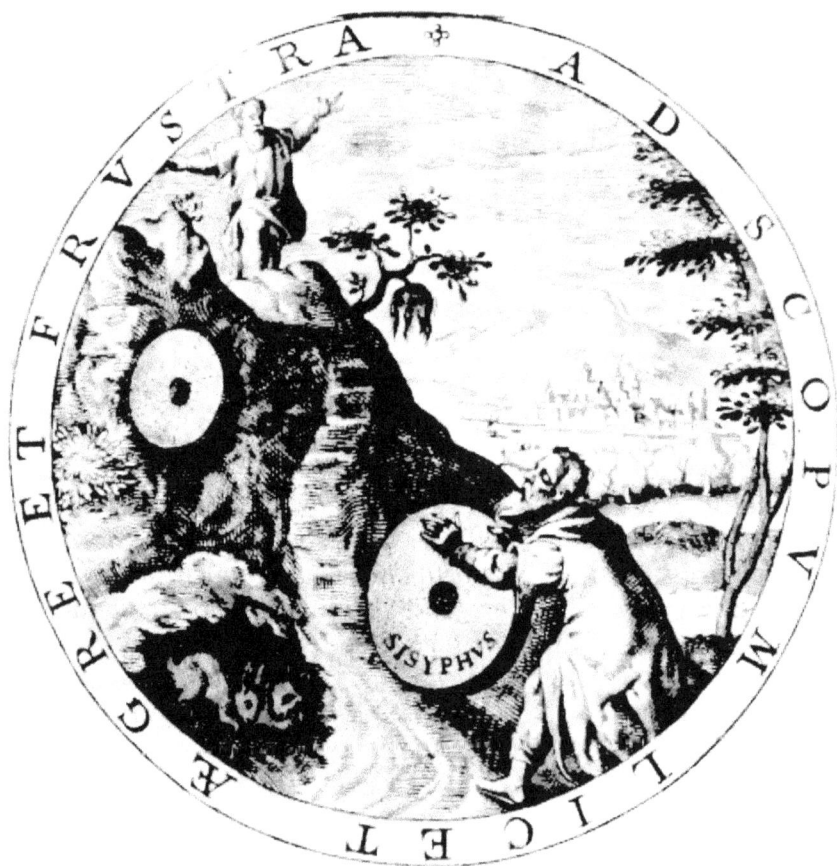

A Foole, in Folly taketh Paine,
Although he labour still in vaine.
(Wither, 1.11)

A Foole, in Folly taketh Paine,
Although he labour still in vaine. (Wither, 1.11)

A Massie Mil-stone up a tedious Hill,
With mighty Labour, Sisyphus doth roll;
Which being rais'd-aloft, downe-tumbleth, still,
To keepe imployed his afflicted Soule.
On him, this tedious Labour is impos'd;
And (though in vaine) it must be still assayd:
But, some, by no Necessity inclos'd,
Upon themselves, such needlesse Taskes have layd.
Yea, knowing not (or caring not to know)
That they are worne and weary'd out in vaine,
They madly toyle to plunge themselves in Woe;
And, seeke uncertaine Ease, in certaine Paine.

Such Fooles are they, who dreame they can acquire
A Minde-content, by Lab'ring still for more:
For, Wealth encreasing, doth encrease Desire,
And makes Contentment lesser then before.

Such Fooles are they, whose Hopes doe vainely stretch
To climbe by Titles, to a happy Height:
For, having gotten one Ambitious-Reach,
Another comes perpetually in sight.
And, their stupidity is nothing lesse,
Who dreame that Flesh and Blood may raysed be
Up to the Mount of perfect-Holinesse:
For (at our best) corrupt and vile are we.
Yet, we are bound by Faith, with Love and Hope,
To roll the Stone of Good-Endeavour, still,
As neere as may be, to Perfections top,
Though backe againe it tumble downe the Hill.

So; What our Workes had never power to doe,
God's Grace, at last, shall freely bring us to.

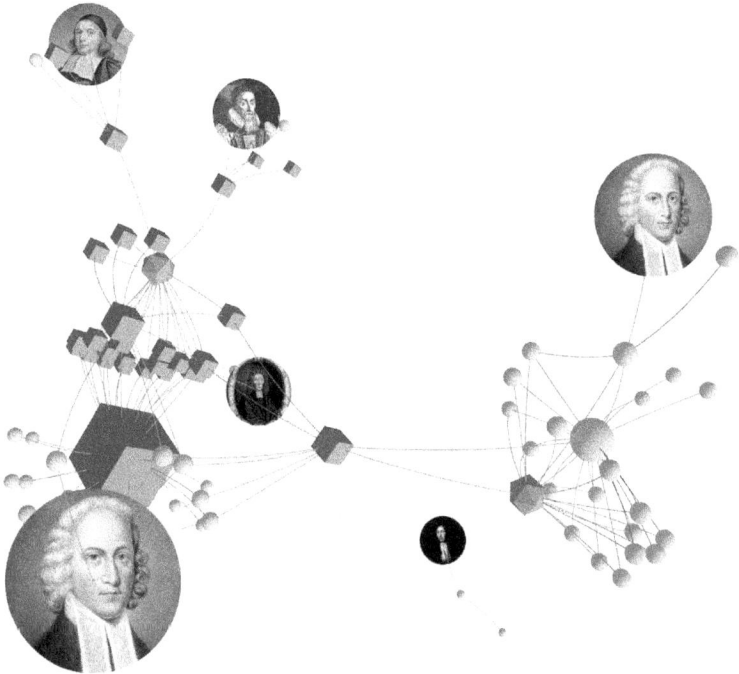

Ascending a Hill

Ass

Plutarch noted that the ass, being the most sluggish of all creatures, had the fattest heart. This is the inspiration for the phrase in Scripture, 'Go make their hearts fat', indicating a dullness of spirit. The 'Ovos', or ass-fish, is a perfect representation of a hedonistic glutton, due to its heart being located in its belly.

— "Images," no. 153

Concerning Misers: *Septitius, the wealthiest of them all, had more land than any elderly man. He denied himself any pleasure and ate only beets and hard turnips. How could I compare this man, whose wealth made him poor? An ass, that's it! He was like an ass carrying costly food on its back. He was a pauper who fed on thorns and hard reeds. (Alciati, 86)*

AURELIA

As the worm's death, followed by its transformation into a glorious flying creature, symbolizes the resurrection of a saint, so the golden spots on the chrysalis represent the preciousness of the saint's dust, even in its state of death, being still united to Christ and precious to Him.

— *"Images," no. 144*

Aurelia, Moth, Butterfly, Worm

BALLAST AND SAILS

If a structure is raised to great heights, its foundation must be laid low and wide, or else it will be in danger of toppling. Likewise, if a person's station in life is elevated, they must have a strong foundation of knowledge and faith, and a great humility, or else they will be at risk of being overthrown. This is also portrayed by ships with large sails, which must have ballast to keep them from capsizing.

— "Images," no. 106

A Ship Aground,
is a Beacon at Sea

(Cats and Farlie, 21)

To him a happy Lot befalls
That has a Ship, and prosp'rous Gales.

(Wither, 1.13)

He, that his Course directly Steeres,
Nor Stormes, nor Windy-Censures fears.

(Wither, 1.37)

When thou art shipwrackt in Estate,
Submit with patience, unto Fate.

(Wither, 4.13)

When thou art shipwrackt in Estate,
Submit with patience, unto Fate. (Wither, 4.13)

When I beheld this Picture of a Boat,
(Which on the raging Waves doth seeme to float)
Forc'd onward, by the current of the Tide,
Without the helpe of Anchor, Oare or Guide,
And, saw the Motto there, which doth imply,
That shee commits her selfe to Destinie;
Me thinkes, this Emblem sets out their estate,
Who have ascribed ev'ry thing to Fate;
And dreame, that howsoe're the businesse goe,
Their Worke, nor hinders, neither helpes thereto.
The leaking Ship, they value as the sound:
Hee that's to hanging borne, shall ne're bee drown'd;
And, men to happinesse ordain'd (say these)
May set their Ship to float, as Fate shall please.

This Fancie, springing from a mis-beleeving
Of God's Decrees; and, many men deceiving,
With shewes of Truth, both causeth much offence
Against God's Mercies, and his Providence;
And brings to passe, that some to ruine runne,
By their neglect of what they might have done.
For, Meanes is to bee us'd, (if wee desire,
The blessing of our safetie to acquire)
Whose naturall effects, if God deny,
Upon his Providence wee must relye,
Still practising what naturall aydes may bee,
Untill no likely ayd untride wee see.
And, when this Non plus wee are forc'd unto,
Stand still, wee may, and wayt what God will do.

Hee that shall thus to Fate, his fortunes leave,
Let mee bee ruin'd, if Shee him deceive.

Sirens: *Birds without wings, maidens without legs, and fish without snouts, yet they sing with a mouth - who would have thought it possible? Nature says these things should not be combined, yet the sirens prove otherwise. The woman with a tail of a black fish lures men in with her beauty; for lust has the power to create monsters. Men are drawn to her by her looks, her words, her spirit - Parthenope, Ligia, and Leucosia. The Muses pluck away their feathers, and Ulysses plays with them—meaning, the wise have no business with harlots. (Alciati, 116)*

Fir tree: *The silver fir tree is raised in the lofty mountains, though it is fit for the depths of the sea. It is at its most useful in times of difficulty. (Alciati, 202)*

Against those prone to vice: *As small as a snail, the remora can stop a ship all on its own. It scorns the power of the wind and oars. Thus, certain men of genius and virtue, who were destined for greatness, can be brought to a halt by a minor event. Similarly, a lawsuit or an infatuation with a woman of ill repute can distract young men from their noble studies. (Alciati, 83)*

(Quarles, 4.13)

Whoever Worldly means employs
For unsophisticated Joys,
Will be deceiv'd; in God alone
True, solid Happiness is found.

Upon a Danger Springing From an Unseasonable Contest With the Steersman (Boyle, 4.8)

This discourse being ended, Eugenius who was look'd upon by us as the most experienced as well as concerned angler among us, descrying at a good distance a place which he judged might be more convenient for our sport, than that we were in, where the fish began to bite but slowly; we walk'd on along the river till he lighted upon a youth, that by his habit seem'd to belong to some boat or other vessel; and having enquir'd of him whether he could not be our guide to some place, where the fish would bite more quick, he replied that he easily could, if we would take the trouble of coming to a place on the other side of the river, which his master, who was a fisherman, had baited over night, and would questionless let us make use of for a small gratification. Eugenius, being very well content, call'd away the company, which were led by the youth to a boat belonging to his master, into which being enter'd, the old man who was owner of the boat, hoyst up sails, and began to steer the boat with one of his oars to a place he shewed us at a good distance off; but did it so unskilfully, that since a mariner of his age could scarce mistake so grossly for want of experience in the river, we began to suspect that he had too plentifully tasted a far stronger liquor than that which was the scene of his trade. And as the old man was half drunk, so the youth appeared to be a mere novice, both which we had quickly occasion to take notice of; for some clouds, that were gathering out of the sea, passing over our vessel rais'd in their passage a temporary wind, that to such a slight boat as ours was, might almost pass for a kind of storm; and then the old man gave his directions so ill, and the youth was so little able to execute them punctually, that two of the company, offended at their unskilfullness, began by angry and unseasonable expostulations and clamours, to confound the already disorder'd boatman: and being got up, with no small hazard to the boat, they would perchance, by crossing the watermen in their endeavours, have made it miscarry, had not Lindamor, whose travels made him well acquainted with such cases, earnestly requested them to sit still, and let the watermen do their own work as well as they could; affirming that he had seen more than one of those easily overset boats, cast away by the confused and disagreeing endeavours of the watermen and passengers to preserve it.

This counsel was thought reasonable, since the greater the wind was, and the less the steersman's dexterity, the more necessary it appeared that we should be orderly and quiet, and by leaning our bodies sometimes one way and sometimes another, as occasion required, do what in us lay to keep the vessel upright. And herein we were so prosperous, that soon after the cloud was passed, and the shower it brought with it was over, the wind grew moderate enough to allow us to make some calm reflections on what had happened. This Lindamor, from the thanks that were given him for his advice, took occasion to do in these tearms. Since statesmen and philosophers are wont to compare a commonwealth to a ship, I hope the reflection suggested by what has just now hap. pened, will be the easier pardon'd. The skill of ruling nations is an art no less difficult than noble; for whereas statuaries, masons, carpenters, and other artificers work upon inanimate materials, a Ruler must manage free agents, who may have each of them interests or designs of their own, distinct from those of the prince, and many times repugnant to them: and the prizes that are contended for in government either are, or are thought so valuable, and the concurrents are so concern'd, and consequently so industrious to drive on each his own design; that without mentioning any of those many other things which make good government difficult, these alone may suffice to make it more our trouble than wonder, that the rulers of states and commonwealths should oftentimes mis-govern them. But the publick infelicities of declining states are not always due to the imprudence of the Rulers; but oftentimes those that most resent such imprudency, and by those very resentments encrease the publick disorders they appear so much troubled at. It may be a question whether it be more prejudicial to commonwealths, to have Rulers that are mean statesmen, or to have a multitude of subjects that think themselves to be wise ones, and are forward to censure what is done by their magistrates, either because it is done by their superiors, or because it is not done by themselves.

Ordinary men may often think that imprudent, whilst they consider it only in itself,which its congruity to the rest of the prince's designs may make politick enough; and a private whisper, or the intimation from an unsuspected spy, or an intercepted letter, or divers other things unperceived by those that are not of the state cabal, may make it wise to do several things, which to those that look only at the actions without knowing the motives, may appear unpolitick, (and would indeed be so, were it not for these reasons,) which yet ought to be as little divulged as disobey'd. So that the people's forwardness to quarrel with the transactions of their prince is usually compounded of pride and ignorance, and is most incident to those, that do not sufficiently understand either state affairs or themselves; and whilst they judge upon incompetent information, even when their superiors are in fault, they may themselves be so for censuring them.

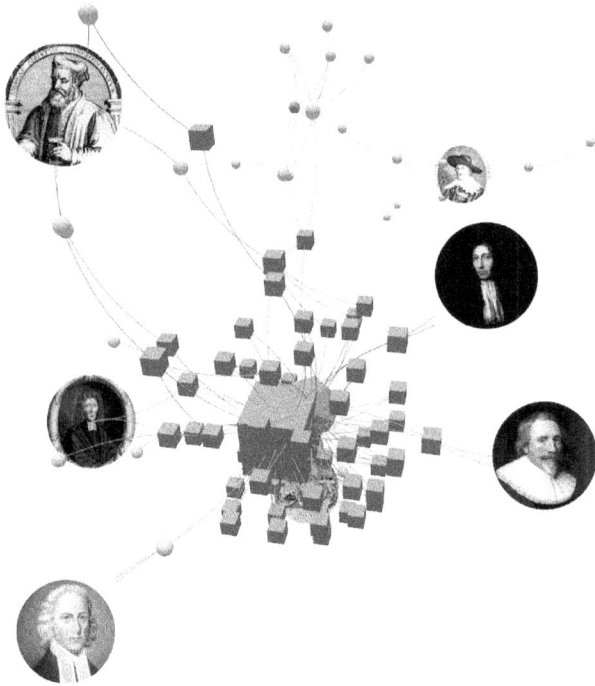

Ballast, Sails, Boat, Ship

BALM

The balsam tree of Gilead, still renowned for its healing properties, was pierced to produce the balm used in Israel and the East. This balm is analogous to the blood of Christ, which was shed to heal the wounds of the soul. Piercing of Christ procured this sovereign balm.

— "Images," no. 75

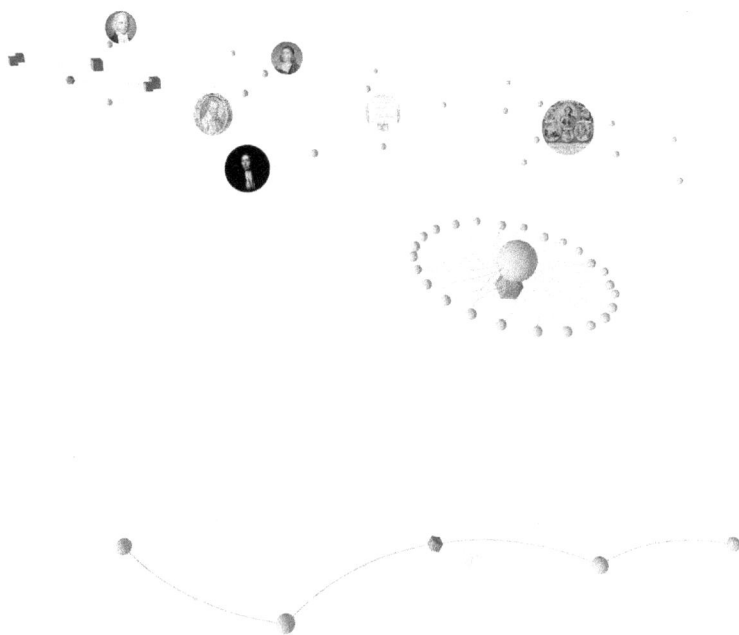

Balm, Heal, Medicine

BEASTS OF PREY

As the sun sets, predators go out to wreak havoc, and this is when caterpillars, noxious bugs, and other harmful pests venture out to feast on the vegetation. But when the sun rises they retreat, which is analogous to the wickedness of the human heart, the adversaries of our souls, and the adversaries of God's church.

— "Images," no. 186

On someone who causes their own trouble: *I, a she-goat, provide milk to a wolf not of my own will, but due to the neglect of the goatherd. As soon as the wolf has grown, it will continue to feed on me - beyond my udder! Submitting does not prevent the evil. (Alciati, 64)*

Forgetfulness gives birth to poverty: *The ravenous lynx, having feasted on a fawn it had caught in its hunger, glanced away or closed its eyes, forgetting the prey in its grasp. It then sought out a new quarry, its forgetfulness so great. Those who have neglected their own foolishly search for what belongs to others. (Alciati, 66)*

When the wolf comes, the oxen leave off fighting to unite in self-defense.

(Cats and Farlie, 189)

When the wolf comes, the oxen leave off fighting to unite in self-defense (Cats and Farlie, 189)

Nor long ago, some oxen of our herds upon the moor,
In furious fight among themselves, as oft I've seen before,
Were suddenly surpris'd to see some Wolves, which, crouching
      low,
Were stealing on the herd to strike an unexpected blow.
Like magic, all at once, th' intestine feuds and bloodshed cease,
As though the common danger had subdued them all to peace:
And quick, -as if impress'd with all the folly of their strife;
Made sensible that Union alone could save the life
Of each and all, – to face the foe they haste a ring to form,

And croup to croup close press'd make front to meet th' impend-
      ing storm.
'Twas just in time! for scarcely were they marshall'd back to back,
When down upon the herd already bursts the rav'ning pack:
But all in vain the Wolves assail; for everywhere they meet
A phalanx of opposing horns, their onset fierce to greet;
And high in air uptoss'd, or disembowell'd on the plain, –
The few remaining take to flight, nor dare th' assault again.
So should confed'rate States and Peoples hush all inward strife,
When from without a foreign foe assails the Nation's life;
All discords then out trodden-'tis by Unity alone
The Free shall save their Freedom, and the Brave preserve their
      own.

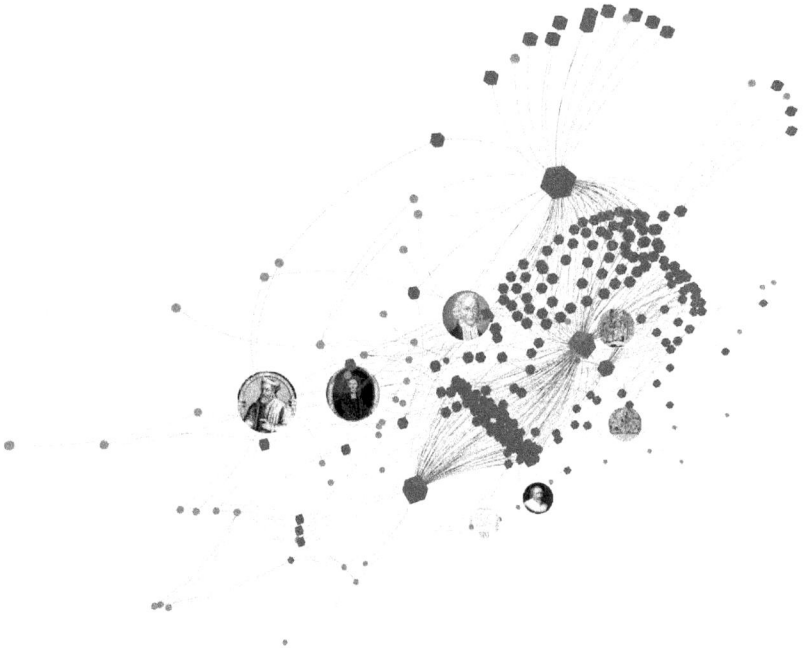

Beasts of Prey

BEE

As the silkworm, so the bee appears to be fashioned as a representation of Christ, who tirelessly labored and gathered the most delectable sustenance, only to be slain at the end of his toil, leaving behind his stores for the pleasure of his killers.

— *"Images," no. 198*

Upon Bees Fighting (Hall, 62)

What a pity it is to see these profitable, industrious creatures fall so furiously upon each other and thus sting and kill each other in the very mouth of the hive! I could like well to see the bees do this execution upon wasps and drones, enemies to their common stock; this savors but of justice. But to see them fall foul upon those of their own wing, it cannot but trouble their owner, who must needs be an equal loser by the victory of either. There is no more perfect resemblance of a commonwealth, whether civil or sacred, than in an hive. The bees are painful and honest compatriots, laboring to bring wax and honey to the maintenance of the public state; the wasps and drones are unprofitable and harmful hangbys which live upon the spoil of others' labors. Whether as common barattorst or strong thieves or bold parasites, they do nothing but rob their neighbors. It is an happy sight when these feel the dint of justice and are cut off from doing further mischief. But to see well-affected and beneficial subjects undo themselves with duels, whether of law or sword, to see good Christians of the same profession shedding each others' blood upon quarrels of religion, is no other than a sad and hateful spectacle; and so much the more by how much we have more means of reason and grace to compose our differences and correct our offensive contentiousness. Oh God who are at once the Lord of Hosts and Prince of Peace [Gen. 32: 2; Isa. 8:6], give us war with spiritual wickedness and peace with our brethren.

Upon Wasps Falling into a Glass (Hall, 63)

See you that narrow-mouthed glass which is set near to the hive? Mark how busily the wasps resort to it, being drawn thither by the smell of that sweet liquor wherewith it is baited. See how mannerly they creep into the mouth of it and fall down suddenly from that slippery steepness into that watery trap from which they can never rise; there, after some vain labor and weariness, they drown and die. You do not see any of the bees look that way; they pass directly to their hive without any notice taken of such a pleasing bait. Idle and ill-disposed persons are drawn away with every temptation; they have both leisure and will to entertain every sweet allurement to sin and wantonly prosecute their own wicked lusts till they fall into irrecoverable damnation; whereas the diligent and laborious Christian that follows hard and conscionably work of an honest calling is free from the danger of these deadly enticements, and lays up honey of comfort [Rev. 10:9] against the winter of evil. Happy is that man who can see and enjoy the success of his labor; but, however, this we are sure of, if our labor cannot purchase the good we would have, it shall prevent the evil we would avoid.

Whoe'er a Bee-hive does molest,
Altho' in Roguery or Jest,
Great Chance but he will feel a Sting;
The sweetest Joys their Smart will bring.

(Quarles, 1.3)

The bee goes out, and honey home doth bring,
And some who seek that honey find a sting.
Now would'st thou have the honey, and be free
From stinging, in the first place kill the bee.

This bee an emblem truly is of sin,
Whose sweet, unto a many, death hath been.
Now would'st have sweet from sin and yet not
die,
Do thou it, in the first place, mortify.
(Bunyan, 11)

Sweets can sometimes turn bitter: *The Ly-
dian child, having ventured away from his
mother, soon found himself under attack from
you, the merciless bees. He had thought of you
as gentle birds, yet a venomous serpent could
not have been as cruel. Ah, you offer stings in
return for the sweet honey you give; alas, o
misery, no kindness comes without you.*
(Alciati, 112)

By Paine, on Pleasures we doe seize;
And, we by Suff'rance, purchase Ease.
(Wither, 1.23)

The Bees, will in an Helmet breed;
And, Peace, doth after Warre, succeed.
(Wither, 2.28)

By Paine, on Pleasures we doe seize;
And, we by Suff'rance, purchase Ease. (Wither, 1.23)

The lick'rish Beare to rob the Honey-Bees
Among their stinging-Swarms thrusts in his pawes;
Adventureth to climbe up hollow Trees,
And from their Cells, the well fill'd Combes he drawes:
Right so, the Sensuall-Man that he may gaine
His bruitish Lust, a thousand perills dares;
And, that his Lawlesse-will he may attaine,
Nor Conscience, Credit, Cost, nor Labour spares.

'Twere shamefull basenesse, therefore, if that he
Who knoweth Vertue, and is thought her Lover,
Should so by any Perills frighted bee,
To make him such Affections to give-over.
For, why should that Vaine-Crew whose Valour springs
From beastly Fury, or inflamed-Passion,
Enabled be to compasse bolder things,
Then Sober-Wit, and Grave Consideration?
Or, why should lisping-Wantons, for their Lust
So much adventure as one finger, there,
Where we our Lives in hazard would not thrust
For Vertues Glory, if it needfull were?
For, though her Sweetnesse fast is closed in
With many Thornes, and such a Prickling-guard,
That we must smart, before that Prize we winne,
The Paine is follow'd, with a Rich Reward.
By Suff'ring, I have more Contentment had,
Then ever I acquir'd by Slothfull Ease;
And, I by Griefe, so joyfull have beene made,
That I will beare my Crosse, while God shall please.

For, so at last my Soule may Ioy procure,
I care not, in my Flesh what I endure.

BIRDS

The inhabitants of this world can be divided into three parts: those of the earth, those of the waters beneath, and those of the air or heavens. The birds of the air, with their glorious plumage, symbolize the inhabitants of heaven, who use their wings to praise their Creator with sweet music. The fishes of the waters beneath show the inhabitants of hell, as the waters in Scripture are the place of the dead and of destroyers. The miseries of death and God's wrath are likened to the sea, deeps, floods, and billows.

— *"Images," no. 82*

Upon the sight of many small Birds chirping about a dead Hawk (Flavel, 1.2)

Hearing a whole quire of Birds chirping and twinking together, it ingaged my curiosity a little to enquire into the occasion of that convocation, which mine eye quickly inform'd me of; for I perceived a dead Hawk in the bush, about which they made such a noise, seeming to triumph at the death of their enemy; and I could not blame them to sing his knell, who like a Cannibal was wont to feed upon their living bodies; tearing them limb from limb, and scaring them with his frightful appearance. This Bird which living was so formidable, being dead the poorest Wren or Titmouse fears not to chirp or hop over. This brings to my thoughts the base and ignoble ends of the greatest Tyrants and greedy ingroffers of the world, of whom (whilst living) men were more afraid than birds of a Hawk, but dead became objects of contempt and scorn. The death of such Tyrants is both inglorious and unlamented; When the wicked perish, there is shouting, Prov. 11:10.

Upon the singing of a blind Finch by night (Flavel, 1.7)

A Dear friend, who was a great observer of the works of God in nature, told me, That being entertain'd with a sight of many rarities at a friends house in London; among other things, his friend shewed him a Finch, whose eyes being put out, would frequently sing, even at midnight. This Bird in my opinion, is the lively Emblem of such careless and unconcerned persons, as the Prophet describes, Amos 6. 4, 5, 6. who chant to the viol, when a dismal night of trouble and affliction hath overshadowed the Church. You would have thought it strange to have heard this Bird sing in the night, when all others are in a deep silence; except the Owl, an unclean Bird, and the Nightingal which before we made the Emblem of the Hypocrite. And as strange it is, that any except the profane and hypocritical, should so unseasonably express their mirth and jollity; that any of Sions children Should live in pleasure, whilest she herself lyes in tears. The people of God in Psal. 137. tell us, in what postures of sorrow they sate; even like birds, with their heads under their wings, during the night of their Captivity. How shall we sing the Lords song in a strange land? 'Tis like enough, such as can sing and chaunt in the night of the Churches trouble, have well feathered their nests in the dayes of her prosperity; however let them know, that God will turn their unseasonable mirth into a sadder note; and those that now sit sad and silent, shall shortly sing for joy of heart, when the winter is past, the rain over and gone, the flowers appear again upon the earth, and the time of the singing of Birds is come.

Every Bird Sings According to his Beak
(Cats and Farlie, 213)

Every Cock Scratches Toward Himself
(Cats and Farlie, 229)

The Goose Hisses Well, But It Don't Bite
(Cats and Farlie, 165)

On the Cackling of a Hen (Bunyan, 41)

Every Bird Sings According to his Beak (Cats and Farlie, 213)

'Tis an old Saying and a true,
That ev'ry bird sings its own note;
Nor can it any other do
But as permits its beak and throat.
Whene'er you rove thro' field or wood,
And well attend with ears and eyes,
You'll find the Proverb just and good,
Whate'er the bird in shape or size.
Those which a hook'd harp beak have got,
Are for the most part Birds of Prey,
And bent alone on War, they wot
No note of song or minstrelsy.
Whene'er near rivers, lake or flood
You chance a flat-beak'd bird to meet,
From groping in the slush and mud,
Be sure his voice is never sweet.
The birds with longer flute-like beak,
Might more be thought to song inclin'd,
But in their thrumming note and shriek,
No turn for melody you'll find.
I therefore say,–as far as size
And shape of beak,–nor fear protest,
That of all birds beneath the skies,
The little beaks they sing the best.
E'en thus among mankind, we see,
God gives the little now and then,
A talent rare and quality
Which He gives not to bigger men.
Of little beaks, what bird like he
Which night-thro' sings in wood and dale?
That feather'd Soul of Harmony,
That little beak, the Nightingale!
And would you seek a tuneful throat,
You'll find throughout the feather'd throng,
The greater beak the harsher note,
The smaller beak the sweeter song.

As with the Fowls of earth and air,
Not so with Man–he hath no beak,
But in his mouth beyond compare
The nobler Godlike power to speak!
And when he speaks in spirit kind,
What note of bird more softly sweet
To breathe the music of the mind,
When kindred hearts and spirits meet!
But when the mouth of Man outpours
The blast of Passion's wrathful breath,
The Lion not more fiercely roars
His angry note of blood and death!
Hence what befalls mankind between,
Comes from a deeper source express'd,
Where sits, by ev'ry eye unseen
But God's, the impulse of the breast.
The Mouth commands, implores, decries,
As moves the Heart, and gives thereto
The tone which most its will implies,
By force or softness to subdue.
Hence ye who speak in bitter tone,
And fiercely wound another's heart,
Beware, and learn to curb thine own,
Lest it repay thee smart for smart.
As "by his ears the Ass is known,"
A truth which no one can impeach,
"The Man," as Proverbs long have shewn,
"Is known as truly by his speech."

On the Cackling of a Hen (Bunyan, 41)

The hen, so soon as she an egg doth lay,
(Spreads the fame of her doing what she may.)
About the yard she cackling now doth go,
To tell what 'twas she at her nest did do.
Just thus it is with some professing men,
If they do ought that good is, like our hen
They can but cackle on't where e'er they go,
What their right hand doth their left hand must know.

A hen lays every day, but an ostrich only once a year (Cats and Farlie, 133)

Birds of One Feather will Flocke Together (Cats and Farlie, 109)

It is a crime for scholars to speak ill of other scholars: *Ah, Procne! Why dost thou so cruelly take the singing cicada and prepare a dreadful feast for thy young? Is it just for one chatterer to do harm to another? Is it fair for a singer of the spring to harm another of the same? Is it right for a guest to harm another guest? Is it proper for one with wings to harm another with wings? Lay down thy quarry, for it is a wicked deed for one who sings to be consumed by another. (Alciati, 180)*

A small kitchen is not big enought for two gluttons: *No reward lies in the small; a single orchard cannot satisfy two robins. Likewise, two fig-peckers cannot find contentment in a single grove. (Alciati, 94)*

A hen lays every day, but an ostrich only once a year (Cats and Farlie, 133)

Hear now what has befallen me; I'm nicely taken in!
All through my Wife! who thought at once a mine of wealth to
     win
A Dealer shew'd this Ostrich and its egg to her one day,
And making her believe 'twas such a wondrous bird to lay;
I bought it at her bidding – brought it home, and, like her,
     thought
A Bird that lay such eggs as that, could not be dearly bought.
Hens' eggs (thought I), however good, were at the best but small,
And, as compar'd to Ostrich eggs, were of no size at all.
Off such an egg as that, why, two could make a dinner quite,
"Twas big enough to satisfy a ploughman's appetite.
Such was my mind: but very soon I'd reason to regret
I'd parted with my money, or an Ostrich ever met.
It eat! Oh! such a bird to eat as that I never saw!
No end of food and things could satisfy its hungry maw;
But Eggs! not one it laid! though all the while I did my best
With hay and straw and feathers soft to make the bird a nest.
When, after waiting long, 'twas just about the month of May-
I found one egg! Eh! now, thought I, it has begun to lay!
But all my joy was very short, for from that time till now,
It hasn't laid another egg, nor will it any how.
Yet all this while our Hens, as is with Hens the usual way,
They've always laid at intervals, and often ev'ry day.
At length, all patience losing, and my temper put about,
I went up to the Ostrich, and I call'd to him; Turn out!
Away with you, you rav'nous brute, you shall no longer stay!
You're big enough, and eat enough, and yet no eggs you lay.
I see how 'tis with you, you're all appearance, nothing more;
In buying you I've learnt what I ought well t' have known before:
The biggest things are not the best, the brightest often dross;
And when we grasp at profit most, we oft get greater loss.

Upon the sight of a Robbin-red-breast picking up a worm from a mole-hill then raising (Flavel, 1.5)

Observing the Mole working industriously beneath, and the Bird watching so intently above; I made a stand to observe the issue. When in a little time the bird descends and seizes upon a worm, which I perceived was crawling apace from the enemy below that hunted her, but fell to the share of another which from above waited for her. My thoughts presently suggested these Meditations from that occasion; me thought this poor worm seem'd to be the Emblem of my poor soul, which is more endangered by its own lusts of pride and covetousness, than this worm was by the Mole and Bird; my pride, like the aspiring Bird watches for it above; my covetousness, like this subterranean Mole, digging for it beneath. Poor soul! what a sad Dilemma art thou brought to? If thou go down into the caverns of the earth, there thou art a prey to thy covetousness that hunts thee; and if thou aspire, or but creep upward, there thy pride waits to ensnare thee. Distressed soul! whither wilt thou go? ascend thou mayest, not by a vain elation, but by a heavenly conversation, beside which, there is no way for thy preservation; the way of life is above to the wise, &c.

Again, I could not but observe the accidental benefit this poor harmless Bird obtained by the labour of the Mole, who hunting intentionally for her self, unburroughed and ferrited out this worm for the Bird, who possibly was hungry enough, and could not have been relieved for this time, but by the Mole, the fruit of whose labours she now fed upon. Even thus the Lord oft-times makes good his word to his people: The wealth of the wicked is laid up for the just. And again, The earth shall help the woman. This was fully exemplified in David, to whom Nabal that churlish muck-worm speaks all in possessives. Shall I take my bread &c. and give it to one I know not whom; and yet David reaps the fruit of all the pains and toyl of Nabal at last. Let it never incourage me to idleness, that God sometimes gives his people the fruit of uthers sweat; but if providence reduce me to necessity, and disable me from helping my self, I doubt not then but it will provide instruments to do it. The Bird was an hungry and could not dig.

Upon the Sight of a Cockfight (Hall, 24)

How fell these creatures out? Whence grew this so bloody combat? Here was neither old grudge nor present injury. What then
is the quarrel? Surely nothing but that which should rather unite
and reconcile them, one common nature; they are both of one
feather. I do not see either of them fly upon creatures of different kind; but while they have peace with all others, they are at
war with themselves. The very sight of each other was sufficient
provocation. If this be the offence, why doth not each of them
fall out with himself, since he hates and revenges in another the
being of that same which himself is?

Since man's sin brought debate into the world, nature is become
a great quarreler. The seeds of discord were scattered [Prov. 6:14]
in every furrow of the creation and came up in a numberless
variety of antipathies, whereof yet none is more odious and
deplorable than those which are betwixt creatures of the same
kind. What is this but an image of the woeful hostility which
is exercised betwixt us reasonables, who are conjoined in one
common humanity if not religion?

We fight with and destroy each other more than those creatures
that want reason to temper their passions. No beast is so cruel to
man as himself; where one man is slain by a beast, ten thousand
are slain by man. What is that war which we study and practice
but the art of killing? Whatever Turks and pagans may do, O
Lord, how long shall this brutish fury arm Christians against each
other? While even devils are not at enmity with themselves but
accord in wickedness, why do we men so mortally oppose each
other in good?

Oh Thou that are the God of peace, compose the unquiet hearts
of men to an happy and universal concord, and at last refresh
our souls with the multitude of peace.

Upon the Sight and Noise of a Peacock (Hall, 83)

I see there are many kinds of hypocrites. Of all birds this makes the fairest show and the worst noise, so as this is an hypocrite to the eye. There are others, as the blackbird, that looks foul and sooty but sings well, this is an hypocrite to the ear. There are others that please as well both in their show and voice but are cross in their carriage and condition, as the popinjay, whose colors are beautiful and noise delightful yet is apt to do mischief in scratching and biting any hand that comes near it. These are hypocrites both to the eye and ear. Yet there is a degree further (beyond the example of all brute creatures) of them whose show, whose words, whose actions are fair but their hearts are foul and abominable. No outward beauty can make the hypocrite other than odious. For me, let my profession agree with my words, my words with my ac-tions, my actions with my heart; and let all of them be approved of the God of truth.

BIRTH

Children enter the world naked and dirty, crying and powerless, to signify the spiritual nakedness, depravity of nature, and wretchedness of condition they are born with. There are many things in the world that are not direct reflections of divine things, yet they signify them; such as children's crying upon entering the world representing their sorrow. Man's birth, like that of the beasts, signifies his ignorance and brutishness, and his agreement with the beasts in many aspects. Men, born filthy and out of filth, come into the world with their backs to God and heaven, and their faces to the earth and hell, symbolizing the natural state of their hearts.

— *"Images," nos. 10, 25, 122*

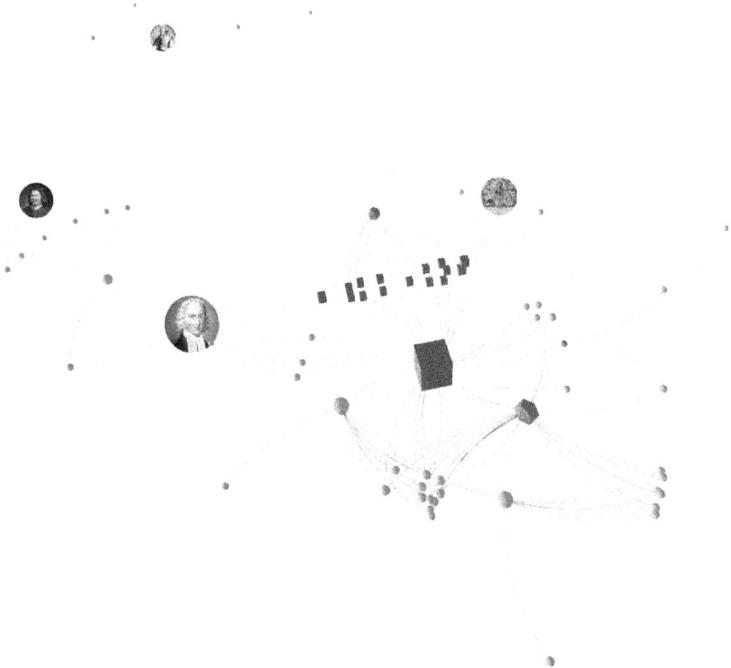

Birth

BLESSING

From the moment a seed is sown in the ground, it is exposed to many dangers that can destroy it. It can be taken by birds, eaten by worms, scorched by the sun, choked by weeds or thorns, and even when the fruit is ripe, it can be killed by a honey-dew. Similarly, the soul of a believer is exposed to various trials, from which some may be overcome and others may hold out for a longer time. But the greatest trial of all is great worldly and spiritual prosperity, as it can lead to spiritual pride and a sorrowful state.

— *"Images," no. 165*

Blessing

BLOOD

The heart is the source of life, and thus it should be guarded carefully. For, as Proverbs 4:23 states, "Keep thy heart with all diligence; for out of it are the issues of life."

— *"Images," no. 6*

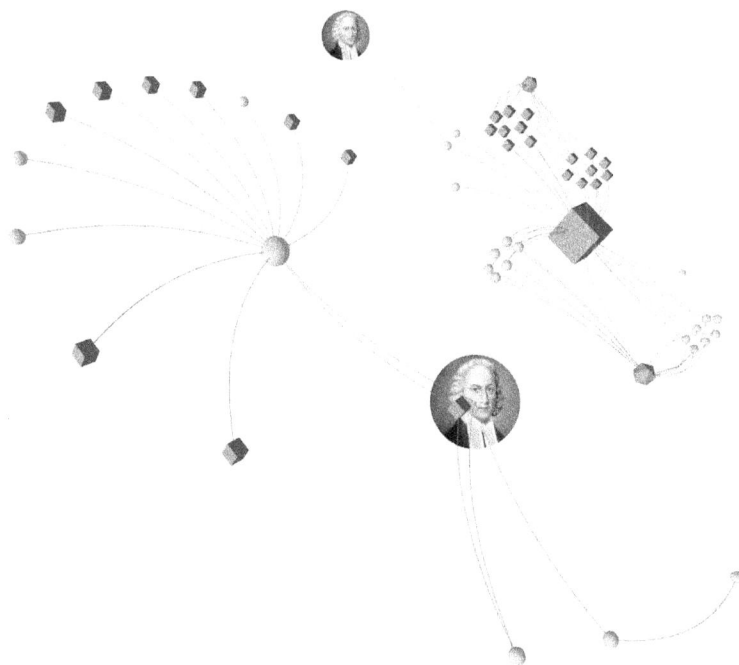

Blood

Blossoms

Of the countless blossoms that adorn a tree, so few become ripe fruit; and of the immense number of seeds released yearly, so few become a plant; and the vast amount of seeds, both of plants and animals, that never become anything, appear to be a reminder: how few are saved from the multitude of mankind, and especially how few of the professed Christians remain sincere until the end, and how, out of many, only a few are chosen.

— *"Images,"* no. 60

Upon the Promising Fruitfulness of a Tree (Bunyan, 25)

Upon the Promising Fruitfulness of a Tree (Bunyan, 25)

A comely sight indeed it is to see
A world of blossoms on an apple-tree:
Yet far more comely would this tree appear,
If all its dainty blooms young apples were.
But how much more might one upon it see,
If all would hang there till they ripe should be.
But most of all in beauty 'twould abound,
If then none worm-eaten should there be found.
But we, alas! do commonly behold
Blooms fall apace, if mornings be but cold.
They too, which hang till they young apples are,
By blasting winds and vermin take despair,
Store that do hang, while almost ripe, we see
By blust'ring winds are shaken from the tree,
So that of many, only some there be,
That grow till they come to maturity.

Comparison

This tree a perfect emblem is of those
Which God doth plant, which in his garden grows,
Its blasted blooms are motions unto good,
Which chill affections do nip in the bud.
Those little apples which yet blasted are,
Show some good purposes, no good fruits bear.
Those spoiled by vermin are to let us see,
How good attempts by bad thoughts ruin'd be.
Those which the wind blows down, while they are green,
Show good works have by trials spoiled been.
Those that abide, while ripe upon the tree,
Show, in a good man, some ripe fruit will be.
Behold then how abortive some fruits are,
Which at the first most promising appear.
The frost, the wind, the worm, with time doth show,
There flows, from much appearance, works but few.

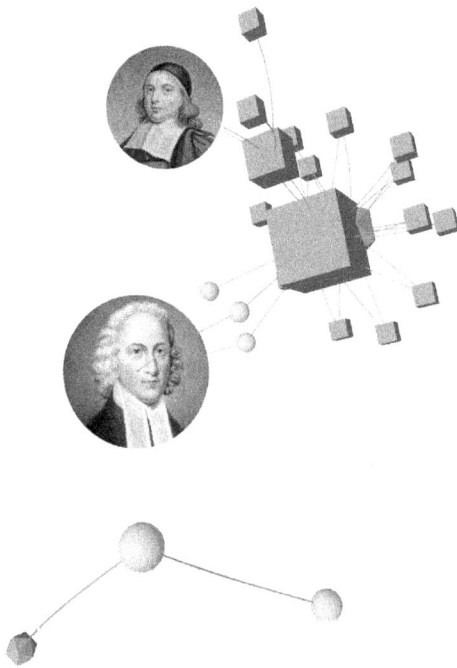

Blossom

BODY OF MAN

The Apostle reasoned in such a way, from what is found in the human body to what should be in the spiritual body of Christ or the Church of God, demonstrating that more than mere analogy is intended. This implies that one is a real symbol of the other; otherwise his arguments would not be as powerful as his words imply.

— "Images," no. 130

Concerning gluttony: *A man was portrayed with the neck of a crane, his stomach bloated; in his grasp he held a mew or pelican. That was the image of Dionysius, and Apicius, and all those whom luxurious gluttony made renowned. (Alciati, 91)*

BOWELS

The depths of man's body are filled with uncleanness, his bowels filled with dung - a symbol of the natural corruption and filthiness of the heart. His inwards are laden with filth and dung, signifying the spiritual depravity and wickedness of the inner man, often represented by the heart, bowels, belly, and veins. The many turns and twists of the bowels signify the complex, hidden, and deceitful ways of the heart. Proverbs 20:27, Proverbs 18:8, Proverbs 26:22, Proverbs 20:30, and Proverbs 22:18.

— *"Images," nos. 109, 115*

Bowels

BREAD

*The threshing of grain and the burning of sacrifice repre-
sent the suffering of Christ, and the instruments used in
both are symbols of the instruments of Christ's suffering.
The oxen, whose labor trod out the corn, are offered as
a sacrifice, symbolizing Christ, who not only was the
sacrifice but the priest, actively providing us with heavenly bread. Gideon was told to build an altar to God
near the threshing floor and wine press, for the manner
of obtaining wine in the press signifies the shedding of
blood, and the threshing of wheat for bread symbolizes
the suffering inflicted on Christ's body. Baking bread is
a type of the suffering of Christ, as the showbread is an
offering made by fire unto the Lord. All offerings made
by fire under the Mosaic law are types of Christ, and
their suffering the fire is a symbol of Christ's suffering.*

— *"Images," nos. 187, 197*

Thy price one penny is in time of plenty,
In famine doubled, 'tis from one to twenty.
Yea, no man knows what price on thee to set
When there is but one penny loaf to get.

This loaf's an emblem of the Word of God,
A thing of low esteem before the rod
Of famine smites the soul with fear of death,
But then it is our all, our life, our breath.
(Bunyan, 37)

Why should I feare the want of Bread?
If God so please, I shall bee fed.
(Wither, 4.47)

Why should I feare the want of Bread?
If God so please, I shall bee fed. (Wither, 4.47)

The faithlesse Iewe's repining currishnesse,
The blessed Psalmist, fitly did expresse,
By grinning-dogs, which howling roame by night,
To satisfie their grudging appetite.
Here, therefore, by an Emblem, wee are showne,
That, God, (who as hee lists, bestowes his owne)
Providing so, that none may bee unfed,
Doth offer to the Dogges, the Childrens bread.

And, by this Emblem, wee advised are,
Of their presumptuous boldnesse to beware,
Who bound God's Mercie; and, have shut out some
From hope of Grace, before the Night is come:
Since, to the Dogs, his meat is not denide,
If they returne, (though not till Evening-tide.)

Moreover, wee, some notice hence may take,
That, if provision, God, vouchsafes to make,
For Lyons, Dogs, and Ravens, in their need,
Hee will his Lambes, and harmlesse Turtles feed:
And, so provide, that they shall alwayes have
Sufficient, to maintaine the Life hee gave.

I must confesse, I never merit shall,
The Crummes, which from thy Childrens table fall:
Yet, thou hast oft, and freely fed mee, Lord,
Among thy Children, at thy Holy-board:
Nor have I, there, been fill'd with Bread alone;
But, on the blessed Bodie of thy Sonne,
My Soule hath feasted. And, if thou dost grant
Such favours, Lord! what can I feare to want?

For, doubtlesse, if thy Sonne thou please to give,
All other things, with him, I shall receive.

Bread

BREAD-CORN

The Bible uses bread-corn to symbolize the saints. The wicked are likened to clusters of grapes, while the godly are compared to bread-corn. They are referred to as Christ's wheat, which He will gather into His barn and storehouse. Wheat and other bread-corn are sown and grow before winter, and are then seemingly killed by the cold season, only to revive in the spring and grow taller than before, bearing fruit. This is a vivid representation of the resurrection of the saints, as after their conversion they may fall away and remain in a cold, dormant state, only to reawaken and grow taller than before, never faltering until they reach perfection. This is also an apt description of the Christian church, which after being planted by the apostles and thriving for a time, fell into a long period of suffering before being restored to glory and fruitfulness at the destruction of Antichrist. This is alluded to in Hosea 14:7 and Isaiah 37:30-31, which speak of Israel and the church reviving as the corn.

— "Images," no. 108

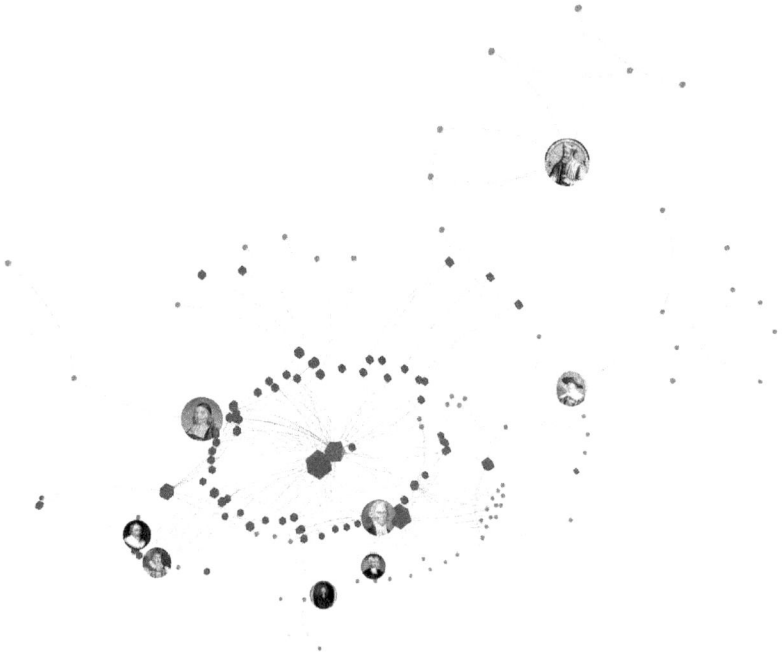

Bread-corn

BREATH

The breath of life is likened to the Spirit of God, with Scripture providing the example. As God commanded in Ezekiel 37:9–10, the breath of life was breathed into the slain so that they could live. This is similar to the Spirit of God entering into the soul, as seen in Ezekiel 37:13–14 and John 20:22. Thus, the breath of life is a symbol of the Holy Ghost, giving life to the dead.

— *"Images," no. 62*

Breath

BRIDLE

The tongue and another part of the body come with a natural restraint, a reminder of the necessity to control both.

— *"Images," no. 104*

Doe not the golden Meane, exceed,
In Word, in Passion, nor in Deed.
(Wither, 3.35)

Doe not the golden Meane, exceed,
In Word, in Passion, nor in Deed. (Wither, 3.35)

As is the head-strong Horse, and blockish Mule,
Ev'n such, without the Bridle, and the Rule,
Our Nature growes; and, is as mischievous,
Till Grace, and Reason, come to governe us.
The Square, and Bridle, therefore let us heed,
And, thereby learne to know, what helpes wee need;
Lest, else, (they fayling, timely, to bee had)
Quite out of Order, wee, at length, bee made.

The Square, (which is an usefull Instrument,
To shape foorth senselesse Formes) may represent
The Law: Because, Mankind, (which is by Nature,
Almost as dull, as is the senselesse-creature,)
Is thereby, from the native-rudenesse, wrought;
And, in the Way of honest-living taught.
The Bridle, (which Invention did contrive,
To rule, and guide the Creature-sensitive)
May type forth Discipline; which, when the Law
Hath school'd the Wit, must keepe the Will in awe.
And, hee that can by these, his Passions bound,
This Emblems meaning, usefully, hath found.

Lord, let thy sacred Law, at all times, bee
A Rule, a Master, and a Glasse to mee;
(A Bridle, and a Light) that I may, still,
Both know my Dutie, and obey thy Will.
Direct my Feet; my Hands, instruct thou so,
That I may neither wander, nor mis-doe.
My Lookes, my Hearing, and my Wordes confine,
To keepe still firme, to ev'ry Word of thine.

On thee, let also my Desires attend:
And, let me hold this temper, till mine end.

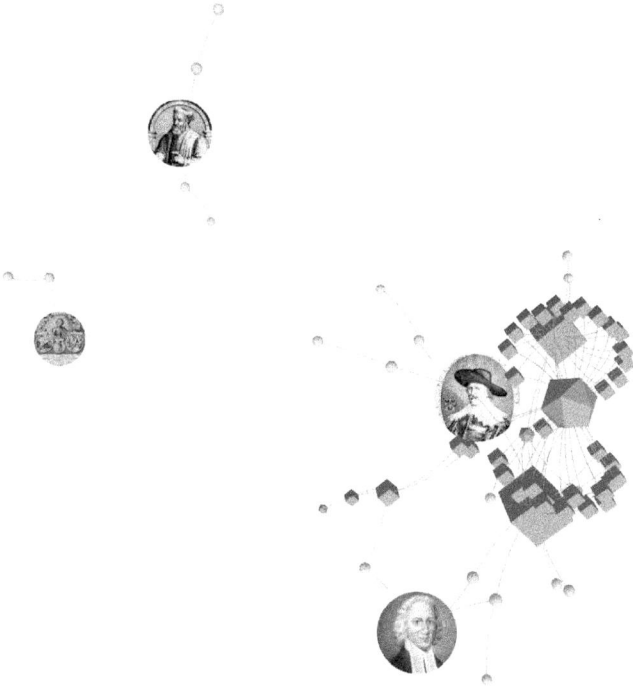

Bridle

BUBBLE

The grandeur of a bubble that is blown up to its fullest size and painted with beautiful colors is a vivid image of the fleeting nature of earthly glory. Those who place their joy in the things of this world, when they are most prosperous, surrounded by honors, wealth, and pleasure, often die suddenly and all their glory is gone in an instant. This is seen in Psalms 37:35–36, where it is said that the wicked man is like a green bay tree, yet he passes away and is not found. Similarly, Hosea 10:7 speaks of Samaria's king being cut off like foam on the water.

— *"Images," no. 191*

This World's so vain and full of Trouble,
That if it's ballanc'd with a Bubble,
The light-blown Film will weigh down all
The other's rich and mighty Ball.
(Quarles, 1.4)

BURNING USELESS THINGS

Many things, when they are of no use, are good for burning, and that is what people do with them. This is said of fruitless branches in John 15:6, "and men gather them, and cast them into the fire, and they are burned." That is the way people get rid of useless material, like the wood of fruitless trees, brambles, thorns, and bushes when they are clearing land. It is the same in spiritual matters.

— "Images," no. 88

I pine, that others may not perish,
And waste my Selfe, their Life to cherish.
(Wither, 1.15)

I pine, that others may not perish,
And waste my Selfe, their Life to cherish. (Wither, 1.15)

Observe I pray you, how the greedy Flame
The Fewell, on an Altar doth consume.
How it destroyeth that which feedes the same,
And how the Nourisher away doth fume.

For, so it fares with Parents that uphold
Their thriftlesse Children in unlawfull Pleasures:
With Cares, it weares them out, ere they are old;
And ere their Lives consume, consumes their Treasures.
So fares it with such Wantons as doe feede
Unchast Desires; for, ev'ry day they grow
Untill their Longings, their Supplies exceede,
And, quite devoure those men that fed them so.
So fares it with all those that spend their Youth
In lab'ring to enrich ungratefull Men,
Who, growing Great, and Wealthy, by their Truth,
Returne them Smoke and Ashes backe agen.
So fares it with good States-men, who to keepe
A thankelesse Common-wealth in happy Peace,
Deprive their Mindes of Rest, their Eyes of Sleepe,
And, waste themselves, that others may encrease.
And, so it fares with Men that passe away
Their time in Studies, (and their Healths impaire)
That helps to other men become they may,
And, their defective Knowledges, repaire.

But, let my Flesh, my Time, and my Estate,
Be so consum'd; so spent; so wasted bee,
That they may nourish Grace, and perfit that
For which all these were first bestowd'd on me:

So when I quite am vanish'd out of seeing,
I shall enjoy my Now-concealed-Being.

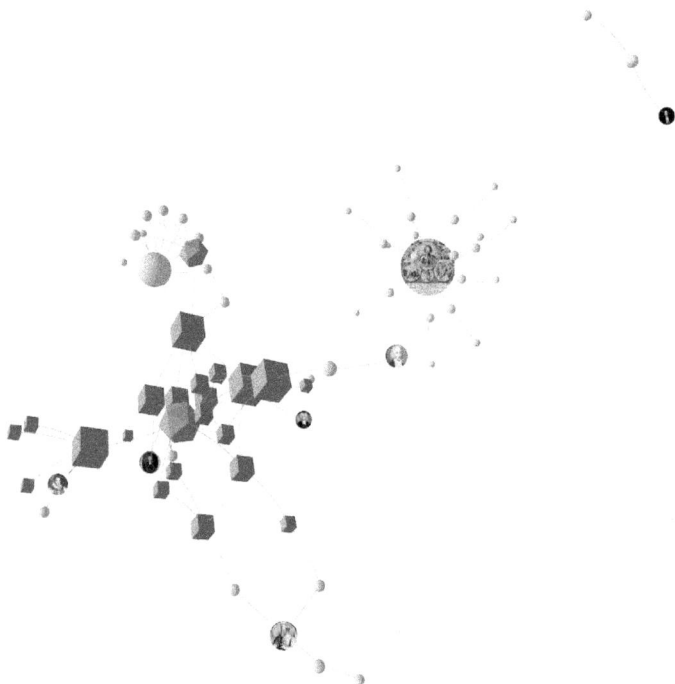

Burning

CANDLE

The life of man is likened to the flame of a candle or lamp, which is feeble when first lit, can be extinguished by a breath or gust of wind, and can be snuffed out by its own fuel when there is an excess of it. This is seen in the Bible, such as 1 Kings 11:36 and 15:4, where it is stated that God gave David a lamp in Jerusalem. Job 18:6, 21:17, Proverbs 13:9, 24:20 and 20:20 also use the analogy of a candle or lamp being put out to represent the destruction of a wicked person.

— "Images," no. 52

Upon a Lanthorn and Candle Carried Bye, on a Windy Night (Boyle, 6.3)

As there are few controversies more important, so there are not many that have been more curiously and warmly disputed than the question, whether a publick or private life be preferable? But perhaps this may be much of the nature of the other question, whether a married life or a single life ought to be chosen? that being best determinable by the circumstances of particular cases. For though indefinitely speaking, one of the two may have advantages above the other, yet they are not so great, but that special circumstances may make either of them the more eligible to particular persons. They that find themselves furnished with abilities to serve their generation in a publick capacity, and virtue great enough to resist the temptations to which such a situation is usually exposed, may not only be allowed to embrace such an employment, but obliged to seek it. But he whose parts are too mean to qualifie him to govern others, and perhaps to enable him to govern himself or manage his own private concerns, or whose graces are so week, that 'tis less to his virtues, or his ability of resisting, than to his care of shunning the occasions of sin, that he owes his escaping the guilt of it, had better deny himself some opportunities of doing good, than expose himself to probable temptations. For there is such a kind of difference betwixt virtue shaded by a private, and shining forth in a publick life, as there is betwixt a candle carried aloft in the open air, and inclosed in a lanthorn; in the former place it gives more light, but in the latter 'tis in less danger of being blown out.

I pine, that others may not perish,
And waste my Selfe, their Life to cherish.
(Wither, 3.50)

This Day, my Houre-glasse, forth is runne;
Thy Torch, to Morrow, may bee done. (Wither, 3.50)

There is no Day, nor minute of the Day,
In which, there are not many sent away
From Life to Death; or, many drawing-on,
Which, must within a little while, bee gone.
You, often, view the Grave; you, often, meet
The Buriers, and the Mourners, in the street,
Conveying of some Neighbour, to that home,
Which must, e're long, your dwelling-place become.
You see the Race, of many a youthfull Sonne
Is finish'd, e're his Father's Course is done;
And, that, the hand of Death, regardeth neither
Sexe, Youth, nor Age; but, mingleth all together.
You, many times, in your owne houses, heare
The groanes of Death, and, view your Children, there,
Your loving Parents, or, beloved Wives,
To gaspe for breath, and, labour for their lives.

Nay, you your selves, do sometime find the paines
Of Sicknesse, in your Bowels, and your Vaines.
The Harbingers of Death, sometime, begin
To take up your whole Bodie, for their Inne.
You beare their heavie Aches, on your back;
You feele their twinges, make your heartstrings crack;
And, sometime, lye imprison'd, and halfe dead,
With Age, or with Diseases, on your bed:
Yet you deferre your ends; and, still contrive,
For temp'rall things; as if you thought to live
Six Ages longer: or, had quite forgot,
That, you, and others, draw one common-Lot.

But, that, you might not, still, the same forget,
This Emblem, and this Motto, here were set.

A Vertue hidden, or not us'd,
Is either Sloth, or Grace abus'd.
(Wither, 3.47)

A Vertue hidden, or not us'd,
Is either Sloth, or Grace abus'd. (Wither, 3.47)

The World hath shamelesse Boasters, who pretend,
In sundry matters, to be skill'd so well,
That, were they pleased, so their houres to spend,
They say, they could in many things excell.
But, though they make their hearers to beleeve,
That, out of Modestie their Gifts they hide,
In them wee very plainely may perceive,
Or Sloth, or Envy, Ignorance, or Pride.

When other mens endeavours they peruse,
They either carpe at what they cannot mend;
Or else of Arrogance doe those accuse,
Who, to the publike view, their Workes commend.
If these men say, that they can Poetize,
But, will not; they are false in saying so:
For, he, whose Wit a little that way lies,
Will doing bee, though hee himselfe undoe.
If they, in other Faculties are learned,
And, still, forbeare their Talents to imploy;
The truest Knowledge, yet, is undiscerned,
And, that, they merit not, which they injoy.
Yea, such as hide the Gifts they have received,
(Or use them not, as well as they are able)
Are like fayre Eyes, of usefull sight bereaved;
Or, lighted-Candles, underneath a Table.
Their glorioust part, is but a Painted-cloath,
Whose Figures, to the wall-ward, still are hung.
Their hidden Vertues, are apparant Sloth;
And, all their life, is to the publike wrong:

For, they doe reape the Fruits, by many sowne,
And, leave to others, nothing of their owne.

My Substance, and my Light, are spent,
In seeking other mens content.
(Wither, 3.31)

My Substance, and my Light, are spent,
In seeking other mens content. (Wither, 3.31)

If this nigh-wasted Candle, you shall view,
And, heed it well, it may enlighten you
To looke with more compassion, on their paines,
Who rob themselves, to multiply your gaines.
The Taper burnes, to give another light,
Ev'n till it selfe, it hath consumed quite;
And, all the profit, which it thence doth winne,
Is to be snufft, by ev'ry Commer-in.

This is the Lot of some, whom I have knowne,
Who, freely, all their life-time, have bestowne
In such industrious labour, as appeares,
To further others profits, more then theirs;
And, all their Patrimonies, well nigh spent,
The ruining of others, to prevent.
The wit, the strength, and all the pow'r they had,
(Which might, by probability, have made
Good meanes to raise them, in this world, as high,
As most, who climbe to wealthy dignity)
Ev'n these, they have bestow'd, to better them,
Who their indeavours, for their paines, contemne.

These are those Lamps, whose flames, from time to time,
Have through each Age, and through-out ev'ry Clime,
To one another, that true Light convey'd,
Which Ignorance, had, els, long since betray'd
To utter darknesse. These, despightfull Pride
Oft snuffs; and, oft, to put them out, hath try'd.
But, from the brightnesse of such Lights, as they,
We got our Light of knowledge, at this day.

To them, God make us kinder; and to Him,
More thankfull, that we gain'd such light by them.

Those Fooles whom Beauties Flame doth blinde,
Feele Death, where Life they thought to finde.
(Wither, 1.40)

Those Fooles whom Beauties Flame doth blinde, Feele Death, where Life they thought to finde. (Wither, 1.40)

When you doe next behold the wanton Flyes
About the shining Candle, come to play,
Untill the Light thereof hath dimm'd their Eyes,
Or, till the Flame hath sing'd their Wings away:
Remember, then, this Emblem; and, beware
You be not playing at such harmefull Games:
Consider, if there sit no Female, there,
That overwarmes you, with her Beauties Flames,
Take heed, you doe not over dally so
As to inflame the Tinder of Desire;
But, shun the Mischiefe, e're too late it grow,
Lest you be scorched in that Foolish-Fire.

For, as those Wandring-Fires which in the Night,
Doe leade unwary Trauellers astray,
Alluring them, by their deceiving Sight,
Till they have altogether lost their way:
Right so fantasticke Beauty doth amaze
The Lust-full Eye, allures the Heart aside,
Captives the Senses (by a sudden blaze)
And, leaves the Iudgement wholly stupify'd.
Nay, if Men play too long about those Torches,
Such is the Nature of their wanton Flame,
That, from their Bodies (unawares) it scorches
Those Wings and Feet, on which they thither came.
It wasteth (ev'n to nothing) all their Wealth,
Consumes their precious Time, destroyes their Strength,
Bespots their Honest-Fame, impaires their Health,
And (when their Fatall Thread is at the length)

That thing, on which their Hope of Life is plac't,
Shall bring them to Destruction, at the last.

At first the Candle burns but dim,
And a mere smoaky Snuff will seem:
For Life, just kindled in the Mother,
What is it more than Smoak and Smother?
(Quarles, 6.1)

How first God lighted up the Soul
In Man, a Lump of heavy Mould;
And how the Soul and Body's join'd,
Deep searching Reason cannot find.
(Quarles, 6.2)

The Candle's lighted, but I doubt
A Puff of Wind will blow it out;
Such is our Life, and such our Breath,
Each Moment liable to Death.
(Quarles, 6.3)

Snuff not your Candle down too low,
The more it's trimm'd the less 'twill fhew:
So of your Bodies be not nice—
You may, you know, be over-wise.
(Quarles, 6.4)

Let Boreas blow, the Taper's screen'd,
Nor can be puff'd by any Wind;
Thus the good Man need never fear,
Since he is still in Angel's Care.
(Quarles, 6.5)

Death, why so fast? i pray stop your Hand,
And let my Glass run out its sand:
As neither Death nor Time will stay,
Let us improve the present Day.
(Quarles, 6.6)

When Sol's in his meridian Blaze,
No other Lights can shew their Face:
When God reveals his glorious Light,
Our brightest Day's as dark as Night.
(Quarles, 6.7)

The Sun eclips'd, appears forlorn;
A Candle in a darken'd Horn
Helps none: and such that Merit is
Which none but its Possessor sees.
(Quarles, 6.8)

Scarce more than Smoak the candle gives,
When it the feeble Light receives:
What is an Infant, when its born?
A Creature naked and forlorn.
(Quarles, 6.9)

Youth is a giddy, hair-bran'd Thing,
And seems as born to laugh and sing;
Joy is its Bent; but thought and Care
Let older heads and Shoulders bear.
(Quarles, 6.10)

The Youth is now advanc'd to Man,
And thirty merry Years has ran;
Reason must now assume her Place,
And plan the Method of his Race.
(Quarles, 6.11)

At Forty we become sedate,
Steady in Action or Debate;
Error and Truth distinctly know,
And then are wise, if ever so.
(Quarles, 6.12)

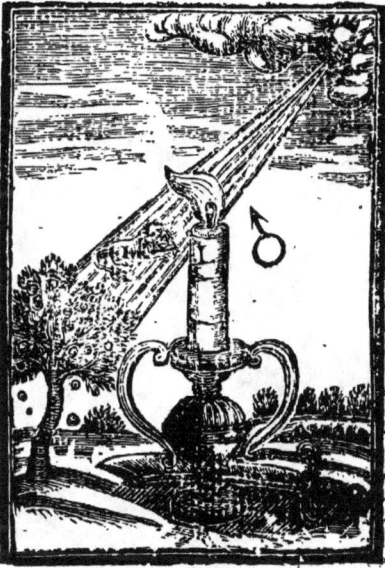

The Sun from his Meridian Height,
Gradual defends with weaker Light:
Of Fifty turn'd, Man down-hill goes,
Till a mere Shade on Earth he grows.
(Quarles, 6.13)

Sixty is come, with Silver Locks;
Death at his Door gives warning Knocks:
Nature and Strength are both decay'd;
His Death-bed too is ready made.
(Quarles, 6.14)

The Sun at last is sunk below,
A feeble Glimmer's all his Shew:
So Man, to Seventy arriv'd,
Can only say, I once have liv'd.
(Quarles, 6.15)

When God withdraws his chearing Light,
The Soul is sunk in dismal Night;
But his Return the Cloud dispels,
Comforts, and Love, and Grace reveals.
(Quarles, 1.13)

Fire, Cough, Love, And Money, Are Not Long Concealed
(Cats and Farlie, 209)

Fire, Cough, Love, And Money, Are Not Long Concealed (Cats and Farlie, 209)

THIS Candle I would carry so
That neighbours cannot see
A gleam of Light that may in aught
Reveal a glimpse of me;
For if I can, no one will watch
Me then, and I may go
Where'er I lift, without the fear
That any one will know.
But still, in spite of all I do,
I fear the light is seen;
Its rays still stream thro' all the holes
And Lanthorn's chinks between;
Whatever care I take, howe'er
I strive to shade it o'er,
Some gleams pierce thro' behind, or at
The side, or thro' the door.
My neighbour's very old, and as
Old people often are,
He's very much afflicted with
A cough, and bad catarrhe;
But ne'ertheless, strange though it seem,
As ev'ry one must own,
The good man has a great dislike
To lie at night alone.
He's courting a young maiden now,
And while he's so engaged,
He strives his best to stop the cough, -
But 'twill not be assuag'd:
And while he sits and looks his best,
To make his courtship sure,
The sprightly lass, tho' striving all
She can to look demure,
Says, that is not the Music a
Young Maiden's heart to gain,
And bids him rest content to sleep
Alone, and not complain:

But if a Wife he's bent to have,
The best thing he can do,
Is one of his own age to choose,
Who has a bad cough too.
A fellow who to gain his bread,
Runs errands here and there,
Found recently, a purse well fill'd
With ducats, in the Square:
With joy elate he took it home,
And to his Wife he said:
Look here! dear Trijn! I've found a prize!
Our fortune now is made!
But you! you must not breathe a word;
So mind you what you do! No one,
Trijn, save yourself, must aught
Of this good Wind-fall know!
No longer now with messages
Will I run here and there;
But like a Burgher live at ease,
And have the best of cheer!
Therefore stitch thou this purse inside
Thy sleeve, or else somewhere.
Trijn swore she would, and with an oath
To take the best of care.
But, mark! e'en from that very time,
The Wife began to spend;
Dress fine, prate large, and treat or this
Or that dear-gossip-friend;
The Man, too, he will go no more
With messages—not he;
Such paltry jobs he says are quite
Beneath his dignity.
The Daughter, the is dress'd as fine-
The babe put out to nurse,
"Tis wondrous strange! but money ne'er
Will stop within the purse!
At length the truth gets wind, and lo!
The man is prisoner made,
And mourns within a cell, that he

Had left an honest trade.
The sprightly Trijn in sorrow blames
Her foolish spendthrift-riot;
And all because the money would
Not rest in peace and quiet.

Upon the Sight of a Pound of Candles Falling to the Ground (Bunyan, 36)

Of the Fly at the Candle (Bunyan, 23)

But be the candles down, and scattered too,
Some lying here, some there? What shall we do?
Hold, light the candle there that stands on high,
It you may find the other candles by.
Light that, I say, and so take up the pound
You did let fall and scatter on the ground.

Comparison

The fallen candles do us intimate
The bulk of God's elect in their laps'd state;
Their lying scattered in the dark may be
To show, by man's lapsed state, his misery.
The candle that was taken down and lighted,
Thereby to find them fallen and benighted,
Is Jesus Christ; God, by his light, doth gather
Who he will save, and be unto a Father.

What ails this fly thus desperately to enter
A combat with the candle? Will she venture
To clash at light? Away, thou silly fly;
Thus doing thou wilt burn thy wings and die.
But 'tis a folly her advice to give,
She'll kill the candle, or she will not live.
Slap, says she, at it; then she makes retreat,
So wheels about, and doth her blows repeat.
Nor doth the candle let her quite escape,
But gives some little check unto the ape:
Throws up her heels it doth, so down she falls,
Where she lies sprawling, and for succour calls.
When she recovers, up she gets again,
And at the candle comes with might and main,
But now behold, the candle takes the fly,
And holds her, till she doth by burning die.

Comparison

This candle is an emblem of that light
Our gospel gives in this our darksome night.
The fly a lively picture is of those
That hate and do this gospel light oppose.
At last the gospel doth become their snare,
Doth them with burning hands in pieces tear.

Meditations Upon a Candle
(Bunyan, 14)

Meditations Upon a Candle (Bunyan, 14)

Man's like a candle in a candlestick,
Made up of tallow and a little wick;
And as the candle when it is not lighted,
So is he who is in his sins benighted.
Nor can a man his soul with grace inspire,
More than can candles set themselves on fire.
Candles receive their light from what they are not;
Men grace from Him for whom at first they care not.
We manage candles when they take the fire;
God men, when he with grace doth them inspire.
And biggest candles give the better light,
As grace on biggest sinners shines most bright.
The candle shines to make another see,
A saint unto his neighbour light should be.
The blinking candle we do much despise,
Saints dim of light are high in no man's eyes.
Again, though it may seem to some a riddle,
We use to light our candles at the middle.
True light doth at the candle's end appear,
And grace the heart first reaches by the ear.
But 'tis the wick the fire doth kindle on,
As 'tis the heart that grace first works upon.
Thus both do fasten upon what's the main,
And so their life and vigour do maintain.
The tallow makes the wick yield to the fire,
And sinful flesh doth make the soul desire
That grace may kindle on it, in it burn;
So evil makes the soul from evil turn.
But candles in the wind are apt to flare,
And Christians, in a tempest, to despair.
The flame also with smoke attended is,
And in our holy lives there's much amiss.
Sometimes a thief will candle-light annoy,
And lusts do seek our graces to destroy.
What brackish is will make a candle sputter;
'Twixt sin and grace there's oft' a heavy clutter.
Sometimes the light burns dim, 'cause of the snuff,

Sometimes it is blown quite out with a puff;
But watchfulness preventeth both these evils,
Keeps candles light, and grace in spite of devils.
Nor let not snuffs nor puffs make us to doubt,
Our candles may be lighted, though puffed out.
The candle in the night doth all excel,
Nor sun, nor moon, nor stars, then shine so well.
So is the Christian in our hemisphere,
Whose light shows others how their course to steer.
When candles are put out, all's in confusion;
Where Christians are not, devils make intrusion.
Then happy are they who such candles have,
All others dwell in darkness and the grave.
But candles that do blink within the socket,
And saints, whose eyes are always in their pocket,
Are much alike; such candles make us fumble,
And at such saints good men and bad do stumble.
Good candles don't offend, except sore eyes,
Nor hurt, unless it be the silly flies.
Thus none like burning candles in the night,
Nor ought to holy living for delight.
But let us draw towards the candle's end:
The fire, you see, doth wick and tallow spend,
As grace man's life until his glass is run,
And so the candle and the man is done.
The man now lays him down upon his bed,
The wick yields up its fire, and so is dead.
The candle now extinct is, but the man
By grace mounts up to glory, there to stand.

CARCASS

The looming shadow of everlasting death is a grim re-
minder of the agonies and suffering that come with it.
The corpse's pallid, ghastly appearance, the putrefac-
tion and corruption of the body, and being consumed by
worms are all symbols of the wretchedness of hell. The
body's entombment in the silent grave is a metaphor for
the eternity of the anguish of hell. Ravens, who feed on
carrion, are a representation of the demons who prey
upon the souls of the dead. The stench of a decaying
carcass is a vivid depiction of the spiritual corruption of
a wicked soul, which the devil relishes. Likewise, dead
bodies signify the departed souls of the deceased, and
the devil does not take hold of the wicked until they
have passed away. Furthermore, the putrefaction of the
body is an emblem of a soul in the state of eternal death.
The name of the wicked shall rot, and they shall be an
abomination to all flesh, as Isaiah 66:24 states. Ravens,
being birds of the air, are a type of the devil, as Christ
mentioned in the parable of the sower and the seed
[Matthew 13:3–8]. The devil is the prince of the power
of the air, and his darkness reflects the sin, sorrow, and
death of Scripture.

— *"Images," nos. 1, 51, 61*

Carcass

Cat and Mouse

The way of a cat with a mouse it has taken captive is a symbol of the devil's dealings with many wicked men. The mouse is a symbol of the unclean and wicked, as described in Leviticus 11:29 and Isaiah 66:17. The cat makes a game of the mouse, and the devil likewise toys with wicked men. The mouse makes many attempts to escape, but never quite succeeds, until finally it yields its life to its enemy and is devoured. Similarly, many wicked men, particularly false religious followers and sinners exposed to the gospel, are taken captive by Satan and never quite escape their sins, until they are ultimately destroyed by him.

— *"Images," no. 73*

When Magistrates confined are,
They revell, who were kept in feare.
(Wither, 4.7)

When Magistrates confined are,
They revell, who were kept in feare. (Wither, 4.7)

A Tyrannous, or wicked Magistrat,
Is fitly represented by a Catt:
For, though the Mice a harmfull vermine bee,
And, Cats the remedie; yet, oft wee see,
That, by the Mice, far lesse, some house-wives leese,
Then when they set the Catt to keepe the Cheese.
A ravenous Cat, will punish in the Mouse,
The very same Offences, in the house,
Which hee himselfe commits; yea, for that Vice,
Which was his owne (with praise) he kills the Mice;
And, spoyleth not anothers life alone,
Ev'n for that very fault which was his owne,
But feeds, and fattens, in the spoyle of them,
Whom hee, without compassion did condemne.
Nay, worse than so; hee cannot bee content,
To slaughter them, who are as innocent,
As hee himselfe; but, hee must also play,
And sport his wofull Pris'ners lives away;
More torturing them, 'twixt fruitlesse hopes and feares,
Than when their bowels, with his teeth he teares:
For, by much terrour, and much crueltie,
Hee kills them, ten times over, e're they die.

When, such like Magistrates have rule obtain'd,
The best men wish their powre might be restrain'd:
But, they who shun enormities, through Feare,
Are glad when good-men out of Office are.
Yea, whether Governours bee good or bad,
Of their displacings wicked-men are glad;

And, when they see them brought into disgraces,
They boldly play the Knaves before their faces.

Cat and mouse

CAVERNS

The grandeur of the heavens, with their glimmering light, their clouds and hues, speaks to us of the joy and splendor of the blessed in the afterlife. In stark contrast, the depths of the earth remind us of the misery and horror of the damned. This serves to remind us of the vast difference between the two realms, and of the infinite power, wisdom, holiness, and love of God in the spiritual world. The magnificence of the visible world is only a mere reflection of the magnitude of the spiritual world, and of the divine goodness, light, knowledge, holiness, and happiness that will be bestowed upon it. Thus, the grandeur of the heavens, the height of the sky, and the beauty of the clouds are often compared to the greatness of God's mercy and truth.

— *"Images," nos. 21, 212*

Caverns

CHAFF

The ore containing gold and silver, the stone with gems, the husk and chaff with the grain, the shell and pod with the kernel, all symbolize the mixture of grace and sin in the hearts of the saints in this world. Affliction, like a furnace or threshing, separates them more and more, and death finally separates the dross and chaff.

— "Images," no. 163

Chaff

CHAOS

When God began to create the world and bring it into order, it was in a state of chaos and confusion, "without form and void, and darkness was upon the face thereof" (Genesis 1:2). Before God works a great and glorious work in the church or world, things are often in a dark, confused and woeful state. Thus, we can expect this to be the case before the glorious times of the church of God. After this confusion, light will be the first thing to appear—light to explain and defend the truth. The doctrines of the gospel will begin to shine forth with clear and irresistible light, just as the lower world was, at first, an image of confusion and emptiness.

— *"Images," no. 72*

Chaos

CHARMING BY SERPENTS

As birds and squirrels are charmed and destroyed by serpents, so sinners under the gospel often find themselves bewitched by their own desires. Despite their fears and remorse, they cannot tear themselves away from their beloved sins. Warnings and checks of conscience may make them back away, but they return again and again, going further and further until they are taken by Satan. The only way to save them is for Christ to come and crush the serpent's head.

— "Images," no. 63

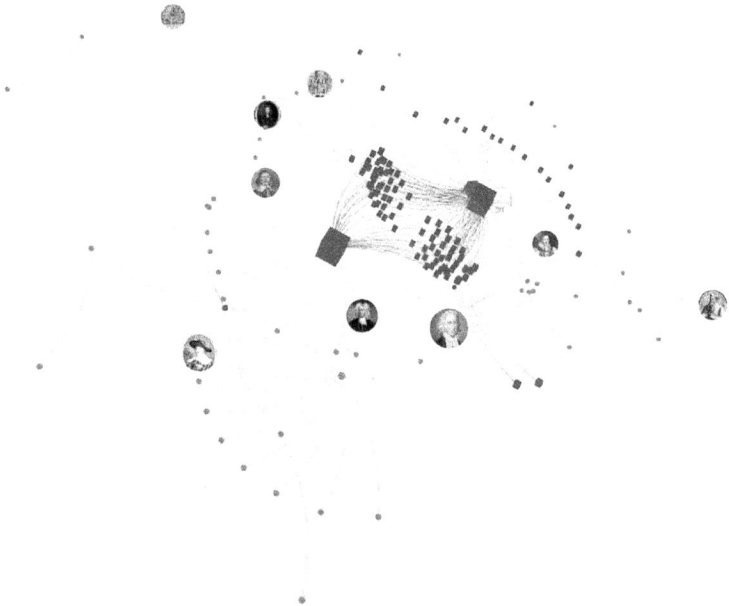

Charming Serpents

CHILDREN

The journey from childhood to adulthood is akin to the progress of the righteous and the church towards greater knowledge, holiness, and joy. This is evident in the Apostle's words in 1 Corinthians 13:11, "When I was a child, I spoke as a child, I understood as a child; but when I became a man, I put away childish things."

— *"Images," no. 42*

Children

CITIZENS OF ROME

The constitution of the spiritual polity of the heavenly Jerusalem, or the Church of Christ, is much like that of the Roman polity of the time of Christ and His apostles. It includes many who are called and considered citizens of the heavenly city, even though they live in other cities far away and have never seen heaven. These people have their citizenship in heaven, even though they are currently living in another country.

— *"Images," no. 91*

Citizen of Rome

CLOCK

The wheels of a watch or clock revolve in different directions, some clockwise, some counterclockwise, yet all serve the same purpose - to show the time or make the clock strike. In the same way, God's providence may appear to be contrary to His promises, one man going one way, another going another, good men one way and wicked men another, yet all eventually achieve God's will and end up in His intended purpose.

— *"Images," no. 178*

Make use of Time, that's comming on;
For, that is perish'd, which is gone.
(Wither, 4.49)

Make use of Time, that's comming on;
For, that is perish'd, which is gone. (Wither, 4.49)

This Glasse declares, how Time doth passe away;
And, if the Words, about it, rightly say,
Thy Time that's gone, is lost: and, proofe will shew,
That, many find both Words, and Emblem, true.
How fast their Time departs, they best perceive,
From whom it steales, before they take their leave,
Of what they love; and, whose last houre is gone,
Before their chiefest businesses are done.

How fast it slides, ev'n they are also taught,
(Too late, perhaps) who never kept in thought
Their ending-day; but, always did presume,
Or, largely hope upon the Time to come;
The present-howres, nor thankfully enjoying,
Nor, honestly, nor usefully employing.

That, yeares expir'd, are lost, they likewise find:
For, when their understanding brings to mind,
How fondly (or, how ill perchance) they spent
Their passed age; they see, with discontent,
The Time, not onely lost, but, worse than so;
Lost, with a thousand other Losses moe:
And, that, when they shall need it, wealth nor pow'r,
Can purchase them, one minute of an howre.

Consider this, all ye that spend the prime,
The noone tide, and the twilight of your Time,
In childish play-games, or meere worldly things;
As if you could, at pleasure, clip Times wings,
Or turne his Glasse, or, had a Life, or twaine
To live, when you had fool'd out this in vaine.

Short is the present; lost Times-passed bee;
And, Time to come, wee may not live to see.

Pursue thy Workes, without delay,
For, thy short houres runne fast away.
(Wither, 4.4)

Pursue thy Workes, without delay,
For, thy short houres runne fast away. (Wither, 4.4)

Though this bee but the picture of that Glasse,
By which thou measur'st how thine houres doe passe,
Yet, sleight it not; for, much 'twill profit thee,
To ponder what the Morals of it bee.
And, 'tis an Emblem, whence the Wise may learne,
That, which their persons, neerely doth concerne.

The brittle Glasse, serves fitly to expresse
The Bodie's frailtie, and much crasinesse.
Foure Pillars, which the glassie worke empale,
Instruct thee, that the Vertues Cardinall,
To guard the Manhood, should bee still employ'd,
Lest else the feeble fabrick bee destroy'd.
The Sand, still running forth, without delay,
Doth shew, that Life-time, passeth fast away,
And, makes no stop: yea, and the Motto too,
(Lest thou forgetfull prove) informes thee so.

By viewing this, Occasion, therefore, take,
Of thy fast-flying Houres, more use to make;
And, heedfull bee, to shunne their common crime,
Who take much care to trifle out the time;
As if it merited their utmost paine,
To lose the gemme, which most they seeke to gaine.
Time-past is lost already: Time-to-come,
Belongs, as yet, thou knowst not unto whom.
The present-houres are thine, and, onely those,
Of which thou hast Commission to dispose;
And, they from thee, doe flye away so fast,
That, they are scarcely knowne, till they are past.

Lord, give mee grace, to minde, and use Time so,
That, I may doe thy worke, before I goe.

What cannot be by Force attain'd,
By Leisure, and Degrees, is gain'd.
(Wither, 1.49)

What cannot be by Force attain'd,
By Leisure, and Degrees, is gain'd. (Wither, 1.49)

Some Foolish-Boyes (and such a Boy was I)
When they at Schoole have certaine houres to passe,
(To which they are compell'd unwillingly)
Much time they spend in shaking of the Glasse:
Thus, what they practise, to make-short their stay,
Prolongs it more; for while they seeke to force
The Sands, to runne more speedily away,
They interrupt them; and, they passe the worse.

Right so, in other things, with us it fares;
(And, seeming wise, we act a foolish part)
For, otherwhile, what Time alone prepares,
We seeke to make the subject of an Art.
Sometimes, by Rashnesse, we endeavour what
We ought with Leisure, and Advice, to doe:
But, if a good Successe doth follow, that,
Our Wit was nothing helpefull thereunto.
Sometime, againe, we prosecute a thing
By Violence; when our desir'd effect,
No other meanes so well to passe can bring,
As Love and Gentlenesse, which we neglect.

But, let this Emblem teach us to regard
What Way of Working, to each Worke pertaines:
So, though some Portion of our Hopes be barr'd,
We shall not, altogether, lose our paines.
Some things are strong, and, othersome are weake;
With Labour, some; and, some with Ease be wrought:
Although the Reed will bend, the Kexe will breake;
And, what mends one thing, makes another naught.

Marke this; And, when much Haste will marre thy Speed,
That, then, thou take good Leisure; take thou Heed.

313

Upon an Hour Glass (Bunyan, 42)

Upon an Hour Glass (Bunyan, 42)

This glass, when made, was, by the workman's skill,
The sum of sixty minutes to fulfil.
Time, more nor less, by it will out be spun,
But just an hour, and then the glass is run.
Man's life we will compare unto this glass,
The number of his months he cannot pass;
But when he has accomplished his day,
He, like a vapour, vanisheth away.

CLOTHES OFF IN SLEEP

At nightfall, individuals lay down to rest, removing their garments. In the same way, when one falls into spiritual slumber, they must be vigilant to keep their garments on, lest they walk exposed and be shamed. This lesson was taught to the Israelites when they were rebuilding Jerusalem in difficult times, for they did not take off their clothes (Nehemiah 4:23).

— *"Images," no. 121*

Upon his Lying down to Rest (Hall, 25)

What a circle there is of human actions and events! We are never without change, and yet that change is without any great variety. We sleep and wake and wake and sleep, and eat and evacuate, labor in a continual interchange. Yet hath the infinite wisdom of God so ordered it that we are never weary of these perpetual iterations, but with no less appetite enter into our daily courses than if we should pass them but once in our life. When I am weary of my day's labor, how willingly I undress myself and betake myself to my bed; and ere morning, when I have wearied of my restless bed, how glad am I to rise and renew my labor!

Why am I not more desirous to be unclothed of this body that I may be clothed upon with immortality? What is this but my closest garment which, when it is once put off, my soul is at liberty and ease? Many a time have I lain down before in desire of rest, and after some tedious changing of sides have risen sleepless, disappointed, languishing. In my last uncasing, my body shall not fail of repose nor my soul of joy; and in my rising up neither of them shall fail of glory. What hinders me, O God, but my infidelity from longing for this happy dissolution? The world hath misery and toil enough, and heaven hath more than enough blessedness to perfect my desires of my last and glorious change. I believe. Lord, help my unbelief [Mark 10:24].

COIN

Kings imprint their image and name on coins as a sign of ownership; similarly, God marks his saints as his own treasure, his jewels, likened to coins. He engraves his image on their hearts and inscribes his name, as seen in Revelation. He claims them as his own and proudly recognizes them as his special possession.

— "Images," no. 138

Upon the Sight of a Piece of Money under the Water (Hall, 59)

I should not wish ill to a covetous man if I should wish all his coin in the bottom of the river. No pavement could so well become that stream; no sight could better fit his greedy desires, for there every piece would seem double; every teston would appear a shilling, every crown an angel. It is the nature of that element to greaten appearing quantities; while we look through the air upon that solid body, it can make no other representations. Neither is it otherwise in spiritual eyes and objects. If we look with carnal eyes through the interposed mean of sensuality, every base and worthless pleasure will seem a large contentment. If with weak eyes we shall look at small and immaterial truths aloof off, in another element of apprehension every parcel thereof shall seem main and essential. Hence every knack of heraldry in the sacred genealogies and every scholastical quirk in disquisitions of divinity are made matters of no less than life and death to the soul. It is a great improvement of true wisdom to be able to see things as they are and to value them as they are seen. Let me labor for that power and staidness of judgment that neither my senses may deceive my mind nor the object may delude my sense.

COLORS

It is a sign that the magnificence of the colors of light was created as a symbol of the various beauties and graces of the Spirit of God. This is seen in the colors of the rainbow, the precious stones of the breastplate of the high priest, and the precious stones of the foundations and gates of the new Jerusalem. These colors can also be seen in the temple of Solomon and the new Jerusalem. The jasper and sardine stone are used to reference the light of the new Jerusalem, and the streets of the city are said to be like clear glass. The hangings of the tabernacle and temple, and the ephod and breastplate, are of blue, purple, and scarlet. These colors represent the spiritual beauties and graces of the Spirit of God, as well as the moral goodness of God. White is often used in Scripture to signify holiness, and the one and same white light contains a great variety of rays. The Spirit of God is also represented by a variety of gifts, though there is one body and one Spirit.

— "Images," no. 58

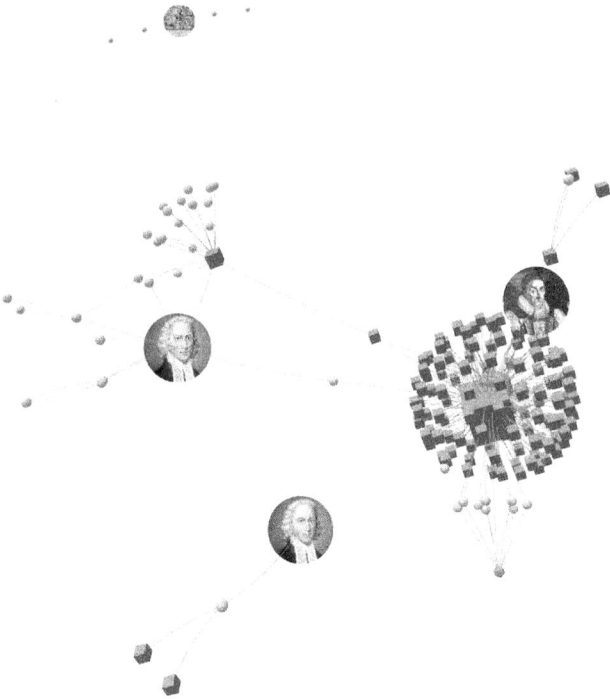

Colors

CONCEPTION

The very first thing that appears in the formation of an animal and its embryo is the beating heart. This is a vivid illustration of how a new creature is formed - the first thing is a fresh heart, a new desire, a new life principle that, though small, is strong, energetic and vigorous. It yearns for holiness and strives for everything that makes up the new creature, and is the source of the entire being. It seeks perfection and from it emanates the many aspects that make up the new creature, gradually becoming more and more visible until the creature is whole and reaches its highest potential.

— "Images," no. 190

Conception

CORN

Grinding corn to powder, baking in an oven, and pressing out the juice of the grape - all of these processes represent the suffering of Christ in order for us to receive spiritual nourishment. The fat of the kidneys of wheat and the pure blood of the grape in Deuteronomy 32:14 are analogous to the fat and blood of the sacrifices offered to God, and oil, a type of the grace of the Holy Spirit, is procured by treading and pressing olives. All of these acts and substances point to the suffering of Christ, which brings us the benefits of His grace and the nourishment of His Spirit.

— *"Images," nos. 48, 68*

A Whole Mill to Grind a Peck of Corn
(Cats and Farlie, 173)

A Whole Mill to Grind a Peck of Corn (Cats and Farlie, 173)

Eh! Master, what is all this work,
This hamm'ring, sawing, clatter?
Each morning that I wake of late
I wonder what's the matter!
What is't that you are building here?
A Mill, forsooth! but surely
So large a Mill as this will be
A loss of money purely;
For in this sack of yours I feel
So little corn for grinding,
That when you've made it into meal
"Twill scarce be worth your minding.
A Hand-mill would be large enough
To grind this corn, good neighbour!
And if you'd be advised by me
You'd cease your useless labour.
You may rely, this Mill of yours
Will yield you little profit,
'Twill soon stand still, or, what is worse,
You'll be obliged to let it:
Don't spend your money thus, my friend,
"Tis hard enough to find it;
Who only hath a peck of corn
Need build no Mill to grind it.

Corn

CORONATION

On the Day of Judgment, mankind will gather in great assemblies to witness the great things that will be seen. This is like the coronation of a prince, when the saints receive their crown of glory with Christ. It is like a court of judicature, or an execution, or a wedding, or a great triumph. All these events are a shadow of what will be on the Day of Judgment, when there will be a joyful assembly, a splendid show, and a solemn procession.

— "Images," no. 180

Coronation

CORPSE

The death of the body symbolizes spiritual and eternal death, and the putrid smell of a corpse is a sign of the wicked's everlasting shame and contempt, as Proverbs 10:7 states. As Isaiah 66:24 says, those who have sinned against the Lord will suffer for eternity, and all will be repulsed by them.

— *"Images," no. 51*

Upon the Sight of a Coffin Stuck with Flowers (Hall, 86)

Too fair appearance is never free from just suspicion. While here was nothing but mere wood, no flower was to be seen here; now that this wood is lined with an unsavory corpse, it is adorned with this sweet variety. The fir whereof that coffin is made yields a natural redolence alone; now that it is stuffed thus noisomely, all helps are too little to countervail that scent of corruption.

Neither is it otherwise in living. Perpetual use of strong perfumes argues a guiltiness of some unpleasing savor. The case is the same spiritually; an over-glorious outside of profession implies some inward filthiness that would fain escape notice. Our uncomely parts have more comeliness put on; too much ornament imports extreme deformity. For me, let my show be moderate, so shall I neither deceive applause nor merit too deep censure.

O with what Diligence and Care
These dainty Bodies we repair
Yet a few Years when come and gone,
Grim Death will strip us Skin from Bone.
(Quarles, 5.8)

A wealthy man's inheritance: The Trojans and allies of Patroclus clashed as the former seized him in his borrowed armor. Hector obtained the arms as the Greeks kept his body. This scene is repeated when a wealthy individual passes away. A great disagreement ensues, yet eventually the heir settles it, granting something to the crows and vultures. (Alciati, 159)

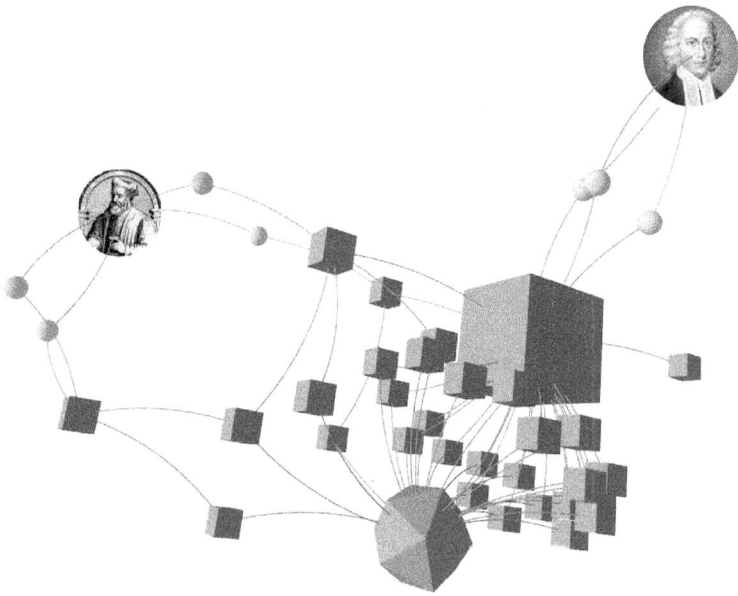

Corpse

CORRECTION OF CHILDREN

That a child ought to be disciplined, and the good that comes of disciplining them, is a type of the truth that applies to God's children.

— *"Images," no. 129*

Behold, you may, the Picture, here,
Of what, keepes Man, and Childe, in feare.
(Wither, 2.31)

Behold, you may, the Picture, here,
Of what, keepes Man, and Childe, in feare. (Wither, 2.31)

These, are the great'st Afflictions, most men have,
Ev'n from their Nursing-cradle, to their Grave:
Yet, both so needfull are, I cannot see,
How either of them, may well spared bee.
The Rod is that, which, most our Child-hood feares;
And, seemes the great'st Affliction that it beares:
That, which to Man-hood, is a plague, as common
(And, more unsufferable) is a Woman.

Yet, blush not Ladies; neither frowne, I pray,
That, thus of Women, I presume to say;
Nor, number mee, as yet, among your foes;
For, I am more your friend, then you suppose:
Nor smile ye Men, as if, from hence, ye had
An Argument, that Woman-kinde were bad.
The Birch, is blamelesse (yea, by nature, sweet,
And gentle) till, with stubborne Boyes, it meet:
But, then, it smarts. So, Women, will be kinde,
Untill, with froward Husbands, they are joyn'd:
And, then indeed (perhaps) like Birchen boughes,
(Which, else, had beene a trimming, to their House)
They, sometimes prove, sharpe whips, and Rods, to them,
That Wisdome, and Instruction doe contemne.

A Woman, was not given for Correction;
But, rather for a furtherance to Perfection:
A precious Balme of love, to cure Mans griefe;
And, of his Pleasures, to become the chiefe.
If, therefore, she occasion any smart,
The blame, he merits, wholly, or in part:

For, like sweet Honey, she, good Stomackes, pleases;
But, paines the Body, subject to Diseases.

(Quarles, 4.4)

Fear to offend thy gracious God,
And then thou need'st not fear his Rod;
But if thou fear'st not to offend,
Well may'st thou fear a dreadful End.

Upon the Disobedient Child
(Bunyan, 47)

Upon the Disobedient Child (Bunyan, 47)

Children become, while little, our delights!
When they grow bigger, they begin to fright's.
Their sinful nature prompts them to rebel,
And to delight in paths that lead to hell.
Their parents' love and care they overlook,
As if relation had them quite forsook.
They take the counsels of the wanton's, rather
Than the most grave instructions of a father.
They reckon parents ought to do for them,
Though they the fifth commandment do contemn;
They snap and snarl if parents them control,
Though but in things most hurtful to the soul.
They reckon they are masters, and that we
Who parents are, should to them subject be!
If parents fain would have a hand in choosing,

The children have a heart will in refusing.
They'll by wrong doings, under parents gather,
And say it is no sin to rob a father.
They'll jostle parents out of place and power,
They'll make themselves the head, and them devour.
How many children, by becoming head,
Have brought their parents to a piece of bread!
Thus they who, at the first, were parents joy,
Turn that to bitterness, themselves destroy.
But, wretched child, how canst thou thus requite
Thy aged parents, for that great delight
They took in thee, when thou, as helpless, lay
In their indulgent bosoms day by day?
Thy mother, long before she brought thee forth,
Took care thou shouldst want neither food nor cloth.
Thy father glad was at his very heart,
Had he to thee a portion to impart.
Comfort they promised themselves in thee,
But thou, it seems, to them a grief wilt be.
How oft, how willingly brake they their sleep,
If thou, their bantling, didst but winch or weep.
Their love to thee was such they could have giv'n,
That thou mightst live, almost their part of heav'n.
But now, behold how they rewarded are!
For their indulgent love and tender care;
All is forgot, this love he doth despise.
They brought this bird up to pick out their eyes.

COUNTERFEITS OF GRACE

In the natural and spiritual worlds alike, there are numerous counterfeits of what is excellent. Diamonds have imitations, gold can be forged, and even the balm of Gilead and other great medicines can be imitated. The same is true of grace.

— "Images," no. 170

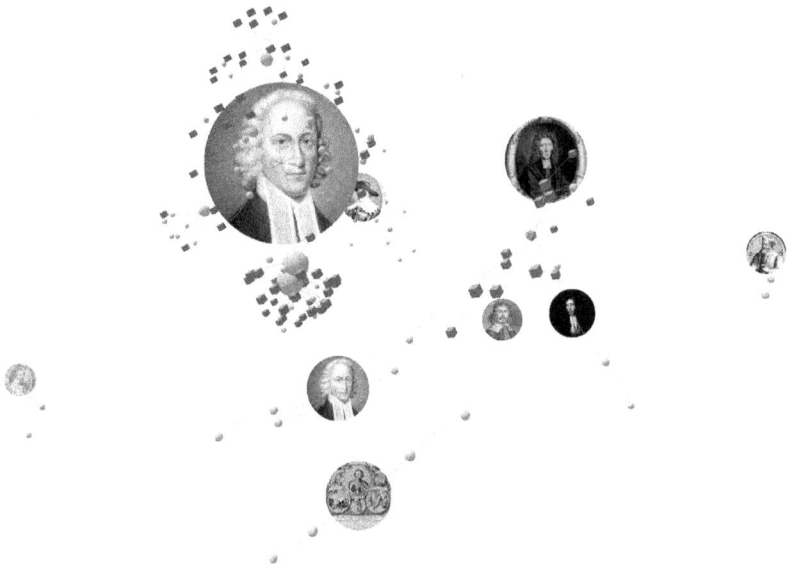

Counterfeit grace

Courts

The grandeur of courts of justice, the solemnity of executions, the joy of weddings, and the pageantry of triumphs all hint at what will be when the great Day arrives.

— *"Images," no. 180*

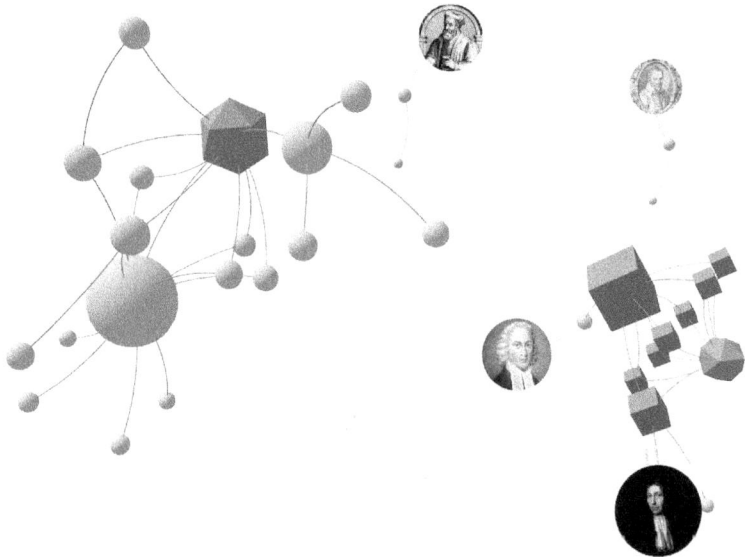

Courts

CREATION OF THE WORLD

When God began to create the world, it was a chaotic mess, "formless and void, with darkness covering its face" (Genesis 1:2). This is often the way it is when God is about to do a great and glorious work in the church or world, or in someone's life. Before God's work begins, things are usually in a dark, confused and desperate state, with no hope of improvement. So too, it will be before the glorious times of the church of God come. Light will be the first thing to appear, bringing clarity and strength to the truth. The world, which was previously formless and void, was a reflection of the emptiness and confusion that was to come.

— *"Images," no. 72*

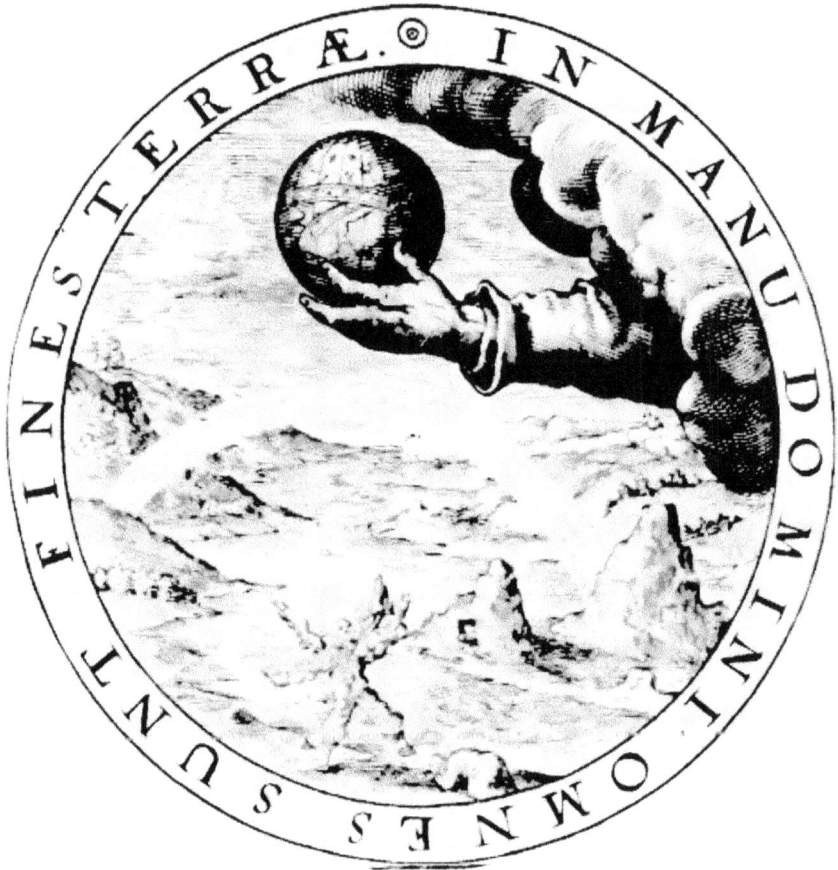

The Earth is God's, and in his Hands
Are all the Corners of the Lands.
(Wither, 4.2)

The Earth is God's, and in his Hands
Are all the Corners of the Lands. (Wither, 4.2)

Long since, the sacred Hebrew Lyrick sayd,
(A Truth, which never justly was denayd)
That, All the world is God's; and that his hands
Enclose the limits of the farthest Lands.
The selfe same Truth affirmes, that likewise, there,
By him, their clodds, and furrowes warred are,
And, that with dewes and showres, he doth so blesse
The dwellings of the barren Wildernesse,
That, those Inhabitants (whom some conceiv'd,
Of usefull, and all pleasant things bereav'd)
Their labors, with advantage, doe employ,
And, fetch their yearely Harvests home, with joy.

Why then should wee, that in God's Vineyard live,
Distrust that all things needfull hee will give?
Why should his Garden doubt of what it needs,
Since hee oft waters barren Rocks and Weeds?
Why should his Children, live in slavish feare,
Since hee is kind to those that strangers are?
Or, whither from his presence, can we flie,
To whom the furthest hiding-place is nigh.

And, if I may, from lower objects clime,
(To questioning, in matters more sublime)
Why should I thinke, the Soule shall not bee fed,
Where God affoords, to Flesh, her daily Bread?
Or, dreame, that hee, for some, provided none,
Because, on us, much Mercie is bestowne?
'Tis true enough, that Hell devoureth all,
Who shall be found without the Churches pale;

But, how farre that extends, no Eye can see,
Since, in Gods hands, Earth's farthest Corners bee.

Creation

CROCODILE

The crocodile is an example of how quickly and destructively something can grow if left unchecked. Just like a crocodile, sin is easy to crush in its beginning, but if ignored it can become powerful, strong, and hard to kill, growing worse and worse for as long as it lives. This was seen in the old world with Cain's family, with idolatry after the Flood, and with the kingdom of Antichrist and Satan's Mahometan kingdom. It is likely that the same will occur with the last apostacy before the end of time.

— "Images," no. 177

True Vertue is a Coat of Maile,
'Gainst which, no Weapons can prevaile.
(Wither, 2.50)

True Vertue is a Coat of Maile,
'Gainst which, no Weapons can prevaile. (Wither, 2.50)

Lord, what a coyle men keepe, and, with what care
Their Pistolls, and, their Swords doe they prepare,
To be in readinesse? and, how they load
Themselves with Irons, when they ride abroad?
How wise and wary too, can they become,
To fortifie their persons up at home,
With lockes, and barres? and such domestick-Armes,
As may secure their bodies, there, from harmes?

However, when all's done, we see, their foes
Breake in, sometimes, and worke their overthrowes.
For, though (about themselves, with Cable-quoiles,
They could inclose a hundred thousand miles)
The gunshot of a slanderous tongue, may smite,
Their Fame quite through it, to the very White.
Yea, more (though, there, from others, they were free)
They wounded, by themselves, to death might be,
Except their Innocence, more guards them, than
The strength of twenty royall Armies, can.

If, therefore, thou thy Spoylers, wilt beguile,
Thou must be armed, like this Crocodile;
Ev'n with such nat'rall Armour (ev'ry day)
As no man can bestowe, or take away:
For, spitefull Malice, at one time or other,
Will pierce all borrowed Armours, put together.
Without, let Patience durifie thy Skin;
Let Innocencie, line thy heart within;
Let constant Fortitude, unite them so,
That, they may breake the force of ev'ry blow:

And, when thou thus art arm'd, if ill thou speed;
Let me sustaine the Mischiefe, in thy steed.

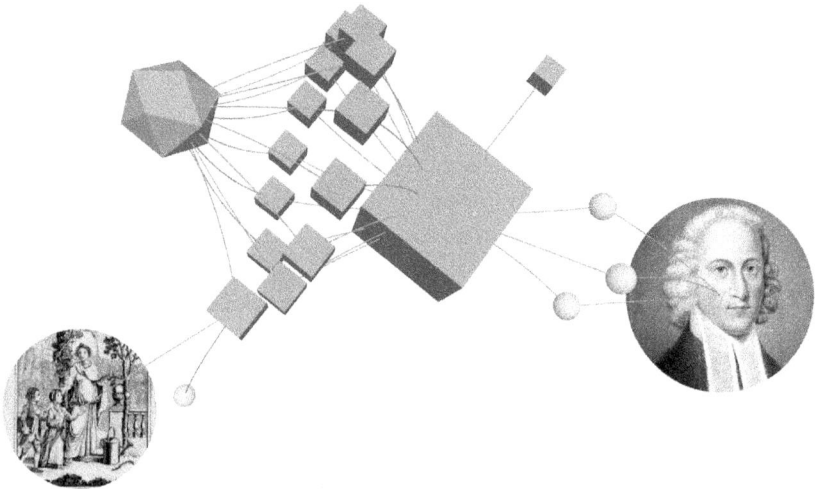

Crocodile

CROWING OF THE COCK AT BREAK OF DAY

The crowing of the cock and the song of the spring birds rouse men from slumber, signifying the introducing of a glorious day of the church by ministers preaching the Gospel. Peter's awakening from deep sleep brought by the crowing of the cock, symbolizes the awakening of Christ's church and the rousing of the wise virgins from their backsliding state, brought by the preaching of the Gospel, to introduce the morning of glorious times.

— "Images," no. 110

Upon the Crowing of a Cock (Hall, 90)

How harshly did this note sound in the ear of Peter, yea, pierced his very heart [Mark 14:66-72]! Many a time had he heard this bird and was no whit moved with the noise. Now there was a bird in his bosom that crowed louder than this, whose shrill accent, conjoined with this, astonished the guilty disciple

The weary laborer, when he is awakened from his sweet sleep by this natural clock of the household, is not so angry at this troublesome bird nor so vexed at the hearing of that unseasonable sound as Peter was when this fowl awakened his sleeping conscience and called him to a timely repentance. This cock did but crow like others, neither made or knew any difference of this tone and the rest. There was a divine hand that ordered this morning's note to be a summons of penitence; He that foretold it had fore-appointed it. That bird could not but crow then, and all the noise in the high priests' hall could not keep that sound from Peter's ear. But oh Saviour, couldst Thou find leisure, when thou stoodst at the bar of that unjust and cruel judgment amidst all that bloody rabble of enemies, in the sense of all their fury and the expectation of Thine own death, to listen unto this monitor of Peter's repentance and upon the hearing of it to cast back Thine eyes upon Thy denying, cursing, abjuring disciple? Oh mercy without measure and beyond all possibility of our admiration, to neglect Thyself for a sinner, to attend the repentance of one when Thou wert about to lay down thy life for all!

Oh God, Thou art still equally merciful. Every elect soul is no less dear unto thee. Let the sound of Thy faithful monitors smite my ear and let the beams of thy merciful eyes wound my heart so as I may go forth and weep bitterly [Matt. 26:75].

Watch and Protect: *The crowing of the cock heralds the oncoming Dawn, reminding toiling hands of a new day's labor. The bronze bell summons the alert mind to contemplate loftier matters. Both are placed upon sacred towers. Here stands a lion, its vigilant gaze ever open, guarding the entrance to the temple. (Alciati, 15)*

Crowing Cock

DAM AND YOUNG BIRDS

The similarity between the young birds in a nest and a dam to Christ and his saints is clear. The dam shelters and protects them, just as Christ shelters and protects his saints. They are brought forth by the dam, and the soul is brought forth by the warmth and heat of Christ and the Holy Spirit. The nest of the dam provides a safe place for the birds, just as the church provides a safe place for the saints. The manner in which the dam feeds the young birds is akin to the manner in which Christ feeds his saints. The birds grow and eventually fly away to sing in the Firmament, just as the saints are nourished up to glory.

— *"Images," no. 125*

A favor should be reciprocated: In her nest, the stork, tender and caring, looks after her young. She dreams of the day when her children will take care of her, when she is an old woman and in need of help. Her devoted chicks do not let her down, and they support her when she is weak, and feed her with their own mouths. (Alciati, 30)

Parental love: *Before the season of spring, the white ring-dove builds her nest in the frigid north and broods over her prematurely laid eggs. To make a softer bed for her young, she plucks her own feathers and, left bare, she succumbs to the cold winter air. O Colchian and Procne, how can you not feel shame when a bird dies out of love for her offspring? (Alciati, 194)*

Dam and young birds

DAY AND NIGHT, THEIR VICISSITUDES

By the ever-changing nature of this world, God shows us that we should not anticipate eternal joy and success, but should instead prepare ourselves for a variety of successes and hardships.

— *"Images," no. 100*

Each Day a Line, small tasks appeares:
Yet, much it makes in threescore Yeares.
(Wither, 3.24)

Each Day a Line, small tasks appeares:
Yet, much it makes in threescore Yeares. (Wither, 3.24)

Here's but one Line; and, but one Line a Day,
Is all the taske our Motto, seemes to lay:
And, that is thought, perhaps, a thing so small,
As if it were as good bee nought at all.
But, be not so deceiv'd; For, oft you see
Small things (in time) great matters, rise to be:
Yea, that, which when the same was first begun,
A Trifle seem'd, (and easie to be done)
By long nelect of time, will burthensome,
And, at the last, impossible, become.

Great Clarkes, there are, who shall not leave behinde them,
One good Weekes worke, for Future-Times to minde them,
(In Callings, either Humane, or Divine)
Who, by composing but each Day a Line,
Might Authors, of some famous Workes appeare,
In sixtie, seventie, or in eightie yeare;
To which, ten hundred thousands have arrived
Of whom, we see no signe that ev'r they lived.
And, with much pleasure, wee might all effect,
Those needfull Works, which often we neglect,
(Untill too late). If we but, now and then
Did spare one houre to exercise the penn.

For, still, one-Line, another draweth on,
And, Line by Line, great Workes at last are done.
Whereas, dis-use, and many dayes mispent,
Without their Lines, let in discouragement,
Or, bring Despaire; which doth so sottish make us,
That we, to no endeavour can betake us.

Marke this, and, labour in some honest Way,
As much as makes, at least, One Line a Day.

Sweet is Retirement to the Soul,
Since there she Christ enjoys to Full;
In whom she places her Delight,
Who is her Solace Day and Night.
(Quarles, 4.7)

The pious Soul with Sin oppress'd,
And utter Darkness fore distress'd,
Strives to grope out her gloomy Way,
And will at length discover Day.
(Quarles, 3.1)

DEATH

The Wise One pondered the fate of the spirit of man, which ascends, and the spirit of a beast, which descends to the ground. He saw in this a sign that the spirit of man returns to the Lord who gave it, while the spirit of a beast fades away with its body, returning to the earth, and ultimately to nothing.

— *"Images," no. 65*

Live, ever mindfull of thy dying;
For, Time is always from thee flying.
(Wither, 4.27)

Whil'st thou dost, here, injoy thy breath,
Continue mindfull of thy Death.
(Wither, 3.34)

Where er'e we dwell, the Heav'ns are neere;
Let us but fly, and wee are there.
(Wither, 3.18)

In Death, no Difference is made,
Betweene the Scepter, and the Spade.
(Wither, 1.48)

As soone, as wee to bee, begunne;
We did beginne, to be Undone.
(Wither, 1.45)

Death no Losse, but rather, Gaine;
For wee by Dying, Life attaine.
(Wither, 1.21)

This Ragge of Death, which thou shalt see,
Consider it; And Pious bee.
(Wither, 1.8)

By Knowledge onely, Life wee gaine,
All other things to Death pertaine.
(Wither, 1.1)

(Quarles, 1.7)

Sinner, behold thy Danger here!
How can'st thou sleep, and Hell so near?
At thee grim Death has took his Aim–
Will nothing break thy pleasing Dream?

As, to the World I naked came,
So, naked-strips I leave the same.
(Wither, 1.12)

As, to the World I naked came,
So, naked-stript I leave the same. (Wither, 1.12)

Thrice happy is that Man whose Thoughts doe reare
His Minde above that pitch the Worldling flies,
And by his Contemplations, hovers where
He viewes things mortall, with unbleared eyes.
What Trifles then doe Villages and Townes
Large Fields or Flockes of fruitfull Cattell seeme?
Nay, what poore things are Miters, Scepters, Crownes,
And all those Glories which Men most esteeme?
Though he that hath among them, his Delight,
Brave things imagines them (because they blinde
With some false Lustre his beguiled sight)
He that's above them, their meane-Worth may finde.

Lord, to that Blessed-Station me convey
Where I may view the World, and view her so,
That I her true Condition may survey;
And all her Imperfections rightly know.
Remember me, that once there was a Day
When thou didst weane me from them with content,
Ev'n when shut up within those Gates I lay
Through which the Plague-inflicting Angel went.
And, let me still remember, that an Houre
Is hourely comming on, wherein I shall
(Though I had all the World within my powre)
Be naked stript, and turned out of all.
But minde me, chiefely, that I never cleave
Too closely to my Selfe; and cause thou me,
Not other Earthly things alone to leave,
But to forsake my Selfe for love of Thee:

That I may say, now I have all things left,
Before that I of all things, am bereft.

Depths

The heavens, so pure and beautiful, show their sublimity and glory when the air is still and the colors are vibrant. Little clouds add to the picture, reminding us of the exalted purity of the blessed inhabitants. In stark contrast, the dark and dismal abyss of the earth reveals the vast difference between the joy of the saints and the suffering of the damned. This highlights the ineffable glory of one and the unspeakable horrors of the other.

— *"Images," no. 21*

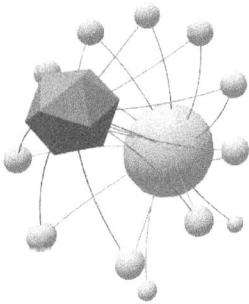

Depths

DIAMOND

True grace is like pure gold, maintaining its worth after being tested in the fire. It is also like a diamond, able to withstand a hard strike of the hammer yet remain unharmed.

— *"Images," no. 162*

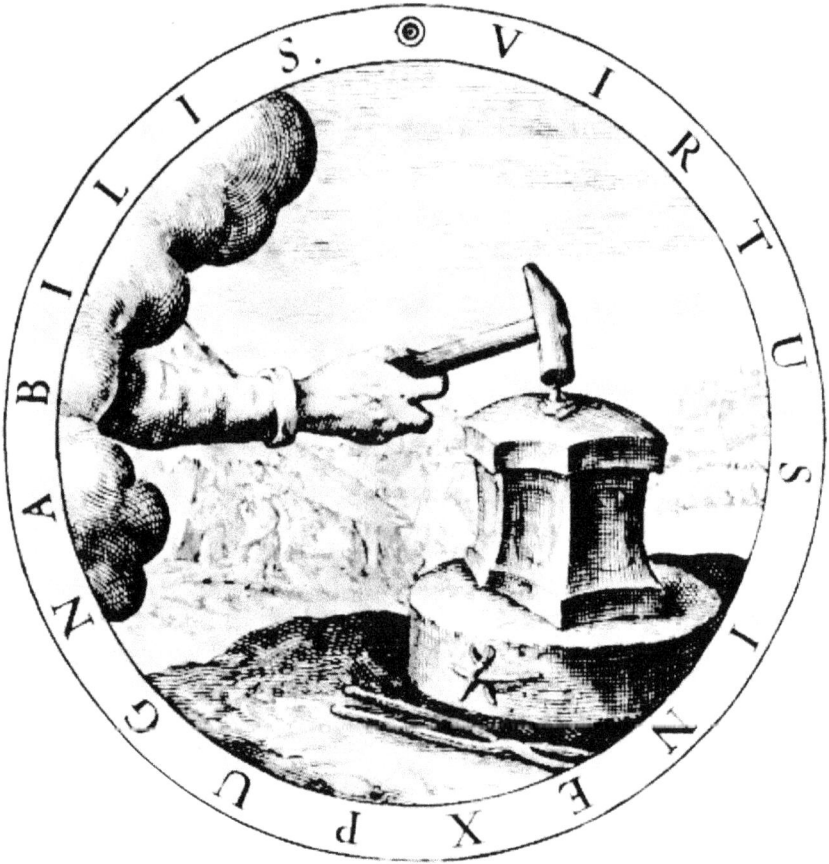

True Vertue, firme, will always bide,
By whatsoever suffrings tride.
(Wither, 3.37)

True Vertue, firme, will alwayes bide,
By whatsoever suffrings tride. (Wither, 3.37)

This is a well-knowne Figure, signifying,
A man, whose Vertues will abide the trying:
For, by the nature of the Diamond stone,
(Which Violence, can no way worke upon)
That Patience, and long-suffering is intended,
Which will not bee with Injuries offended;
Nor yeeld to any base dejectednesse,
Although some bruising Pow'r, the same oppresse;
Or, such hard streights, as theirs, that hamm'rings feele,
Betwixt an Anvile, and a Sledge of Steele.

None ever had a perfect Vertue, yet,
But, that most Pretious-stone, which God hath set
On his right hand, in beaming-Majestie,
Upon the Ring of blest ETERNITIE.
And, this, is that impenitrable Stone,
The Serpent could not leave impression on,
(Nor signe of any Path-way) by temptations,
Or, by the pow'r of sly insinuations:
Which wondrous Mysterie was of those five,
Whose depth King Solomon could never dive.

Good God! vouchsafe, ev'n for that Diamond-sake,
That, I may of his pretiousnesse, partake,
In all my Trialls; make mee alwayes able
To bide them, with a minde impenitrable,
How hard, or oft so'ere, those hamm'rings bee,
Wherewith, Afflictions must new fashion mee.
And, as the common Diamonds polish'd are,
By their owne dust; so, let my errours weare

Each other out; And, when that I am pure,
Give mee the Lustre, Lord, that will endure.

Diamond

DIRT IN OUR EYES

If one's eyes are clogged with dirt, it significantly impedes their vision. This illustrates how much it clouds the vision of men when their sight is preoccupied with worldly matters. To achieve clarity of sight, we must free our eyes of worldly concerns and focus on the spiritual, as Christ said: "If your eye is single, your whole body will be full of light. But if your eye is evil, your whole body will be full of darkness" [Matthew 6:22–23].

— *"Images," no. 145*

Upon a Pair of Spectacles (Hall, 104)

I look upon these not as objects but as helps; as not meaning that my sight should rest in them but pass through them and by their aid discern some other things which I desire to see. Many such glasses my soul hath and useth: I look through the glass of the creatures at the power and wisdom of their maker; I look through the glass of the Scriptures at the great mystery of redemption and the glory of an heavenly inheritance; I look through God's favors at His infinite mercy, through His judgments at His incomprehensible justice. But as these spectacles of mine presuppose a faculty in the eye and cannot give me sight when I want it but only clear that sight which I have, no more can these glasses of the creatures, of Scriptures, of favors and judgments enable me to apprehend those blessed objects except I have an eye of faith whereto they may be presented. These helps to an unbelieving man are but as spectacles to the blind. As the natural eyes, so the spiritual have their degrees of dimness, but I have ill improved my age if, as my natural eyes decay, my spiritual eye be not cleared and confirmed. But at my best I shall never but need spectacles till I come to see as I am seen [1 Cor. 13:12].

DIRT OF THE HANDS AND FEET

We cannot traverse the world without our feet becoming sullied. Whatever it is that people do with their hands, they too will become soiled, necessitating regular cleansing. This world is filled with sin and temptation, and our every action is blemished by it. We cannot do any work without our guilt and contamination increasing, so we must rely on the cleansing power of the blood of Christ.

— *"Images," no. 195*

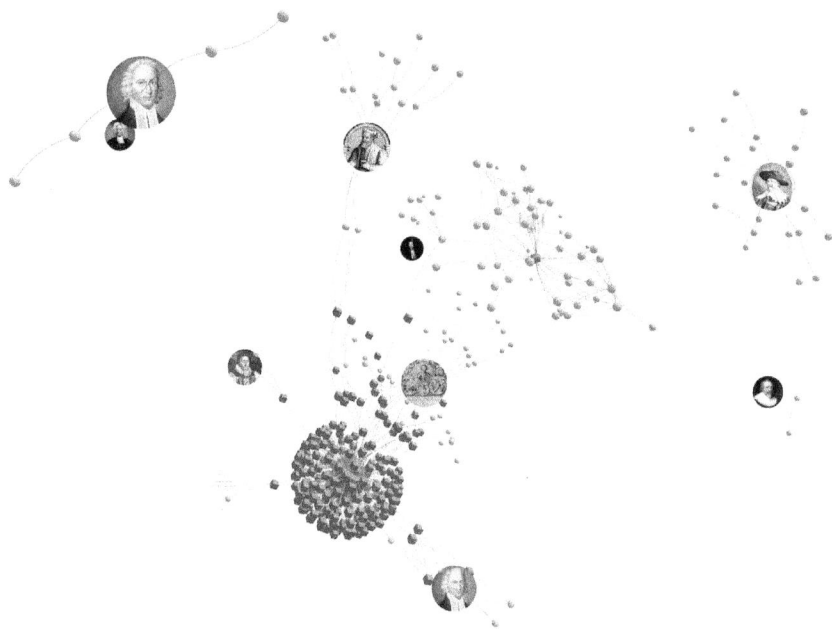

Dirt of hands and feet

DIRTINESS OF THE WORLD

This planet is stained with filth. Everywhere we go, we encounter contamination that soils the soles of those who venture forth. Our roads are mired in grime, suggesting that the world is rife with elements that can taint the spirit, that material matters and worldly pursuits and socializing can be corrupting.

— *"Images," no. 116*

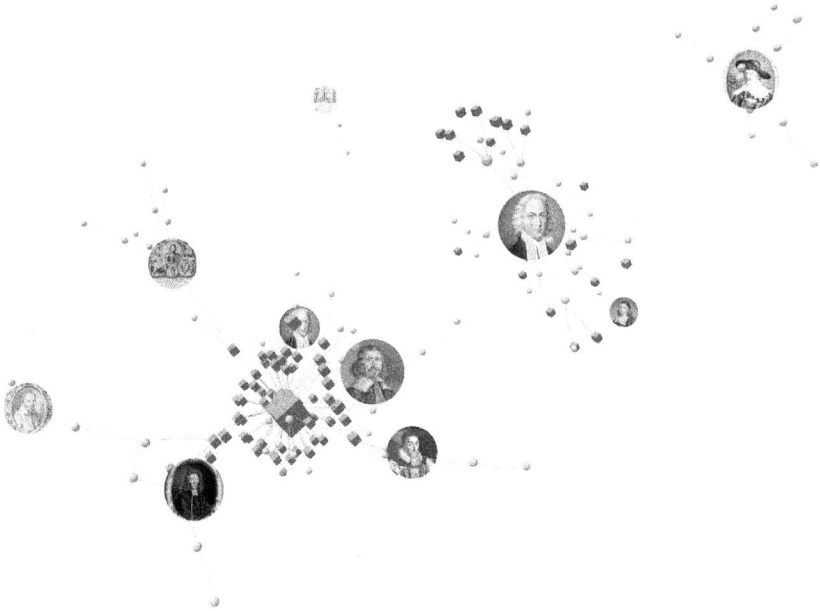

Dirt of the world

DRAGONS

The owls and dragons of the night produce a sorrowful, screeching sound that echoes through the darkness. This sound, referred to in the Bible in Micah 1:8 and Job 30:28-29, is said to be like the wailing of devils and other spirits that are doomed to an eternity of darkness. The mournful noise serves as a reminder of their wretchedness and despair.

— "Images," no. 204

Dragons

Dross

The ore containing gold and silver, the stone sheltering gems, the husk and chaff concealing grain, the shell and pod preserving the kernel; all these are symbols of the mixtures of grace in the hearts of saints on earth. Affliction acts like a furnace, threshing and winnowing, separating these mixtures more and more until death brings ultimate purification. This mixture is referred to as "dross" and "tun" in Scripture.

— "Images," no. 163

If Love Divine should once but dart
It's Rays into th' enlighten'd Heart,
It melts its Dross, its Gold refines,
And the whole Soul illustrious shines.
(Quarles, 5.5)

The World, tho' turned upside down,
And in whatever Light it's shewn,
You'll find its Riches but a Dross,
And ev'ry Pleasure has its. Cross.
(Quarles, 1.6)

EARTH, ITS SMALLNESS

The earth is so insignificant compared to the vastness of the heavens that if we were to stand there, the highest palaces and mountains we marvel at now would appear miniscule. Even if the earth were to be magnified many millions of times, it would still be too small to be seen, nothing more than a speck. This serves to illustrate how worldly honors, pleasures, and profits, even the entire world, are so much less than heavenly glory that when the saints reach heaven, it will seem infinitely insignificant.

— *"Images," no. 47*

Earth, smallness

ECLIPSE

The moon sometimes eclipses the sun in its conjunction, signifying both Christ's incarnation and death. His taking on human flesh was a veil that hid his divine glory, and his death was a consequence of his coming to save those who would ultimately put him to death. This eclipse of the sun is a type of Christ's death, as he could not be held by death for long due to his divine worthiness. The sun's resurrection from the dead is a figure of the church's resurrection, as it is begotten again to a living hope and made partaker of the life and power of Christ's resurrection. It is also a reminder that when God's people are in their greatest glory, He is wont to bring some great calamity to keep them from being exalted in their prosperity.

— "Images," no. 76

(Quarles, 3.7)

When God is pleas'd to hide his Face,
The Soul, impatient, sighs and prays,
She may to Favour be restor'd,
And feel the Comforts of her Lord.

EMBALMING OF DEAD BODIES

The sweet-smelling ointments used in the past to anoint and preserve the dead were a sign of the joy of the souls of the saints, anointed by the Holy Spirit. In particular, when the bodies of Jacob and Jesus were embalmed, Jesus' body symbolized the entire church of saints. When in the state of death, the souls of the righteous are blessed and perfumed, while those of the wicked perish in a horrible spiritual stench and putrefaction. The preservation of Christ's body from corruption signifies the happiness of the departed soul, while the rotting and loathsomeness of unburied bodies symbolizes the misery of the damned at the end.

— WJE, 24:963

Embalming

EMBRYO

The initial spark of life is the punctum saliens, the heart, which begins to beat as soon as it is formed. This is a vivid illustration of the formation of a new being, with a new heart, a new spirit and impulse. This, though small, is energetic and forceful, and almost seems to pulsate and struggle, desiring holiness and aiming towards all that is part of the new creature, and having the capacity to generate and sustain the entirety. It is always striving for perfection, and from this originates the various aspects of the new creature, which manifest and become more and more developed, until the new being reaches its ultimate completion.

— "Images," no. 190

Embryo

ERECT POSTURE OF MEN

Man is made to stand upright on the earth, his gaze set towards the heavens, signaling that he was created to have his eyes on the heavens and his feet on the ground. Beasts, however, are made to look down to the earth, seeking sustenance with their mouths in the dust and on the ground. This speaks to the difference between man and beast, for the highest good of the beasts is of an earthly nature, whereas man's true joy lies in the heavens.

— "Images," nos. 98, 133

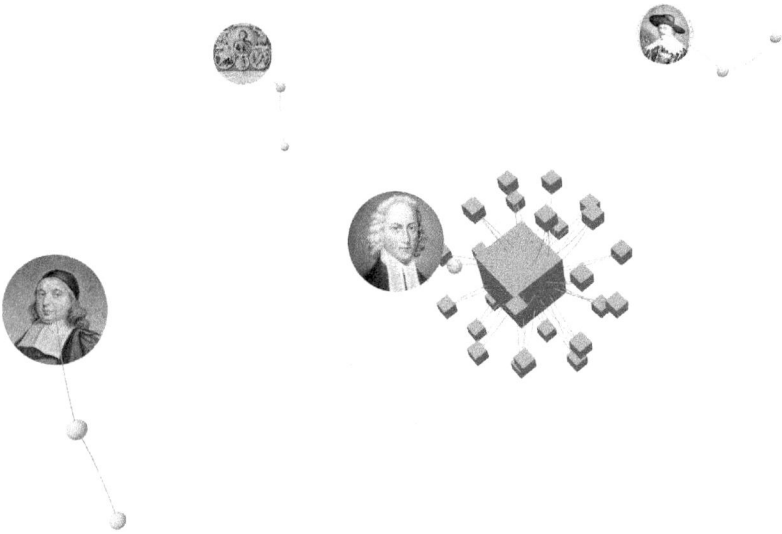

Erect posture

FADING OF THE GRASS, LEAVES AND FLOWERS

The beauty of the land is fleeting, its grass and leaves, its flowers, all fading away in time. In winter, all is destroyed, the most captivating, the crown of its glory, the flowers of the trees and fields, fading the quickest. The glory of the sky, however, never fades, its brightness and light remaining constant through the seasons, lasting through ages. This is in stark contrast to earthly glory, riches and pleasure, which wither like a leaf or grass or flower, compared to the glory and joy of heaven that never fades away, as many passages in the Bible describe.

— "Images," no. 123

All Flesh, is like the wither'd Hay,
And, so it springs, and fades away.
(Wither, 4.48)

Time, is a Fading-flowre, that's found
Within Eternities wide round.
(Wither, 2.40)

FALL OF BODIES RAISED HIGH

The higher one is raised in the sky, the more severe and quick their descent. The greater the height from which someone falls, the more devastating their fall. And if they plunge into water, the farther they fall, the more forcefully they are submerged. This holds true for faith too. Those who have been lifted to great heights in understanding, riches, worldly honor, spiritual blessings, and religious enlightenment and joy, will feel the effects of their fall even more intensely should they backslide and become hypocrites.

— *"Images," no. 159*

The Higher the Rise the Greater the Fall
(Cats and Farlie, 121)

The Higher the Rise the Greater the Fall (Cats and Farlie, 121)

A tortoise of ambitious mind,
Such as in Men we sometimes find,
Puff'd up with an egregious sense
Of his superior excellence,
Much wish'd to change his lot on earth
For one more fitted to his worth;
Which in his self-conceit he deem'd

Too little by his friends esteem'd-
Who neither would allow nor see
That he possess'd a quality
Of form or of intelligence,
Beyond their Tortoise common-sense.
Resolv'd ne'erless that they should be
Convinc'd of his ability
To shine where they could never hope
With his superior mind to cope,
Seeing one day the bird of Jove
Alighting from the clouds above,
He urged him with address polite
To bear him upward in his flight;
That he might prove to all his race
How qualified he was to grace
A station more exalted than
Their weak intelligence could scan:
Whence he at once might grasp and see
The glories of the land and sea,
And like the eagle gaze upon
The full effulgence of the sun,
High up above the puny ken
Of grov'lling Tortoises and men.
The Eagle, quick as thought to see
The silly reptile's vanity,
Express'd himself but too content
To do what from the first he meant:
And seizing him right quickly too,
He upward with the Tortoise flew,
So high into the realms of light,
That almost losing sense and sight,
The Tortoise wished himself again
Below upon the humble plain.
But upward still the Eagle rose,
As though pretending to disclose
A range of view as high and wide
As most would satisfy his pride.
Like silver threads the rivers flow,
And wind some thousand feet below : -

Like mole-hills are the mountains high-
In vast expanse- Earth, sea and fky
Lit up and flooded with a light
Too glorious for the reptile's sight.
Anon, the Eagle asks him how
He liked the change from things below?
If higher yet he'd like to rise?
And felt at home? and how the skies
Agreed with his abilities?
When lo! the Tortoise, all dismay,
Had not a single word to say!
With scornful and derisive shriek,
Unloosing then both claws and beak,
The Eagle lets the Tortoise go;
Which, dash'd upon the rocks below,
Became his prey, and learnt–too late–
The ills that on ambition wait.

E'en so at Courts, when men of low degree,
And menial minds, are raised to rank and place;
How oft are they uplifted but to be
Cast down with greater force and more disgrace!

FALLS

The sea in a storm and the powerful force of rivers express the great wrath of God and the suffering of those who experience it. The Bible often compares suffering to being overwhelmed by water. For example, Psalms 88:7 and Psalms 42:7 compare God's wrath to waves and billows. Job 27:20 states that terrors take hold like waters, and Hosea 5:10 says God will pour out His wrath like water. Psalms 42:7 further compares God's wrath to cataracts of water, with deep calling out to deep at the noise of its waterspouts. God's wrath is also represented by hail, stormy winds, dark clouds, and thunder.

— *"Images," no. 27*

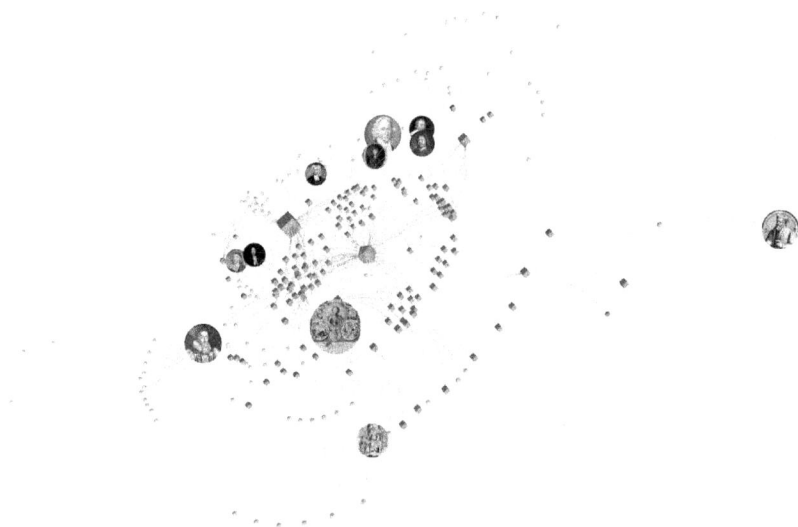

Falls

FIRE, ENKINDLING IT IN A MORNING

When we first rise in the morning, we stoke the fire to life. Likewise, when Christians awaken from spiritual slumber, they reignite their faith.

— *"Images," no. 137*

Upon His Making of a Fire (Boyle, 3.2)

How many fruitless blasts have I been spending upon this sullen fire! twas not through the greenness of the wood that made it so uneasie to be kindled; but t'was alone the greatness of the loggs, on which the fire could take no hold, but through the intervention of such smaller sticks as were at first wanting here: witness that I had no sooner laid on a little brush-wood, but the flame, from those kindled twiggs, invading and prevailing on the billets, grew suddenly great enough to threaten to make the house itself part of its fuel, and turn it to such ashes as it reduces the wood into. Methinks the blaze of this fire should light me to discern something instructive in it. These blocks may represent our necessary, these sticks our less important religious practices, and this aspiring flame the subtile inhabiter of that of Hell. Twill be but successlessly that the Devil can attempt our grand resolves, till he have first master'd our less considerable ones; and made his successes against them not only degrees but instruments, in the destroying of the others. Our more neglected and seemingly trivial affections, having once receiv'd his fiery impressions, do easily impart them to higher faculties, and serve to kindle solider materials. It is therefore the safest way to be faithful, even to our lesser determinations and watchful over our less important passions; and whensoever we find ourselves tempted to violate the former or neglect the latter, not so barely to cast one eye on the inconsiderableness of what we are intic'd to, as not to fix the other upon the consequences that may attend it: and therein to consider the importance of what such slighted things may, as they are managed, proye instrumental either to endanger or preserve.

Upon the Blowing of the Fire (Hall, 22)

We beat back the flame not with a purpose to suppress it but to raise it higher and to diffuse it more. These afflictions and impulses which seem to be discouragements are indeed the merciful incitements of grace. If God did mean judgment to my soul, He would either withdraw the fuel or pour water upon the fire, or suffer it to languish for want of new motions. But now that He continues to me the means and opportunities and desires of good, I shall misconstrue the intentions of my God if I shall think His crosses sent rather to damp than to quicken His spirit in me. O God, if Thy bellows did not sometimes thus breathe upon me in spiritual repercussions, I should have just cause to suspect my estate. These few weak gleeds of grace that are in me might soon go out if they were not thus refreshed. Still blow upon them till they kindle; still kindle them till they flame up to Thee.

(Quarles, 2.1)

Feeble and dim is Nature's Light,
The Fire by blowing is more bright:
The Light of Grace will plainly shew,
How little of ourselves we know.

Upon the Kindling of a Charcoal Fire (Hall, 26)

There are not many creatures but do naturally affect to diffuse and enlarge themselves. Fire and water will neither of them rest contented with their own bounds. Those little sparks that I see in those coals, how they spread and enkindle their next brands! It is thus morally both in good and evil, either of them dilates itself to their neighborhood, but especially this is so much more apparent in evil by how much we are more apt to take it. Let but some spark of heretical opinion be let fall upon some unstable, proud, busy spirit, it catcheth instantly and fires the next capable subject; they two have easily inflamed a third, and now the more society, the more speed and advantage of a public combustion. When we see the Church on a flame, it is too late to complain of the flint and steel. It is the holy wisdom of superiors to prevent the dangerous attritions of stubborn and wrangling spirits, or to quench their first sparks in the tinder.

But why should not peace and truth be as successful in dilating itself to the gaining of many hearts? Certainly these are in themselves more winning if our corruption had not made us indisposed to good. Oh God, out of an holy envy and emulation at the speed of evil, I shall labor to enkindle others with these heavenly flames. It shall not be my fault if they spread not.

Upon a Coal Covered with Ashes (Hall, 37)

Nothing appears in this heap but dead ashes. Here is neither light, nor smoke, nor heat, and yet, when I stir up these embers to the bottom, there are found some living gleedst which do both contain fire and are apt to propagate it. Many a Christian's breast is like this hearth. No life of grace appears there for the time, either to his own sense or to the apprehension of others; while the season of temptation lasteth, all seems cold and dead. Yet still at the worst there is a secret coal from the altar of heaven [Isa. 6:6] raked up in their bosom, which, upon the gracious motions of the Almighty, doth both betray some reminders of that divine fire and is easily raised to a perfect flame. Nothing is more dangerous than to judge by appearances. Why should I deject myself or censure others for the utter extinction of that spirit which doth but hide itself in the soul for a glorious advantage?

FISHES

The sea is seen as a symbol of Hell, with its creatures embodying the inhabitants of the underworld. In Scripture, the waters are associated with the dead, the Rephaim, and the wrath of God. The deep sea is likened to the miseries of death and God's wrath, with its floods and billows coming to represent the suffering of the damned.

— *"Images," no. 82*

Each Deplores His Own Lot
(Cats and Farlie, 61)

THE Fish that in the Weel are taken,
When they find no issue more,
Feel the stronger wish awaken
To be where they were before:
But the Fish that see them in it,
Think it far more pleasant there;
And they strive their best to win it,
Swimming round it ev'rywhere.
Thus it is that men, like Fishes,
Ne'er contented with their lot,
Ever restless in their wishes,
Craving more than what they've got;–
In their greed of wealth and station,
Coveting yet more and more,
Oft in change of situation,
Find it worse than t'was before.

Upon the Fish in the Water
(Bunyan, 8)

The water is the fish's element;
Take her from thence, none can her death
    prevent;
And some have said, who have transgressors
    been,
As good not be, as to be kept from sin.

The water is the fish's element:
Leave her but there, and she is well content.
So's he, who in the path of life doth plod,
Take all, says he, let me but have my God.

The water is the fish's element,
Her sportings there to her are excellent;
So is God's service unto holy men,
They are not in their element till then.

Upon Fishing With a Counterfeit Fly (Boyle, 4.3)

Being at length come to the river side, we quickly began to fall to the sport for which we came thither, and Eugenius finding the fish forward enough to bite, thought fit to spare his flies, till he might have more need of them, and therefore ty'd to his line a hook furnished with one of those counterfeit flies which in some neighbouring countries are much used, and which being made of the feathers of wild fowl, are not subject to be drench'd by the water, whereon those birds are wont to swim. This fly being for a pretty while scarce any oftener thrown in, than the hook it hid was drawn up again with a fish fasten'd to it, Eugenius looking on us with a smiling countenance, seem'd to be very proud of his success; which Eusebus taking notice of, whilst (says he) we smile to see how easily you beguile these silly fishes that you catch so fast with this false bait, possibly we are not much less unwary ourselves; and the world's treacherous pleasures do little less delude me and you. For Eugenius, (continues he,) as the Apostles were fishers of men in a good sense, so their and our grand adversary is a skilful fisher of men in a bad sense, and too often in his attempts to cheat fond mortals, meets with a success as great and as easy, as you now find yours. Certainly that tempter, as the Scripture calls him, does sadly delude us, even when we rise at his best baits, and as it were his true flies: for alas! the best things he can give are very worthless, most of them in their own nature, and all of them in comparison of what they must cost us to enjoy them. But however riches, power, and the delights of the senses are real goods in their kind, though they be not of the best kind: yet alas! many of us areso fitted for deceits, that we do not put this subtle angler to make use of his true baits to catch us! We suffer him to abuse us much more grossly, and to cheat us with empty titles of honor, or the ensnaring smiles of great ones, or disquieting drudgeries disguis'd with the specious names of great employments: and though these, when they must be obtained by sin, or are proposed as the recompenses for it, be, as I was going to say, but the devil's coun terfeit flies; yet, as if we were fond of being deceiv'd, we greedily swallow the hooks for flies that do but look like such; so dim-sighted are we, as well to what vice shews, as to what it hides. Let us not then, (concludes Eusebius,) rise at baits whereby we may be sure to be either grossly, or at least exceedingly deceiv'd; for whoever ventures to commit a sin to taste the sweets that the fruition of it seems to promise, certainly is so far deceiv'd, as to swallow a true hook for a bait, which either proves but a counterfeit fly, or hides that under its alluring shew, which makes it not need to be a counterfeit one to deceive him.

Upon a Fish's Struggling After Having Swallowed the Hook (Boyle, 3.4)

Fortune soon offer'd Eusebius a fair opportunity to confirm this last part of his reflection, for he had scarce made an end of it, when a large fish, espying the fly that kept my hook swimming, rose swiftly at it, and having greedily chop'd it up, was hastily swimming away with it, when I struck him, and thereby stopt for a while his progress; but finding himself both arrested and wounded, he struggled with so much violence, that at length he broke my slender line, and carry'd away a part of it, together with the annex'd hook and bait. If philosophers (says hereupon Eusebius) be not too liberal in allowing brutes to think, we may well suppose that this fish expected a great deal of pleasure from the bait he fell upon so greedily, and that when once he had got it into his mouth, he might well look upon it as his own, and those other fishes that saw him swallow it, and swim away with it, did probably envy his good fortune; but yet he does not enjoy his wish, though he seems to have the thing wish'd for within his power; for by the same action in which he sucked the fly, he likewise took in the hook, which does so wound and tear his tender gills, and thereby put him into such restless pain, that no doubt he wishes that the hook, bait and all, were out of his torn jaws again, the one putting him to too much torment to let him at all rellish the other. Thus men which do what they should not, to obtain any object of sensual desires, whatever pleasures they may before hand fancy to themselves in their success, are oftentimes, even when they obtain their ends, disappointed of their expectations; sometimes conscience, reason, or honour, making them, (even when their desires are not of the worst sort,) do as David did, when he had, more vehemently than became a pious general, long'd for water out of the well at Bethlehem, and by the strange venterrousness of his bold and affectionate officers obtained it, could not find it in his heart to drink it, but pour'd it untasted on the ground. But when the things we so long for must be criminally obtain'd, then it, often fares with them as it did with Judas; who, after having betrayed a master, that was incomparably more worth than all the world, and thereby for ever lost himself for a few pieces of silver, seem'd to have it in his power, without having it in his will to enjoy them, and in a desperate but not unseasonable fit of anguish and remorse, did of his own accord disburthen himself of that money which he had sold his conscience to get; so that though he had what he sought, he had not what he expected. And when what he had coveted was in his possession, he had the guilt of acquiring it without the power of enjoying it. Even in cases far less heinous, (concludes Eusebius,) when men seem to have got what they aimed at, and to have carried it away as their booty, the wound thereby inflicted on injur'd conscience, puts them to so much deserved pain, that the wishes they are thus criminally possest of they do not enjoy but detest.

Fish

FIXED STARS

The heavens above us are more permanent and unchanging than the heavens nearer to us. The planets in these heavens move and change their positions, they are dark and not as bright, and some of them wax and wane in light. The sun and moon experience eclipses. But in the heavens above, the stars are fixed and bright, never waxing or waning, and never eclipsing, showing that the highest heavens are an unshakable kingdom of enduring and brilliant glory.

— "Images," no. 143

Fixed Stars

FLAX

The flax, so delicate and frail, resembles the spiritual clothing we receive through Christ. He, being tender and weak, had no beauty or form (Isaiah 53:2). He was bruised and beaten, yet still provided us with a garment of protection. Through great suffering, Christ gave us his righteousness, like a fine linen, clean and white, and presented us to the Father without blemish.

— "Images," no. 46

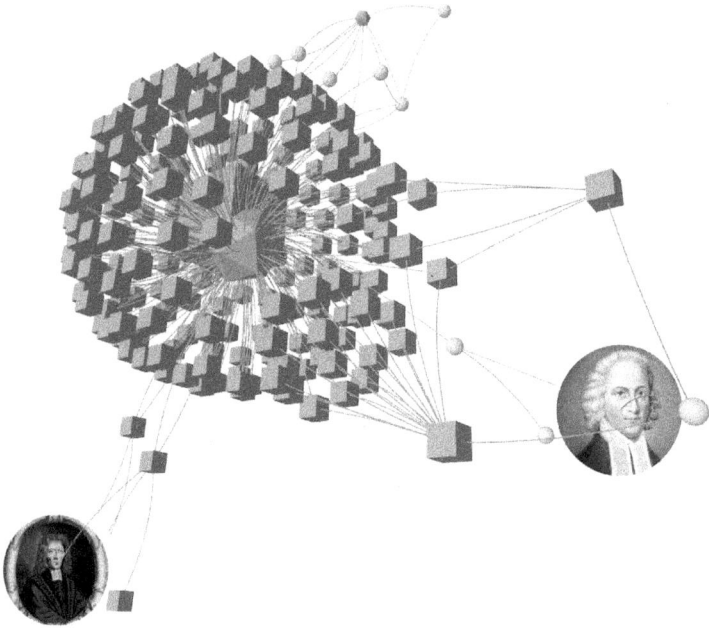

Flax

FLIES (INSECTS) IN SUMMER

As summer lingers on, noisome and hurtful insects come to thrive. Even a slight frost may only chill them, and they will revive again when the weather warms up. Similarly, when prosperity and comfort linger in a person or church, harmful and corrupting influences gradually multiply until they swarm, and it is hard to root them out. Even when the comforts are withdrawn, much of the contrary must be endured before these insects are killed, just as the worms in the manna.

— *"Images," no. 182*

Upon a Glow-Worm That He Kept Included in a Crystal Vial (Boyle, 5.5)

If this unhappy worm had been as despicable as the other rep-
tiles, that crept up and down the hedge whence I took him, he
might, as well as they, have been left there still; and his own
obscurity, as well as that of the night, had preserved him from
the confinement he now suffers; and if, as he sometimes for a
pretty while withdraws that luminous liquor, that is as it were
the candle to this dark lanthorn, he had continued to forbear
the disclosing of it, he might have eluded my search, and es-
caped his present confinement. Rare qualities may sometimes be
prerogatives without being advantages; and though a needless
ostentation of one's excellencies may be more glorious, a modest
concealment of them is usually more safe; and an unseasonable
disclosure of flashes of wit, may sometimes do a man no other
service, than to direct his adversaries how they may do him a
mischief.

And as though this worm be lodged in a crystalline prison,
through which it has the honour to be gazed at by many eyes,
and among them by some that are said to shine more in the day,
than this creature does in the night; yet no doubt, if he could
express a sense of the condition he is in, he would bewail it, and
think himself unhappy in an excellency which procures him at
once captivity and admiration. This oftentimes is the fate of a
great wit: the light that ennobles him tempts inquisitive men to
keep him, as upon the like score we do this glow-worm, from
sleeping. This conspicuousness is not more a friend to his fame,
than an enemy to his quiet; for men allow such persons much
praise, but little rest. They attract the eyes of others, but are not
suffer'd to shut their own; and find that they are reduced, for
that imaginary good call'd fame, to pay that real blessing, liberty.

And as, though this luminous creature be himself imprison'd in
so close a body as glass, yet the light that ennobles him is not
thereby restrain'd from diffusing itself; so there are certain truths
that have in them so much of native light or evidence, that by
the personal distresses of the proposer, it cannot be hidden or
restrained, but in spight of prisons, it shines freely, and procures

the teachers of it admiration, even where it cannot procure them liberty.

Upon the Flies Gathering to a Galled Horse (Hall, 31)

How those flies swarm to the galled part of this poor beast and there sit feeding upon that worst piece of his flesh, not meddling with the other sound parts of his skin! Even thus do malicious tongues of detractors. If a man have any infirmity in his person or actions, that they will be sure to gather unto and dwell upon; whereas his commendable parts and well-deservings are passed by without mention, without regard. It is an envious self-love and base cruelty that causeth this ill disposition in men. In the meantime this only they have gained: it must needs be a filthy creature that feeds upon nothing but corruption.

The gnat stings the eyes of the lion
(Cats and Farlie, 221)

The gnat stings the eyes of the lion (Cats and Farlie, 221)

FRIENDS! come here and list to me!
Something strange I would relate;
Should it prove of use to thee,
That will me well compensate.
Though so strong the Lion be,
Though so full of Majesty,
Though his eyes fo fiercely gleam,
And so terrible he seem;
That no man, whoe'er he be,
Can unmov'd his anger see;
Yet the gnat, though he's so small,
And so slight of limb withal,
Is so wondrous brave and keen,
That the Lion oft is seen
Fill'd with dread as soon as he
Gnats perceives but two or three!
Yet the gnat doth not attack
Slyly, or behind his back;
But, first, like a gen'rous foe,
Scorning all advantage low,
When the Lion comes in fight,
Sounds his challenge to the fight;
And forthwith bids him prepare
All his fiercest wrath to bear.
Nor doth he assault his foe
Where he least defence can show;
Though so small, yet keenly bold,
Like a Paladin of old,
He the Lion scorns t' assail,
On the flank or on the tail
Front to front in open fight,
Heedless of the Lion's might,
Headlong at his face he flies,
And attacks his rage-lit eyes.
Where the Lion best can see
All his foe's hostility,
There the gnat, his rage despite,

Rushing 'mid their flashing light,
Deeply stings the fount of sight;
Till half blind and mad with pain,
The Lion flees across the plain.

Let Arrogance by this be taught,
That whatsoe'er its Strength and Size,
There's nothing with more danger fraught
Than what is little, to despise;
There's neither man nor brute so great
But, like the Lion pictur'd here,
May learn to rue the wrath and hate
Of that which seem'd too small to fear.

Even the smallest things should be feared: *The beetle, though weaker than his foe, used cunning to wage war. He concealed himself in the feathers of an eagle, soaring to the highest heavens, and reached his enemy's nest. He destroyed the eggs, bringing an end to the young's hope of life, and, avenging himself, he flew away. (Alciati, 169)*

Of the Boy and the Butterfly
(Bunyan, 22)

Of the Boy and the Butterfly (Bunyan, 22)

Behold how eager this our little boy
Is for this Butterfly, as if all joy,
All profits, honours, yea, and lasting pleasures,
Were wrapt up in her, or the richest treasures,
Found in her, would be bundled up together,
When all her all is lighter than a feather.
He halloos, runs, and cries out, Here, boys, here,
Nor doth he brambles or the nettles fear.
He stumbles at the mole-hills, up he gets,
And runs again, as one bereft of wits;
And all this labour and this large outcry,
Is only for a silly butterfly.

Comparison

This little boy an emblem is of those
Whose hearts are wholly at the world's dispose,
The butterfly doth represent to me,
The world's best things at best but fading be.
All are but painted nothings and false joys,
Like this poor butterfly to these our boys.
His running through nettles, thorns, and briars,
To gratify his boyish fond desires;
His tumbling over mole-hills to attain
His end, namely, his butterfly to gain;
Doth plainly show what hazards some men run.
To get what will be lost as soon as won.
Men seem in choice, than children far more wise,
Because they run not after butterflies;
When yet, alas! for what are empty toys,
They follow children, like to beardless boys.

Upon a Glow worm (Hall, 49)

What a cold candle is lighted up in the body of this sorry worm! There needs no other disproof of those that say there is no light at all without some heat, yet sure an outward heat helps on this cool light. Never did I see any of these bright worms but in the hot months of summer; in cold seasons, either they are not or appear not when the nights are both darkest and longest and most uncomfortable. Thus do false-hearted Christians in the warm and lightsome times of free and encouraged profession; none shine more than they. In hard and gloomy seasons of restraint and persecution, all their formal light is either lost or hid; whereas true professorst either like the sunshine ever alike or like the stars shine fairest in the frostiest nights. The light of this worm is for some show but for no use. Any light that is attended with heat can impart itself to others, though with the expence of that subject wherein it is; this doth neither waste itself nor help others. I had rather never to have light than not to have it always; I had rather not to have light than not to communicate it.

Upon the Pismire
(Bunyan, 33)

Upon the Pismire (Bunyan, 33)

Must we unto the pismire go to school,
To learn of her in summer to provide
For winter next ensuing. Man's a fool,
Or silly ants would not be made his guide.
But, sluggard, is it not a shame for thee
To be outdone by pismires? Pr'ythee hear:
Their works, too, will thy condemnation be
When at the judgment-seat thou shalt appear.
But since thy God doth bid thee to her go,
Obey, her ways consider, and be wise;
The piss-ant tell thee will what thou must do,
And set the way to life before thine eyes.

Upon Gnats in the Sun (Hall, 52)

What a cloud of gnats is here! Mark their motion; they do nothing but play up and down in the warm sun and sing, and when they have done sit down and sting the next hand or face they can seize upon. See here a perfect emblem of idleness and detraction. How many do thus miserably misspend their good hours who, after they have wasted the succeeding day in vain and merely unprofitable pastime, sit down and backbite their neighbors? The bee sings too sometimes, but she works also and her work is not more admirable than useful; but these foolish fliest do nothing but play and sing to no purpose. Even the busiest and most active spirits must recreate, but to make a trade of sport is for none but lazy wantons.

The bee stings too but it is when she is provoked; these draw blood unoffended and sting for their own pleasure. I would be glad of some recreation but to enable and sweeten my work. I would not but sting sometimes where is just cause of offence. But God bless me from those men which will ever be either doing nothing or ill.

Upon the Stinging of a Wasp (Hall, 88)

How small things may annoy the greatest! Even a mouse troubles an elephant; a gnat, a lion; a very flea may disquiet a giant. What weapon can be nearer to nothing than the sting of this wasp, yet what a painful wound hath it given me! That scarce-visible point, how it envenoms and rankles and swells up the flesh! The tenderness of the part adds much to the grief.

And if I be thus vexed with the touch of an angry fly, Lord, how shall I be able to endure the sting of a tormenting conscience? As that part is both most active and most sensible, so that wound which it receives from itself is most intolerably grievous. There were more ease in a nest of hornets than under this one torture. Oh God, howsoever I speed abroad, give me peace at home; and whatever my flesh may suffer, keep my soul free.

Thus pained, wherein do I find ease but in laying honey to the part infected? That medicine only abates the anguish. How near hath nature placed the remedy to the offence! Whensoever my heart is stung with the remorse for sins, only Thy sweet and precious merits, oh blessed Saviour, can mitigate and heal the wound; they have virtue to cure me, give me grace to apply them. That sovereign receipt shall make my pain happy; I shall thus applaud my grief. It is good for me that I was thus afflicted.

Insects

FLOWER FALLS TO MAKE WAY FOR FRUIT

When man was first created, his life was innocent, holy, pleasant, and happy, like a fair and pleasant blossom. But when man fell, the blossom faded and fell off, making way for the incarnation of Christ. Christ, God-man, is the tree of life to both angels and men, providing them with bread of life and its blessed consequences.

— WJE 15:394–95

Flower Falls

FLOWERS

Beauty may be seen in the petals of a flower and its sweet scent may fill the air, but it is the fruit that we must use to judge the tree. Similarly, people may speak of religious matters in a way that seems attractive and pleasing, and the pious may feel they are expressing themselves deeply, enjoying the words and believing they have a spiritual significance... yet it may all be for naught.

— *"Miscellanies," no. 1000*

Upon Being Presented With a Rare Nosegay by a Gardener (Boyle, 5.4)

Lindamor: Here is indeed a present for which I must still think myself this fellow's debtor, though he thinks I have overpaid him. "Tis pity these rarities were not more suitably addressed, and worn by some of nature's other master-pieces, with whom they might exchange a graceful lustre, and have the ornament they confer reflected back upon them. But one who had never been a lover, would perhaps say, that that wish were more civil to the flowers than to the ladies, of whom there are few which these soft polished skins, and orient tinctures, would not easilier make foils than prove such to them. For (not to name the rest) this lovely fragrant rose here, wears a blush that needs not do so, at any colour the spring itself can, amongst all her charming rarities, shew. Yes; here are flowers above the flattery of those of rhetorick; and besides two or three unmingled liveries, whose single colours are bright and taking enough to exclude the wish of a diversity, here is a variety of flowers, whose dyes are so dexterously blended, and fitly checquered, that every single flower is a variety. I envy not Arabia's odours, whilst that of this fresh blusher charms my sense; and I find my nose and eyes so ravishingly entertained here, that the bee extracts less sweetness out of flowers. Surely this gardener leads a happy life! he inherits nothing of Adam, but that primitive profession that employed and recompensed his innocence, and such a gay and privileged plot of his Eden, as seems exempted from the general curse; and, instead of the thorns and thistles that are the unthankful earth's wonted productions, brings him forth lillies and tulips, and gratefully crowns his culture (for toil I cannot think it) with chaplets of flowers.

Eusebius: I perceive, Lindamor, that you judge of the delight-fullness of this man's calling, only by these lovely and fragrant productions of it, and you see these curious flowers in their prime, without seeing by what practices, and degrees, they have been brought from despicable seeds to this perfection and lustre; and perhaps, if you considered that a gardener must be digging in the violent heats of the summer, must be afraid of the bitter cold of the winter, must be watchful against surprising frosts in the spring, and must not only prune, and water, and weed his ground, but must, to obtain these gawdy and odoriferous flowers, submit to deal with homely and stinking dung; if, Lindamor, you would take notice of these and some other toils and hardships that attend a gardener's trade, you would, I doubt not, confess, that his employments, like his bushes, bring him thorns as well as roses.

And now give me leave, Lindamor, to tell you, that this may be applied to the condition of some studious persons, that you and know. Forwhen we hear a learned or eloquent sermon, or read some book of devotion, or perhaps some occasional discourse handsomely written; we are apt to envy the preacher or the writer, for being able to say some things that instruct or please us so much. But alas, Lindamor, though we see not these productions of the brain till they are finished, and consequently fitted to appear with their full advantages abroad, yet, to bring them to that pass, the author may perhaps undergo many a trouble that we dream not of. For he that has to do with difficult or weighty subjects, cannot present us a fine pair of gloves, or a fine collation, which may be had, at an hour's warning, from the next milliner's or confectioner's. For to be able to write one good book on some subjects, a man must have been at the trouble to read an hundred. To grow capable to give a better rendering of a Greek text, he must perchance have perused Suidas, Stephanus, and Hesychius, and I know not how many Lexicographers and Scholiasts. To be qualified to make a translation of an Hebrew word or phrase, that shall illuminate a dark text or clear a difficulty, or more fitly agree with his notion or accommodation of a place in Scripture, a man must not only, like a school boy, have learned an Hebrew grammar, and turned over Buxtorf's, Schindler's, and other dictionaries, but (which is worse,) he must in many cases hazard his eyes and patience in conversing with such Jewish writings, not only as Elias his Tishbi, and Kimchi's Michlol; but to gain a little Rabbinical learning, and find out some unobvious signification of a word or phrase, he must devour the tedious and voluminous rapsodies, that make up the Talmud; in which he can learn little but the art of saying nothing in a multitude of words. Even when a man sets himself to write those smooth composures, where eloquence is con'spicuous, and seems chiefly to be designed, the author seldom comes by his contentment on as easie terms as the readers come by theirs; for, not to mention that sometimes periods, that in a well printed book look very handsomely and run very evenly, were not in the written copy without interlining and transcriptions, those that are scholars themselves can hardly write any thing without having an ambition, or at least a care to approve their discourses to them that are so too. In the judgement of such perusers, to be able to write well, one must not only have skill in the subject, but be well skilled in the way of writing, lest the matter be blemished by the manner of handling it. For though an author's natural parts may make his book abound with wit, yet without the help of art he will scarce make it free from faults. To be well stocked with comparisons, (which, when skilfully managed, make the most taking passages of fine pieces,) one must sometimes survey and range through the works of nature and art, which are the chief warehouses, where variety of similitudes are to be had; and to obtain those pleasing ornaments, there is oftentimes required no less pains than to devise useful notions. As one must search the ditches amongst briars and weeds, not only to find medicinal herbs, but to gather primroses and violets. So that, Lindamor, to conclude, if we consider the trouble that applauded composures do oftentimes cost their authors, we should be sensible we owe more, than most men think we do, to those to whom we owe good books. But then, unless they find recompense for their labours in the satisfaction of promoting piety, or in the well natured pleasure they feel themselves in pleasing others, I should scarce doubt but that some of the writers we think so happy, may rather deserve our esteem than our envy.

Upon the Sight of Tulips and Marigolds, etc. in His Garden (Hall, 55)

These flowers are true clients of the sun. How observant they are of his action and influence! At even they shut up as mourning for his departure, without whom they neither can nor would flourish; in the morning they welcome his rising with a cheerful openness; and at noon are fully displayed in a free acknowledgement of his bounty. Thus doth the good heart unto God. "When thou turnedst away thy face I was troubled," saith the man after God's own heart [Ps. 102:2]. "In thy presence is life, yea, the fullness of joy" [Ps. 16: 11]. Thus doth the carnal heart to the world; when that withdraws his favor he is dejected and revives with a smile. All is in our choice; whatsoever is our sun will thus carry us. Oh God, be Thou to me such as Thou art in Thyself. Thou shalt be merciful in drawing me, I shall be happy in following Thee.

Whil'st I, the Sunne's bright Face may view,
I will no meaner Light pursue.
(Wither, 4.1)

Whil'st I, the Sunne's bright Face may view, I will no meaner Light pursue. (Wither, 4.1)

When, with a serious musing, I behold
The gratefull, and obsequious Marigold,
How duely, ev'ry morning, she displayes
Her open brest, when Titan spreads his Rayes;
How she observes him in his daily walke,
Still bending towards him, her tender stalke;
How, when he downe declines, she droopes and mournes,
Bedew'd (as 'twere) with teares, till he returnes;
And, how she vailes her Flow'rs, when he is gone,
As if she scorned to be looked on
By an inferiour Eye; or, did contemne
To wayt upon a meaner Light, then Him.
When this I meditate, me-thinkes, the Flowers
Have spirits, farre more generous, then ours;
And, give us faire Examples, to despise
The servile Fawnings, and Idolatries,
Wherewith, we court these earthly things below,
Which merit not the service we bestow.

But, oh my God! though groveling I appeare
Upon the Ground, (and have a rooting here,
Which hales me downward) yet in my desire,
To that, which is above mee, I aspire:
And, all my best Affections I professe
To Him, that is the Sunne of Righteousnesse.
Oh! keepe the Morning of his Incarnation,
The burning Noone-tide of his bitter Passion,
The Night of his Descending, and the Height
Of his Ascension, ever in my sight:

That imitating him, in what I may,
I never follow an inferiour Way.

Flowers

FOOD

The preparation of our food, with boiling, roasting, and other methods to make it clean, healthy, and enjoyable to us, serves as a metaphor for God's dealings with his people, individuals, and chosen nations, and his visible church, to make them suitable for him. Christ's suffering, even unto death, must come before we can receive spiritual nourishment from him. This is symbolized by meal being ground to powder, cast into poisoned pottage and healed, and baked in the oven or by the fire. All of our food is prepared by fire, which is a reminder of Christ's suffering in order to be our spiritual food.

— *"Images," no. 189*

Upon the Sight of Sweetmeats Very Artificially Counterfeited in Wax (Boyle, 6.2)

The shape and colours of the best sweetmeats of these kinds are here so luckily represented by a skilful hand, that art seems to have designed rather to rival nature, than barely to imitate her; and a lover of junkets that approaches not too near to these, must have much quickness of sight, or but little of appetite, if such inviting objects do not tempt him both to mistake and to desire them. But though at this distance these alluring sweetmeats appear very pleasing, yet if one should be so unadvised as to endeavour to eat them, instead of enjoying them more fully by the taste than he did by the sight, he would both spoil and disfigure them, and perhaps be so near choaking himself, that he would more earnestly wish them out of his mouth, than ever he wished them in it.

There are some pleasures and conditions too in the world, which make so fine a shew at a distance, that in those that gaze at them aloof off, they frequently beget envy at them and wishes for them; and yet he that calmly beholds them takes the best way of injoying them; since that which, whilst 'tis but aimed at, is expected to be very satisfactory, upon a nearer and fuller fruition, would be so far from proving so, and would so little be as sweet to the palate as pleasing to the eye, that it would not only cease to afford them any delight, but would make them wish they had let those deluding sweets alone, and would make attainments more uneasie and troublesome than ever desire was.

Upon the Sight of a Full Table at a Feast (Hall, 81)

What a great variety is here of flesh, of fish, of both, of neither, as if both nature and art did strive to pamper us! Yet, methinks, enough is better than all this. Excess is but a burden, as to the provider so to the guest. It pities and grieves me to think what toil, what charge hath gone to the gathering of all these dainties together, what pain so many creatures have been put to in dying for a needless sacrifice to the belly. What a penance must be done by every accumbent in sitting out the passage through all those dishes! What a task the stomach must be put to in the concoction of so many mixtures! I am not so austerely scrupulous as to deny the lawfulness of these abundant provisions upon just occasions. I find my Saviour Himself more than once at a feast; this is recorded as well as His one long fast. Doubtless our bountiful God hath given us His creatures not for necessity only but for pleasure. But these exceedings would be both rare and moderate, and when they must be require no less patience than temperance.

Might I have my opinion, oh God, give me rather a little with peace and love. He whose provision for every day was thirty measures of fine flour, and threescore measures of meal, thirty oxen, an hundred sheep, besides venison and fowl? yet can pray, "Give me the bread of sufficiency." Let me have no perpetual feast but a good conscience, and from these great preparations, for the health of soul and body, let me rise rather hungry than surcharged.

(Quarles, 1.11)

Luxurious Feeding is not good,
And Health is hurt for want of Food;
O'er Nature hold an even Rein,
And well observe the Golden Mean.

FOXES

Foxes are remarkable foes of the church of God, likened to the "little foxes that spoil the vines" of Canticles 2:15. These represent either the subtle sins that can easily damage the graces of the saints, or sly deceivers who corrupt and spoil young converts in times of religious revival. Both are dangerous and must be taken seriously.

— *"Images," no. 148*

Mind, not outer appearance, rules: *A fox came across a theatrical director's storeroom, and saw a human head that had been crafted with such finesse that the only thing it was missing was breath. It was as if it were alive. She picked it up in her paws and exclaimed, "What a head this is! But it lacks a brain!" (Alciati, 189)*

FRUIT

Christ often uses symbols of spiritual matters in the world to prove his point, such as the idea that one can tell a tree by its fruit (Matthew 12:33). These symbols are not just used to explain his point, but to demonstrate the validity of his words.

— *"Images," no. 26*

Upon the sight of many sticks lodged in the branches of a choice fruit Tree (Flavel, 3.4)

How is this Tree batter'd with stones, and loaded with sticks that have been thrown at it? whilest those that grow about it being barren, or bearing harsher fruit, escape untouched! Surely, if its fruit had not been so good, its usage had not been so bad: and yet it is affirmed, that some trees, as the Walnut &c. bear the better, for being thus bruised and battered.

Even thus it fares, in both respects with the best of men; the more holy, the more envied and persecuted; every one that passes by will have a fling at them. Methinks I see, how devils and wicked men walk round about the people of God whom he hath enclosed in armes of power, like so many boys about an Orchard, whose lips water to have a fling at them. But God turns all the stones of reproach into precious stones to his people, they bear the better for being thus batter'd.

(Quarles, 1.2)

Adam, behold thy Apple now,
Pregnant with ev'ry human Woe;
The Moniters soon will make their Way,
And all the world must be their Prey.

Like Melons, Friends Are to Be Found in Plenty,
of Which Not Even One Is Good in Twenty
(Cats and Farlie, 225)

One Rotten Apple Infects All in the Basket
(Cats and Farlie, 101)

On fruitfulness that destroys itself: *I am
a chestnut tree, planted at a crossroads by a
rustic. Boys now hurl stones at me, and my
branches are mutilated, my bark damaged. All
sides are assaulted by the stones cast at me with
eagerness. What greater dishonor could befall
a barren tree? I sadly bear the fruit of my own
destruction. (Alciati, 193)*

Upon an excellent, but irregular Tree (Flavel, 3.6)

Seeing a Tree grow somewhat irregular, in a very neat Orchard, I told the Owner it was pity that Tree should stand there; and that if it were mine, I would root it up, and thereby reduce the Orchard to an exact uniformity. It was replyed to this purpose, that he rather regarded the fruit than the form; and that this slight inconveniency was abundantly preponderated by a more considerable advantage. This Tree said he, which you would root up, hath yielded me more fruit than many of those Trees which have nothing else to commend them, but their regular scituation [situation]. I could not but yield to the reason of this answer, and could wish it had been spoken so loud, that all our Uniformity men had heard it, who will not stick to root up many hundred of the best bearers in the Lords Orchard, because they stand not in an exact order with other more conformable, but less beneficial Trees, who do *perdere substanitiam propter accidentia,* destroy the fruit, to preserve the form.

Fruit

FRUITS WHEN RIPE ARE RED

Until corn is threshed, ground, and baked, it is not ready to nourish us, as the bread from heaven. In the same way, fruits must ripen or have their juices become like blood before they can be eaten. This is like the fruit of the tree of life, which is only available to us through Christ's death, which was the shedding of his blood.

— *"Images," no. 112*

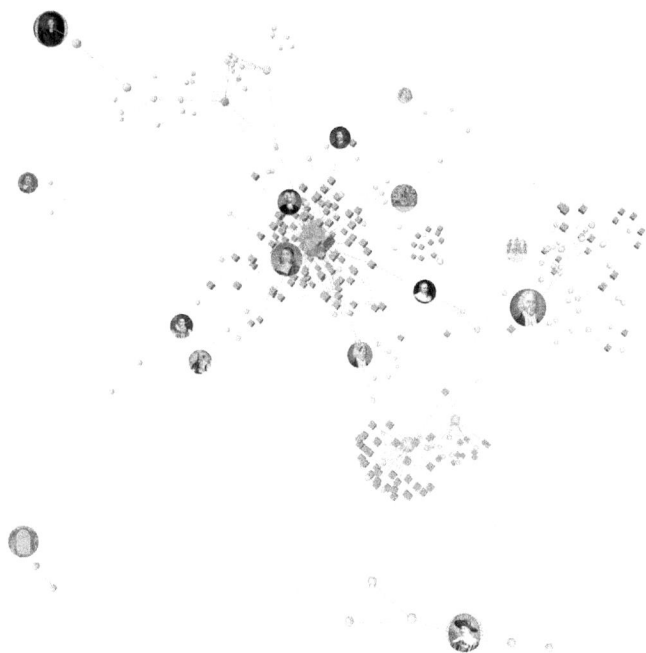

Fruits ripe and red

FRUITS WHEN RIPE EASILY GATHERED

When the fruit is ripe, it is ready to be taken. It does not cling to the tree, but rather parts from it without any harm done. In the same way, a saint ready for heaven leaves this world without any struggle or pain (Job 5:26).

— "Images," no. 192

The Ripe Pear Falls Ready to the Hand (Cats and Farlie, 113)

WOULD'ST early be successful in thy suit,
Nor languish long in Love's consuming flame?-
In Beauty's garden, shun the unripe fruit,
And breathe thy passion to the riper dame.
The fruit that's green clings longest to the tree,
Nor willing yields to leave the parent spray;
While that which has attain'd maturity,
Warm'd to the core beneath the sunny ray,
Yields to the touch-and quickly comes away.

FUEL FOR THE FIRE

Many things, when they are of no use, are burned. This is what people do with barren branches, as stated in John 15:6: "Men gather them, cast them into the fire, and they are burned." This is how men discard of useless items, such as timber from barren trees, briers, thorns, and bushes in clearing land. This is also true in spiritual matters.

— "Images," no. 88

Fuel for the Fire

FURNACES

I think it is ordained that such intense heat is needed to refine metals, signifying the intensity of God's wrath and the extreme suffering which purifies the world of its impurities and saves the saints (who are likened to gold). The heat of the furnace releases the metal from its ore and dross, just as the suffering of Jesus Christ, the due wrath of God, saves the saints from their sins.

— "Images," no. 31

Furnaces

GARMENTS

We, in our fallen state, need garments to hide our nakedness, having lost our primitive glory which was unnecessary in our state of innocence. God has provided us with clothing that represents Jesus Christ and His righteousness, whether it be the coats of skins He made for our first parents, fleeces of sheep for the Lamb of God, or the silkworm's clothing that comes at its death. We also have spiritual clothing in Christ, represented by the small, weak, and unadorned flax plant that is beaten and bruised, yielding its coat for our clothing. Through His great suffering, Christ yields us His righteousness, a fine linen, clean and white, presenting us spotless to the Father.

— "Images," no. 46

Upon the Putting on of his Clothes (Hall, 70)

What a poor thing were man if he were not beholden to other creatures! The earth affords him flax for his linen, bread for his belly; the beasts, his ordinary clothes; the silkworm, his bravery; the back and bowels of the earth, his metals and fuel; the fishes, fowls, beasts, his nourishment. His wit indeed works upon all these to improve them to his own advantage, but they must yield him materials else he subsists not. And yet we fools are proud of ourselves, yea, proud of the cast suits of the very basest creatures. There is not one of them that have so much need of us. They would enjoy themselves the more if man were not. Oh God, the more we are sensible of our own indigence, the more let us wonder at this all-sufficiency in Thyself and long for that happy condition wherein Thou (which art all-perfection) shalt be all in all to us.

Upon Apparel (Bunyan, 17)

Upon Apparel (Bunyan, 17)

God gave us clothes to hide our nakedness,
And we by them do it expose to view.
Our pride and unclean minds to an excess,
By our apparel, we to others show.

Though he endeavour all he can,
An Ape, will never be a Man.
(Wither, 1.14)

Though he endeavour all he can, An Ape, will never be a Man. (Wither, xx)

What though an Apish-Pigmie, in attire,
His Dwarfish Body Gyant-lyke, array?
Turne Brave, and get him Stilts to seem the higher?

What would so doing, handsome him I pray?
Now, surely, such a Mimicke sight as that,
Would with excessive Laughter move your Spleene,
Till you had made the little Dandiprat,
To lye within some Auger-hole, unseene.

I must confesse I cannot chuse but smile,
When I perceive, how Men that worthlesse are,
Piece out their Imperfections, to beguile,
By making showes, of what they never were.
For, in their borrow'd-Shapes, I know those Men,
And (through their Maskes) such insight of them have;
That I can oftentimes disclose (ev'n then)
How much they savour of the Foole or Knave.

A Pigmey-spirit, and an Earthly-Minde,
Whose looke is onely fixt on Objects vaine;
In my esteeme, so meane a place doth finde,
That ev'ry such a one, I much refraine.
But, when in honour'd Robes I see it put,
Betrimm'd, as if some thing of Worth it were,
Looke big, and on the Stilts of Greatnesse, strut;
From scorning it, I cannot then forbeare.
For, when to grosse Unworthinesse, Men adde
Those Dues, which to the Truest-worth pertaine;
Tis like an Ape, in Humane-Vestments clad,
Which, when most fine, deserveth most disdaine:

And, more absurd, those Men appeare to me,
Then this Fantasticke-Monkey seemes to thee.

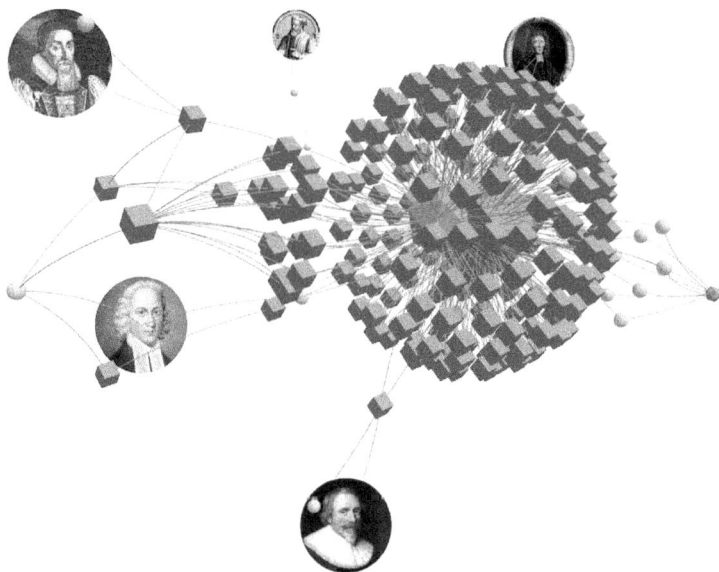

Garments, clothes

GRAFTING

The God of nature and disposer of all things has two distinct meanings for the act of grafting trees. One is to represent the ingrafting of the soul into Christ, where the believer is the scion and Christ is the stock. This is signified by the cutting off from one's own stock, being emptied of oneself, and being united to a new head of influence. The other meaning is the union of Christ, the heavenly branch, with mankind. This is signified by the scion being taken from a good tree and grafted into a bad tree, which is then changed for the better. The good fruit from the grafted tree is the scion's fruit, not the fruit of the stock and root.

— *"Images," no. 166*

Grafting

GRASSHOPPERS

As winter nears, grasshoppers and other idle insects that do not store food for the winter, like ants and bees, sing more than ever before. This is similar to what is described in Matthew 24:37–39, where it is said that people were living life as usual and unaware of the coming flood until it was upon them. Similarly, the Son of Man's coming will be unexpected and sudden.

— *"Images," no. 102*

Grasshoppers

GRAVE

This world devours men as it does their bodies; our mother, who brought us forth and nourished us, is cruel and hungry for the flesh of her children. She swallows up mankind, generation after generation, and is never sated. Those who rely on worldly things for happiness are undone and ruined by the earth, made miserable forever.

— *"Images," no. 157*

Upon the Sight of a Grave Digged up (Hall, 8)

The earth, as it is a great devourer, so also it is a great preserver too: liquors and fleshes are therein long kept from purifying and are rather heightened in their spirits by being buried in it. But above all, how safely doth it keep our bodies for resurrection, we are here but laid up for custody. Balms and serecloths and leads cannot do so much as this lap of our common mother. When all these are dissolved into her dust (as being unable to keep themselves from corruption), she receives and restores her charge. I can no more withhold my body from the earth than the earth can withhold it from my Maker. O God, this is Thy cabinet or shrine wherein Thou pleasest to lay up the precious relics of Thy dear saints until the jubilee of glory. With what confidence should i commit myself to this sure reposition while I know Thy word just, Thy power infinite!

To Learning, I a love should have,
Although one foot were in the Grave.
(Wither, 2.25)

To Learning, I a love should have,
Although one foot were in the Grave. (Wither, 2.25)

Here, we an Aged-man described have,
That hath one foot, already, in the Grave:
And, if you marke it (though the Sunne decline,
And horned Cynthia doth begin to shine)
With open-booke, and, with attentive eyes,
Himselfe, to compasse Knowledge, he applyes:
And, though that Evening, end his last of dayes,
Yet, I will study, more to learne, he sayes.

From this, we gather, that, while time doth last,
The time of learning, never will be past;
And, that, each houre, till we our life lay downe,
Still, something, touching life, is to be knowne.
When he was old, wise Cato learned Greeke:
But, we have aged-folkes, that are to seeke
Of that, which they have much more cause to learne;
Yet, no such minde in them, wee shall discerne.
For, that, which they should studie in their prime,
Is, oft, deferred, till their latter-time:
And, then, old-age, unfit for learning, makes them,
Or, else, that common dulnesse overtakes them,
Which makes ashamed, that it should be thought,
They need, like little-children, to be taught.
And, so, out of this world, they doe returne
As wise, as in that weeke, when they were borne.

God, grant me grace, to spend my life-time so,
That I my duety still may seeke to know;
And, that, I never, may so farre proceed,
To thinke, that I, more Knowledge, doe not need:

But, in Experience, may continue growing,
Till I am fill'd with fruits of pious-knowing.

If God should spare us 'till we say,
We don't desire another Day
Grim Death but little Work would have,
And few Inhabitants the Grave.
(Quarles, 3.12)

From Earth deriv'd, to Earth return;
Earth in our Birth, and in our Uurn;
Let no Man boast his noble Birth,
Since all must own their Mother Earth.
(Quarles, 3.5)

Grave, tomb

GRAVITY

Gravity, attraction, or the mutual pull of all things to one another, preserves the entirety of the material universe. This connection between parts of the world is a kind of love or charity in the spiritual realm, with its beauty, harmony, order, regularity, life, motion, and general well-being depending on it.

— *"Images," no. 79*

Gravity

GREATNESS OF THE WORLD

The grandeur of the universe, its unfathomable expanse, and the tremendous altitude of the heavens are but a shadow of the infinite greatness, height, and glory of God's work in the spiritual realm. His power, wisdom, holiness, and love are beyond comprehension, and the greatness of the moral and natural good, the knowledge, holiness, and joy that will be bestowed upon it is immeasurable. Thus, these characteristics of the physical world are often compared to His divine attributes in scripture, such as "Your mercy is higher than the heavens, your faithfulness reaches to the clouds" (Psalm 108:4) and "You have set your glory above the heavens" (Psalm 8:1).

— *"Images," no. 212*

Greatness of the world

Ground producing plants

The grace of the gospel is like the rain that often falls from the sky, bringing holiness to the lives of God's people. It is like a seed planted in the earth, a living thing in something that is lifeless. Holiness beautifies and adorns that which is otherwise vile, and though it starts small, it grows and is refreshed by God. It has many branches, is tender and easily wounded, and passes through many changes before it reaches its fullness. Eventually, it increases to great heights, and when it is ripe, it is gathered in.

— WJE, 11:139

The Ground brings forth all needfull things;
But, from the Sunne, this vertue springs.
(Wither, 2.42)

The Ground brings forth all needfull things;
But, from the Sunne, this vertue springs. (Wither, 2.42)

We doe acknowledge (as this Emblem showes)
That Fruits and Flowres, and many pleasant-things,
From out the Ground, in ev'ry season growes;
And, that unto their being, helpe it brings.
Yet, of it selfe, the Ground, we know is dull,
And, but a Willing-patient, whereupon
The Sunne, with Beames, and Vertues wonderfull,
Prepareth, and effecteth, what is done.
We, likewise, doe acknowledge, that our eyes
Indowed are with faculties of Seeing,
And, with some other nat'rall properties,
Which are as much our owne, as is our Being.
However, till the Sunne imparts his light,
We finde, that we in darkenesse doe remaine,
Obscured in an everlasting night;
And, boast our Seeing-faculties, in vaine.

So, we, by nature, have some nat'rall powers:
But, Grace, must those abilities of ours
First move; and, guide them, still, in moving, thus,
To worke with God, when God shall worke on us:
For, God so workes, that, no man he procures
Against his nature, ought to chuse, or shun:
But, by his holy-Spirit, him allures;
And, with sweet mildnesse, proveth ev'ry one.
The Sunne is faultlesse of it, when the birth
Of some bad Field, is nothing else but Weeds:
For, by the selfe-same Sun-shine, fruitfull Earth
Beares pleasant Crops, and plentifully breeds.

Thus, from our selves, our Vices have increase,
Our Vertues, from the Sunne of Righteousnesse.

Ground producing plants

GROWTH OF CHILDREN

As we journey from youth to adulthood, this is mirrored in the growth of the saintly and the church in grace, knowledge, holiness, and joy—as argued by the Apostle in 1 Corinthians 13:11, "When I was a child, I spoke as a child, I understood as a child: but when I became a man, I put away childish things."

— "Images," no. 42

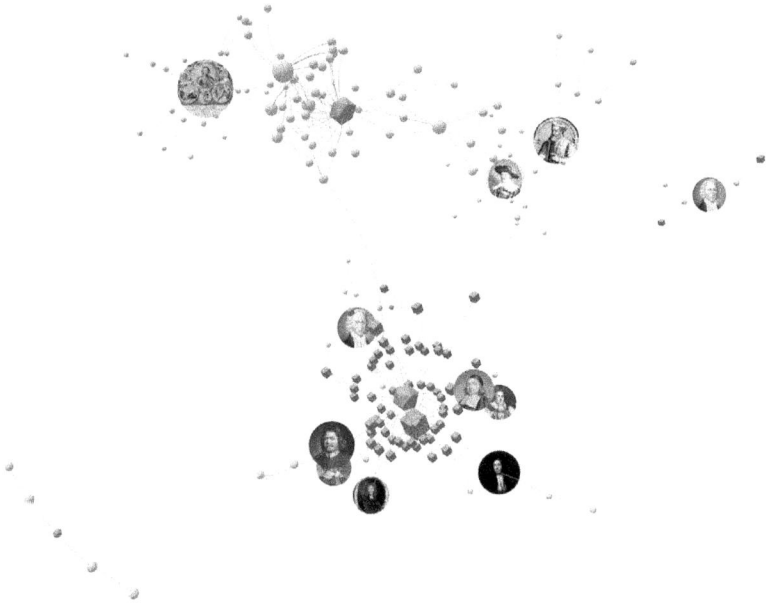

Growth of children

HARVEST, SUCCEEDED BY WINNOWING

A time of gathering is followed by a period of sifting, to divide the wheat from the straw and chaff. Likewise, after the elect are brought to Christ, there are trials and afflictions to separate them from their corruptions. This is often seen after a great harvest in the church of God, as after Christ's ascension and the Reformation. Christ likened the struggles of the righteous to the sifting of wheat (Luke 22:31).

— "Images," no. 94

Upon the Fanning of Corn (Hall, 45)

See how in the fanning of this wheat the fullest and greatest grains lie ever the lowest, and the lightest take up the highest place, It is no otherwise in mortality: those which are most humble are fullest of grace, and oft times those have most conspicuity which have the least substance. To affect obscurity or submission is base and suspicious, but that man whose modesty presents him mean to his own eyes and lowly to others is commonly secretly rich in virtue. Give me rather a low fullness than an empty advancement.

Of Little-Gaines, let Care be had;
For, of small Eares, great Mowes are made.
(Wither, 1.50)

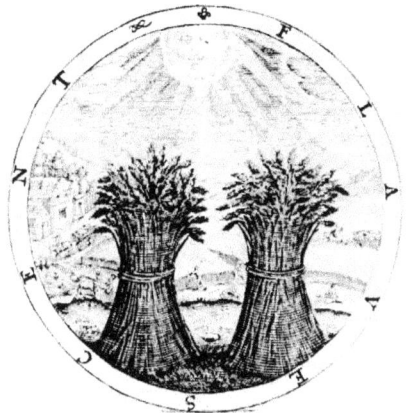

Those Fields, which yet appeare not so,
When Harvest comes, will yellow grow.
(Wither, 1.44)

Harvest

Head and body

The head is the seat of the soul, though the soul is also throughout the body. The Godhead resides in Jesus Christ and also in believers, united with the Head. The head provides life and guidance for the body, and the body carries the head. This is symbolic of the relationship between civil and religious leaders and their people.

— *"Images," nos. 24, 193*

He, that concealed things will finde,
Must looke before him, and behinde.
(Wither, 3.4)

He, that concealed things will finde,
Must looke before him, and behinde. (Wither, 3.4)

That Head, which in his Temple, heretofore,
The well-knowne figure of old Ianus bore,
Retain'd the forme, which pictur'd here you finde;
A Face before him, and a Face behinde.
And this old Hieroglyphicke doth comprize
A multitude of Heathenish Mysteries;
Which, wee omitting, will insist on what
This Emblem's Motto, chiefely poynteth at.

In true Divinity, 'tis God alone,
To whom, all hidden things are truely knowne.
Hee, onely, is that ever-present-being,
Who, by the vertue of his pow'r all-seeing,
Beholds, at one aspect, all things that are,
That ever shall be, and that ever were.

But, in a Morall-sense, we may apply
This double-face, that man to signifie,
Who (whatsoere he undertakes to doe)
Lookes, both before him, and behinde him, too.
For, he shall never fruitfully forecast
Affaires to come, who mindes not what is past:
And, such as doe not, oft, before them looke,
May lose the labour, that's already tooke.
By, sometimes, looking backward, we behold
Those things, which have been done in times of old;
By looking wisely forward, we foresee
Such matters, as in future-times will bee:
And, thus, we doe not onely fruits receive,
From that short space of time, in which we live;

But, by this meanes, we likewise have a share,
In times to come, and, times that passed are.

Head and body

HEART

The blood flows from the heart, signifying that "from the heart come the matters of life" (Proverbs 4:23).

— *"Images," no. 6*

He that with Heaven is in Love,
Whose Heart is set on Things above,
Will never rest till he's assur'd,
That his Salvation is secur'd.
(Quarles, Proem)

When Vanity holds up the Glass,
Beauty we see and comely Grace;
But search thy Heart, and there thou'lt see
More than enough to humble thee.
(Quarles, 2.6)

The Hearts of Kings are in God's Hands;
And, as He lists, He Them commands.
(Wither, 3.46)

The Heart of him, that is upright,
In Heavenly-knowledge, takes delight.
(Wither, 2.29)

The Sacrifice, God loveth best,
Are Broken-hearts, for Sin, opprest.
(Wither, 2.15)

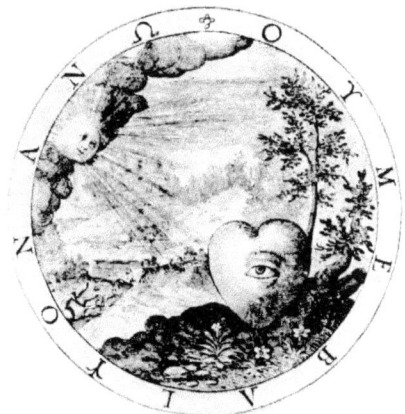

The Minde should have a fixed Eye
On Objects, that are plac'd on High.
(Wither, 1.43)

Heart

Heat of summer

The heat of summer is akin to the trials and sufferings of those devoted to the divine; it evaporates the puddles of snowmelt. These pools of water, which at first appear plentiful, quickly dry up due to their lack of a steady source. Plants and herbs, unable to reach deep into the soil, wither away. Even the most beautiful flowers and promising fruits succumb to the summer heat, while those that are strong and healthy are bettered and brought to their perfect ripeness.

— *"Images," no. 96*

Heat of summer

HEAVEN, ITS HEIGHT

The great expanse of the sky above the land, tower-ing higher than any mountain or tower, illustrates the immeasurable and unimaginable joy of heaven, which surpasses any pleasure found on earth.

— *"Images," no. 124*

(Quarles, 5.14)

The Soul transported, views her Home,
The Heaven, where she hopes to come;
In Contemplation she is lost,
Of Father, Son and Holy Ghost.

Heavens, visible

The sky is adorned with radiant celestial bodies, signi-fying the joy and glory of the heavenly beings; the sun symbolizes Christ and the moon, the church.

— *"Images," no. 4*

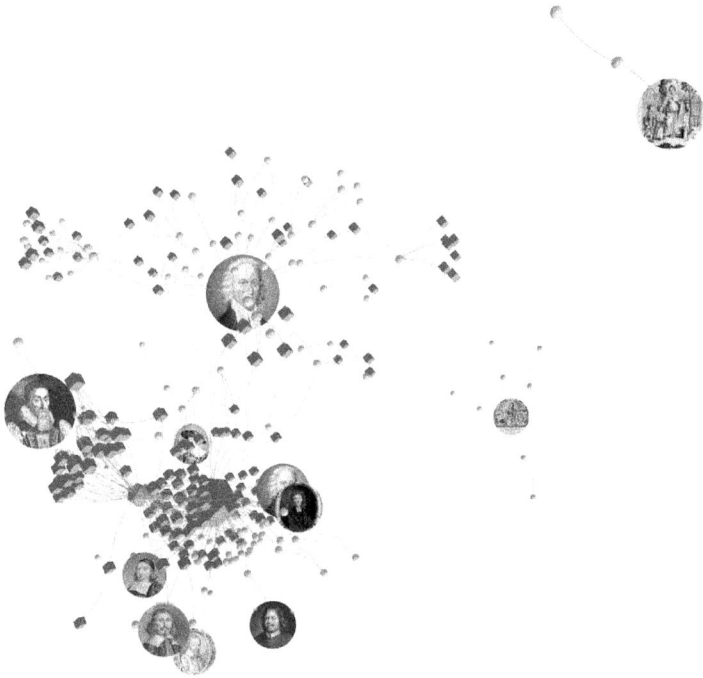

Heavens, visible

HIEROGLYPHICS

It is certain that the Greeks gave the name "hieroglyph-ics" to the symbols used by the ancients, as these were seen as a sacred form of writing to preserve and pass on religious mysteries. The first wise men of antiquity used symbols to represent spiritual and intellectual truths, taking inspiration from the natural world. This early hieroglyphic language likely derived from the belief that the visible world reflects the invisible; that its properties, shapes, and motions are copies, images, and shadows of the attributes, qualities, and laws of the unseen.

— *"Images," no. 206*

When thou a Dangerous-Way dost goe,
Walke surely, though thy pace be slowe.
(Wither, 1.19)

When thou a Dangerous-Way dost goe,
Walke surely, though thy pace be slowe. (Wither, 1.19)

Experience proves, that Men who trust upon
Their Nat'rall parts, too much, oft lose the Day,
And, faile in that which els they might have done,
By vainely trifling pretious Time away.

It also shewes, that many Men have sought
With so much Rashnesse, those things they desir'd,
That they have brought most likely Hopes to nought;
And, in the middle of their Courses, tir'd.
And, not a few, are found who so much wrong
Gods Gratiousnesse, as if their thinkings were,
That (seeing he deferres his Judgements long)
His Vengeance, he, for ever, would forbeare:
But, such as these may see wherein they faile,
And, what would fitter be for them to doe,
If they would contemplate the slow-pac'd Snaile;
Or, this our Hieroglyphicke looke into:

For, thence we learne, that Perseverance brings
Large Workes to end, though slowly they creepe on;
And, that Continuance perfects many things,
Which seeme, at first, unlikely to be done.

It warnes, likewise, that some Affaires require
More Heed then Haste: And that the Course we take,
Should suite as well our Strength, as our Desire;
Else (as our Proverbe saith) Haste, Waste may make.
And, in a Mysticke-sense, it seemes to preach
Repentance and Amendment, unto those
Who live, as if they liv'd beyond Gods reach;
Because, he long deferres deserved Blowes:

For, though Just-Vengeance moveth like a Snaile,
And slowly comes; her comming will not faile.

Hieroglyphics

HIGH BUILDINGS AND TOWERS

Tall towers and other lofty things often struck by thunder, and mountainous regions more prone to angry thunder and lightning, point to how pride and arrogance particularly arouse God's rage, as seen in Isaiah 2:11–17.

— "Images," no. xx

High buildings and towers

HILLS

The hills and mountains, symbolic of heaven, stand for greatness and any achievement of the highest order. Climbing these peaks, with their rocks and steep inclines, is not easy, just as attaining any level of excellence requires hard work and effort.

— *"Images," no. 66*

Hills

HOG

An animal such as a hog is often seen as a representation of a human being who is of the earth and fleshly in nature. This is exemplified in the fact that the hog is of no use until its death; it cannot be ridden like a horse, pull like an ox, give milk like a cow, or provide wool like a sheep; it is only kept alive to be slaughtered.

— *"Images," no. 176*

Her favours, Fortune, oft imparts,
To those that are of no deserts.
(Wither, 4.16)

A sudden Death, with Shame, is due
To him, that, sweares What is untrue.
(Wither, 1.38)

A Life, with good-repute, Ile have,
Or, winne an honourable Grave.
(Wither, 2.48)

A Life, with good-repute, Ile have,
Or, winne an honourable Grave. (Wither, 2.48)

In this our Emblem, you shall finde exprest
A Man, incountring with a Savage-beast;
And, he resolveth (as his Motto sayes)
To live with honour; or, to dye with praise.
I like the Resolution, and the Deed,
In which, this Figure teacheth to proceed.
For, us, me thinkes, it counselleth, to doe,
An act, which all men are oblig'd unto.
That ugly Bore (wherewith the man in strife
Here seemes to be) doth meane a Swinish-life,
And, all those beastly Vices, that assay
To root becomming Vertues quite away;
Those Vices, which not onely marre our features,
But, also, ruinate our manly natures.

The harmefull fury, of this raging Bore,
Oppose couragiously, lest more and more,
It get within you; and, at last, appeare
More prevalent, then your defences are.
It is a large-growne Pig, of that wilde Swine,
Which, ev'ry day, attempts to undermine
Our Safeties Fort: Twas he, which long agoe,
Did seeke the Holy-Vineyards overthrow:
And, if we charge him not with all our power,
The Sire, or hee, will enter and devoure.

But, what's our Strength, O Lord! or, what are wee
In such a Combate, without ayde from thee?
Oh, come to helpe us, therefore, in this Fight;
And, let us be inabled in thy might:

So, we shall both in life-time, Conquests have;
And, be victorious, also, in the Grave.

Better days are on the way: At the start of the new year, a customer presented me with the snouts of a wild boar. "Here," he said, "Take this as a treat for your appetite." The boar charges forward without ever looking back, tearing up the ground with its wide mouth. This is the same for men: to not let hope fall behind and strive to make the future even better. (Alciati, 45)

IMAGES OF DIVINE THINGS IN GOD'S WORKS

The things of this world are ordered and created to be a sign of spiritual matters. The Apostle Paul used this idea to make an argument for the resurrection in 1 Corinthians 15:36, "Thou fool, that which thou sowest is not quickened, except it die." If sowing and the growth of seeds were not meant to be a representation of the resurrection, the Apostle's argument would not have any meaning. The same goes for the argument about the validity of a testament in Hebrews 9:16–17.

— *"Images," no. xx*

Seed and resurrection

INFLUENCES OF THE STARS

The stars wield a power over the earth and its inhabitants, similar to the authority God has granted to angels to govern the affairs of the world.

— *"Images," no. 140*

God, by their Names, the Stars doth cal;
And, hee is Ruler of them all.
(Wither, 4.43)

God, by their Names, the Stars doth cal;
And, hee is Ruler of them all. (Wither, 4.43)

Some say, (and many men doe these commend)
That, all our deeds, and Fortunes doe depend
Upon the motions of celestiall Spheres;
And, on the constellations of the Starres.
If this were true, the Starres, alone, have bin
Prime cause of all that's good, and of all sinne.
And, 'twere (me thinkes) injustice to condemne,
Or, give rewards to any, but to them.
For, if they made mee sinne, why for that ill,
Should I be damn'd, and they shine brightly, still?
If they inforc'd my goodnesse, why should I
Bee glorified for their Pietie?
And, If they neither good nor ill constraine,
Why then, should wee of Destinie complaine?

For, if it bee (as tis) absurd to say,
The starres enforce us (since they still obay
Their just Commander) 'twere absurder, farre,
To say, or thinke, that God's Decree it were,
Which did necessitate the very same,
For which, we thinke the starres might merit blame.
Hee made the starres to bee an ayd unto us,
Not (as is fondly dream'd) to helpe undoe us:
(Much lesse, without our fault, to ruinate,
By doome of irrecoverable Fate)
And, if our good Endeavors, use wee will,
Those glorious creatures will be helpfull still
In all our honest wayes: For, they doe stand
To helpe, not hinder us, in God's command;

And, hee not onely rules them by his pow'rs,
But, makes their Glory, servant unto ours.

Influence of the stars

INHERITANCE

The death of one's parents brings children to their inheritance, a shadow of believers receiving their inheritance through God's free and sovereign gift in His Word. This is clear in the Apostle's words in Hebrews 9:15–17, where the death of Christ brings believers to the possession of their blessings.

— "Images," no. 41

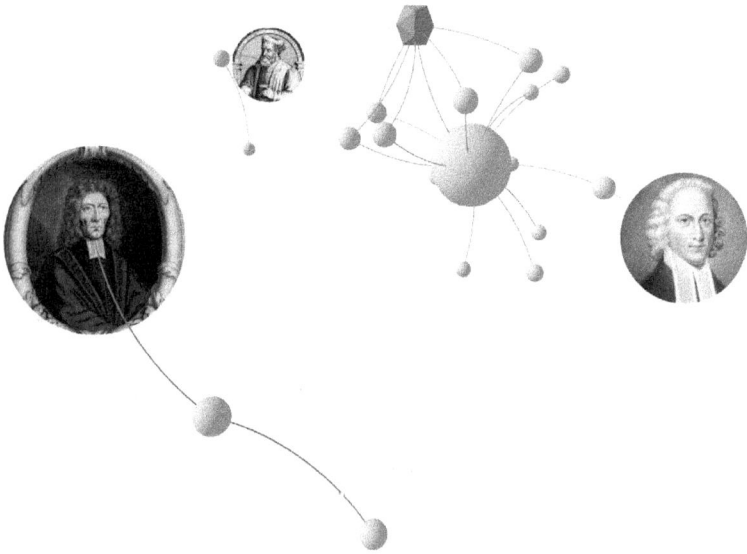

Inheritance

INWARDS

Man's insides are filled with filth and depravity, signi-
fying the inner man— often symbolized by the heart,
bowels, belly, and veins— is rife with spiritual corrup-
tion and wickedness. The many folds and turns of the
bowels demonstrate the myriad complexities, hidden
twists and turns, ploys, and deceptions that exist within
their hearts.

— *"Images," no. 115*

Ill-gotten gains: *'The rapacious kite, overcome by nausea from gluttony, cried out: "Oh, mother! My innards are spilling from my mouth!" She replied: "What is there to complain about? Why do you think these innards are yours, when you live off of stolen goods and spew out only what belongs to others?" (Alciati, 129)*

JUDGMENT DAY

On the Day of Judgment, great assemblies and processions will gather to witness the crowning of the saints in glory with Christ. This is echoed by the grand gatherings at coronations, court cases, executions, weddings, and triumphs. All of these are a mere shadow of what will take place on the Last Day.

— *"Images," no. 180*

Repent, or God will breake the thread,
By which, thy doome hangs o're thy head.
(Wither, 4.5)

Repent, or God will breake the thread,
By which, thy doome hangs o're thy head. (Wither, 4.5)

Marke well this Emblem; and, (when in a thread,
You see the Globe, there, hang above their head,
Who in securitie, beneath it sit)
Observe likewise, the Knife, that threatens it;
The smallnesse of the Twine; and, what a death
Would follow, should it fall on those beneath:
And (having well observ'd it) mind, I pray,
That, which the word about it, there, doth say:
For, it includes a Caveat, which wee need
To entertaine, with a continuall heed.

Though few consider it, wee finde it thus
(Throughout our lives) with ev'ry one of us.
Destruction hangeth in a single thread,
Directly over every Sinner's head.
That Sentence is gone forth, by which wee stand
Condemn'd to suffer death. The dreadfull hand,
Of God's impartiall Iustice, holds a Knife,
Still ready, to cut off our thread of life;
And, 'tis his mercie, that keepes up the Ball
From falling, to the ruine of us all.

Oh! let us minde, how often wee have bin,
Ev'n in the very act of Deadly-sinne,
Whilst this hung over us; and, let us praise,
And love him, who hath yet prolong'd our dayes:
Yea, let our thankfulnesse, bring forth such fruit,
As, to the benefit may somewhat suit:
For, though a sudden-Death may not ensue,
Yet, (since Times Axe, doth every minute hew

The Root of Life) the Tree, e're long, must fall;
And, then perhaps, too late, repent wee shall.

(Quarles, 3.11)

When God provok'd by crying Sins,
To deal his Judgments once begins,
Who shall his furious Wrath abide?
Ev'n he whom his own Hand shall hide.

Upon Fire (Bunyan, 49)

Upon Fire (Bunyan, 49)

Who falls into the fire shall burn with heat;
While those remote scorn from it to retreat.
Yea, while those in it, cry out, O! I burn,
Some farther off those cries to laughter turn.

Comparison

While some tormented are in hell for sin;
On earth some greatly do delight therein.
Yea, while some make it echo with their cry,
Others count it a fable and a lie.

Judgment Day

KERNEL

The husk, chaff, shell and pod of life's mixtures that accompany grace in a saint's heart are separated more and more by affliction, akin to a threshing process which separates the grain from the other parts.

— *"Images," no. 163*

Kernel

LAMP

The flame of a candle or lamp, the way it is lit and its feeble light, the ways of extinguishing it, its vulnerability to a gust of wind, its being extinguished by its own fuel when there is too much of it, the manner of lighting one by another, and its going out when burnt out, all appear to be symbolic of human life. 1 Kings 11:36 states, "That David may always have a lamp before me in Jerusalem." Similarly, 1 Kings 15:4 reads, "Nevertheless for David's sake did the Lord his God give him a lamp in Jerusalem." And 2 Kings 8:19 and 2 Chronicles 21:7 also make mention of this. Job 18:6 states, "His candle shall be put out with him"; Job 21:17 reads, "How oft is the candle of the wicked put out! and how oft cometh their destruction upon them!" Likewise, Proverbs 13:9, Proverbs 24:20 and Proverbs 20:20 refer to this symbol.

— *"Images," no. 52*

Lamp

Lancing a Wound

The spiritual wound of our hearts must be probed to the depths and lanced, even if it is painful, so that it can be cured. The surgeon may appear to heal the wound without causing much distress, but it will not do the patient any good. We must be made aware of the fountain of sin and corruption within us and the dire state we are in by nature, so that a complete and lasting cure can be achieved.

— *"Images," no. 39*

The Infection of the Heart, Acts 5:3 (Harvey, 1)

Whilst thou enclin'st thy Voyce-enveigled ear,
The subtill Serpents Syren-Songs to hear,
Thy heart drinks deadly poyson drawn from Hell,
And with a Vip'rous brood of sin doth swell.

Laws of nature

I am aware that in nature there are certain phenomena that cannot be explained by the regular laws of nature, yet appear to be governed by a specific law for this purpose - to illustrate some spiritual concept, such as the captivation of birds and squirrels by serpents.

— *"Images," no. 16*

Laws of nature

LEVIATHAN

Mystically, Satan is the ruler of all those who are proud,
as the leviathan is a symbol of him.

— *"Images," no. 37*

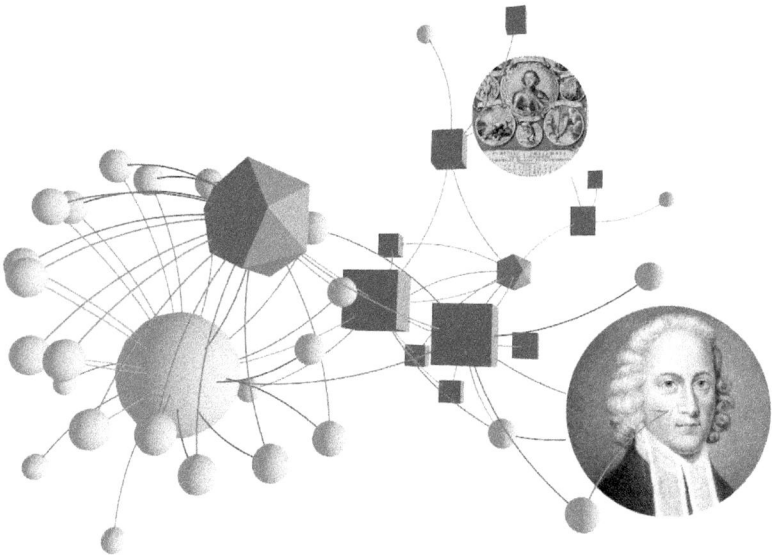

Leviathan

LIGHT

*The beauty and grace of the Spirit of God are repre-
sented by the many colors of light, just as the sweet
spices of the holy anointing oil, the sweet incense, and
the various sweet odors of the different spices and sweet
fruits are used to signify the divine beauty and excellency. The colors of the rainbow, the precious stones of
the breastplate of the high priest, and the foundations
and gates of the New Jerusalem are all symbols of this.
Joseph's coat of many colors is a representation of the
robe of righteousness, and the white light of the sun
is used to signify the moral goodness of God and the
virtues and graces of the saints. The same Spirit of God
is also said to be like a variety of lights, with many gifts
coming from the same source.*

— *"Images," no. 58*

The World's an intricate Meander,
In which a-while poor Christians wander;
But he who has a heav'nly Ray
To guide him, shall not lose his Way.
(Quarles, 4.2)

The Heart replenished with Grace,
Is comforted with heav'nly Rays;
Excludes the World and all its Toys,
Still open to diviner Joys.
(Quarles, 2.14)

Let Your Light Shine Before Men
(Cats and Farlie, 53)

Let Your Light Shine Before Men (Cats and Farlie, 53)

Anxious. tempest toss'd and weary,
To the seaman's gladden'd sight,
'Mid the night-storm, what so cheery
As the gleaming beacon's light?
Though the wild waves wilder threaten,
Calmer now, he steers his way
To the long desir'd haven,
Guided by its friendly ray.
Like unto that beacon, truly,
He of upright heart and mind,
Holding high his light should shew the
Heav'nward way to all mankind.
Christian! lift your light on high then,
Let it shine o'er all, and shew,
In this darksome world to all men,
How and where that men should go.

LIGHT, MORE OF IN A YEAR THAN DARKNESS

God shortens the night, or time of darkness, by refracting the atmosphere and reflecting light in the morning and evening twilight. This symbolizes how God shortens days of tribulation for the sake of His church. He gives light in the darkness through the moon and stars, which represent divine support and comfort for His people in times of trouble. They have guidance and direction from innumerable promises and declarations of God's Word, as from so many stars, and further comfort in God's ordinances in His church, which is the antitype of the moon's light.

— "Images," no. 103

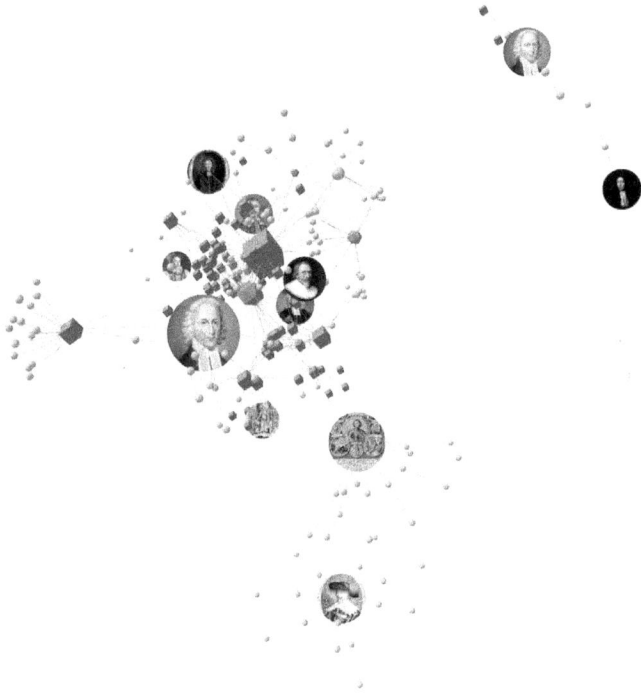

Light more than darkness

LIGHTNING

The intensity of lightning's heat is a reminder of the tremendous might and terror of God's anger.

— *"Images," no. 33*

Lightning

LIGHT OF THE SUN NOT
DIMINISHED BY WIND

The sun's beams cannot be scattered, nor their light broken, by the fiercest winds here on Earth: a fitting image for the light of righteousness from Christ, which cannot be disrupted by the storms and upheavals of life. The sun's light is so pure and subtle, and the luminary itself so far above, that the wind can have no hold on it. This is a clear symbol of the unshakeable spiritual light.

— *"Images," no. 97*

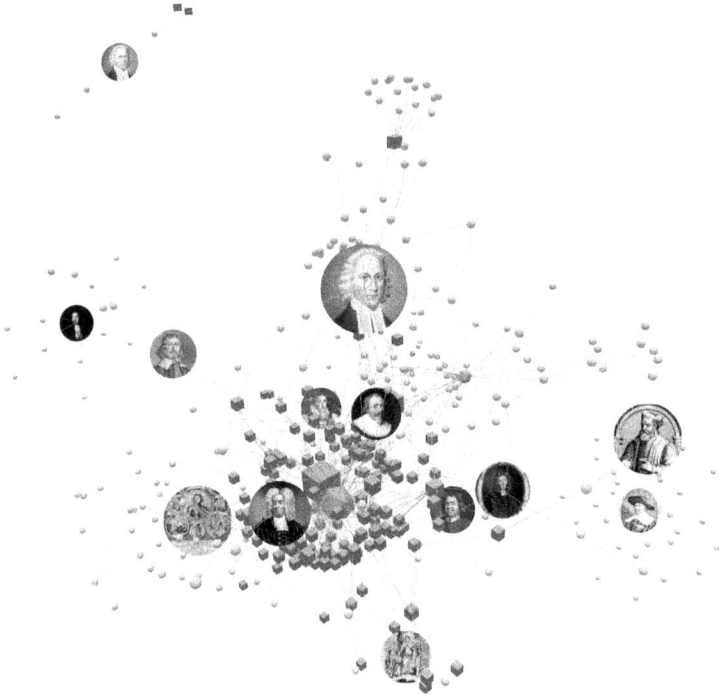

Light of sun and wind

LION

The terror of the lion, tiger, crocodile and other beasts illustrates the sheer horror and astonishment of those that become victims of the devil.

— "Images," no. 131

Do not wrestle with the dead: *As Hector lay dying from the Aeacidean's spear, he could not help but cry out, despite the taunts of his enemies as they prepared chains to bind his feet to his chariot. "Go ahead and do as you please," he said, "even the timid hare will pluck the beard of a lion when his life is no more!" (Alciati, 154)*

LOVE TO WOMEN

Man's nature is constructed in such a way that it is able to form a deep and powerful love for a woman when the right one and opportunity arise, representing the immense love of Christ for His church. Furthermore, a man's jealousy of his beloved's faithlessness is so intense and fierce, mirroring the jealousy of Christ when He sees His people giving their affections to someone else.

— *"Images," no. 32*

(Quarles, 5.15)

The Soul, inspired from above,
Breathes nothing but the Fire of Love;
Fears nothing but that lest her Lover
Should prove to her a wand'ring Rover.

LUMINARIES

The heavens are ablaze with radiant bodies, symbolizing the joy and glory of those who inhabit the heavenly realms. The sun stands for Christ and the moon for the church.

— *"Images," no. 4*

Hee, over all the Starres doth raigne,
That unto Wisdome can attaine.
(Wither, 1.31)

Hee, over all the Starres doth raigne,
That unto Wisdome can attaine. (Wither, 1.31)

I Am not of their Minde, who thinke the Sun,
The Moone, the Planets, and those glorious Lights
Which trim the Sphæres, doe in their Motions run
To no more purpose, then to please our Sights.
Nor for distinguishment of Nights, and Dayes,
Or of the Seasons, and the Times, alone,
Can I suppose the Hand of God displayes
Those many Starres, we nightly gaze upon:
For, both by Reason, and by Common-sense
We know (and often feele) that from above
The Planets have, on us, an Influence;
And, that our Bodies varie, as they move.

Moreover, Holy Writ inferres, that these
Have some such pow'r; ev'n in those Places, where
It names Orion, and the Pleiades;
Which, Starres of much inferiour Nature are.

Yet, hence conclude not, therefore, that the Minde
Is by the Starres constrained to obey
Their Influence; or, so by them inclin'd,
That, by no meanes resist the same we may.
For, though they forme the Bodies temp'rature,
(And though the Minde inclineth after that)
By Grace another Temper we procure,
Which guides the Motions of Supposed Fate.
The Soule of Man is nobler then the Sphæres;
And, if it gaine the Place which may be had,
Not here alone on Earth, the Rule it beares,
But, is the Lord, of all that God hath made.

Be wise in him; and, if just cause there bee,
The Sunne and Moone, shall stand and wayt on thee.

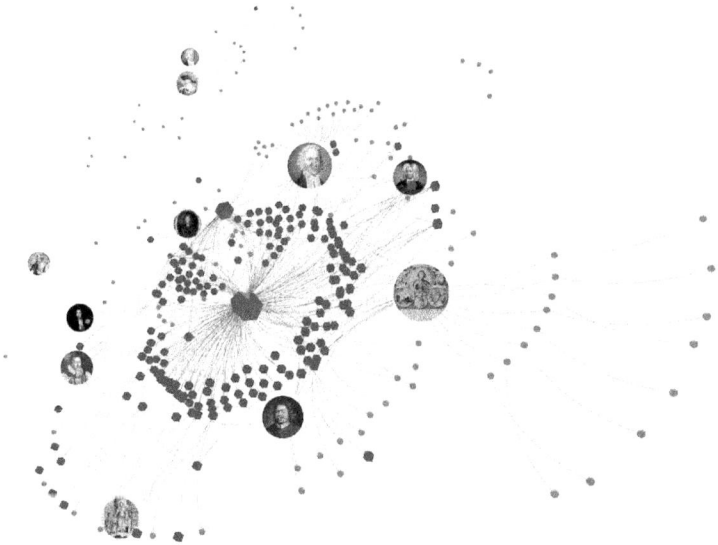

Luminaries

Marriage

The union of marriage is seen as a great mystery, symbolizing the bond between Christ and the Church (Ephesians 5:32). By "mystery" we can understand to mean something of a spiritual nature. If God intended this to represent something spiritual, why not many other aspects of human society and the world?

— *"Images," no. 12*

They, best injoy their Hearts desires,
In whom, Love, kindles mutuall-fires.
(Wither, 3.44)

Where Lovers fitly matched be,
In mutuall-duties, they agree.
(Wither, 3.28)

Thy seeming-Lover, false will bee,
And, love thy Money, more than Thee.
(Wither, 2.21)

Of the Spouse of Christ
(Bunyan, 44)

Of the Spouse of Christ (Bunyan, 44)

Who's this that cometh from the wilderness,
Like smokey pillars thus perfum'd with myrrh,
Leaning upon her dearest in distress,
Led into's bosom by the Comforter?
She's clothed with the sun, crowned with twelve stars,
The spotted moon her footstool she hath made.
The dragon her assaults, fills her with jars,
Yet rests she under her Beloved's shade,
But whence was she? what is her pedigree?
Was not her father a poor Amorite?
What was her mother but as others be,
A poor, a wretched, and a sinful Hittite.
Yea, as for her, the day that she was born,
As loathsome, out of doors they did her cast;
Naked and filthy, stinking and forlorn;
This was her pedigree from first to last.
Nor was she pitied in this estate,
All let her lie polluted in her blood:
None her condition did commiserate,
There was no heart that sought to do her good.
Yet she unto these ornaments is come,
Her breasts are fashioned, her hair is grown;
She is made heiress of the best kingdom;
All her indignities away are blown.
Cast out she was, but now she home is taken,
Naked (sometimes), but now, you see, she's cloth'd;
Now made the darling, though before forsaken,
Barefoot, but now as princes' daughters shod.
Instead of filth, she now has her perfumes;
Instead of ignominy, her chains of gold:
Instead of what the beauty most consumes,
Her beauty's perfect, lovely to behold.
Those that attend and wait upon her be
Princes of honour, clothed in white array;
Upon her head's a crown of gold, and she
Eats wheat, honey, and oil, from day to day.
For her beloved, he's the high'st of all,

The only Potentate, the King of kings:
Angels and men do him Jehovah call,
And from him life and glory always springs.
He's white and ruddy, and of all the chief:
His head, his locks, his eyes, his hands, and feet,
Do, for completeness, out-go all belief;
His cheeks like flowers are, his mouth most sweet.
As for his wealth, he is made heir of all;
What is in heaven, what is on earth is his:
And he this lady his joint-heir doth call,
Of all that shall be, or at present is.
Well, lady, well, God has been good to thee;
Thou of an outcast, now art made a queen.
Few, or none, may with thee compared be,
A beggar made thus high is seldom seen.
Take heed of pride, remember what thou art
By nature, though thou hast in grace a share,
Thou in thyself dost yet retain a part
Of thine own filthiness; wherefore beware.

Honoring marriage: *The viper stands at the shore of the sea, aflame with love, and vomits out poisonous bile. He sends out loud hisses, hoping to draw in the murena fish. At the same time, the murena yearns for the embrace of her partner. Marriage is a sacred thing, and each partner owes loyalty to the other. (Alciati, 192)*

MILDEW

From the moment a seed is sown in the ground, it is exposed to numerous dangers that can destroy it. Birds may peck it up, worms may eat it, the sun may scorch it, weeds or thorns may choke it, and honey-dews may damage it when it is grown tall and the fruit is still green. Similarly, the soul is exposed to various trials and temptations, some of which may prove too much for it. Of all these, however, the greatest danger is that of spiritual pride brought on by great worldly and spiritual prosperity. Even when a person has arrived at a great height in their faith, the sweet joys and comfort they experience can bring them into a state of languishing sorrow if they become too proud.

— *"Images," no. 165*

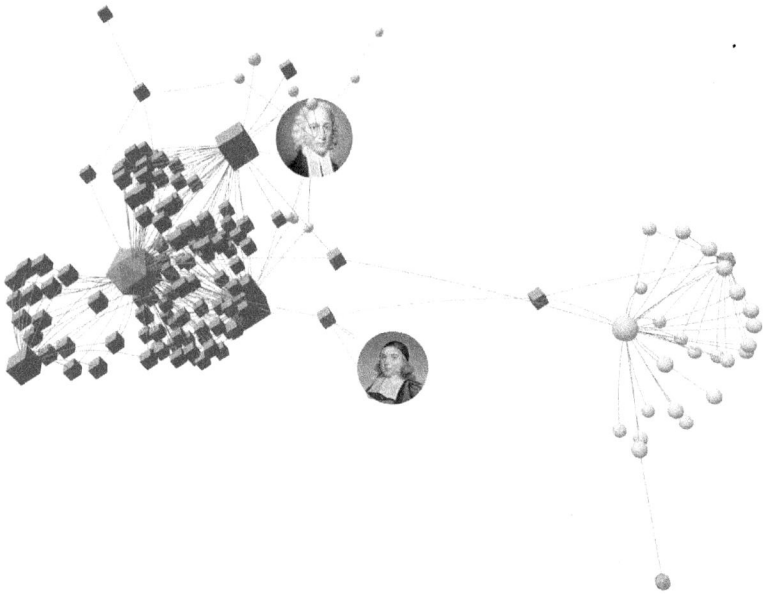

Mildew and plants

MILK

The Word of God is represented by milk, symbolizing its purity and sweetness. It is the nourishment of the saints in this life, as they are children in the faith. Its whiteness and purity signify holiness, which is the natural delight of a spiritual nature, satisfying the spiritual appetite.

— *"Images," no. 113*

Concerning those who degenerate: *You have ruined a promising start with a disappointing result, behaving like a she-goat who knocks over the bucket of her own milk, spilling her own wealth. (Alciati, 141)*

MIRACLES

God has made the material world subordinate to the spiritual and moral world, sometimes setting aside the ordinary course of things to serve the purpose. This is seen in miracles, as when the sun stood still in Joshua's time. To demonstrate the importance of the spiritual world, there are some things in the ordinary course of events that are quite different from the ordinary laws of nature, to symbolize spiritual matters.

— "Images," no. 43

Miracles

MOLE

The mole does not open his eyes until he is dead. A wicked man does not believe in Hell until he is in it. Tacitus wrote that the mole, after living underground for a long time, starts to see when he dies. This is like a wicked, earthly-minded man who does not see or think of Heaven or Hell until he is close to judgement. Then, he begins to understand what he could not be convinced of before.

— "Images," no. 179

Of the Mole in the Ground (Bunyan, 20)

Of the Mole in the Ground (Bunyan, 20)

The mole's a creature very smooth and slick,
She digs i' th' dirt, but 'twill not on her stick;
So's he who counts this world his greatest gains,
Yet nothing gets but's labour for his pains.
Earth's the mole's element, she can't abide
To be above ground, dirt heaps are her pride;
And he is like her who the worldling plays,
He imitates her in her work and ways.
Poor silly mole, that thou should'st love to be
Where thou nor sun, nor moon, nor stars can see.
But O! how silly's he who doth not care
So he gets earth, to have of heaven a share!

MOON

The moon, a representation of earthly glory and all the good of this world, is ever-changing, waxing and waning. It is rarely in its full splendor for long, and when it is, it is often eclipsed. Its radiance is fleeting and it is near its decline when it is at its brightest.

— *"Images," no. 139*

Shee shall increase in glory, still,
Untill her light, the world, doth fill.
(Wither, 2.49)

Shee shall increase in glory, still,
Untill her light, the world, doth fill. (Wither, 2.49)

What in this Emblem, that mans meanings were,
Who made it first, I neither know nor care;
For, whatsoere, he purposed, or thought,
To serve my purpose, now it shall be taught;
Who, many times, before this Taske is ended,
Must picke out Moralls, where was none intended.

This knot of Moones (or Crescents) crowned thus,
Illustrate may a Mystery to us,
Of pious use (and, peradventure, such,
As from old Hieroglyphicks, erres not much)
Old-times, upon the Moone, three names bestow'd;
Because, three diverse wayes, her selfe she show'd:
And, in the sacred-bookes, it may be showne,
That holy-Church, was figur'd by the Moone.

Then, these three Moones in one, may intimate
The holy-Churches threefold blest estate.
The Moone, still, biding in our Hemisphære,
May typifie the Church, consisting, here,
Of men, yet living: when she shewes her light
Among us here, in portions of the night;
The Church it figures, as consist she may
Of them, whose bodies in the Grave doe stay;
And, whose blest spirits, are ascended thither,
Where Soule and Body meet, at last, together.
But, when the Moone is hidden from our eyes,
The Church-triumphant, then, she signifies;
Which, is a Crescent yet, that, some, and some,
Must grow, till all her parts together come:

And, then, this Moone shall beames, at full, display;
Lord, hasten this great Coronation-day.

Wasted efforts: *The dog looked up at the moon, as if it were a reflection of himself. He thought he saw another dog in the sky, so he yelped; yet the wind carried his cries away, and the moon continued on its journey, unheeding. (Alciati, 165)*

MORNING

The morning of the day and the spring of the year are striking emblems of the start of the church's glorious times.

— *"Images," no. 111*

Upon the Sun's Reflection Upon the Clouds in
a Fair Morning (Bunyan, 16)

Upon a Lowering Morning
(Bunyan, 12)

Look yonder, ah! methinks mine eyes do see
Clouds edged with silver, as fine garments be;
They look as if they saw that golden face
That makes black clouds most beautiful with
   grace.
Unto the saints' sweet incense, or their prayer,
These smoky curdled clouds I do compare.
For as these clouds seem edged, or laced with
   gold,
Their prayers return with blessings manifold.

Well, with the day I see the clouds appear,
And mix the light with darkness everywhere;
This threatening is, to travellers that go
Long journeys, slabby rain they'll have, or
   snow.
Else, while I gaze, the sun doth with his
   beams
Belace the clouds, as 'twere with bloody
   streams;
This done, they suddenly do watery grow,
And weep, and pour their tears out where
they go.

Comparison

Thus 'tis when gospel light doth usher in
To us both sense of grace and sense of sin;
Yea, when it makes sin red with Christ's
   blood,
Then we can weep till weeping does us good.

MOUNTAINS

Nothing on this Earth can reach the heavens, not even the highest of things, for all are too small. It may appear that some things ascend to the stars, like the tips of mountains that seem to touch the sky. But when we approach them, we are still just as far away from the heavenly things as we were before. Therefore, nothing here on Earth can bring us true joy, though some of the greatest things may appear to do so. Those that have experienced them, however, find that they are as far from joy as those in a lower state of life.

— "Images," no. 175

Mountains

NAMES

If God had such regard for people's names so that they could represent something special about them, why do we presume He would not do the same with spiritual matters, such that they could be signified and symbolized through them? It appears that the Holy Spirit's purpose is to instruct us in divine secrets through the names given to people without any special orders from God or intention from those who gave the name, as is seen in Hebrews 7:2. It is not a trivial matter for the world to be created to signify divine things.

— *"Images," nos. 30, 132*

Names

NIGHT, THE TIME OF BEASTS OF PREY RANGING AND DEVOURING

In the evening, the predators roam and wreak havoc, but when the light of day arrives, they retreat to their lairs. Likewise, in the moral darkness of our time, the devil prowls, like a lion, seeking to devour the innocent; yet when the Sun of Righteousness rises, he will be banished to the depths of the abyss. Psalms 104:21–22.

— *"Images," no. 211*

The bat: *Only in the evening does it take flight, its vision dimmed in the light. Bearing wings, yet possessing the traits of a mouse, the bat is seen in diverse ways. For some, it is a symbol of debtors, hidden and afraid of being found out. Philosophers, too, are likened to the bat, for while they search for the divine, they are blind to the truth and misguided. Lastly, the shrewd who try to stay on both sides of the fence, yet are trusted by none. (Alciati, 62)*

NURSING OF A CHILD, IMAGE OF NOURISHING GRACE IN THE HEART

Those who have tasted the sweetness of Christ's Word and grace will long for more of it. The Word of God is likened to a mother's milk, providing nourishment for a newborn soul. Christians in this world, being in an imperfect state, need to grow and the Word of God is the proper means for this. The Apostle notes that those who have experienced the grace of the Lord Jesus Christ and the sweetness of the gospel of the Word of his grace will have an appetite for the Word and desire to grow.

— WJE, 11:139

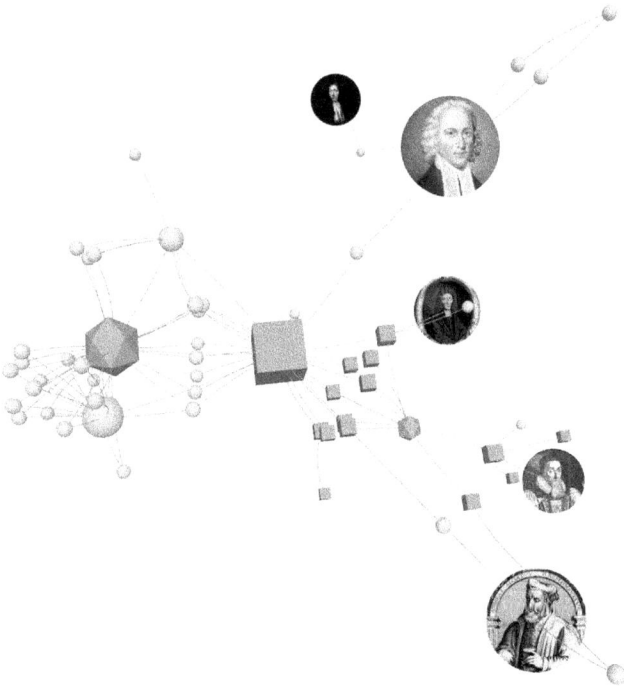

Nursing

OWLS

The doleful cries of owls and dragons fill the night air,
a reminder of the misery and wailing of the spirits con-
demned to darkness. The Scripture speaks of these crea-
tures in Micah 1:8, "I will make a wailing like dragons,
and mourning as the owls"; and Job 30:28–29, "I went
mourning without the sun: I stood up and I cried in the
congregation. I am a brother to dragons, and a compan-
ion to owls." The sorrowful sounds of these birds of the
night symbolize the suffering of the damned.

— *"Images," no. 204*

Upon the Sight of an Owl in the Twilight (Hall, 65)

What a strange melancholic life doth this creature lead, to hide her head all day long in an ivy-bush and at night, when all other birds are at rest, to fly abroad and vent her harsh notes! I know not why the ancients have sacred this bird to wisdom, except it be for her safe closeness and singular perspicacity; that when other domestical and airy creatures are blind, she only hath inward light to discern the least objects for her own advantage. Surely thus much wit they have taught us in her, that he is the wisest man that would have least to do with the multitude; that no life is so safe as the obscure; that retiredness, if it have less comfort, yet less danger and vexation; lastly, that he is truly wise who sees by a light of his own when the rest of the world sit in an ignorant and confused darkness, unable to apprehend any truth save by the helps of an outward illumination.

Had this owl come forth in the daytime, how had all the little birds flocked wondering about her, to see her uncouth visage, to hear her untuned notes! She likes her estate never the worse, but pleaseth herself in her own quiet reservedness. It is not for a wise man to be much affected with the censures of the rude and unskillful vulgar, but to hold fast unto his own well chosen and well fixed resolutions. Every fool knows what is wont to be done, but what is best to be done is known only to the wise.

Upon Sight of a Bat and Owl (Hall, 120)

These night-birds are glad to hide their heads all day, and if by some violence they be unseasonably forced out of their secrecy, how are they followed and beaten by the birds of the day! With us men it is contrary: the sons of darkness do with all eagerness of malice pursue the children of the light [John 12:38; 1 Thess. 5:5] and drive them into corners and make a prey of them. The opposition is alike, but the advantage lies on the worse side. Is it for that the spiritual light is no less hateful to those children of darkness than the natural night is to those cheerful birds of the day? Or is it for that the sons of darkness, challenging no less propriety in the world than the fowls do in the lightsome air, abhor and wonder at the conscionable as strange and uncouth? Howsoever, as these bats and owls were made for the night, being accordingly shaped foul and ill-favored, so we know these vicious men (however they may please themselves) have in them a true deformity fit to be shrouded in darkness, and as they delight in the work of darkness so they are justly reserved to a state of darkness.

Hee that is blind, will nothing see,
What light soe're about him bee.
(Wither, 4.45)

By Studie, and by Watchfulnesse,
The Jemme of Knowledge, we possesse.
(Wither, 2.17)

We best shall quiet clamorous Thronges,
When, we our selves, can rule our Tongues.
(Wither, 2.1)

Before thou bring thy Workes to Light,
Consider on them, in the Night.
(Wither, 1.9)

PLANTS

The grass and other vegetation, flourishing green and pleasant, appear to be rejoicing, blossoming, and bearing fruit due to the heavens, rain, wind, and the sun's light and heat. This is a vivid representation of our spiritual welfare being dependent on God's grace and the outpouring of His Holy Spirit. The Old Testament often uses these images to portray spiritual matters, and this is seen in Scripture.

— *"Images," no. 13*

Upon the strange means of preserving the life of Vegetables (Flavel, 4.8)

I observe that plants and herbs are sometimes killed by frosts, and yet without frosts they would neither live nor thrive; they are sometimes drowned by water, and yet without water they cannot subsist; they are refreshed and cheered by the heat of the Sun, and yet that heat sometimes kills and scorches them up. Thus lives my soul, troubles and afflictions seem to kill all its comforts; and yet without these, its comforts could not live. The Sun-blasts of prosperity sometimes refresh me, and yet those Sun-blasts are the likeliest way to wither me; By what seeming contradictions is the life of my spirit preserved? what a mistery? what a Paradox is the life of a Christian?

Truth, oft oppressed, wee may see,
But, quite supprest it cannot bee.
(Wither, 3.38)

Truth, oft oppressed, wee may see,
But, quite supprest it cannot bee. (Wither, 3.38)

This is that fruitfull Plant, which when it growes,
Where wholesome Water in abundance flowes,
Was, by the Psalmist, thought a likely Tree,
The Emblem, of a blessed-man, to bee:
For, many wayes, it fitly typifies,
The Righteous-man, with his proprieties;
And, those true Vertues, which doe helpe increase
His growing, in the state of Blessednesse.

The Palme, (in this our Emblem, figur'd, thus)
Depressed with a Stone, doth shew to us
The pow'r of Truth: For, as this Tree doth spread,
And thrive the more, when weights presse downe the head;
So, Gods eternall Truth (which all the pow'r
And spight of Hell, did labour to devoure)
Sprung high, and flourished the more, thereby,
When Tyrants crush'd it, with their crueltie.
And, all inferiour Truths, the same will doe,
According as they make approaches to
The best Perfection; or, as they conduce
To God's due praise, or some such pious use.

Lord, still, preserve this Truth's integritie,
Although on ev'ry side, the wicked prie,
To spie how they may disadvantage it.
Yea, Lord, though Sinners in high place doe sit,
(As David saith) yet, let them not oppresse
Thy Veritie, by their imperiousnesse.
But, make both Her, and her Professors, bide
The Test, like Silver seven times purifide.

That, all Truths lovers, may with comfort see,
Shee may deprest, but, not, oppressed bee.

On momentary happiness: *A gourd sprouted close to a lofty pine tree, and it grew quickly, its foliage becoming thick. It wound its branches around the pine and even outgrew it. The gourd thought it was superior to other trees. The pine spoke to it then: "Your glory is fleeting, for winter will soon come and destroy you." (Alciati, 125)*

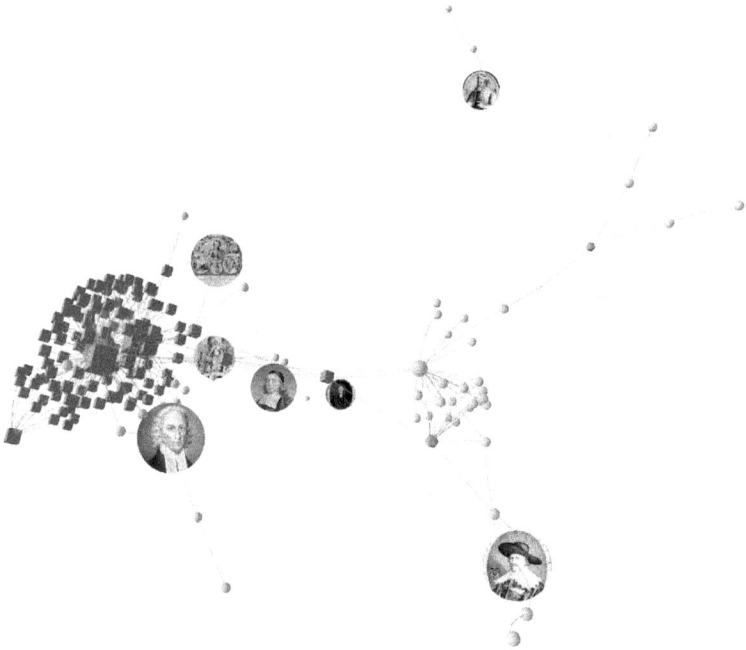

Plants

PLOWING

God, like a wise farmer, tends to His people. He plows the hard ground, softening it and making it even so that it can receive His seed. He only afflicts them as much as is necessary to prepare them for spiritual good. He provides what is best for them, bestowing blessings that are suited to their needs. The husbandman has discretion in managing his field, and God, the source of all wisdom and prudence, has even more in dealing with His people.

— *"Images," no. 44*

Ere thou a fruitfull-Cropp shalt see,
Thy ground must plough'd and harro'wd be.
(Wither, 3.10)

The Husbandman, doth sow the Seeds;
And, then, on Hope, till Harvest, feeds.
(Wither, 2.44)

The Tilling of the Heart, Ezekiel 36:9
(Harvey, 27)

The Husbandman, doth sow the Seeds;
And, then, on Hope, till Harvest, feeds. (Wither, 2.44)

The painfull Husbandman, with sweaty browes,
Consumes in labour many a weary day:
To breake the stubborne earth, he digs and ploughes,
And, then, the Corne, he scatters on the clay:
When that is done, he harrowes in the Seeds,
And, by a well-cleans'd Furrow, layes it drye:
He, frees it from the Wormes, the Moles, the Weeds;
He, on the Fences, also hath an eye.
And, though he see the chilling Winter, bring
Snowes, Flouds, and Frosts, his Labours to annoy;
Though blasting-windes doe nip them in the Spring,
And, Summers Meldewes, threaten to destroy:
Yea, though not onely Dayes, but Weekes, they are
(Nay, many Weekes, and, many Moneths beside)
In which he must with payne, prolong his care,
Yet, constant in his hopes he doth abide.
For this respect, Hope's Emblem, here, you see
Attends the Plough, that men beholding it,
May be instructed, or else minded be,
What Hopes, continuing Labours, will befit.
Though, long thou toyled hast, and, long attended
About such workings as are necessary;
And, oftentimes, ere fully they are ended,
Shalt finde thy paines in danger to miscarry:
Yet, be not out of hope, nor quite dejected:
For, buryed Seeds will sprout when Winter's gone;
Unlikelier things are many times effected;
And, God brings helpe, when men their best have done.

Yea, they that in Good-workes their life imploy;
Although, they sowe in teares, shall reape in joy.

Plowing

POISONOUS ANIMALS

Serpents and spiders, creatures that are both venomous and harmful, often seek to conceal themselves or lurk in secret spots. In this way, they are symbolic of devils and the sinful desires of mankind.

— *"Images," no. 127*

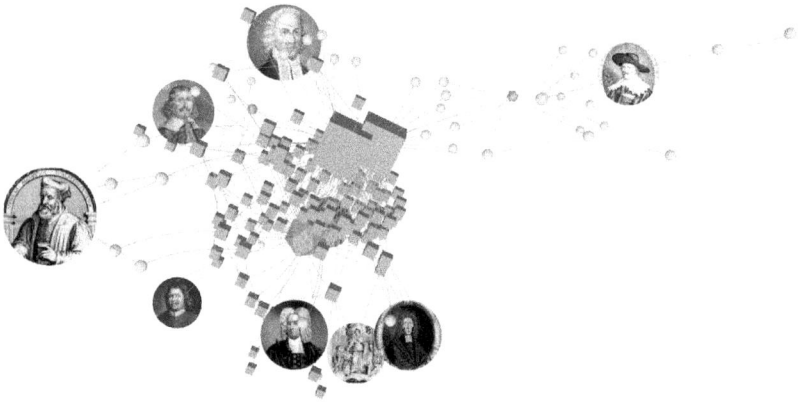

Poisonous animals

PRUNING

Husbandmen take to trimming their trees after winter has passed, just prior to the start of spring, for the sake of new life and joy. Similarly, God wounds His saints before reviving them, after long periods of dormancy, to cleanse them and get them ready for renewal and solace. He leads them into grief and speaks tenderly to them (Hosea 2:14).

— *"Images," no. 172*

Upon the Sight of a Tree Lopped (Hall, 116)

In the lopping of these trees experience and good husbandry hath taught men to leave one bough still growing in the top the better to draw up the sap from the root. The like wisdom is fit to be observed in censures which are intended altogether for reformation, not for destruction. So must they be inflicted that the patient be not utterly discouraged and stripped of hope and comfort, but that while he suffereth he may feel his good tendered and his amendment both aimed at and expected. Oh God, if Thou shouldest deal with me as I deserve, Thou shouldest not only shred my boughs but cut down my stock and stock up my root. And yet Thou dost but prune my superfluous branches and cherishest the rest. How unworthy am I of this mercy if, while Thou art thus indulgent unto me, I be severe and cruel to others perhaps less ill-deserving than myself!

No Inward Griefe, nor outward Smart,
Can overcome a Patient-Heart.
(Wither, 1.28)

No Inward Griefe, nor outward Smart, Can overcome a Patient-Heart. (Wither, 1.28)

Some Trees, when Men oppresse their Aged Heads,
(With waighty Stones) they fructifie the more;
And, when upon some Herbs, the Gard'ner treads,
They thrive and prosper, better then before:
So, when the Kings of Ægypt did oppresse
The Sonnes of Jacob, through their Tyrannies;
Their Numbers, every day, did more encrease,
Till they grew greater then their Enemies.

So, when the Jewes and Gentiles, joyn'd their Powre
The Lord, and his Annoynted, to withstand;
(With raging Furie, lab'ring to devoure
And roote the Gospel, out of ev'ry Land)
The more they rag'd, conspired, and envy'd,
The more they slander'd, scorn'd, and murthered;
The more, the Faithfull, still, were multiply'd:
And, still, the further, their Profession spred.
Yea, so it spred, that quite it overthrew
Ev'n Tyranny it selfe; that, at the last,
The Patience of the Saints, most pow'rfull grew,
And Persecutions force, to ground was cast.

The selfe-same Pow'r, true Patience, yet retaines,
And (though a thousand Suff'rings wound the same)
She still hath Hope enough to ease her paynes;
That Hope, which keepeth off, all Feare and Shame:
For, 'tis not Hunger, Cold, nor Fire, nor Steele,
Nor all the Scornes or Slanders, we can heare,
Nor any Torment, which our Flesh can feele,
That conquers us; but, our owne Trayt'rous Feare.

Where, Honest Mindes, and Patient Hearts, are Mates
They grow victorious, in their Hardest-Fates.

Rain

The sustenance of mankind descends from the sky in the form of rain. Our clothing, homes and even our bodies are mostly made of that same rain. This reminds us of the source of our blessings and that we are sustained by the gifts of God's generosity, reliant on Him entirely.

— *"Images," no. 196*

With Patience, I the Storme sustaine;
For, Sun-shine still doth follow Raine.
(Wither, 1.26)

With Patience, I the Storme sustaine;
For, Sun-shine still doth follow Raine. (Wither, 1.26)

The little Squirrell, hath no other Food
Then that which Natures thrifty hand provides;
And, in purveying up and downe the Wood,
She many cold wet Stormes, for that, abides.
She lyes not heartlesse in her Mossie Dray,
Nor feareth to adventure through the Raine;
But skippeth out, and beares it as she may,
Untill the Season waxeth calme againe.

Right thus, have I and others, often far'd;
For, when we first into the World were brought,
We found but little, for our Use prepar'd,
Save that, which by Hard-Labour, must be sought.
In many Stormes, unheeded, we are faine
To seeke out needfull things; and, smilingly
To jest, at what some others would complaine:
That, none might laugh at our Necessity.
Yea, some have liv'd on Huskes, whil'st others fed
On that which was their Labours due Reward;
And, were pursu'd (till they almost were dead)
Without the Worlds Compassion or Regard.
Yet, by Enduring, they out liv'd the Blast
Of Adverse-Fortune; and, with good successe,
(Expecting calmer Seasons) at the last,
Arrived at the Port of Happinesse.

Their Suffring-much, hath made their Suffrings none;
And brought forth Hopes, by which, perceive they may,
That Nights have but their Turnes; and (they once gone)
Their Darkenesse, makes much welcomer, the Day.

All Griefe shall have an ending, I am sure;
And, therefore, I with Patience, will Endure.

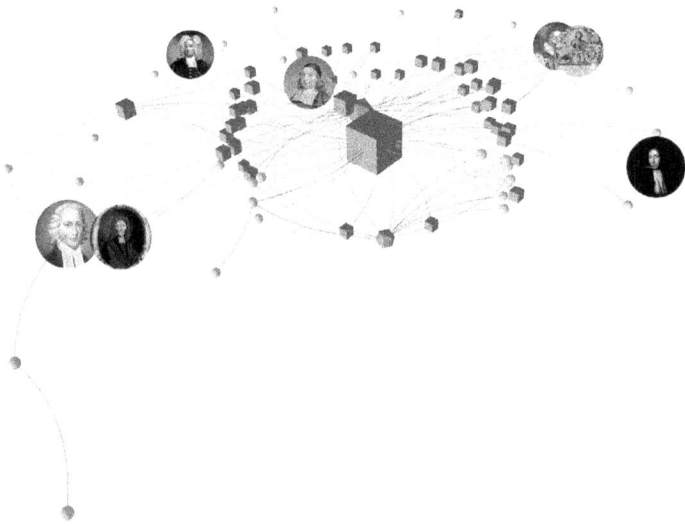

Rain

RAINBOW

God has revealed that nature's works are intended to symbolize and indicate spiritual matters, particularly in the case of the rainbow.

— *"Images," no. 55*

Let none in troublous times repine;
For, after Stormes, the Sun will shine.
(Wither, 4.32)

Let none in troublous times repine;
For, after Stormes, the Sun will shine. (Wither, 4.32)

Discourage not your selves, although you see
The weather blacke, and stormes prolonged be.
What though it fiercely raines, and thunders loud?
Behold, there is a Raine-bow in the Cloud,
Wherein, a trustfull promise may be found,
That, quite, your little-worlds, shall not be drown'd.
The Sun-shine, through the foggy mists appeare,
The lowring Skie, begins againe to cleare;
And, though the Tempest, yet, your eyes affright,
Faire weather may befall you, long ere night.

Such comfort speakes our Emblem, unto those,
Whom stormie Persecution doth enclose;
And, comforts him, that's for the present sad,
With hopes, that better seasons may bee had.
There is nor trouble, sorrow, nor distresse,
But mitigation hath, or some release.
Long use, or time, the storme away will turne,
Else, Patience makes it better to be borne.
Yea, sorrowes lowring dayes, will come and goe,
As well as prosp'rous houres of Sunshine doe;
And, when 'tis past, the paine that went before,
Will make the following pleasure seeme the more.
For, hee, hath promis'd, whom we may beleeve,
His blessing, unto those that mourne and grieve;
And, that, though sorrow much dejects their head,
In ev'ry need, wee shall be comforted.

This promise I beleeve; in ev'ry griefe,

Performe it, Lord, and helpe my unbeliefe:

So, others viewing how thou cheerest mee,
Shall, in all sorrows, put their trust in thee.

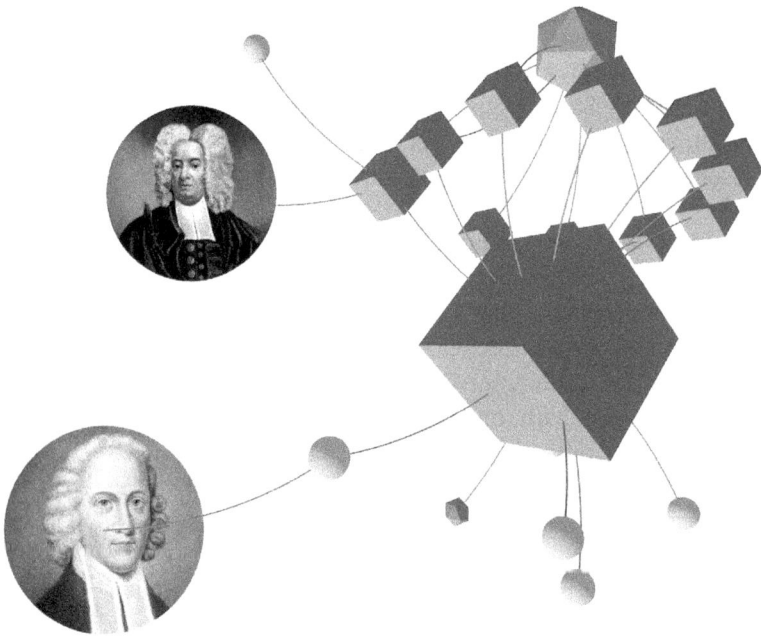

Rainbow

RAVENS

Ravens that feed on carrion appear to be like devils who feast upon the souls of the dead. The corruption of such souls is more abhorrent than the stench of a decaying corpse. The devil takes pleasure in them, like a carcass is a reminder of a wicked soul in an abominable state. Ravens do not consume an animal until it is dead, and the devil does not take hold of the wicked until they are dead. The body in such a state is a representation of a soul in eternal death.

— *"Images," no. 61*

Killing a Crow (Out of a Window) in a Hog's Trough, and Immediately Tracing the Ensuing Reflection With a Pen Made of One of His Quills (Boyle, 5.1)

Long and patiently did I wait for this unlucky crow, wallowing in the sluttish trough, (whose sides kept him a great while out of the reach of my gun,) and gorging himself with no less greediness, than the very swinish proprietaries of the feast; till at length having guzzled and croaked enough, when by hovering over his beloved dainties he had raised himself high enough to prompt me to fire at him, my no less unexpected than fatal shot in a moment struck him down, and turning the scene of his delight into that of his pangs, made him abruptly alter his note, and change his triumphant chant for a dismal and tragick noise. This method is not unusual to divine justice towards brawny and incorrigible sinners, whose souls no less black than this inauspicious bird's feathers, do wear already the livery of the prince of darkness, and with greediness do the works of it; whose delights are furnished (as the feasts of crows are by carrion) by their own filthy lusts, or other people's faults, and who by the oaths and curses wherewith they offend Christian ears while they live, and by the ill odour they leave behind them when they are dead, do but too much justifie my resembling them to these hateful creatures.

Such sensual and obdurate epicures God oftentimes suffers to run on their long career in paths of their own chusing, without checking them in the fruition of those joys, which are to be their only portion, till at length their iniquity filling up the determinate measure, He cuts them off in the height of their enjoyments. And employing oftentimes their own sins for their executioners, He precipitates them headlong from the pinacle of their delights, into the bottomless pit, which one of their predecessors (the rich man in the Parable) called, as he sadly found it, the Place of Turment, where the luscious sweets of sin are so dearly reckoned for, that their sense sadly convinces them of (what their sensuality kept them from believing) the folly of gaining any thing at the rate of losing their own souls. Thus the insolent Philistines found themselves ill protected by their vainly celebrated God, and his much stronger temple, though in the latter there were thousands of them, without any enemy but one, that they had sent for to be a friend to their mirth. For in the very midst of all the triumphs of a solemn festival, whilst they were insulting over captive Samson's blindness, they could not see their own approaching destiny, though it were then so near that the next fit of laughter had not time to pass their mouths, ere an unexpected vengeance (the provoked Deity lending an omnipotent arm to Sampson's hand) confounded in one ruine, the Idol with the worshippers, and suddenly turn'd the whole temple into an altar, with which the Priests themselves fell surprised sacrifices to that tragical solemnity. Thus the revelling Belshazzar, in the midst of his magnificent and royal feast, saw an intruding hand, which by its manner of appearing, as well as by what it wrote, was able to mar the supper, without impairing the dainties. And that monarch, whom even a siege could not reduce below a condition of feasting, though he were carouzing in the consecrated cups, had such a brimmer of trembling put into his hand, as both presaged, and perchance began, the destiny approaching him under the designs of the noble Cyrus, whose conquering sword, guided by Providence, and made the sword of Justice, did, that very same night, let out his wine, and blood, and life together.

Upon the Same Subject (Boyle, 5.2)

'Tis hard, upon such an occasion, to avoid making some reflections upon the mutability of worldly conditions! how little did this crow imagine, a quarter of an hour since, that in so short a time, his body should be as senseless, and as stinking carrion, as that he was wont to feed it with: that his feathers should wear so unlucky a kind of mourning for his destruction, and that I should write his epitaph with one of his own quills! sure, since a few minutes can turn the healthiest bodies into breathless carcasses, and put those very things, which we had principally relied on, into the hands of our enemies, it were little less than madness to repose a distrustless trust in these transitory possessions, or treacherous advantages, which we enjoy but by so fickle a tenure. No; we must never venture to wander far from God, upon the presumption that death is far enough from us; but rather in the very height of our jollity we should endeavour to remember, that they who feast themselves to day, may themselves prove feasts for the worms tomorrow.

Just vengeance: *A raven clutched a scorpion in its claws, lifting him high into the sky, intent on satisfying its own hunger. But the scorpion, injecting its venom into the bird's body, caused it to plummet into the depths of the sea. A humorous sight: the one who had intended to destroy another was himself destroyed, ending his own life by his own deviousness. (Alciati, 173)*

Upon the Sight of a Raven (Hall, 68)

I cannot see that bird but I must needs think of Elijah and wonder less at the miracle of his faith than of his provision [1 Kings 17:2-7]. It was a strong belief that carried him into a desolate retiredness to expect food from ravens. This fowl, we know is ravenous; all is too little that he can forage for himself; and the prophet's reason must needs suggest to him that in a dry barren desert bread and flesh must be great dainties, yet he goes aside to expect victuals from that purveyance. He knew this fowl to be no less greedy than unclean, unclean as in Law and in the nature of his feed. What is his ordinary prey but loathsome carrion? Yet since God had appointed him this cater, he stands not upon the nice points of a fastidious squeamishness but confidently depends upon that uncouth provision; and accordingly these unlikely purveyors bring him bread and flesh in the morning and bread and flesh in the evening.

Not one of those hungry ravens could swallow one morsel of those viands which were sent by them to a better mouth. The River of Cherith sooner failed him than the tender of their services. No doubt Elijah's stomach was often up before his incurious diet came, when expecting from the mouth of his cave out of what coast of heaven these his servitors might be descried. Upon the sight of them he magnified with a thankful heart the wonderful goodness and truth of his God and was nourished more with his faith than with his food. Oh God, how infinite is Thy providence, wisdom, power! We creatures are not what we are but what Thou wilt have us; when Thy turn is to be served, we have none of our own. Give me but faith and do what Thou wilt.

Ravens

REMEDY FROM EVIL, WHY OUR MERCIES ARE BESTOWED AS SUCH

In accordance with the great plan of God's grace towards mankind, many of our outward mercies and good things are bestowed as a means of deliverance, protection, or remedy from some calamity or other that we may be exposed to. Thus, God provides us with clothing not only to cover our nakedness, but to make us look beautiful. He gives us food to keep us from famishing and satisfy our hunger, as well as to bring us pleasure. He provides us with drink to quench our thirst, and means to defend us from the elements and wild beasts. He gives us breath to keep us alive, and sleep to rest us when we are weary. He even provides us with light to guide us in the darkness and medicine to heal us when we are sick. However, these mercies are not just a means of protection from the evils we face, but also a means of positive blessedness and glory, as seen in the redemption of Christ.

— "Images," no. 188

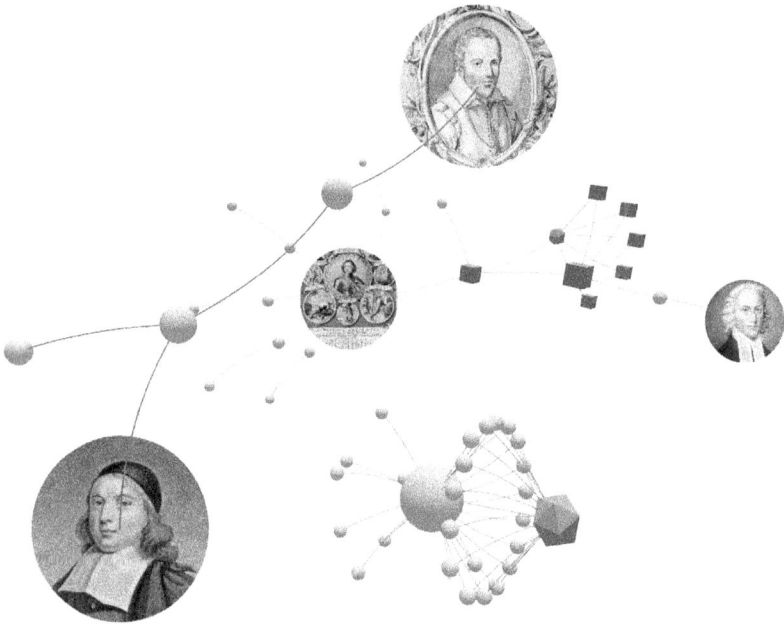

Remedy, medicine

REVOLUTIONS OF THE HEAVENLY BODIES

The revolutions of the spheres of the heavens symbolize the wheels of providence. In the system of the world, the lesser wheels within the greater make multiple revolutions, while the greater wheel makes one. This is analogous to the manner of divine providence, which is nothing more than the revolutions of wheels, both large and small. This is reflected in the history of the visible world, which is symbolized by a great wheel that completes one revolution - beginning with God and ending in chaos. This wheel contains another wheel which completes two revolutions, the first beginning with the creation and the second with the coming of Christ. This wheel in turn contains other wheels, each of which represent significant periods and themes in Old Testament history and the history of the church. The revolutions of the wheels of providence are mirrored by the heavenly bodies, which measure time and influence sublunary things, symbolizing the angels, the ministers of God's providence. The changes of time are represented by the revolutions of the heavenly bodies, which are the great measurers of time.

— *"Images," no. 154*

The motion of the World, this day,
Is mov'd the quite contrarie way.
(Wither, 4.11)

The motion of the World, this day,
Is mov'd the quite contrarie way. (Wither, 4.11)

What was this Figures meaning, but to show,
That, as these kinde of Shell-fish backward goe,
So now the World, (which here doth seeme to take
An arseward Iourney on the Cancer's backe)
Moves counterwise; as if delight it had,
To runne a race, in Courses retrograde:
And, that, is very likely to be true,
Which, this our Emblem, purposeth to shew.

For, I have now, of late, not onely seene,
What backward motions, in my Friends have beene;
And, that my outward Fortunes and Affaires,
Doe of themselves, come tumbling downe the staires:
But, I have also found, that other things,
Have got a wheeling in contrary Rings;
Which Regresse, holding on, 'tis like that wee,
To Iewes, or Ethnicks, backe shall turned bee.

Some punie Clerkes, presume that they can teach
The ancient holy Doctors, how to preach.
Some Laicks, learne their Pastors how to pray.
Some Parents, are compelled to obay
Their Sonnes; and, so their Dignitie to lose,
As to be fed and cloth'd, at their dispose.
Nay, wee have some, who have assay'd to draw,
All backward, to the Bondage of the Law;
Ev'n to those abrogated Rites and Dayes,
By which, the wandring Iew markes out his wayes.
And, to pursue this Round, they are so heady,
That, they have made themselves, and others giddy.

Doe then, these froward Motions, Lord, restraine,
And, set the World in her due course againe.

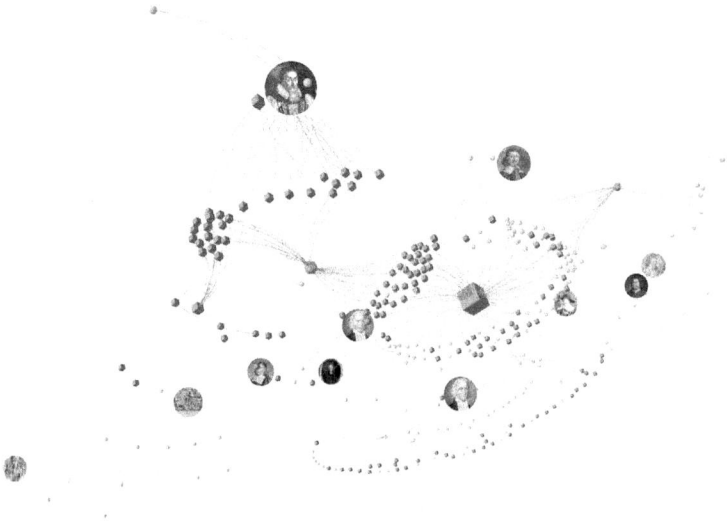

Revolution of the heavens

Rising and setting of the sun

The setting of the sun symbolizes the death of Christ, while its rising is a representation of His resurrection. It was likely for this reason that those who were cursed were taken down and buried as soon as the sun had set. This signified that the curse was removed by the death of Christ. He became a curse for us, and by His death, the curse was removed from the land of Israel, or the land of the Church, so that it was no longer defiled. The people of God do not have the curse remaining with them, for their sins and abominations have been buried forever from God's sight by Christ's death. Christ's body was taken down and buried before the sun had set, so that it would not be left in the open air on the Sabbath day. This was probably done so that Christ, although He was a curse, was not subject to the same curse that was removed by the setting of the sun. The rising of the sun is a type of the resurrection of Christ, and it is fitting that the type is repeated often, but the antitype is only once, just as the daily sacrifices of old.

— *"Images," no. 50*

On the Rising of the Sun (Bunyan, 24)

Look, look, brave Sol doth peep up from be-
    neath,
Shows us his golden face, doth on us breathe;
He also doth compass us round with glories,
Whilst he ascends up to his highest stories.
Where he his banner over us displays,
And gives us light to see our works and ways.
Nor are we now, as at the peep of light,
To question, is it day, or is it night?
The night is gone, the shadows fled away,
And we now most sure are that it is day.
Our eyes behold it, and our hearts believe it;
Nor can the wit of man in this deceive it.
And thus it is when Jesus shows his face,
And doth assure us of his love and grace.

Of the Going Down of the Sun (Bunyan, 30)

What, hast thou run thy race, art going down?
Thou seemest angry, why dost on us frown?
Yea, wrap thy head with clouds and hide thy
    face,
As threatening to withdraw from us thy
    grace?
O leave us not! When once thou hid'st thy
    head,
Our horizon with darkness will be spread.
Tell who hath thee offended, turn again.
Alas! too late, intreaties are in vain.

Comparison

Our gospel has had here a summer's day,
But in its sunshine we, like fools, did play;
Or else fall out, and with each other wrangle,
And did, instead of work, not much but
    jangle.
And if our sun seems angry, hides his face,
Shall it go down, shall night possess this
    place?
Let not the voice of night birds us afflict,
And of our misspent summer us convict.

RIVERS

Like rivers that never cease to flow, the Spirit of God is compared to a river of goodness that never runs dry. The saints who live in this Spirit are like the trees that grow and flourish by the river's side, nourished by its waters. It is only those with a small soul that are easily disturbed and troubled by the slights and ill-treatment of others; like the small streams that are easily disturbed and make much noise, whereas the mighty rivers remain calm and unruffled. Proverbs 16:32 reminds us that those who are slow to anger are greater than the mighty, and those who can control their spirits are more powerful than those who capture cities.

— *"Images," no2. 15, 71*

Upon a Fall Occasioned by Coming Too Near the River's Brink (Boyle, 4.5)

It was not long after this that Eugenius chanceing to spy a little nook, which seem'd to promise him a more convenient station for his angling, he invited Lindamor to share the advantage with him, and began to walk thitherward along the river's brink, which the abundant moisture of the waters that glided by it had adorned with a pleasant verdure: but he had not marcht very far, when chancing to tread on a place where the course of the water had worn off the bank, and made it hollow underneath, he found the earth faulter under him, and could not hinder his feet from slipping down with the turf that betray'd him: nor could he have escap'd so, had not his endeavours to cast the weight of his body towards the bank been assisted by Lindamor, who though not so near the brink as to be in danger, was not so far off but that he was able to catch hold of him and draw him to the firm land. The noise that Lindamor made, when he saw his friend falling, quickly drew Eusebius and me thither, where, after I had awhile made myself merry with the disaster I found to be so harmless, Eusebius (who arrived there a little later) ask'd him how he came to fall; and Eugenius answering that he thought he trod upon firm ground, because he saw the bank look to the very edge as if it differ'd not from the rest of the field which it terminated; Eusebius took occasion from thence to tell him, you may from this take notice, that 'tis not safe travelling upon the confines of what is lawfull and what is sinful, no more than upon the borders of two hostile nations. When we suppose that thus far we may go towards that which is sinfull, without committing it, we are wont with more boldness than considerateness to conclude, that we need not scruple to venture, or rather that we shall run no venture, having firm footing all the way. But 'tis much to be fear'd, that when we allow ourselves to come as far as the utmost verge of what is lawfull, and to do that which, in the casuist's language, is tantum non to sin; the natural proclivity of our minds to evil, which carries them downwards, as weight does our bodies, will sometime or other make us find hollow ground, where we presume to find it firm. He that today will go towards sin as far as he thinks he may, is in danger of going to-morrow further than he should; and it is far more easy for him to feel secure than to be safe, who walks upon the brink of a precipice. He was a wise man that as soon as he had forbidden his son to enter into the path of the wicked, and to go in the way of evil men, subjoins, (as the best course to conform to the prescriptions,) avoid it, pass not by it, turn from it, and pass away: God's indulgence leaves us a latitude to comply with our infirmities and necessities, and to give us opportunities of exercising a pious jealousie over ourselves, and of shewing how much we fear to offend him. But a wary Christian will say in this case, as Saint Paul did in almost a like, all things are lawfull for me, but all things are not expedient. And he must often go further than he can with prudence, that will always go as far ar he thinks he can with innocence.

Upon the Good and Mischief That Rivers Do (Boyle, 4.6)

This discourse being ended, we all, as it were by common consent, applied ourselves again to prosecute the sport that had invited us to the river: but we had not angled very long, before we were disturbed by a loud and confused noise, which we soon discover'd to proceed from a ship, that together with some barges, and other lesser boats, were by the help of a favourable breath of wind, sailing up the river towards London. The sight of these laden vessels, together with the prospect of the Thames, which (as it happened in that place) seem'd in various windings and meanders, wantonly to fly, and to pursue itself; this sight, together with that of the rich and flourishing verdure, which the waters in their passage bestow'd upon all the lands that were on either side any thing near their banks, invited Eugenius to fall upon the praises of that excellent river, which not only imparts fertility and plenty here at home, by inriching all the places that have the advantage to be near it, but helps to bring us home; what. ever the remoter parts of the world, and the Indies themselves, whether East or West, have of rare or usefull.

Lindamor having both applauded and recruited these commendations, methinks, (says he,) that amongst other good things wherewith this river may furnish us, it may supply us with a good argument against those modern stocks, who are wont, with more eloquence than reason, to declaim against the passions, and would fain persuade others (for I doubt whe. ther they be so persuaded themselves) that the mind ought to deal with its affections, as Pharaoh would have dealt with the Jews' males, whom he thought it wise to destroy, least they might one day grow up into a condition to revolt from him. But because the passions are sometimes mutinous, to wish an apathy is as unkind to us, as it would be to our country to wish we had no rivers, because sometimes they do mischief, when great or sudden rain swells them above their banks.

When I consider (says Eusebius) that of the immaculate and divine Lamb himself 'tis recorded in the Gospel, that He look'd round about upon certain Jews with indignation, being grieved for the hardness of their hearts; so that two passions are ascribed to Christ himself in one verse; and when I consider too, the indifferency and consequently the innocence of passions in their own nature, and the use that wise and virtuous persons may make of them, I cannot think we ought to throw away, or so much as to wish away, those instruments of piety, which God and nature has put into our hands. But (continues Eusebius) as I do not altogether disallow Lindamor's comparison be. tween rivers and the passions, so he must give me leave to add this to it, that as rivers, when they overflow, drown those grounds, and ruine those husbandmen, which, whilst they flow'd calmly betwixt their banks, they fertilized and enrich'd; so our passions, when they grow exorbitant and unruly, destroy those virtues, to which they may be very serviceable whilst they keep within their bounds.

Instances of this truth (pursues Eusebius) are but too obvious; our being councill'd by the Apostle to be angry and not to sin, argues that passion of anger not to be incompatible with innocence, whilst 'tis confin'd within the limits of moderation. But when once anger is boil'd up into rage, or choler with an habitual fury, or appetite of revenge, it makes more havock in the world than beasts and inundations. The greatest part of those rivers of blood that are shed in battels, though spilt by anger, do rather irritate than appease the unnatural thirst of that insatiate fury. I will not tell Lindamor, that even that noblest and best of passions, Love, as gentle and amiable as it appears, when once it comes to degenerate by growing unruly, or being misplaced, is guilty of far more tragedies than those that have the fortune to be acted on theatres, or to furnish the writers of romances; and that which perchance at first seems to be but an innocent love, being not duely watched and regulated, may, in time, grow to disobey or deceive parents, to violate friendships, to send challenges, and fight duels, to betray the honor of harmless virgins, to rebel against kings, procure the ruine of monarchies and common-wealths; and in a word to make thousands miserable, and those it possesses most of all.

And as for the desire of excelling others, as great and noble things as it makes men undertake, whilst it aspires only to a transcendancy in virtue and in goodness; when that passionate desire, by making men too greedy of superiority in fame and power, degenerates into ambition, how many vices are usually set to work by this one passion! the contempt of laws, the violation of oaths, the renouncing of allegiance, the breach of leagues and compacts, the murther of one's nearest relations, (if they be more nearly related to a crown) and all the other crimes and miseries, that are wont to beget or attend civil wars, are the usual as well as dismal productions of this aspiring humour in a subject. Nor does it less mischief when harbour'd in a prince's breast for the undoing of his own people; and the subversion of his neighbours' states, the sacking of cities, the slaughter of armies, the dispeopling of provinces, are sacrifices that are more frequently offer'd up to ambition than able to satisfie it. For what can quench this thirst of rule and fame, or hinder the attempts to which it stimulates him, who can find in his heart to destroy armies and to ruine provinces, that he may be taken notice of as being able to do so?

Certainly (subjoins Eusebius,) he very well knew the frame of human spirits, that said by the pen of an Apostle; from whence come warrs and brawlings among you? come they not hence, even of your lusts that war in your members: James 4. 1. I doubt whether plagues, wars, and famines have done more mischief to mankind than anger and ambition, and some other inordinate passions; for these do frequently bring upon men those publick and other fatal calamities, either as judgements which they provoke God to inflict, or as evils, which, as proper consequents, naturally flow from those mischevious practices, to which unbridled passions hurry the criminally unhappy persons they have enslav'd.

Wherefore (concludes Eusebius, casting his eyes upon Lindumor) as the usefulness of a river hinders us not from making good the banks, and if it need be, making damms to confine it within its limits, and prevent its inundations; so the usefulness of the passions should not hinder us from watchfully employing the methods and expedients afforded us by reason and religion, to keep them within their due bounds, which they seldome overflow, without shewing to our cost, that, as 'tis observed of fire and water, they cannot be so good servants, but that they are worse masters.

Upon the Comparing of Lands Seated at Differing Distances From the River (Boyle, 4.7)

This last discourse, to which the river had afforded us the occasion, inviting me to survey as much of it as was within my view a little more attentively, gave me an opportunity of taking notice of a manifest difference betwixt those lands that lay near it, and those whose situation was remoter from it; and having acquainted Eusebius with what I had observed, which his own eyes could not but bear witness to; one (says he) that should only consider how swiftly this stream runs along these flow. ery meadows towards the sea, would be apt to conclude, that certainly these grounds retain none of the water which runs from them so hastily and so plentifully, especially since we can see no channels, nor other manifest inlets, and receptacles, that should divert and retain the fugitive water.

But (continues Eusebius) though these grounds have not any patent passages, whereby to derive water and fatness from the river, and therefore must suffer the greatest part of it to run by them undiverted; yet still some of the cherishing and fertilizing moisture is from time to time soak'd in by the neighbouring ground, and (perhaps by blind pores and crooked channels) so dispersed thorow the whole fields, that they have thereby water, and, in that vehicle, fertility convey'd to them: which you, will not doubt if you do but with me take notice how much the lands, that lye on both sides near the course of the river, are more verdant and flourishing, and more rich than those less happy grounds, to whom their remoteness denies the advantage of so improving a neighbourhood.

Thus (resumes Eusebius) many a pious person that is an assiduous attendant on the means of grace, and has a care to place himself as it were in the way, by which the ordinances of God, especially those of reading, and expounding of the Scriptures, are wont freely and copiously to flow, is (especially upon any fit of melancholly or distress of mind) apt to be extremely discouraged from prosecuting that course of duties, and by looking upon the little that he remembers of so many excellent sermons as he has heard, he is often inclined to conclude, not only that he has lost all the good sermons that he has already heard, but that for such as he, there is little to be expected from them for the future.

But though to lose so much of a thing so precious as the doctrine of salvation, be that which is oftentimes a fault, and always an unhappiness, yet 'tis a far less mischief to forget sermons, than to forsake them. The one may be but an effect of a weak memory, the other is that of a depraved will, perverted by laziness, impatience, or some greater fault. We should scarce allow it for a rational proceeding, if one in a consumption, or disentery, because he grows not fat with feeding, should resolve to renounce eating and drinking.

If you but compare these despondent Christians we are considering, with the careless sensualists that fly a rowing sermon, as they should do what it would deter them from, you will easily discern a sufficient disparity between them, to invite you to conclude, that the instructiveness of preaching may, like the moisture of the river, be convey'd, but by little and little at a time, and by unperceiv'd passages, and yet be able to impart fertility: for though much run by, yet commonly something will stick, which we may safely conclude, though we can discern it no other way, that it will disclose itself by the effects. For 'tis not always to those who remember the most of them, that sermons do the most good; as water retain'd in ponds makes not the bottom flourishing but the banks. The efficacy of a sermon is better collected from the impression it has on the understanding and affections, than from what it leaves on the memory. Whether we retain the particulars faithfully or no, and carry them home with us; yet if a sermon leave us devouter than it found us, if we go from God's ordinances with a love to them, and a rellish of them, and a purpose to frequent them, we may be despondents, but are not altogether non-proficients. That incorruptable seed by which we are regenerated, being once thrown into an honest heart, may, as our Saviour intimates, grow up we know not well how, and though perhaps by insensible degrees, yet at length attain maturity.

What you have been saying, (subjoins Lindamor) when he perceived that Eusebius had done speaking, suggests to me a reflection that till now I did not dream of; and though it differ from that wherewith you have been pleased to entertain us, yet because 'tis applicable to the same purpose, and occasioned by the same river, I shall without scruple, though after your discourse not without blushes, tell you that it is this. I, among many others who live near it, have often resorted in hot weather to this river, to bathe myself in it; and after what I have been hearing, I now begin to consider, that though incomparably the greater part of the river ran by me without doing me any good, and though, when I went out of it, I carried away little or none of it with me, yet whilst I stayed in it, that very stream whose waters run so fast away from me, washed and carried off whatever foulness it might find sticking to my skin; and besides, not only cooled me, and refreshed me by allaying the intemperate heat that discomposed me, and made me faint, but also helped me to a good stomach for some while after.

Thus (resumes Lindamor), I have sometimes found, that a moving sermon, though it did not find me qualified to derive from it the advantages it questionless afforded better auditors, and when I went from it I found I had retain'd so little of it, that it seem'd to have almost totally slipt out of my memory; yet the more instructive and pathetic passages of it had that operation upon me as to cleanse the mind from some of the impurities it had contracted by conversing to and fro in a defiling world, without suffering pollutions to stay long and settle where they began to be harbour'd. Besides, I found that a course of such sermons as I have been mentioning, did oftentimes (and if it had not been my own fault, would have always done so) both allay those inordinate heats that tempting objects are too apt to excite, refresh my drooping spirits that continually needed to be revived, and raise in me an appetite to the means of grace, which are piety's true and improving aliments. So that, (concludes Lindamor,) though I seldome let sermons do me all the good they may and should, yet I dare not forsake them, because I forget them; since 'tis to do a man some good to make him less bad than he was, and to give a value and inclination for the means of growing better than he is.

Bad things from a bad neighbor: *A flood swept away two containers, one of metal, the other crafted from clay by a potter. The metallic one asked the earthen one if it wanted to be taken along, so that together they could brave the raging waters. The clay vessel answered: "It matters not to me what you want: let not proximity bring me harm. For if a wave pushes you against me or me against you, I, being fragile, will shatter, and only you will remain." (Alciati, 166)*

ROMAN TRIUMPH

The Roman triumph was a reflection of Christ's ascension. The general of the Roman armies was dispatched from Rome, the great city of the world, with the highest authority of the state, to hostile lands and the enemies' country to battle against the foes of Rome. Likewise, Christ, the leader of the Lord's armies, was sent out of Heaven, the preeminent city of the universe, by the highest authority of Heaven to this distant land, the land of Heaven's adversaries, to wage war against them. Upon achieving a remarkable and great victory, he returned to Rome in triumph and entered the city in a glorious manner. Similarly, Christ, having fought the fierce battle and attained a glorious and complete victory, came back to Heaven, the place from which he had set out, in a triumphant and majestic way. When Rome heard of his success, they bestowed upon him the title of Imperator. Thus, when Christ had conquered his enemies, he was honored with the ultimate power and authority in Heaven and on earth.

— "Images," no. 81

Roman triumph

Roses

Roses blossom atop briers, signifying that all fleeting joys are tinged with sorrow. But what it truly implies is that true contentment and glory can only be achieved through carrying Christ's cross, living a life of self-denial and dedication, and enduring all hardships for Him. The rose, the most majestic of all blooms, is the last to appear. The prickly bush grows first, but the ultimate reward is the exquisite and fragrant rose.

— "Images," no. 3

Of the Rose-Bush
(Bunyan, 29)

Of the Rose-Bush (Bunyan, 29)

This homely bush doth to mine eyes expose
A very fair, yea, comely ruddy rose.
This rose doth also bow its head to me,
Saying, Come, pluck me, I thy rose will be;
Yet offer I to gather rose or bud,
Ten to one but the bush will have my blood.
This looks like a trapan, or a decoy,
To offer, and yet snap, who would enjoy;
Yea, the more eager on't, the more in danger,
Be he the master of it, or a stranger.
Bush, why dost bear a rose if none must have it.
Who dost expose it, yet claw those that crave it?
Art become freakish? dost the wanton play,
Or doth thy testy humour tend its way?

Comparison

This rose God's Son is, with his ruddy looks.
But what's the bush, whose pricks, like tenter-hooks,
Do scratch and claw the finest lady's hands,
Or rend her clothes, if she too near it stands?
This bush an emblem is of Adam's race,
Of which Christ came, when he his Father's grace
Commended to us in his crimson blood,
While he in sinners' stead and nature stood.
Thus Adam's race did bear this dainty rose,
And doth the same to Adam's race expose;
But those of Adam's race which at it catch,
Adam's race will them prick, and claw, and scratch.

Upon His Distilling Spirit of Roses in a Limbick (Boyle, 1.2)

One who knew how well I love the scent of roses, and were ignorant of the uses of this way of distillation, would, questionless,
think me very ill advised thus hastily to deprive myself of the
flowers I most love, and employ art to make them wither sooner
than nature would condemn them to do. But those that know
both the fading condition of flowers (which unimproved by art,
delight but whilst they are, what they cannot long be, fresh), and
the exalting efficacy of this kind of distillation, will think this
artificial way, that chymists take, of spoiling them, is an effect
as well of their providence, as their skill: for that pleasing and
sprightly scent, that makes the rose so welcome to us, is as short-
lived and perishing as the flower that harbours it is fading; and
though my limbick should not, yet a few days inevitably would
make all these roses wither. But by this way of ordering my roses,
though I cannot preserve them, I can preserve that spirituous
and ethereal part of them, for whose sake it is, that I so much
prize and cherish this sort of flowers; which by this means I
preserve, not indeed in the fading body, but in the nobler and
abstracted quintessence; which purer and lastinger portion of
them, will be more highly fragrant than ordinary roses are wont
to be, (even whilst they are fresh,) in that season when those
flowers that have not been thus early and purposely destroyed,
will, according to the course or nature to which they are left,
wither and putrific.

Thus, he that sees a charitable person, liberally part with that
money which others are so fond of, if he be a stranger to the
operations of faith, and the promises of the Gospel, will be apt
to mistake the Christian's liberality for folly or profusion; and to
think that he is fallen out with his money. But he that remembers
how clear a prospect, and how ab. solute a disposal of the future,
the Scripture of truth (to use an angel's expression) ascribes
to him, that bid his disciples make themselves friends with the
uncertain Mammon, that when we fail, they may receive us into
everlasting habitations; and he that likewise considers not only
the transitory nature of worldly possessions, (from which their
perishing or our's will be sure ere long to divorce us,) but the
inestimable advantage, with which we shall receive in Heaven

whatever we employ in pious uses here on earth, will conclude this way of parting with our wealth, the surest and gainfullest way of preserving it. Since the Christian, by parting but with what (however) he could not long keep, shall by God's munificent goodness, obtain a much more valuable treasure, that he shall never lose: so that thus to sacrifice wealth to charity, is not an early loss of it, but the right way of securing it; for by this gainful way, when we shall in another world be past the possibility of possessing our riches in kind, such an employment of them may help us to enjoy them, and thus laid up, they may there procure us, what they could never here afford us, (HAPPINESS.)

Upon the Sight of Roses and Tulips Growing Near One Another (Boyle, 6.5)

'Tis so uncommon a thing to see tulips last till roses come to be blown, that the seeing them in this garden grow together, as it deserves my notice, so methinks it should suggest to me some reflection or other on it. Perhaps it may not be an improper one, to compare the difference betwixt these two kinds of flowers to the disparity which I have often observed betwixt the faces of those young ladies, that are only very handsome, and those that have a less degree of beauty, recompensed by the accession of wit, discretion, and virtue. For tulips, whilst they are fresh, do indeed by the lustre and vividness of their colours, more delight the eye than roses; but then they do not only quickly fade, but as soon as they have lost that freshness and gawdiness, that solely endeared them, they degenerate into things not only undesirable but distastefull. Whereas roses, besides the moderate beauty they disclose to the eye, do not only keep their colour longer than tulips, but when that decays, retain a perfumed odour, and divers useful qualities and virtues, that survive the spring, and recommend them all the year. Thus those unadvised young ladies, that because nature has given them beauty enough, despise all other qualities, and even that regular diet which is ordinarily requisite to make beauty itself lasting, not only are wont to decay betimes, but as soon as they have lost that youthful freshness, that alone endeared them, quickly pass from being objects of wonder and love, to be so of pity, if not of scorn. Whereas those that were as solicitous to enrich their minds, as to adorn their faces, may not only with a mediocrity of beauty bevery desirable, whilst it lasts, but notwithstanding the recess of that and youth, may by the fragrancy of their reputation, and those virtues and ornaments of the mind that time does but improve, be always sufficiently endeared to those who have merit to discern, and value such excellencies, and whose esteem and friendship is alone worth being concerned for. In a word, they prove the happiest, as well as the wisest ladies, that whilst they possess the desirable qualities that youth is wont to give, neglect not the acquist of those that age cannot take away.

SCARLET AND PURPLE ROBES OF PRINCES

At the time of Christ's arrival, kings were known to wear robes of purple and scarlet, symbolizing the apparel of the King appointed by God. Isaiah 63 stated that this King would be red in his garments, stained with his own blood and the blood of his enemies. Therefore, in his last suffering, Christ wore a robe of scarlet and purple, though those who put it on him did not understand its significance.

— "Images," no. 150

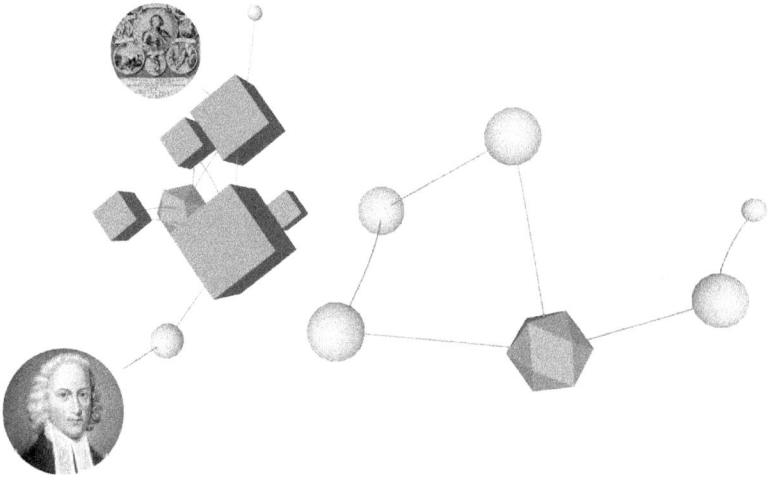

Scarlet and purple robes

SEA

The wise man points to the natural world, citing Ecclesiastes 1:7: "All the rivers run into the sea; yet the sea is not full."

— *"Images," no. 22*

Upon the Sight of a Branch of Corral Among a Great Prince's Collection of Curiosities (Boyle, 6.6)

The present and future condition of a Christian, especially of a Martyr, is not ill represented by what we take notice of in corral; for whilst that shrub yet lives and remains fastned to its native earth or soil, it grows in an obscure region of the world, and is perpetually surrounded and overflown by the brackish and unpleasant. waters of the sea, and oftentimes exposed to the irregular agitations of its waves. Besides, the substance of this plant (as those that should know inform us is but soft and tender under water, and its colour but sad and unlively; nor is it, like the tulip or the rose bush, adorned with any pleasant verdure, and much less does it flourish with gawdy colours. Whilst it remains under water the excellency of it does so. little disclose itself, that men sail over it, without suspecting or dreaming they have any thing precious under their feet, and by the fishes in whose element it grows 'tis pass'd by wholly unregarded. But when this unheeded corral comes to be torn off from its root, and pluck'd out of it's soil, and so is killed in the capacity of a plant, it then exchanges the dark and unquiet place it was confined to, for a more elevated and lightsome region, and instead of sharing the fate of common shrubs and flowers, first to degenerate into fading colours, and offensive smells, and then to perish either by rottenness or fire; our corral by the violence offered to it acquires a delightful redness, together with a solidity and a durableness, that makes it a thing so lovely and immortal, that it serves for an ornament for the cabinets of the curious: and what stupid fishes do not at all regard, those nobler creatures men do so highly prize, that oftentimes it finds place even among the rarities of princes.

Thus a true Christian, whilst he is yet confin'd to the region of the animal life, lives oftentimes in an obscure and low condition, and far from that prosperous state wherein the world's favorites are wont to flourish; he is almost perpetually exposed to pressures, and afliction, and either most men consider him not at all, or those, that look at his out-side only, are apt to despise him because he is so homely. And he is not only in such seemingly forlorn condition as made the Psalmist complain of himself, that all the waves of the sea pass'd over him; but (like those plants of corral that, not growing so near the shore are constantly cover'd with water, as well as sometimes disordered by storms,) the calamities that do, as it were, overwhelm him, are never altogether removed, even in the intervals of those tem. pestuous fits which increase his distresses. But when the violence of sickness, or the fury of a persecutor shall have taken away his life, he must be then translated into a higher and happier region, where afflictions and distresses will be all left behind. And when the sensual idolizers of their bodies shall be condemned to have those as loathsome as were their minds, and as restless as their guilty consciences, his body will obtain new and glorious qualities like that of his Redeemer, and his soul shall find no less happy a transfiguration; the mortal part will be swallow'd up. in life; that perfection which is but in part shall be done away. These newly acquired excellencies of the whole man will never after vanish or decay: and he that liv'd unregarded by the stupid inhabitants of the earth shall be joyfully welcomed into the blest society of celestial spirits; and what is infinitely more, be graciously welcom'd and dignified by the Son of God himself. Men should not therefore by a Christian's present state take their measures of his future state, but rather should remember that he who said of such, they shall be mine in the day when I make up my special treasures, is one whose estimate of persons and conditions we may safely rely upon, since he is able to make any of them such as he pleases to pronounce them. Consequently we may look upon the constant Christian's differing condition with his eyes who said; we are now the sons of God, and it does not indeed yet appear what we shall be, but we know that when he shall appear we shall be like him, who would be like himself alone, did not his goodness vouchsafe to exalt those that love him to a likeness, which makes them very unlike the gloriousest things we here admire, by incomparably transcending them.

Upon the Sight of a Fair Pearl (Hall, 111)

What a pure and precious creature is this, which yet is taken out of the mud of the sea! Who can complain of a base original when he sees such excellencies so descended? These shellfishes that have no sexes and therefore are made out of corruption, what glorious things they yield to adorn and make proud the greatest princesses! God's great work goes not by likelihoods. How easily can He fetch glory out of obscurity who brought all out of nothing!

An Innocent no Danger feares,
How great soever it appeares.
(Wither, 1.10)

An Innocent no Danger feares,
How great soever it appeares. (Wither, 1.10)

When some did seeke Arion to have drown'd,
He, with a dreadlesse heart his Temples crown'd;
And, when to drench him in the Seas they meant,
He playd on his melodious Instrument;
To shew, that Innocence disdayned Feare,
Though to be swallow'd in the Deeps it were.
Nor did it perish: For, upon her Backe
A Dolphin tooke him, for his Musick's sake:
To intimate, that Vertue shall prevaile
With Bruitish Creatures, if with Men it faile.

Most vaine is then their Hope, who dreame they can
Make wretched, or undoe, an Honest-Man:
For, he whom Vertuous Innocence adornes,
Insults o're Cruelties; and, Perill scornes.
Yea, that, by which, Men purpose to undoe him,
(In their despight) shall bring great Honours to him.

Arion-like, the Malice of the World,
Hath into Seas of Troubles often hurl'd
Deserving Men, although no Cause they had,
But that their Words and Workes sweet Musicke made.
Of all their outward Helps it hath bereft them;
Nor meanes, nor hopes of Comfort have beene left them;
But such, as in the House of Mourning are,
And, what Good-Conscience can afford them there.
Yet, Dolphin-like, their Innocence hath rear'd
Their Heads above those Dangers that appear'd.
God hath vouchsaf'd their harmelesse Cause to heed,
And, ev'n in Thraldome, so their Hearts hath freed,

That, whil'st they seem'd oppressed and forlorne;
They Ioyd, and Sung, and Laugh'd the World to scorne.

SEED

John 12:24, "Verily, verily, I say unto you, Except a corn of wheat fall into the ground and die, it abideth alone: but if it die, it bringeth forth much fruit." If we observe the shadows of divine things, we can hear God speaking to us and see divine things excellently represented. This will help to confirm the Scriptures, for there is a strong agreement between them.

— *"Images," no2. 23, 70*

The Seeding of the Heart, Luke 8:15 (Harvey, 28)

The Seeding of the Heart, Luke 8:15 (Harvey, 28)

Lest the field of miny heart should unto thee,
Great Husband-man that mad'st it, barren be,
Manure the ground, then come thy self and seed it,
And let thy servants water it, and weed it.

SERPENTS

One who is bitten by a venomous snake is greatly inclined to sleep and resistant to being kept awake; however, if they do drift off in such a situation, it can be fatal. The same is true for those who are bitten by the ancient serpent, the devil.

— *"Images," no. xx*

Upon the Sight of a Snake (Hall, 75)

I know not what horror we find in ourselves at the sight of a serpent. Other creatures are more loathsome and some no less deadly than it, yet there is none at which our blood riseth so much as at this. Whence should this be but out of an instinct of our old enmity? We were stung in Paradise and cannot but feel it. But here is our weakness: it was not the body of the serpent that could have hurt us without the suggestion of sin, and yet we love the sin while we hate the serpent. Every day are we wounded with the sting of that old serpent and complain not, and so much more deadly is that sting by how much it is less felt. There is a sting of guilt and there is a sting of remorse; there is mortal venom in the first, whereof we are the least sensible; there is less danger in the second. The Israelites found themselves stung by those fiery serpents in the desert [Num. 21:6], and the sense of their pain sent them to seek for cure. The world is our desert, and as the sting of death is sin so the sting of sin is death. I do not more wish to find ease than pain; if I complain enough I cannot fail of cure. Oh Thou, which art the true brazen serpent lifted up in this wilderness [Num. 21:9; John 3:14], raise up mine eyes to Thee and fasten them upon thee. Thy mercy shall make my soul whole, my wound sovereign.

The World with various Face is seen,
As it is chang'd by Lust or Spleen;
These are the Demons scourge it round,
And all its Happiness confound.
(Quarles, 1.5)

From adversity, enduring fame (Alciati, 132)

A sparrow had placed her brood in the branches of a plane tree, unaware of the lurking danger of a cruel serpent. The snake devoured all the chicks and their poor mother, and for this heinous act, it was transformed into stone. If Calchas can be believed, this story of suffering and sorrow will live on for eternity.

How ever thou the Viper take,
A dang'rous hazzard thou dost make.
(Wither, 4.39)

How ever thou the Viper take,
A dang'rous hazzard thou dost make. (Wither, 4.39)

This Figure warnes us, that wee meddle not
With matters, whereby nothing may bee got,
Save harme or losse; and, such as once begun,
Wee may, nor safely doe, nor leave undone.
I should bee loath to meddle in the strife
Arising 'twixt a Husband, and his Wife;
For, Truth conceal'd, or spoke, on either side,
May one or th'other grieve, or both divide.
I would not with my most familiar Mate,
Be Partner in the whole of my estate;
Lest I, by others errors, might offend,
Or, wrong my Family, or, lose my Friend.
I would not, willingly, in my distresse,
From an unworthy hand, receive redresse;
Nor, when I need a Suretie, would I call
An Unthrift, or a roaring Prodigall:
For, either these I thanklesly must shun,
Or, humour them, and be perhaps undone.
I would not heare my Friend unwisely prate
Those things, of which I must informe the State:
And, seeme unfriendly; or, else leave to doe,
That, which a stronger Band obligeth to.

Nor would I, for the world, my heart should bee
Enthrald by one, that might not marry mee;
Or, such like passions, bee perplexed in,
As hang betwixt a Vertue, and a Sinne;
Or, such, as whether way soe're I went,
Occasion'd guilt, or shame, or discontent:

For, howsoe're wee mannage such like things,
Wee handle winding Vipers, that have stings.

Serpent, snake

SHEEP

We are all clothed in the wool of the Lamb, the righteousness of Christ. As it is written in Acts 8:32, "As a lamb dumb before his shearers"."We were all guilty of crucifying Christ; our sins were the nails that pierced him, and we are the ones who reap the benefits of his suffering. By his death, brought on by our sins, we are granted the privilege of wearing his fleece.

— "Images," no. 2

Upon the Sight of a Crow Pulling of Wool from the Back of a Sheep (Hall, 28)

How well these creatures know whom they may be bold with! That crow durst not do this to a wolf or a mastiff; the known simplicity of this innocent beast gives advantage to this presumption.

Meekness of spirit commonly draws on injuries; the cruelty of ill natures usually seeks out those, not who deserve the worst, but who will bear most.

Patience and mildness of spirit is ill bestowed where it exposes a man to wrong and insultation. Sheepish dispositions are best to others, worst to themselves. I could be willing to take injuries, but I will not be guilty of provoking them by lenity. For harmlessness let me go for a sheep, but whosoever will be tearing my fleece let him look to himself!

Who, Patience tempts, beyond her strength,
Will make it Fury, at the length.
(Wither, 4.44)

Who, Patience tempts, beyond her strength,
Will make it Fury, at the length. (Wither, 4.44)

Although wee know not a more patient creature,
Than is the Lambe, (or, of lesse harmfull nature)
Yet, as this Emblem shewes, when childish wrong,
Hath troubled, and provok'd him overlong,
Hee growes enrag'd; and makes the wanton Boyes,
Bee glad to leave their sports, and run their wayes.

Thus have I seene it with some Children fare,
Who, when their Parents too indulgent were,
Have urg'd them, till their Doting grew to Rage,
And, shut them wholly from their Heritage.
Thus, many times, a foolish man doth lose
His faithfull Friends, and justly makes them foes.
Thus, froward Husbands; and, thus, peevish Wives,
Doe foole away the comfort of their lives;
And, by abusing of a patient-Mate,
Turne dearest Love, into the deadliest Hate:
For, any wrong may better bee excused,
Than, Kindnesse, long and wilfully abused.

But, as an injur'd Lambe, provoked, thus,
Well typifies how much it moveth us,
To finde our Patience wrong'd: So, let us make
An Emblem of our selves, thereby to take
More heed, how God is moved towards them,
That, his long suffring, and his Love contemne.
For, as wee somewhat have of every Creature,
So, wee in us, have somewhat of his Nature:
Or, if it bee not sayd the same to bee,
His Pictures, and his Images are wee.

Let, therefore, his long-suffring, well be weigh'd,
And, keepe us, to provoke him, still afraid.

Upon the Sight of a Goat (Hall, 124)

This creature is in an ill name. It is not for any good qualities that God hath made choice of the goat to resemble the wicked and reprobate soul [Lev. 16:20-22]. It is unruly and salacious and noisome. I cannot see one of them but I presently recall to my thoughts the woeful condition of those on the left hand whom God hath set aside to so fearful a damnation [Matt. 25:33]. They are here mixed with the flock. Their color differs nothing from the sheep, or if we do discern them by their rougher coat and odious scent we sever ourselves from them. But the time shall come when He shall sever them from us Who hath appointed our innocence to the fold and their harmfulness to an everlasting slaughter. Onwards if they climb higher than we and feed upon those craggy cliffs which we dare scarce reach to with our eyes, their boldness is not greater than their danger, neither is their ascent more perilous than their ruin deadly.

A man ignorant and wealthy: *Phryxus, perched atop the invaluable fleece, braved the waves. Aboard the gilded ram, he sailed fearlessly across the ocean. What strange sight was this? A man of limited wit, yet abundant in riches, guided by the whims of a spouse or servant. (Alciati, 190)*

Upon the Sight of a Well-fleeced Sheep (Hall, 121)

What a warm winter coat hath God provided for this quiet innocent creature, as indeed how wonderful is His wisdom and
goodness in all His purveyances! Those creatures which are
apter for motion and withal most fearful by nature hath He
clad somewhat thinner and hath allotted them safe and warm
burrows within the earth. Those that are fit for labor and use
hath He furnished with a strong hide. And for man, whom He
hath thought good to bring forth naked, tender, helpless He hath
ended his parents and himself with that noble faculty of reason
whereby he may provide all manner of helps for himself. Yet,
again, so bountiful is God in His provisions that He is not lavish,
so distributing His gifts that there is no more superfluity than
want. Those creatures that have beaks have no teeth, and those
that have shells without have no bones within. All have enough,
nothing hath all. Neither is it otherwise in that one kind of man
whom He meant for the lord of all. Variety of gifts is here mixed
with a frugal dispensation; none hath cause to boast, none to
complain. Every man is as free from an absolute defect as from
perfection I desire not to comprehend, oh Lord, teach me to do
nothing but wonder.

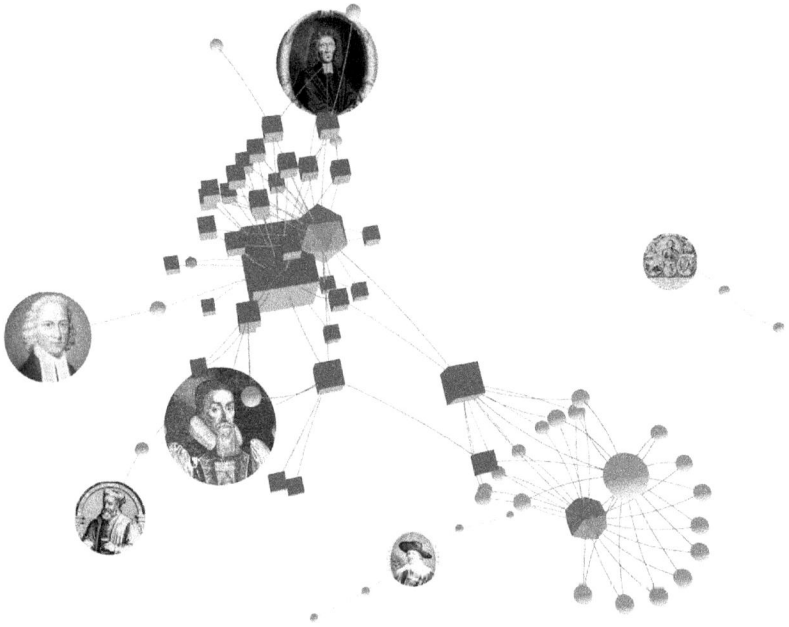

Sheep

SHOWER OF RAIN

In Scripture, the spring season is likened to an outpour-ing of the Spirit of God. Like a seed sown in rocky soil, it may look promising at first, but eventually withers away due to lack of sustenance. Flowers bloom and fruits ap-pear, yet many of them will later drop off and come to nothing. Streams flow high, some from snowmelt, and others from living fountains, yet when the spring ends, all streams dry up except those from living springs. A shower of rain is akin to an outpouring of the Spirit, causing water to flow abundantly in the streets and raising streams from living fountains. The shower also brings about mushrooms, good plants, and fruits, yet also blasts many fruits. Similarly, when the saints sing God's praises, hypocrites sing as well, yet the difference in their voices is as stark as the difference between the sweet singing of birds and the croaking of toads and frogs.

— *"Images," no. 155*

The Watering of the Heart, Isaiah 27:3 (Harvey, 29)

The Watering of the Heart, Isaiah 27:3 (Harvey, 29)

Close downwards tow'rds the earth, open above
Tow'rds heaven mine heart is. O let thy love
Distill in fructifying dews of grace
And then mine heart will be a pleasant place.

Silkworm

The silkworm is a symbol of Christ and His great work. It spends its life weaving something that is used to make beautiful clothing, and in the end, it dies in the process. Similarly, Christ was obedient unto death and His righteousness was accomplished in His dying. But He rose again, just as the worm rises again, as a more glorious creature. The worm leaves behind its web, which is used to make clothing, and rises as a perfectly white butterfly, signifying the purity of grace with which He rose as our Savior. In His resurrection, He was justified.

— *"Images," no. 142*

Silkworm

SILVER AND GOLD FROM AMERICA

The alteration of the path of commerce, providing the world with its riches from America, is a sign and herald of what is to come in spiritual matters - when the world will be endowed with spiritual wealth from America.

— *"Images," no. 147*

(Quarles, 2.5)

Gold is the Idol we adore;
He that has That can ne'er be poor,
Yes, he is poor, and wretched too,
Who will for This his Heav'n forego.

SINGING OF SPRING BIRDS

The heralding of spring by the song of birds is like a preacher preaching the Gospel, announcing the joyous day of the church. Many will be stirred and called to preach the Gospel with great zeal, shouting and proclaiming like a trumpet.

— "Images," no. 110

Upon the Hearing of a Swallow in the Chimney (Hall, 33)

Here is music, such as it is, but how long will it hold? When but a cold morning comes in, my guest is gone without either warning or thanks. This pleasant season hath the least need of cheerful notes; the dead of winter shall want and wish them in vain. Thus doth an ungrateful parasite: no man is more ready to applaud and enjoy our prosperity, but when with the times our condition begins to alter, he is a stranger at least. Give me that bird which will sing in winter and seek to my window in the hardest frost. There is no trial of friendship but adversity. He that is not ashamed of my bonds, not daunted with my checks, not aliened with my disgrace is a friend to me. One dram of that man's love is worth a world of false and inconstant formality.

(Quarles, 5.10)

Imprison'd in this Cage of Flesh,
We earnestly Enlargement wish;
In Hopes that God Relief will bring,
The caged Bird its Song will sing.

Singing birds

SKY

The azure hue of the tranquil sky, a hue of pure serenity, is a faint shade. It is the reflection of the faintest and least intense rays of the sun, symbolizing the holiness and meekness of the blessed in heaven.

— *"Images," no. 114*

Upon the Sight of Some Variously-Colour'd Clouds (Boyle, 3.1)

There is amongst us a sort of vain and flanting grandees, who for their own unhappiness and the age's, do but too much resemble these painted clouds; for both the one and the other are elevated to a station, that makes most men look upon them as far above them; and their conspicuousness is often increas'd by the bright sunshine of the prince's favour, which, though it really leaves them creatures of the same frail nature that it found them, does yet give them a lustre and a gawdiness, that much attracts the eyes, and perhaps the envy and respect of those superficial gazers upon things, that are wont to be amused, if not dazzled, with their insignificant out-sides. But the parallel holds further; for as, in spight of these clouds' sublimity and conspicuousness, they are but airy and unsolid things, consisting of vapours, and steer'd by every wind; so the fine people I am comparing them to, in spight of their exaltation, and of all the shew they make, are really but slight persons, destitute of intrinsick and solid worth, and guided either by their own blind lusts and passions, or else by interests as fickle as those, (to which it will be no addition to bay) or as variable as the wind. And as these clouds, though they seem vast as well as high, and are perhaps able for a while to make the sky somewhat dark, have usually but a short duration, and either quickly fall down in rain, or are quite dissipated and made to disappear; so these titled persons, what shew soever their greatness makes, do sometimes, either by a voluntary humility and repentance as it were, descend of their own accord, and by doing good, endeavour to expiate and make amends for their former uselessness, if not mischiefs; or else, after having been for a while stared at, they do (some more slowly and some more abruptly) vanish, without leaving behind them any thing, that can so much as entertain our sight in the very place where before they ingross'd it: and this ruine sometimes happens to the most elevated persons, from that very prince, whose favour made them attract so many eyes; as clouds are oftentimes dispers'd before night by the same sun, that had rais'd and gilded them in the morning.

Poverty stifles the advancement of the brightest minds: *My right hand clutches a stone, while my left holds wings. The feathers lift me, yet the weight of poverty drags me down. My mind could ascend to the highest heights, if only destitution did not weigh me down. (Alciati, 121)*

Sky

SPIDERS

As spiders, confined and unable to catch flies, consume one another, so too will the devils, on the day of judgement, when they are locked in their ultimate anguish and can no longer torment the wretched sons of man, become each other's tormentors.

— *"Images," no. 160*

Upon Occasion of a Spider in his Window (Hall, 15)

There is no vice in man whereof there is not some analogy in the brute creatures. As amongst us men there are thieves by land and pirates by sea that live by spoil and blood, so is there in every kind amongst them variety of natural sharkers: the hawk in the air, the pike in the river, the whale in the sea, the lion and tiger and wolf in the desert, the wasp in the hive, the spider in our window. Amongst the rest, see how cunningly this little Arabian hath spread out his tent for a prey, how heedfully he watches for a passenger. So soon as ever he hears the noise of a fly afar off, how he hastens to his door, and if that silly heedless traveler do but touch upon the verge of that unsuspected walk, how suddenly doth he seize upon the miserable booty and, after some strife, binding him fast with those subtle cords, drags the helpless captive after him into his cave! What is this but an emblem of those spiritual free-booters that lie in wait for our souls? They are the spiders, we the flies. They have spread their nets of sin; if we be once caught, they bind us fast and hail us into hell.

Oh Lord, deliver Thou my soul from their crafty ambushes. Their poison is greater, their webs both more strong and more insensiblyt woven. Either teach me to avoid temptation or make me to break through it by repentance. Oh let me not be a prey to those fiends that lie in wait for my destruction.

From thence, where Nets and Snares are layd,
Make-hast; lest els you be betray'd.
(Wither, 1.18)

From thence, where Nets and Snares are layd, Make-hast; lest els you be betray'd. (Wither, 1.18)

The nimble Spider from his Entrailes drawes
A suttle Thread, and curious art doth show
In weaving Nets, not much unlike those Lawes
Which catch Small-Thieves, and let the Great-ones goe.

For, as the Cob-web takes the lesser Flyes,
When those of larger size breake through their Snares;
So, Poore-men smart for little Injuries,
When Rich-men scape, whose Guilt is more then theirs.

The Spider, also representeth such
Who very curious are in Trifling-things,
And neither Cost, nor Time, nor Labour grutch,
In that which neither Gaine nor Pleasure brings.
But those whom here that Creature doth implye
Are chiefely such, who under cunning shewes
Of simple-Meanings (or of Curtesie)
Doe silly Men unwarily abuse.
Or else, it meanes those greedy-Cormorants
Who without touch, of Conscience or Compassion,
Seeke how to be enricht by others wants,
And bring the Poore to utter Desolation.

Avoyd them therefore, though compell'd by need;
Or if a Storme inforce, (yee lab'ring Bees)
That yee must fall among them; Flie with speed
From their Commerce, when Calmes your passage frees.
Much more, let wastfull Gallants haste from these;
Else, when those Idling-painted-Butterflies,
Have flutter'd-out their Summer-time, in ease,
(And spent their Wealth in foolish Vanities)

The Blasts of Want may force them to be brought
For shelter thither, where they shall be caught.

SPRING OF THE YEAR

The gradual approach of the sun to the earth, bringing with it changes that are often interrupted by clouds and cold, serves as a metaphor for the approach of the church's latter-day glory. As too much warmth and light too quickly would be harmful to the fruits of the earth, so too much spiritual growth too quickly can be damaging to the church and individual souls. The earth's transformation from its winter death to its summer glory is a symbol of the spiritual change that takes place in the world and in particular souls. The spring brings with it a loosening and softening of the ground, along with the most turbulent season of the year.

— *"Images," no. 152*

Spring of year

STARS

The dominion of the stars in the sky, as described in Job 38:31–33, symbolizes the power of angels on earth.

— *"Images," no. 184*

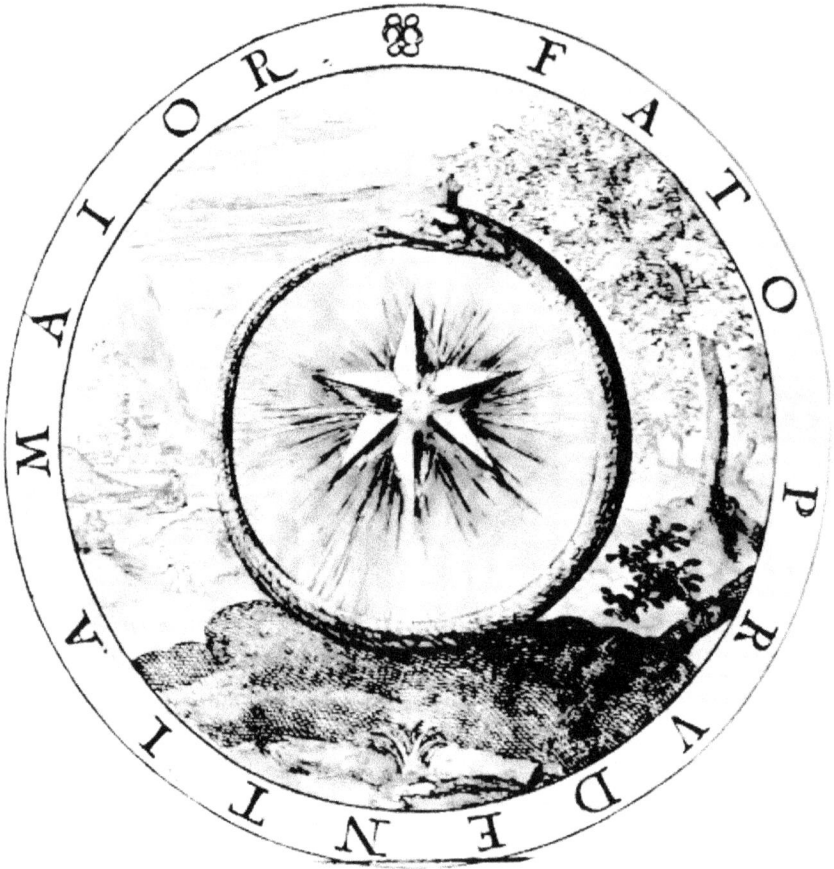

Let none despaire of their Estate,
For, Prudence, greater is, than Fate.
(Wither, 2.12)

Let none despaire of their Estate,
For, Prudence, greater is, than Fate. (Wither, 2.12)

Bee merry man, and let no causelesse feare
Of Constellation, fatall Destinie,
Or of those false Decrees, that publish'd are
By foolish braines, thy Conscience terrifie.
To thee, these Figures better Doctrines teach,
Than those blind Stoikes, who necessitate
Contingent things; and, arrogantly teach
(For doubtlesse truths) their dreames of changelesse Fate.
Though true it bee, that those things which pertaine,
As Ground-workes, to Gods glorie, and our blisse,
Are fixt, for aye, unchanged to remaine;
All, is not such, that thereon builded is.
God, gives men power, to build on his Foundation;
And, if their workes bee thereunto agreeing,
No Power-created, brings that Variation,
Which can disturbe, the Workmans happy being.
Nor, of those workings, which required are,
Is any made unpossible, untill
Mans heart begins that Counsell to preferre,
Which is derived from a crooked-will.

The Starres, and many other things, incline
Our nat'rall Constitutions, divers wayes;
But, in the Soule, God plac'd a Power-divine,
Which, all those Inclinations, overswayes.
Yea, God, that Prudence, hath infus'd, by Grace,
Which, till Selfe-will, and Lust, betrayes a man,
Will keepe him firmely, in that happy place,
From whence, no Constellation move him can.

And, this is that, whereof I notice take,
From this great Starre, enclosed by a Snake.

697

Laziness: *An Essene lounged by a bale of hay, gazing up at the night sky. In his hand, he held a blazing torch, its flames flickering in the darkness. He was cloaked in righteousness, yet his sluggishness was of no service to him or anyone else. (Alciati, 81)*

STRAINING UTENSILS

The way in which many of our tools and body parts are serviceable to us is through being strained, or hard-pressed, or violently agitated. This is true of a bow, a staff, teeth, feet, an ax, a saw, a flail, a rope, a chain, and more. Anything that is not strong enough to bear the strain of such usage is useless. This is also true of true and sincere saints, who are often likened to God's instruments or utensils. They answer God's end and serve and glorify Him by enduring temptation, labor, suffering, and self-denial. In contrast, hypocrites are like a broken tooth, a foot out of joint, a broken staff, a deceitful bow, which fail when pressure is applied.

— *"Images," no. 158*

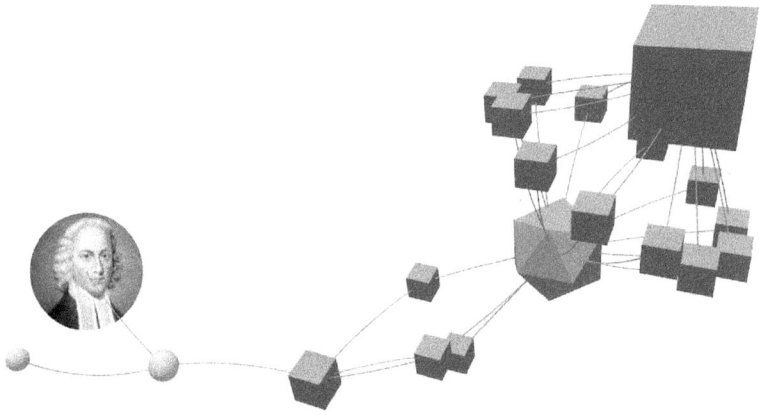

Straining utensils

SUN

The sun has shone for countless ages, its rays a reminder of God's boundless generosity and constancy. It is a symbol of Christ, its light and warmth a representation of his benevolence. Yet its great heat also speaks of the Lamb's fury, a warning of the depths of the wicked's despair. For God's glory and anger are far more powerful than the sun's, making it but a shadow in comparison.

— *"Images," no2. 14, 128*

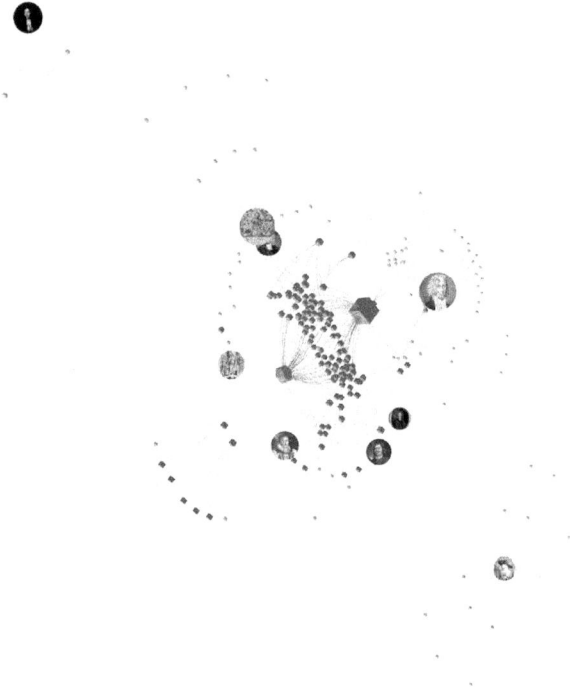

Sun

TEARS

Tears of sorrow, flowing from the eyes, signify godly sorrow, born of spiritual understanding.

— *"Images," no. 173*

Well may he weep a Flood of Tears,
Who feels the Weight of Sins he bears;
Sins which have made his God his Foe,
And brought on him a World of Woe.
(Quarles, 3.8)

The Soul with Sin that's faint and sick,
And Conscience smarting to the Quick,
No Hand can heal, 'till Christ appears,
Who gives her Ease, and dries her Tears.
(Quarles, 3.3)

TELESCOPES, THEIR INVENTION
AND USE OF LATE

Telescopes, which bring the heavens closer and make them visible, were a sign of the greater knowledge of heavenly things that will come in the glorious times of the Christian church.

— *"Images," no. 146*

Looking Through a Perspictive Glass Upon a Vessel We Suspected to Give Us Chase, and to Be a Pyrat (Boyle, 1.7)

Sailing betwixt Rotterdam and Gravesend on Easterday, 1648.

This glass does indeed approach the distrusted vessel, but it approaches it only to our eyes, not to our ship. If she be not making up to us, this harmless instrument will prove no loadstone to draw her towards us, and if she be, it will put us into a better readiness to receive her. Such another instrument in relation to death, is the meditation of it, (by mortals so much and so causelessly abhorr'd;) for though most men as studiously shun all thoughts of death, as if, like nice acquaintances, he would forbear to visit where he knows he is never thought of, or as if we could exempt ourselves from being mortal, by forgetting that we are so; yet does this meditation bring death nearer to us, with. out at all lessening the real distance betwixt us and him. If our last enemy be not yet approaching us, this innocent meditation will no more quicken his pace than direct his steps; and if he be, without hastning his arrival, it will prepare us for his reception. For my part my beardless chin allows me to presume, that by the course of nature, I have yet a pretty stock of sand in the upper part of my hour glass; wherefore, though I am too young to say with Isaac, Behold now I am old and I know not the day of my death; (Gen. 27. 2.) yet since 'tis the wise man's counsel, not to boast ourselves of tomorrow, because we know not what a day may bring forth, I will endeavour (to use our Saviour's tearms,) To take heed to myself, least at any time that day come upon me unawares. (Luke 21. 34.) And as the only safe expedient in order thereto, I will (in imitation of holy Job) all the days of my appointed time wait till my change is come. Job, 14, 24.

THRESHING

In His dealing with His people, God is like a farmer who threshes grain. He does not intend to harm them, but to purify and separate them from their sins, and to make them fit for His use. Just as the farmer uses discretion in threshing grain, so God uses wisdom in the afflictions He brings on His people, varying them according to the individual and only afflicting them in such a way that it is for their benefit.

— *"Images," no. 44*

Threshing

THUNDER

The thunder, with its clouds, carries a hint of the divine grandeur of God, while the blue sky, verdant fields, and blossoms present a reflection of His gentle goodness, grace, and love. Moreover, the lovely rainbow serves as an additional reminder of His beauty.

— "Images," no. 28

Upon the Hearing of Thunder (Hall, 122)

There is no grace whereof I find so general a want in myself and others as an awful fear of the infinite majesty of God. Men are ready to affect and profess a kind of familiarity with God out of a pretence of love, whereas if they knew Him aright they could not think of Him without dread nor name Him without trembling. Their narrow hearts strive to conceive of Him according to the scantling of their own strait and ignorant apprehension, whereas they should only desire to have their thoughts swallowed up with an adoring wonder of His divine incomprehensibleness. Though He thunder not always, He is always equally dreadful; there is none of His works which doth not betray omnipotency. I blush at the sauciness of vain men that will be circumscribing the powerful acts of the Almighty within the compass of natural causes, forbearing to wonder at what they profess to know. Nothing but ignorance can be guilty of this boldness. There is no divinity but in an humble faith, no philosophy but in a silent admiration.

TONGUE; ITS NATURAL BRIDLE

The tongue is naturally restrained and protected by the double row of teeth, as if a strong wall were built around it, signifying that it should be managed with caution.

— *"Images," no. 120*

The Tongue, which every secret speakes,
Is like a Barrell full of leakes.
(Wither, 4.38)

No Heart can thinke, to what strange ends,
The Tongues unruely Motion tends.
(Wither, 1.42)

No Heart can thinke, to what strange ends,
The Tongues unruely Motion tends. (Wither, 1.42)

Well-worthy of our better Heeding were,
That Holy Pen-mans Lesson, who hath sayd,
We should be slow to Speake, and swift to Heare;
If, well, the nature of the Tongue we waigh'd.
For, if we let it loose, it getteth Wings,
And, flies with wanton Carelesnesse, about;
It prateth in all places, of All things;
Tells Truth and Lyes, and babbleth Secrets out.
To speake, of things unknowne, it taketh leave,
As if it had all Knowledge in Possession;
And, Mysteries (which no Man can conceive)
Are thought fit Objects for the Tongues Expression.
With Truth it mixeth Errors; sayes, unsayes;
And, is the Preacher of all Heresies.
That Heart, which gives it motion, it betrayes;
And, utters Curses, Oathes, and Blasphemies.
It spreads all Slanders, which base Envie raiseth;
It moveth Anger, and begetteth Hates:
It blameth Vertue; filthy Deeds it praiseth;
And, causeth Uproares, Murthers, and Debates.
Yea, tis the chiefest Factor for the Devill;
And, yet, with speeches feignedly-sincere,
It otherwhile reproveth what is Evill,
And, will in Lowly-words, a Saint appeare.

Now this is knowne; we, next of all, should learne,
How we may shunne the Mischiefe being knowne;
How, we bad Tongues, in Others, may discerne;
And, how to guide and moderate our Owne.

And, reason good; for, none can apprehend,
What Mischiefe doth an Evill Tongue attend.

Tongue

TONGUES OF SERPENTS

The venomous tongues of wicked men are likened to that of the most poisonous serpents; their corruption of the heart flows out in a deadly manner. It is said of these men that the poison of asps is under their tongues and the tongue is full of deadly poison and a fire, a world of iniquity, that sets the course of nature on fire and is set on fire of hell. Even though mankind can tame every kind of beast, bird, serpent, and creature of the sea, the tongue is an unruly evil that cannot be tamed.

— *"Images," no. 69*

Tongue of serpent

TRAPS

The trapping and destruction of animals and birds through traps, pits, snares and nets, baiting them with what they desire, is a vivid metaphor of what happens in the moral and spiritual world.

— *"Images," no. 167*

Upon His Seeing a Lark Stoop to and Caught With Day-Nets (Boyle, 5.7)

Eusebius: Poor bird! thou wert just now so high upon the wing, that the tired gazers fear'd thou hadst lost thyself in heaven, and in thy fatal stooping from thence, seems to have brought thence a message. Some birds, you know, Lindamor, we usually beguile with chaff, and others are generally drawn in by appropriated baits, and by the mouth, not the eye. But the aspiring lark seems composed of more sprightly and refined materials; she is ever a natural, tho' no native Persian; and the sun makes not a cloudless visit to our horizon, which that grateful creature gives not a welcome to, both by notes, which could he hear them, he would think worthy of him, and by a flight as aspiring as if she meant he should hear them. And in a word, so conspicuous is this creature's fondness of light, that fowlers have devised a way to catch her by it, and pervert it to her ruin; for placing broken looking-glasses upon a moveable frame, betwixt their nets, the unwary bird, while she is gazing upon that glittering light the glass reflects, and sporting herself in those beams, which derive a new glory from their being broken, heedlessly gives into the reach of the surprizing nets, which suddenly cover her, and which the light itself kept her from seeing. The devil is like this fowler, Lindamor, and you and I had perhaps resembled the unhappy lark, if sometimes Providence had not both graciously and seasonably interposed, and, even when we were come near enough to have been covered by the nets, rescued us from them. For it has ever been the old serpent's policy and practice, to take the exact measure of our inclinations, that he may skilfully suit his temptations to them. If, therefore, the tempter find by experience, that you are indisposed to be wrought upon by common temptations to forget the practice of religion, and that you have uncon. cernedness enough not to be much distracted. with the empty and trifling chaff youth is wont to be caught with; and that the very gain, and solider goods of this world, (for which many, who are thought wise men, lose those of the next,) cannot make you so greedy, nor so fond of them as he desires; if the devil have sufficiently observed how uneasie it were to intice you with common baits, he will alter his method straight, and attempt to catch you with light. He knows as well as I do, that you have a curiosity, or rather a greediness of knowledge, that is impatient of being confined. by any other limits than those of knowledge itself; and accordingly, he will let you freely, sport yourself about the glittering intellectual glass, men call philosophy, and suffer you not only to gaze upon all its pieces, and survey a pretty number, but peradventure pry into more than one; and among so numerous, and delighting objects, I fear, that if you will frankly own what my own guilt makes me suspect you of, you must confess, that he had made you so shave your time, that you should scarce have left yourself any for heavenly themes and the meditation of death; which consequently might have then surprised you (had it invaded you;) if Providence, had not mercifully snatch'd you out from between the nets you were allur'd to, before you were quite involv'd in them, and by sickness, or else by means of outward distractions, called your thoughts home by driving them away from those enchanting studies, whose light might much likelier have betrayed you into the net, than have shown it to you.

Lindamor: Though I am not surprised to hear Eusebius, yet I am glad to hear a scholar talk at this rate, and believe with you that many a one that was neither crow, nor woodcock, has perish'd in this snare; and we have known but too many great scholars, so entirely taken up with writing and reading of books, with learning this and teaching that science, that by setting themselves such tasks as requir'd and employ'd. the whole of man, death has undiscernedly stolen upon them, and unawares intruded into their studies, where their restless ambition to enrich the mind never left them leisure to prepare it to leave the body, but made their condition like that of Archimedes who was so busy in tracing his circles, that he took no notice of that victorious enemy who came to dispatch him.

Eusebius: I allow that 'tis the innocence as well as pleasure of knowledge, that deceives those learned men; but they, as well as others, must remember, that even the wholesomest meats may be surfeited on, and there is nothing more unhealthy, than to feed very well and do but little exercise. I take it to be as true of the intellectual as the material world, that it profits not a man if he gain the whole world, and lose his own soul. Let not therefore philosophy any more take up our life so, as not to leave us leisure to prepare for death, and study a science which shall most benefit us in another world, and which alone will do so there: No, we may visit Athens, but we should dwell at Jerusalem; we may take some turns on Parnassus, but should more frequent Mount Calvary; and we must never so busie ourselves about those many things, as to forget that unum necessarium, that good part which shall not be taken away from us.

Deceiving one's own: A duck, fat and blue-feathered, would come and go from her master. She watched as her kin flew through the sky and, with a quack, she joined them, leading them unknowingly into the nets spread for her. The birds cried out in protest, yet she was still, her treacherous act having stained her feathers with the blood of her own. She had been loyal to her master, yet deadly to her own kind. (Alciati, 50)

Anyone who thinks on high things is liable to fall: The fowler, unaware, traps birds with lime and net, his arrow piercing the crane in flight. Yet, as he stomps on a snake, the creature releases a deadly venom, causing the man's death. His bow still drawn, his gaze fixed on the stars, he is unaware of the fate awaiting him. (Alciati, 105)

Gluttony has imprisoned me: *The lord of provisions, a mouse who had nibbled from the master's table, found the oysters with their lips agape. He thrust his whiskered face inside, only to be ensnared by their deceptive shells. As soon as he touched them, the oysters clamped shut, trapping the thief in a dark prison of his own making. (Alciati, 95)*

On weakness: *The gilt-bream, lurking in the depths of the ocean, pounces on the small sardines, who, if they don't flee in alarm, are doomed. But, if they do escape, they are only to be met by the hungry beaks of coots and other waterfowl waiting above. Alas, the weak are never safe from danger. (Alciati, 170)*

Upon The Lark And The Fowler
(Bunyan, 2)

Upon The Lark And The Fowler (Bunyan, 2)

Thou simple bird, what makes thou here to play?
Look, there's the fowler, pr'ythee come away.
Do'st not behold the net? Look there, 'tis spread,
Venture a little further, thou art dead.
Is there not room enough in all the field
For thee to play in, but thou needs must yield
To the deceitful glitt'ring of a glass,
Plac'd betwixt nets, to bring thy death to pass?
Bird, if thou art so much for dazzling light,
Look, there's the sun above thee; dart upright;
Thy nature is to soar up to the sky,
Why wilt thou come down to the nets and die?
Take no heed to the fowler's tempting call;
This whistle, he enchanteth birds withal.
Or if thou see'st a live bird in his net,
Believe she's there, 'cause hence she cannot get.
Look how he tempteth thee with is decoy,
That he may rob thee of thy life, thy joy.
Come, pr'ythee bird, I pr'ythee come away,
Why should this net thee take, when 'scape thou may?
Hadst thou not wings, or were thy feathers pull'd,
Or wast thou blind, or fast asleep wer't lull'd,
The case would somewhat alter, but for thee,
Thy eyes are ope, and thou hast wings to flee.
Remember that thy song is in thy rise,
Not in thy fall; earth's not thy paradise.
Keep up aloft, then, let thy circuits be
Above, where birds from fowler's nets are free.

Comparison

This fowler is an emblem of the devil,
His nets and whistle, figures of all evil.
His glass an emblem is of sinful pleasure,
And his decoy of who counts sin a treasure.
This simple lark's a shadow of a saint,
Under allurings, ready now to faint.
This admonisher a true teacher is,

Whose works to show the soul the snare and bliss,
And how it may this fowler's net escape,
And not commit upon itself this rape.

TRAVAIL

Women endure great hardship in childbirth, symbolizing the church's persecution and suffering in bringing forth Christ and increasing His followers; a representation of the spiritual anguish within the soul when birthing Christ.

— *"Images," no. 18*

Travail

TREE

The Church of God is often likened to a tree, with its many branches, twigs, leaves, flowers, and fruit, all growing from a single stock and root. It is represented by an olive tree, vine, palm tree, lignaloes cedar tree, and more - all of which show the growth and progress of the Church in different ages. The various changes of a tree in different seasons, and the ingrafting of a tree by the husbandmen, represent the abundance of God's goodness and grace that can be seen in the Church. Some trees more than others represent the Church, such as the vine, olive, palm, and apple tree. A tree can even be a lively image of a particular Christian, with regard to the new man, and is so spoken of in Scripture. It can be argued, then, that infants do belong to the Church.

— "Images," no. 99

Upon the Sight of Two Trees, One High, the Other Broad (Hall, 129)

Those trees that shoot up in height are seldom broad, as contrarily those trees that are spreading are seldom tall. It were too much ambition in that plant which would be both ways eminent. Thus it is with men. The covetous man that affects to spread in wealth seldom cares to aspire unto height of honor; the proud man, whose heart is set upon preferment, regards not (in comparison thereof) the growth of his wealth. There is a poor shrub in a valley that is neither tall nor broad nor cares to be either which speeds better than they both. The tall tree is cut down for timber; the broad tree is lopped for firewood, besides that the tempest hath power on them both: whereas the low shrub is neither envied by the wind nor threatened by the axe but fostered rather for that little shelter which it affords the shepherd. If there be glory in greatness, meanness hath security. Let me never envy their diet that had rather be unsafe than inglorious.

They passe through many stormes, and streights, Who rise to any glorious heights.
(Wither, 4.35)

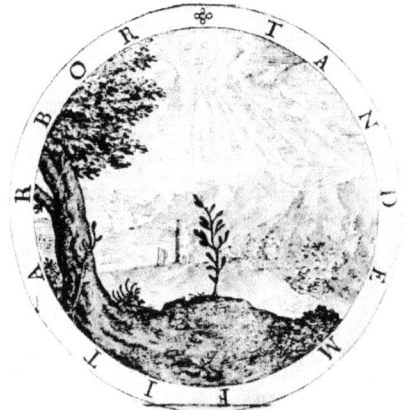

Though very small, at first, it be, A Sprout, at length, becomes a Tree.
(Wither, 1.46)

He that delights to Plant and Set, Makes After-Ages in his Debt.
(Wither, 1.35)

By many Strokes, that Worke is done, Which cannot be perform'd at One.
(Wither, 1.29)

Upon the Barren Fig Tree in God's Vineyard
(Bunyan, 1)

Upon the Barren Fig Tree in God's Vineyard (Bunyan, 1)

What, barren here! in this so good a soil?
The sight of this doth make God's heart recoil
From giving thee his blessing; barren tree,
Bear fruit, or else thine end will cursed be!
Art thou not planted by the water-side?
Know'st not thy Lord by fruit is glorified?
The sentence is, Cut down the barren tree:
Bear fruit, or else thine end will cursed be.
Hast thou been digg'd about and dunged too,
Will neither patience nor yet dressing do?
The executioner is come, O tree,
Bear fruit, or else thine end will cursed be!
He that about thy roots takes pains to dig,
Would, if on thee were found but one good fig,
Preserve thee from the axe: but, barren tree,
Bear fruit, or else thy end will cursed be!
The utmost end of patience is at hand,
'Tis much if thou much longer here doth stand.
O cumber-ground, thou art a barren tree.
Bear fruit, or else thine end will cursed be!
Thy standing nor they name will help at all;
When fruitful trees are spared, thou must fall.
The axe is laid unto thy roots, O tree!
Bear fruit, or else thine end will cursed be.

Tree

TREES OR WOOD GROWING WITHOUT ROOT

Hypocrites are like wood that lies on the surface, with no roots in the ground, yet sprouting leaves in the spring as if alive. But this growth is fleeting; it cannot withstand the scorching summer heat. See Matthew 13:6.

— *"Images," no. 194*

When Hopes, quite frustrate were become,
The Wither'd-branch did freshly bloome.
(Wither, 4.9)

When Hopes, quite frustrate were become,
The Wither'd-branch did freshly bloome. (Wither, 4.9)

Tis true, a wither'd-branch I am, and seeme
To some, as voyd of Hopes, as of esteeme;
For, in their judgements, I appeare to be
A saplesse Bough, quite broken from the Tree,
(Ev'n such as that, in this our Emblem, here)
And, yet, I neither feele Despaire, nor Feare;
For, I have seene (e're now) a little Spray,
(Rent from her Stemme) lye trodden by the way,
Three moneths together; which, when Spring drew on,
To take an unexpected Root begun;
(Yea, grew to bee a Tree) and, growing, stood,
When those great Groves, were fell'd for firing-wood,
Which once had high esteeme; and sprung unhurt,
While that poore Branch, lay sleighted in the durt.
Nay, I have seene such twiggs, afford them shade,
By whom they were the meanest shrippings made,
Of all the Wood; And, you may live to see,
(For ought yet knowne) some such event in mee.

And, what if all who know mee, see me dead,
Before those hopes begin to spring and spread?
Have therefore they that hate me, cause to boast,
As if mine expectations I had lost?
No sure: For, I, who by Faith's eyes have seene,
Old Aarons wither'd Rod grow fresh and greene;
And also viewed (by the selfe-same Eyes)
Him, whom that Rod, most rightly typifies,
Fall by a shamefull Death, and rise, in spight
Of Death, and Shame, unto the glorioust height.

Ev'n I, beleeve my Hope shall bee possest,
And, therefore, (ev'n in Death) in Hope I'le rest.

Tree, wood, and root

TRIAL OF GOLD AND SILVER

The testing of gold and silver in the fire is akin to the trials of the saints and their virtues through persecution and other forms of suffering and sacrifice for God. Not only is their faith validated, but it is refined and improved by the removal of impurities. Such trials of the faithful not only demonstrate their sincerity, but also purify them, strengthening their virtues and separating them from any impure elements.

— *"Images," no. 49*

Upon the Sight of Gold Melted (Hall, 9)

This gold is both the fairest and most solid of all metals, yet is the soonest melted with the fire. Others, as they are coarser, so more churlish and hard to be wrought upon by a dissolution. Thus a sound and good heart is most easily melted into sorrow and fear by the sense of God's judgments [Ps. 51:17], whereas the carnal mind is stubborn and remorseless. All metals are but earth, yet some are of finer temper than others; all hearts are of flesh, yet some are, through the power of grace, more capable of spiritual apprehensions. O God, we are such as Thou wilt be pleased to make us. Give me a heart that may be sound for the truth of grace and melting at the terrors of Thy Law. I can be for no other than Thy sanctuary on earth or Thy treasury of heaven.

All is not Gold, which makes a show;
But, what the Touchstone findeth so.
(Wither, 4.25)

All is not Gold, which makes a show;
But, what the Touchstone findeth so. (Wither, 4.25)

When Silver Medalls, or some coynes of Gold,
Are by the Gold-smith either bought or sold,
Hee doth not only search them with his Eye,
But, by the Scale, their weight will also trie;
Or, by the Touchstone, or the Test, assay
The truenesse of them, and their just Alay.
Now, by their warinesse, who thus proceed,
Wee fairely are admonished, to heed
The faithfulnesse of him wee make our Friend;
And, on whose love wee purpose to depend:
Or else, when wee a Iewell thinke to get,
Wee may bee cheated by a Counterfet.

All is not Gold that glisters: Otherwhile,
The Tincture is so good, it may beguile
The cunningst eye: But, bring it to the Touch,
And, then, you find the value not so much.
Some, keepe the Tincture, brooking, likewise, well
An ordinarie Touch; but, yeeld a Smell,
Which will discover it, if you apply
Unto your Nose, that piece of Chymistrie.
Sometime, when there's enough to give content,
In Colour, in the Touch, and in the Scent;
The Bulke, is more than answers Gold in weight,
And, proves it a sophisticall deceit.
Nay, some, is fully that which you desire,
In all these Properties; and, till the fire
Hath made assayes, you'l thinke you might be bold
To pawne your life, it had been Ophir-gold:

But, to bee false, the Metall's then describe;
And, such are many Friends, when they are tride.

Afflictions Fire consumeth Sinne;
But, Vertue taketh Life therein.
(Wither, 1.30)

Afflictions Fire consumeth Sinne;
But, Vertue taketh Life therein. (Wither, 1.30)

Whether the Salamander be a Beast,
Or Precious-Stone, which overcomes the Flame,
It skills not; Since, by either is exprest
The Meaning which we purpose by the same:
Both brooke the Fire unhurt; And (more then so)
The fiercer and the longer Heats there are,
The livelyer in the same the Beast will grow;
And, much the brighter, will the Stone appeare.

This Crowned-Salamander in the Fire,
May, therefore, not unfitly, signifie
Those, who in Fiery Charriots, doe aspire
Elijah-like, to Immortality:
Or, those Heroicke-spirits, who unharm'd
Have through the Fires of Troubles, and Affliction,
(With Vertue, and with Innocencie arm'd)
Walkt onward, in the Path-way, of Perfection.

The Fiery-Tryall, which like Wood and Hay,
Consumes the Workes of ev'ry Wicked-one;
(And maketh all their Hopes to fume away)
Doth purifie what Faithfull-men have done.
They triumph in the Flames, and shall obtaine
The glorious Crowne of Endless-Happinesse,
When all that show of Blisse appeareth vaine,
Which Worldly men have seemed to possesse.
For, though some Sinnes and Follies, gilded are,
And shine like purest Gold, and Pretious-Stones;
This Test, will finde of what Allay they were,
And, make them knowne but Counterfeited Ones:

For, in this Fornace, all such Wormes expire;
And, none but Vertue liveth in this Fire.

TRUE VINE, TRUE LIGHT

The truth of Christ's being the true Light, Vine and Bread from Heaven is evidenced in Scripture, unlike the mere types and shadows of these things. Heaven is the true holy of holies, in contrast to the tabernacle and temple of the law. Christ has entered into heaven itself, as opposed to the man-made holy places. He is the true Bread from Heaven, unlike the manna of the law which was only a representation. Thus, Christ is the true Vine, Light and Bread of the world, in opposition to the literal vines, light and bread which are only types of Him.

— *"Images," no. 45*

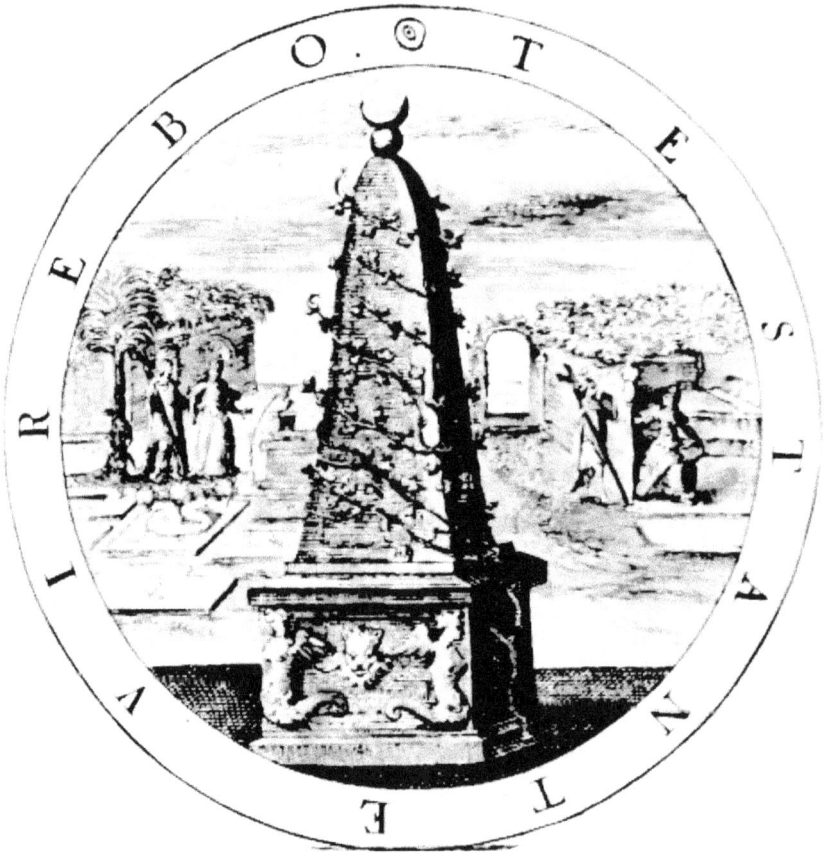

Though weaknesse unto me belong,
In my Supporter, I am strong.
(Wither, 4.18)

Though weaknesse unto me belong,
In my Supporter, I am strong. (Wither, 4.18)

Although there bee no Timber in the Vine,
Nor strength to raise the climbing Ivie-twine,
Yet, when they have a helper by their side,
Or, prop to stay them, like this Pyramide,
One roote sometime, so many Sprayes will beare,
That, you might thinke, some goodly Grove it were:
Their tender stalkes, to climbe aloft, are seene;
Their boughs are cover'd with a pleasant greene;
And, that, which else, had crept upon the ground,
Hath tops of loftie trees, and turrets crown'd.

This Emblem, fitly shadowes out the Natures
Of us, that are the Reasonable-creatures:
For, wee are truely by our nat'rall-birth,
Like Vines undrest, and creeping on the earth;
Nor free from spoyling, nor in case to beare
Good fruits, or leaves, while we are groveling there.
But, if new-borne by Grace, streight borne are wee,
From earthly creepings, by that Living-tree,
Which, here, was planted, meerely to this end,
That, by his pow'r, our weaknesse might ascend.
And, hee our frailtie to himselfe so takes,
So, of his might, the partners us hee makes;
That, hee, in us, doth seeme to hide his pow'rs,
And, make the strength hee gives, appeare as ours.

Continue, Lord, this Grace, and grant wee may,
Firme hold, on our Supporter, always lay:
So climbing, that wee nor neglect, nor hide
His Love; nor over-climbe it, by our Pride.

Thus, our yet staggering weaknesse, shall at length,
Bee fully changed into perfect Strength.

Vine

TWIGS

Young branches are easily bent and steered in another direction, but old trees are harder to move. Similarly, it is easier to turn away from sin in the early stages of life than it is after a long practice of it. A young plant is much simpler to uproot than one that has been firmly rooted in the ground for a long time.

— "Images," no. 34

The Branches may be Trained, but not the Trunk
(Cats and Farlie, 81)

The Branches may be Trained, but not the Trunk (Cats and Farlie, 81)

As I want wood to build a house,
I would cut down this tree:
'Tis a fine stem, although in truth
It somewhat crooked be.
I've sunk this pole, in hopes to bend
It somewhat straighter by;
Yet fear, though I the trunk e'en with
A hundred withies tie–
(It is so stiff in heart and growth,)
That it will never take
A better shape, whatever be
The efforts I may make.
But while here on the ladder,
I Some person hear below!–
Some voice unknown that calls to me,
Holloa! up there! holloa!
And somehow (why I know not) I
Leave off to hear what he
Has got to say, and this is the
Difcourfe he holds to me:
Eh! man, what art about? wouldst bend
A full grown tree like this!
Dost take it for a sapling, eh?–
Why what's with thee amiss!
There is no sense in what thou do'st,
So spare thy labour, friend;
'Tis only when the tree is young
That thou the stem canst bend!
Go, get thee home, and rather let
Thy children have thy care:
The labour that thou here bestow'st,
Were better given there.
Those are the trees whose growth once set
Will give thee most concern;
And from th' experience of my years,
This lesson thou may'st learn:

In tender youth alone, the mind
To Virtue can be train'd;
But that once pass'd, its growth and bend
Are not to be reclaim'd.

UNDOING, EASIER AND QUICKER THAN DOING

It is simpler and quicker to undo than to do in all things, and this carries a lesson in it.

— *"Images," no. 92*

Undoing, destroying, building

VALLEY

Heaven and hell are depicted in Scripture as hills and valleys. Climbing the hills is difficult and requires effort, while descending into valleys is easy and pleasurable. This is an emblem for the difficulty of the path to heaven and the ease of the path to hell. At the bottom of valleys is often water, which in Scripture symbolizes misery and the wrath of God, which is found in hell.

— "Images," no. 64

Valley

Vermin, hurtful

As the sun sets, predators emerge to ravage, and it is then that caterpillars and other pests come out to feast on the vegetation. But when the sun rises, they flee, a fitting illustration of the malevolence of the wicked, the depravity of the heart, and the adversaries of our faith and the church of God.

— "Images," no. 186

Vermin, insects

VOLCANOES

Torrents of liquid fire, spewing from the depths of hell, can be seen as a warning of what is to come: a lake of fire and brimstone, engulfing the wicked, and mighty cataracts of wrath descending from heaven, as mighty torrents of liquid fire have poured down from the likes of Mount Etna and Vesuvius. Such sights presage the ultimate destruction.

— *"Images," no. 84*

Volcanoes, fire, and brimstone

WATCH

Machines for the measuring of time are like wheels, small and large, spinning fast and slow, in different directions, each dependent on the other, all connected and coordinated to produce the same result - a vivid image of how divine providence directs the passage of time from day to day, year to year and age to age.

— *"Images," no. 200*

The Boy and the Watchmaker
(Bunyan, 38)

The Boy and the Watchmaker (Bunyan, 38)

This watch my father did on me bestow,
A golden one it is, but 'twill not go,
Unless it be at an uncertainty:
But as good none as one to tell a lie.
When 'tis high day my hand will stand at nine;
I think there's no man's watch so bad as mine.
Sometimes 'tis sullen, 'twill not go at all,
And yet 'twas never broke nor had a fall.

Watchmaker

Your watch, though it be good, through want of skill
May fail to do according to your will.
Suppose the balance, wheels, and springs be good,
And all things else, unless you understood
To manage it, as watches ought to be,
Your watch will still be at uncertainty.
Come, tell me, do you keep it from the dust,
Yea, wind it also duly up you must?
Take heed, too, that you do not strain the spring;
You must be circumspect in every thing,
Or else your watch, were it as good again,
Would not with time and tide you entertain.

Comparison

This boy an emblem is of a convert,
His watch of the work of grace within his heart,
The watchmaker is Jesus Christ our Lord,
His counsel, the directions of his Word;
Then convert, if thy heart be out of frame,
Of this watchmaker learn to mend the same.
Do not lay ope' thy heart to worldly dust,
Nor let thy graces over-grow with rust,
Be oft' renewed in the' spirit of thy mind,
Or else uncertain thou thy watch wilt find.

Providence and wheels

WATER

The water of a man-made reservoir or fountain can never rise higher than its source, unless given an extra push by some other force. Likewise, humans cannot ascend to a higher level of ability than that provided by nature. We are unable to improve ourselves beyond the natural principles of things like self-love and the like.

— *"Images," no. 161*

Upon a Spring-water (Hall, 51)

How this spring smoketh while other greater channels are frozen up! This water is living while they are dead. All experience teacheth us that well-waters arising from deep springs are hotter in winter than in summer; the outward cold doth keep in and double their inward heat. Such is a true Christian in the evil day; his life of grace gets more vigor by opposition, he had not been so gracioust if the times had been better. I will not say he may thank his enemies but I must say he may thank God for his enemies. Oh God, what can put out that heat which is increased with cold? How happy shall I be if I grow so much more in grace as the world in malice!

Upon the Flint in the Water
(Bunyan, 7)

Upon the Flint in the Water (Bunyan, 7)

This flint, time out of mind, has there abode,
Where crystal streams make their continual road.
Yet it abides a flint as much as 'twere
Before it touched the water, or came there
Its hard obdurateness is not abated,
'Tis not at all by water penetrated.
Though water hath a soft'ning virtue in't,
This stone it can't dissolve, for 'tis a flint.
Yea, though it in the water doth remain,
It doth its fiery nature still retain.
If you oppose it with its opposite,
At you, yea, in your face, its fire 'twill spit.

Comparison

This flint an emblem is of those that lie,
Like stones, under the Word, until they die.
Its crystal streams have not their nature changed,
They are not, from their lusts, by grace estranged.

WAVES

The wrath of God is likened to the tumultuous waves of the sea and the crashing cataracts of rivers, signifying the misery of those who endure it. Scripture often compares misery to being overwhelmed in waters, and God's wrath to waves, billows, and waterpours. Job 27:20 states, "Terrors take hold as waters," and Hosea 5:10 reads, "I will pour out my wrath upon them like water." Psalms 42:7 further compares God's wrath to cataracts of water, exclaiming, "Deep calleth unto deep at the noise of thy waterspouts." Furthermore, it is depicted in hail, stormy winds, dark clouds, and thunder.

— "Images," no. 27

(Quarles, 3.10)

This World's an Ocean deep and wide,
Wherein we're toss'd from Side to Side;
Tumultuous Waves are raging round–
Save me, O Lord, or I am drown'd.

WEEDING A GARDEN

The time for weeding a garden is best after a rainfall - when the ground is moist and the weeds easily pulled. In the same way, purging the church of God requires a time of revival and spiritual awakening. This is the particular time when searching doctrines of religion can be applied and ecclesiastical discipline enforced, and when old corrupt customs and ceremonies can be removed.

— *"Images," no. 205*

Upon a Cornfield Overgrown with Weeds (Hall, 54)

Here were a goodly field of corn if it were not overlaid with weeds. I do not like these reds and blues and yellows amongst these plain stalks and ears; this beauty would do well elsewhere. I had rather see a plot less fair and more yielding. In this field I see a true picture of the world wherein there is more glory than true substance, wherein the greater part carries it from the better, wherein the native sons of the earth outstrip the adventitious brood of grace, wherein parasites and unprofitable hangbys do both rob and over-top their masters. Both field and world grow alike, look alike, and shall end alike. Both are for the fire while the homely and solid ears of despised virtue shall be for the garners of immortality.

WHEAT

A corn of wheat is planted, growing tall and strong until winter arrives, stunting its progress. But when spring arrives, it flourishes even more and reaches its full potential, producing perfect fruit. In the same way, Christ was slain and arose, and His church flourished in the days of the apostles and beyond. Then came a period of affliction, persecution, and darkness, yet we hope that the spring is coming.

— *"Images," no. 90*

Wheat

WHEELS

It is as if God's providence were a wheel, a complex machine of wheels within wheels, so arranged in nature and by God that almost every remarkable device that man creates to do something remarkable or produce an effect is composed of wheels, turning and returning, reflecting the way of progress in divine providence.

— *"Images," no. 89*

The gaining of a rich Estate,
Seemes, many times, restrain'd by Fate.
(Wither, 4.40)

By Guiltines, Death entred in,
And, Mischiefe still pursueth Sinne.
(Wither, 2.7)

Occasions-past are sought in vaine;
But, oft, they wheele-about again.
(Wither, 1.4)

Though Fortune prove true Vertues Foe,
It cannot worke her Overthrowe.
(Wither, 1.6)

The gaining of a rich Estate,
Seemes, many times, restrain'd by Fate. (Wither, 4.40)

Observe this Wheele, and you shall see how Fate
Doth limit out to each man, that Estate
Which hee obtaines; Then, how hee doth aspire
To such a height; and, why hee mounts no higher:
For, whatsoere their Authors understood,
These Emblems, now, shall speake as I thinke good.

The Cornucopias fastned to a Round,
Thus fixt, may shew, that Riches have their bound;
And, can be raised, by mans pow'r or wits,
No higher than Gods Providence permits.
The placing of them on that Wheele, doth show,
That, some waxe Poore, as others Wealthy grow:
For, looke how much the higher, one doth rise,
So much the lower, still, the other lies;
And, when the height of one is at an end,
Hee sinkes againe, that others may ascend.
The many stops, which on this Wheele you spie,
Those many obstacles may typifie,
Which barre all those that unto Wealth aspire,
From compassing the Round of their desire.

The want of Wit, from Riches, barreth some;
Some, cannot rich, because of Sloth, become.
Some, that are wise, and painefull, are deny'd
Encrease of wealth, through Pleasure, or through Pride.
Some, lose much profit, which they else might make,
Because of Conscience, or for Credit sake.
If none of these did hinder, wee have store,
That might bee Rich, who, yet, are very Poore.

And, these, indeed, doe come to be those Fates,
Which keepe most men, from getting large Estates.

Wheels

WINE

The juice of the grape is akin to the blood of Christ, providing us with a refreshing drink to invigorate our souls and bring us joy. The pressure of a winepress is likened to the suffering of God's wrath in Scripture. Bread made of wheat and wine made of grapes are symbols of Jesus Christ, given to us through his suffering and self-sacrifice. Thus, in Deuteronomy 32:14, the bread and wine are referred to as "the fat of the kidneys of wheat" and "the pure blood of the grape," a reference to the parts of sacrificed animals that were offered to God as the most essential parts of the offering.

— *"Images," no. 68*

The New Wine of the Heart, Psalm 104:115 (Harvey, 47)

The New Wine of the Heart, Psalm 104:115 (Harvey, 47)

Christ the true Vine, Grape, Cluster, on the Cross
Trod the Winepress alone, unto the loss
Of Blood, and life. Draw thankful Heart, and spare not:
Here's wine enough for all, save those that care not.

WINTER

The end of the world is foreshadowed by winter's destruction of the land, as symbolized by the Feast of Tabernacles, which took place at the end of the year just before the onset of harsh weather.

— *"Images," no. 136*

Winter

BIBLIOGRAPHY

Alciati, Andrea. *A Book of Emblems: The Emblematum Liber in Latin and English*. London: McFarland, 2004.

———, "Alciato's *Book of Emblems*: The Memorial Web Edition in Latin and English." https://www.mun.ca/alciato/index.html.

Ashworth, William B., Jr. "Natural History and the Emblematic World View." In *Reappraisals of the Scientific Revolution*, 303–32. Cambridge: Cambridge University Press, 1990.

Austen, Ralph. *The Spiritual Use of an Orchard*. New York: Garland, 1982.

Bath, Michael. *Speaking Pictures: English Emblem Books and Renaissance Culture*. Longman Medieval and Renaissance Library. London ; New York: Longman, 1994.

———, John Manning, and Alan R. Young, eds. *The Art of the Emblem: Essays in Honor of Karl Josef Höltgen*. AMS Studies in the Emblem, no. 9. New York: AMS Press, 1993.

———, and Daniel Russell, eds. *Deviceful Settings: The English Renaissance Emblem and Its Contexts: Selected Papers from the Third International Emblem Conference, Pittsburgh, 1993*. AMS Studies in the Emblem, vol. 6. New York: AMS Press, 1999.

Baxter, Richard. *A Christian Directory*. Vol. 1 of *The Practical Works of Richard Baxter*. Morgan, PA: Soli Deo Gloria, 1846.

Bayer, Oswald. *Martin Luther's Theology: A Contemporary Interpretation*. Translated by Thomas H. Trapp. Grand Rapids: Eerdmans, 2008.

Beata, Agrell. "Documentarism and Theory of Literature." In *Documentarism in Scandinavian Literature*, 37–76. Rodopi, 1997.

Bielfeldt, Dennis. "Luther, Metaphor, and Theological Language." *Modern Theology* 6, no. 2 (1990): 121–35.

Bono, James J. *The Word of God and the Languages of Man: Interpreting Nature in Early Modern Science and Medicine*. Science and Literature. Madison: University of Wisconsin Press, 1995. Brown, Robert E. Jonathan Edwards and the Bible. Bloomington, IN: Indiana University Press, 2002.

———. "From Paracelsus to Newton: The Word of God, the Book of Nature, and the Eclipse of the Emblematic World View." In *Newton and Religion: Context, Nature, and Influence,* 45–76. International Archives of the History of Ideas, vol. 161. Boston: Kluwer Academic, 1999.

Boot, Peter. "Mesotext. Digitised Emblems, Modelled Annotations and Humanities Scholarship." Ph.D. diss. University of Utrecht, 2009.

Boss, Robert L. *Visual Edwards Project.* https:www.visualedwards.org.

———. "Jonathan Edwards and the Reinscripturation of the World." Ph.D. diss. Fort Worth, TX: Southwestern Baptist Theological Seminary, 2013.

———. "Allegorical Method." In *The Jonathan Edwards Encyclopedia,* 16–17. Grand Rapids, MI: Eerdmans, 2017.

———. "Cosmology." In *The Jonathan Edwards Encyclopedia,* 114–16. Grand Rapids, MI: Eerdmans, 2017.

———. "Ecology/Environmentalism." In *The Jonathan Edwards Encyclopedia,* 169–71. Grand Rapids, MI: Eerdmans, 2017.

Boyle, Robert, and John Weyland. *The Hon. Robert Boyle's "Occasional Reflections".* London: Printed for T. Cadell [etc.], 1808.

Browne, Thomas. *Pseudodoxia Epidemica, or, Enquiries Into Very Many Received Tenents and Commonly Presumed Truths by Thomas Browne.* London: Printed by T.H. for E. Dod, 1646. https://quod.lib.umich.edu/e/eebo/A29861.0001.001.

Buhler, Pierre, and Tibor Fabiny. *Interpretation Of Texts Sacred And Secular.* Pano Verlag, 1999.

Bunyan, John. *The Pilgrim's Progress.* Westwood, NJ: Barbour, 1970.

———. *Divine Emblems, or, Temporal Things Spiritualized.* London: Bickers & Son, 1867.

———, and George Offor. "Solomon's Temple Spiritualized." In *The Whole Works of John Bunyan.* Grand Rapids: Baker, 1982.

Burns, William E. "'Our Lot Is Fallen Into an Age of Wonders': John Spencer and the Controversy Over Prodigies in the Early Restoration." *Albion: A Quarterly Journal Concerned with British Studies* 27, no. 2 (Summer 1995): 237–52.

Calvin, John. *Institutes of the Christian Religion.* In *The Library of Christian Classics.* Ed. John T. McNeill trans. Ford Lewis Battles. Philadelphia: Westminster, 1960.

Camerarius, Joachim, and Mathias van Somer. *Symboloru[m] & Emblematum Ex Re Herbaria Desumtorum Centuria Vna[-Quarta] Collecta.* Francofurti: Impensis Iohannis Ammonij, 1654.

Cats, Jacob, and Robert Farley. *Moral Emblems: With Aphorisms, Adages, and Proverbs, of All Ages and Nations.* London: Longman, Green, Longman and Roberts, 1860.

Clark, Michael P. "The Eschatology of Signs in Cotton Mather's Biblia Americana." In *Cotton Mather and Biblia Americana, America's First Bible Commentary: Essays in Reappraisal.* Grand Rapids, Mich.: Baker Academic, 2011.

Conforti, Joseph A. *Jonathan Edwards, Religious Tradition & American Culture.* Chapel Hill: University of North Carolina Press, 1995.

Daly, Peter M., ed. *Companion to Emblem Studies.* AMS Studies in the Emblem. New York: AMS Press, 2008.

———, ed. *The English Emblem and the Continental Tradition.* AMS Studies in the Emblem, no. 1. New York: AMS Press, 1988.

———, and Mary V. Silcox. *The Modern Critical Reception of the English Emblem.* K G Saur Verlag Gmbh & Co, January 1992.

Daniel, Stephen H. *The Philosophy of Jonathan Edwards, A Study in Divine Semiotics.* Bloomington, IN: Indiana University Press, 1994.

Daston, Lorraine, and Katharine Park. *Wonders and the Order of Nature, 1150–1750.* New York: Zone Books, 2001.

Davis, Thomas M. "The Traditions of Puritan Typology." In *Typology and Early American Literature,* edited by Sacvan Bercovitch, 11–45. Amherst: University of Massachussetts Press, 1972.

Dawkins, Richard. *The God Delusion.* New York: Houghton Mifflin Company, 2006.

Dawson, David. "Allegorical Intratextuality in Bunyan and Winstanley." *The Journal of Religion* 70 (1990): 189–212.

Daly, Peter. *Literature in the Light of the Emblem.* London: University of Toronto Press, 1998.

Diehl, Huston. *An Index of Icons in English Emblem Books, 1550–1700.* Norman, OK: University of Oklahoma Press, 1986.

———. "Graven Images: Protestant Emblem Books in England." *Renaissance Quarterly* 39, no. 1 (1986): 49–66.

Eco, Umberto. *Art and Beauty in the Middle Ages.* Trans. Hugh Bredin. New Haven: Yale University Press, 1988.

Edwards, Jonathan, Wallace E. Anderson, ed. *Scientific and Philosophical Writings*. Vol. 6 of *The Works of Jonathan Edwards*. New Haven and London: Yale University Press, 1980.

———, Wilson H. Kimnach, ed. *Sermons and Discourses, 1720–1723*. Vol. 10 of *The Works of Jonathan Edwards*. New Haven and London: Yale University Press, 1992.

———, Wallace E. Anderson, Mason I. Lowance Jr., and David H. Watters, eds. *Typological Writings*. Vol. 11 of *The Works of Jonathan Edwards*. New Haven and London: Yale University Press, 1993.

———, David Hall, ed. *Ecclesiastical Writings*. Vol. 12 of *The Works of Jonathan Edwards*. New Haven and London: Yale University Press, 1994.

———, Thomas A. Schafer, ed. *The Miscellanies, a-500*. Vol. 13 of *The Works of Jonathan Edwards*. New Haven and London: Yale University Press, 1994.

———, Kenneth P. Minkema, ed. *Sermons and Discourses, 1723–1729*. Vol. 14, *The Works of Jonathan Edwards*. New Haven and London: Yale University Press, 1997.

———, Stephen J. Stein, ed. *Notes on Scripture*. Vol. 15 of *The Works of Jonathan Edwards*. New Haven and London: Yale University Press, 1998.

———, George S. Claghorn, ed. *Letters and Personal Writings*. Vol. 16 of *The Works of Jonathan Edwards*. New Haven and London: Yale University Press, 1998.

———, Harry S. Stout, Nathan O. Hatch, and Kyle P. Farley, eds. *Sermons and Discourses, 1739–1742*. Vol. 22 of *The Works of Jonathan Edwards*. New Haven and London: Yale University Press, 2003.

———, Douglas A. Sweeney, ed. *The "Miscellanies" 1153–1360*. Vol. 23 of *The Works of Jonathan Edwards*. New Haven and London: Yale University Press, 2004.

———, Peter J. Thuesen, ed. *Catalogues of Books*. Vol. 26 of *The Works of Jonathan Edwards*. Yale University Press, 2008.

———. *Documents on the Trinity, Grace and Faith*. Vol. 37 of *The Works of Jonathan Edwards Online*. edwards.yale.edu. Jonathan Edwards Center at Yale University.

———. *Sermons, Series II, 1737*. Vol. 52 of *The Works of Jonathan Edwards Online*. edwards.yale.edu. Jonathan Edwards Center at Yale University.

Encyclopedia of Life. "Rose." https://eol.org/pages/29911.

Enenkel, Karl A.E., and Paul J. Smith, eds. *Emblems and the Natural World*. Leiden: Brill, 2017.

———. Smith, and P.J., eds. *Early Modern Zoology: The Construction of Animals in Science, Literature and the Visual Arts (Intersections)*. London: BRILL, 2007.

———. *The Invention of the Emblem Book and the Transmission of Knowledge, Ca. 1510–1610*. Leiden ;: Brill, 2019.

Estep, William R. *Renaissance and Reformation*. Grand Rapids: Eerdmans, 1986.

Fabiny, Tibor. *The Lion and the Lamb: Figuralism and Fulfilment in the Bible, Art, and Literature*. New York: St. Martin's Press, 1992.

———. "Edwards and Biblical Typology." In *Understanding Jonathan Edwards: An Introduction to America's Theologian,* edited by Gerald McDermott, 91–108. New York: Oxford University Press, 2008.

Finocchiaro, Maurice A. "Galileo's Letter to the Grand Duchess Christina (1615)." In *The Galileo Affair: A Documentary History,* 87–118. California Studies in the History of Science. Berkeley: University of California, 1989.

Flavel, John. *Husbandry Spiritualized; or, The Heavenly Use of Earthly Things.: Consisting of Many Pleasant Observations, Pertinent Applications, and Serious Reflections; and Each Chapter Concluded with a Divine and Suitable Poem; Directing Husbandmen to the Most Excellent Improvements of Their Common Employments. Whereunto Are Added, by Way of Appendix, Several Choice Occasional Meditations, Upon Birds, Beasts, Trees, Flowers, Rivers, and Several Other Objects; Fitted for the Help of Such as Desire to Walk with God in All Their Solitudes, and Recesses from the World*. Elizabeth Town, NJ: Printed and sold by Shepard Kollock, 1794.

Friedman, Jerome. "The Battle of the Frogs and Fairford's Flies: Miracles and Popular Journalism During the English Revolution." *The Sixteenth Century Journal* 23, no. 3 (1992): 419–42.

Foucault, Michel. *The Order of Things; an Archaeology of the Human Sciences*. New York: Vintage Books, 1973.

Franz, Wolfgang. *Historia Animalium Sacra: In Qua Plerorumque Animalium Praecipuae Proprietates in Gratiam Studiosorum Theologiae.. Breviter Accomodantur*. Germany: Schurer, 1613.

———. *The History of Brutes, or, A Description of Living Creatures : Wherein the Nature and Properties of Four-Footed Beasts Are at Large Described*. London: Printed by E. Okes, for Francis Haley, 1670.

Freeman, Rosemary. *English Emblem Books*. New York: Octagon Books, 1966.

Galilei, Galileo. *Discoveries and Opinions of Galileo*. Translated with introduction and notes by Stillman Drake. Garden City: N.Y., Doubleday, 1957.

Garrett, James Leo. *Baptist Theology: A Four-Century Study*. Macon, Ga.: Mercer University Press, 2009.

Gatta, John. *Making Nature Sacred: Literature, Religion, and Environment in America from the Puritans to the Present*. New York: Oxford University Press, 2004.

Gere, Charles. "The Computer as an Irrational Cabinet." Ph.D. dissertation. London: Middlesex University, 1996.

Gesner, Conrad. *Historiae Animalium, (1551–87)* [online]. Accessed 30 November 2022. Available from https://www.biodiversitylibrary.org/page/ 52773824; Internet.

Goodman, Godfrey. *The Creatures Praysing God: Or, The Religion of Dumbe Creatures*. London: Printed by Felik Kingston, 1622.

Green, Henry. *Shakespeare and the Emblem Writers: An Exposition of Their Similarities of Thought and Expression. Preceded by a View of Emblem-Literature Down to A. D. 1616*. London: Trübner, 1870.

———. *Andrea Alciati and His Books of Emblems a Biographical and Bibliographical Study*. New York: B. Franklin, 1965.

Hall, A. Rupert. *The Revolution in Science, 1500–1750*. New York: Longman, 1983.

Hall, David D. *Worlds of Wonder, Days of Judgment*. New York: Alfred A. Knopf, 1989.

Hall, Joseph. "The Art of Divine Meditation." In *The Works of the Right Reverend Joseph Hall, D. D.* Oxford: Oxford University Press, 1863.

———. "The Invisible World." In *The Works of the Right Reverend Joseph Hall, D. D.* Oxford: Oxford University Press, 1863.

———. "The Remedy of Profaneness." In *The Works of the Right Reverend Joseph Hall, D. D.* Oxford: Oxford University Press, 1863.

Hallyn, Fernand. *The Poetic Structure of the World: Copernicus and Kepler*. Translated by Donld M. Leslie. New York: Zone Books, 1990.

Hamann, J. G., J. M. Bernstein, ed. "Aesthetica in Nuce: A Rhapsody in Cabbalistic Prose (1762)." In *Classic and Romantic German Aesthetics*. New York: Cambridge University Press, 2003.

Hambrick-Stowe, Charles E. *The Practice of Piety: Puritan Devotional Disciplines in Seventeenth-Century New England*. Chapel Hill: University of North Carolina Press, 1982.

Harrison, Peter. "The Metaphor of 'the Book of Nature' and Early Modern Science." In *The Book of Nature in Early Modern and Modern History*, 1–26. Leuven: Peeters, 2006.

Harvey, Christopher. *The School of the Heart*. London: Printed for Lodowick Lloyd, 1676.

Heckscher, William S. "Renaissance Emblems." *The Princeton University Library Chronicle* XV, no. 2 (Winter 1954): 55–68.

Heffernan, Thomas. *Art and Emblem: Early Seventheenth-Century English Poetry of Devotion*. The Renaissance Institute, 1991.

Holbrook, Clyde. Jonathan Edwards, *The Valley and Nature, An Interpretive Essay*. Lewisburg: Bucknell University Press, 1987.

Holifield, E. Brooks. "Edwards as Theologian." In *The Cambridge Companion to Jonathan Edwards*, 144–61. New York: Cambridge University Press, 2007.

Holmes, James Christopher. "The Role of Metaphor in the Sermons of Benjamin Keach, 1640–1704." Ph.D. diss., The Southern Baptist Theological Seminary, 2009.

Höltgen, Karl Josef. *Aspects of the Emblem: Studies in the English Emblem Tradition and the European Context*. With a foreword by Sir Roy Strong. Problemata Semiotica. Kassel, GER: Reichenberger, 1986.

———. *Francis Quarles (1592–1644) Als Meditativer und Emblematischer Dichter*. Buchreihe der Anglia, Zeitschrift Für Englische Philologie. Tübingen: Niemeyer, 1978.

Huff, Peter A. "Calvin and the Beasts: Animals in John Calvin's Theological Discourse." *Journal of the Evangelical Theological Society* 42, no. 1 (1999): 67–75.

Hüllen, Werner. *English Dictionaries 800–1700: The Topical Tradition*. New York: Oxford, 2006.

Huntley, Frank Livingstone. *Bishop Joseph Hall and Protestant Meditation in Seventeenth-Century England: A Study with Texts of The Art of Divine Meditation (1606) and Occasional Meditations (1633)*. Medieval & Renaissance Texts & Studies, vol. 1. Binghamton, N.Y.: Center for Medieval & Early Renaissance Studies, 1981.

———. "Bishop Joseph Huntley and Protestant Meditation." *Studies in the Literary Imagination* 10, no. 2 (Fall 1977): 57–71.

Ingvarsson, Jonas. *Towards a Digital Epistemology: Aesthetics and Modes of Thought in Early Modernity and the Present Age*. London: Palgrave Macmillan, 2021.

Israel, Jonathan I. *Enlightenment Contested: Philosophy, Modernity, and the Emancipation of Man 1670–1752.* New York: Oxford University Press, 2009.

———. *Radical Enlightenment: Philosophy and the Making of Modernity 1650–1750.* New York: Oxford University Press, 2002.

Jenson, Robert W. *America's Theologian, A Recommendation of Jonathan Edwards.* New York: Oxford University Press, 1988.

Jeske, Jeffrey. "Cotton Mather: Physico-Theologian." Journal of the History of Ideas 47, no. 4 (December 1986): 583–94.

Jessey, Henry. *The Lord's Loud Call to England.* London, 1660.

Kalff, Sabine. "Comets—Celestial Objects in the Emblem Tradition of the Late Seventeenth and Early Eighteenth Century." In *Emblems and the Natural World,* 321–50. Leiden: Brill, 2017.

Keach, Benjamin. *Spiritual Melody.* London: Printed for John Hancock in Castle-Alley, 1691.

———. *Tropologia: A Key to Open Scripture Metaphors..: To Which Are Prefixed, Arguments to Prove the Divine Authority of the Holy Bible: Together with Types of the Old Testament.* London: William Hill Collingridge, 1856.

Knight, Janice. "Typology." In *The Princeton Companion to Jonathan Edwards,* edited by Sang Hyun Lee, 190–209. Princeton: Princeton University Press, 2005.

Kreitzer, Larry J. *Seditious Sectaryes: The Baptist Conventiclers of Oxford 1641–1691.* Milton Keynes, UK: Paternoster, 2006.

Kuhn, Thomas S. *The Structure of Scientific Revolutions.* Chicago: The University of Chicago Press, 2012.

Lakoff, George, and Mark Johnson. *Metaphors We Live By.* Chicago: University of Chicago Press, 1980.

———, and Mark Turner. *More Than Cool Reason: A Field Guide to Poetic Metaphor.* The University Of Chicago Press, 1989.

Lane, Belden C. *Ravished by Beauty: The Surprising Legacy of Reformed Spirituality.* New York: Oxford University Press, 2011.

———. "Two Schools of Desire: Nature and Marriage in Seventeenth-Century Puritanism." *Church History* 69 (2000): 372–402.

Lewalski, Barbara Kiefer. *Protestant Poetics and the Seventeenth-Century Religious Lyric.* Princeton: Princeton University Press, 1979.

Lovelace, Richard F. *The American Pietism of Cotton Mather: Origins of American Evangelicalism.* Grand Rapids: Christian University Press, 1979.

Lowance, Mason I. *The Language of Canaan: Metaphor and Symbol in New England from the Puritans to the Trancendentalists.* Cambridge: Harvard University Press, 1980.

Luther, Martin. *Lectures on Genesis Chapters 1–5.* Vol. 1 of *Luther's Works.* Ed. Jaroslav Pelikan. St. Louis, MO: Concordia, 1958.

———. *Schriften.* Vol. 46 of *D. Martin Luthers Werke: Kritische Gesamtausgabe.* Weimar: Hermann Böhlaus Nachfolger, 1912–21.

———. *Tischreden.* Vol. 5 of *D. Martin Luthers Werke: Kritische Gesamtausgabe.* Weimar: Hermann Böhlaus Nachfolger, 1912–21.

Luxon, Thomas H. *Literal Figures: Puritan Allegory and the Reformation Crisis in Representation.* Chicago: University of Chicago Press, 1995.

Manning, John. *The Emblem.* London: Reaktion Books, 2004.

Mardsen, George M. *Jonathan Edwards: A Life.* New Haven: Yale University Press, 2003.

Mather, Cotton. *Brontologia Sacra: The Voice of the Glorious God in Thunder.* London: Printed by John Astwood, 1695.

———. *The Christian Philosopher.* Ed. Winton U. Solberg. Chicago: University of Illinois Press, 1994.

———. *Diary of Cotton Mather.* New York: Frederick Ungar Publishing Co., 1957.

———. *The Wonderful Works of God Commemorated.* Boston: Published by S. Green & sold by Joseph Browning, 1690.

———. Reiner Smolinski, and Kenneth P. Minkema. *A Cotton Mather Reader.* New Haven: Yale University Press, 2022.

Mather, Increase. *A Discourse Concerning Faith and Fervency in Prayer and the Glorious Kingdom of the Lord Jesus Christ,* 1710.

Mather, Samuel. *The Figures or Types of the Old Testament.* London: Printed for N. Hillier, 1705.

Matheson, Peter. *The Imaginative World of the Reformation.* Minneapolis: Fortress Press, 2001.

———. *The Rhetoric of the Reformation.* Edinburgh: T. & T. Clark, 1998.

———. "Thomas Muntzer's Vindication and Refutation: A Language for the Common People?" *The Sixteenth Century Journal* 20, no. 4 (1 December 1989): 603–15.

McClymond, Michael J., and Gerald R. McDermott. *The Theology of Jonathan Edwards.* New York: Oxford University Press, 2012.

———. Review of *Jonathan Edwards's Philosophy of History. The Journal of Religion* 85, no. 1 (2005): 121–23.

McDermott, Gerald R. *Everyday Glory: The Revelation of God in All of Reality.* Grand Rapids, Michigan: Baker Academic, 2018.

———. "Alternative Viewpoint: Edwards and Biblical Typology." In *Understanding Jonathan Edwards: An Introduction to America's Theologian,* edited by Gerald McDermott, 109–12. New York: Oxford University Press, 2008.

McGilchrist, Iain. *The Master and His Emissary: The Divided Brain and the Making of the Western World.* New Haven, CT: Yale University Press, 2019.

———. *The Matter With Things: Our Brains, Our Delusions and the Unmaking of the World.* London: Perspectiva Press, 2021.

Melion, Walter S., Bret Rothstein, and Michel Weemans, eds. *The Anthropomorphic Lens: Anthropomorphism, Microcosmism and Analogy in Early Modern Thought and Visual Arts* (Intersections: Interdisciplinary Studies in Early Modern Culture, 34). London: Brill Academic Pub, 2014.

———. Walter S., and Lee Palmer Wandel, eds., Walter S Melion, and Lee Palmer Wandel. *Early Modern Eyes.* Boston: Brill, 2010.

MiddleKauff, Robert. *The Mathers: Three Generation of Puritan Intellectuals 1596– 1728.* Berkeley: University of California Press, 1999.

Minkema, Kenneth. "'Informing of the Child's Understanding, Influencing His Heart, and Directing Its Practice': Jonathan Edwards on Education." *Acta Theologica* 31, no. 2 (2011): 159–89.

Mooney, James E. *Eighteenth-Century Catalogues of the Yale College Library.* New Haven: Beinecke, 2001.

Muller, Richard A. *Post-Reformation Reformed Dogmatics: The Rise and Development of Reformed Orthodoxy, Ca. 1520 to Ca. 1725.* Grand Rapids: Baker Academics, 2003.

Muntzer, Thomas, Peter Matheson, ed. "Vindication and Refutation." In *The Collected Works of Thomas Muntzer,* 324–50. Edinburgh: T. & T. Clark, 1988.

Noll, Mark. *America's God: From Jonathan Edwards to Abraham Lincoln.* New York: Oxford University Press, 2002.

Ogilvie, Brian W. *The Science of Describing: Natural History in Renaissance Europe.* Chicago: University of Chicago Press, 2006.

Paracelsus. *The Hermetic and Alchemical Writings of Aureolus Philippus Theophrastus Bombast, of Hohenheim, Called Paracelsus the Great. Now for the First Time Faithfully Tr. Into English. Ed. with a Biographical Preface, Elucidatory Notes.* A copious Hermetic vocabulary and index by Arthur Edward Waite. London: J. Elliott and co., 1894.

Paulson, Ronald. *Emblem and Expression: Meaning in English Art of the Eighteenth Century.* Cambridge: Harvard University Press, 1975.

Pearcey, Nancy. *Saving Leonardo: A Call to Resist the Secular Assault on Mind, Morals, and Meaning.* Nashville: B&H, 2010.

Pelikan, Jaroslav. *The Christian Tradition: A History of the Development of Doctrine, Vol. 3: The Growth of Medieval Theology (600–1300).* Chicago: University Of Chicago Press, 1980.

Porter, Roy. *The Creation of the Modern World: The Untold Story of the British Enlightenment.* New York: W.W. Norton & Co., 2001.

Quarles, Francis. *Francis Quarles' Emblems and: Hieroglyphics of the Life of Man, Modernized : In Four Books.* London: Printed for J. Cooke, 1773.

Ramm, Bernard. *Protestant Biblical Interpretation: A Textbook of Hermeneutics.* Grand Rapids: Baker, 1980.

Sharrock, Roger. "Bunyan and the English Emblem Writers." *The Review of English Studies* 21 (1945): 105–16.

Schmidt, Leigh Eric. *Hearing Things: Religion, Illusion, and the American Enlightenment.* Cambridge: Harvard University Press, 2000.

Schreiner, Sonja. "*Orbis Pictus* for Boys—Emblematics for Men: Some Remarks on Learning by Studying Pictures and Interpreting Riddles." In *Emblems and the Natural World,* 629–53. Leiden: Brill, 2017.

Schwanke, Johannes. "Luther on Creation." *Lutheran Quarterly* 16, no. 1 (Spring 2002): 1–20.

Simonson, Harold P. *Jonathan Edwards, Theologian of the Heart.* Grand Rapids: Eerdmans, 1974.

Sloane, Mary Cole. *The Visual in Metaphysical Poetry.* Atlantic Highlands, N.J.: Humanities Press, 1981.

Smolinski, Reiner, and Jan Stievermann, eds. *Cotton Mather and Biblia Americana, America's First Bible Commentary: Essays in Reappraisal.* Grand Rapids, Mich.: Baker Academic, 2011.

Spencer, John. *Things New and Old: Or, A Storehouse of Similes, Sentences, Allegories, Apophthegms, Adages, Apologues, Divine, Moral, Political, &c., with Their Several Applications. Collected and Observed from the Writings and Sayings of the Learned in All Ages to This Present.* London: William Tegg, 1869.

Steltzer, Scott. "Equipping People for Biblical Meditation on Creation at St. Paul's Evangelical Presbyterian Church in Somerset, Pennsylvania." DEdMin Project. Louisville, KY: The Southern Baptist Theological Seminary, 2022.

Stout, Harry S. *The Jonathan Edwards Encyclopedia.* Grand Rapids, MI: Eerdmans, 2017.

Svetlikova, Anna. "Jonathan Edwards' Typology as Language." *Theologica Wratislaviensia* 7 (2012): 159–72.

Sweeney, Douglas A., and Jan Stievermann, eds. *The Oxford Handbook of Jonathan Edwards.* Oxford: Oxford University Press, 2021.

———. *Edwards the Exegete: Biblical Interpretation and Anglo-Protestant Culture on the Edge of the Enlightenment.* New York, New York: Oxford University Press, 2016.

———. *The American Evangelical Story: A History of the Movement.* Grand Rapids: Baker Academic, 2005.

Thuesen, Peter. "Jonathan Edwards as Great Mirror." *Scottish Journal of Theology* 50 (1997): 39–60.

Tillyard, E. M. W. *The Elizabethan World Picture.* New York: Vintage, 1959.

Topsell, Edward. *The Historie of Fovre-Footed Beastes. Describing the True and Liuely Figure of Euery Beast, with a Discourse of Their Seuerall Names, Conditions, Kindes, Vertues (Both Naturall and Medicinall) Countries of Their Breed, Their Loue and Hate to Mankinde, and the Wonderfull Worke of God in Their Creation, Preseruation, and Destruction. Necessary for All Diuines and Students, Because the Story of Euery Beast is Amplified with Narrations Out of Scriptures, Fathers, Phylosophers, Physitians, and Poets: Wherein Are Declared Diuers Hyerogliphicks, Emblems, Epigrams, and Other Good Histories, Collected Out of All the Volumes of Conradvs Gesner, and All Other Writers to This Present Day.* London. Printed by William Iaggard and 1607. The English Experience, Its Record in Early Printed Books Published in Facsimile, no. 561. Amsterdam: Theatrum Orbis Terrarum; New York: Da Capo Press, 1973.

Turner, James. "Ralph Austen, an Oxford Horticulturist of the Seventeenth Century." *Garden History* 6, no. 2 (1978): 39–45.

Roggen, Vibeke. "Biology and Theology in Franzius's *Historia Animalium Sacra* (1612)." In *Early Modern Zoology: The Construction of Animals in Science, Literature and the Visual Arts (Intersections).* London: Brill, 2007.

Ward, W. R. *Early Evangelicalism: A Global Intellectual History, 1670–1789.* New York: Cambridge University Press, 2006.

Westerhoff, Jan C. "A World of Signs: Baroque Pansemioticism, the Polyhistor and the Early Modern Wunderkammer." *Journal of the History of Ideas* 62, no. 4 (October 2001): 633–50.

Westerweel, Bart, ed. *Anglo-Dutch Relations in the Field of the Emblem.* Symbola et Emblemata, vol. 8. Leiden; New York: Brill, 1997.

Wetstein, Henricus, Joseph Mulder, and Daniel de La Feuille. *Symbola et Emblemata.* Amstelaedami: Apud Henricum Wetstenium, 1705.

Whitney, George, and Henry Green. *Whitney's "Choice of Emblemes": A Fac-Simile Reprint : With an Introductory Dissertation, Essays Literary and Bibliographical and Explanatory Notes.* London: Lovell Reeve, 1866.

Wilson, Andrew. *The Creation, the Ground-Work of Revelation, and Revelation the Language of Nature. Or, a Brief Attempt to Demonstrate, That the Hebrew Language is Founded Upon Natural Ideas, and That the Hebrew Writings Transfer Them to Spiritual Objects.* Edinburgh, 1750.

Winship, Michael. "Prodigies, Puritanism, and the Perils of Natural Philosophy: The Example of Cotton Mather." *The William and Mary Quarterly* 51, no. 1 (January 1994): 92–105.

Winslow, Lisanne. *A Great and Remarkable Analogy: The Onto-Typology of Jonathan Edwards* (New Directions in Jonathan Edwards Studies). London: Vandenhoeck & Ruprecht Gmb., 2020.

———. *The History of Brutes, or, A Description of Living Creatures Wherein the Nature and Properties of Four-Footed Beasts Are at Large Described / by Wolfgangus Franzius.. ; and Now Rendred Into English by N.W.* London: Printed by E. Okes, for Francis Haley, 1670. https://quod.lib.umich.edu/e/eebo/A40406.0001.001.

Zakai, Avihu. *Jonathan Edwards's Philosophy of History: The Reenchantment of the World in the Age of Enlightenment.* Princeton: Princeton University Press, 2003.

———. *Jonathan Edwards's Philosophy of Nature: The Re-Enchantment of the World in the Age of Scientific Reasoning.* New York: T&T Clark, 2010.

———. "An Interview with Avihu Zakai" [on-line]. Accessed 8 February 2023. Available from https://www.jesociety.org/an-interview-with-avihu-zakai/; Internet.

INDEX

Below is a brief index of significant names and topics.